Art Goedeke

World Tensions

ELTON ATWATER, KENT FORSTER
and JAN S. PRYBYLA

All of The Pennsylvania State University

World Tensions

Conflict and Accommodation

APPLETON-CENTURY-CROFTS

Educational Division

New York　MEREDITH CORPORATION

6109-6

Library of Congress Card Number: 67-21691

PRINTED IN THE UNITED STATES OF AMERICA
390-04005-3

ACKNOWLEDGMENTS

(Page numbers given are those of this volume.)

POSITION PAPERS

pp. 34–36   Translation from the *Current Digest of the Soviet Press,* published weekly at Columbia University by the Joint Committee on Slavic Studies, appointed by the American Council of Learned Societies and the Social Science Research Council. Copyright 1965, Vol. XVII, No. 18, the Joint Committee on Slavic Studies. Reprinted by permission.

pp. 36–38   From *Speak Truth to Power,* American Friends Service Committee Publication. Reprinted by permission.

pp. 38–39   Reprinted from INDEPENDENCE AND AFTER by Jawaharlal Nehru by permission of The John Day Company, Inc., publisher and of the Office of the Prime Minister of India.

pp. 62–67   Reprinted with omissions from POLITICS AMONG NATIONS, second edition, by Hans J. Morganthau. Copyright, 1948, 1954 by Alfred A. Knopf, Inc.

pp. 67–70   From Thomas I. Cook and Malcolm Moos, *Power Through Purpose,* Baltimore: The John Hopkins Press, 1954. Reprinted by permission.

pp. 70–71   Condensed from POWER AND INTERNATIONAL RELATIONS, by Inis L. Claude, Jr. © copyright 1962 by Random House, Inc. Reprinted by permission.

pp. 92–94   From Sir Arthur Keith, *Evolution & Ethics* (New York, Putnam, 1946, original British edition *Essays on Human Evolution*). Reprinted by permission of Rationalist Press Association Ltd., London.

pp. 94–97   Abridged from ON AGGRESSION by Konrad Lorenz, copyright, © 1963, by Dr. G. Borotha-Schoeler Verlag, Wien; English translation, copyright © 1966, by Konrad Lorenz. Translation by Mrs. M. Latzke. Reprinted by permission of Harcourt, Brace & World, Inc. and of Methuen and Co. Ltd., London.

pp. 97–101   From SOCIAL PSYCHOLOGY, revised edition, by Otto Klineberg, copyright 1954 by Holt, Rinehart and Winston, Inc. Used by permission of the publishers.

pp. 101–106   Reprinted with the permission of Charles Scribner's Sons from the following works by Reinhold Niebuhr: MORAL MAN AND IMMORAL SOCIETY, pages xi–xiii, xx, xxii–xxiv (Copyright 1932 Charles Scribner's Sons; renewal copyright © 1960 Reinhold Niebuhr); THE CHILDREN OF LIGHT AND THE CHILDREN OF DARKNESS, pages 173–176 and 186 (Copyright 1944 Charles Scribner's Sons); and THE IRONY OF AMERICAN HISTORY, pages 40–41 and 149–150 (Copyright 1952 Charles Scribner's Sons). Excerpts from *Moral Man and Immoral Society* reprinted by permission also of Student Christian Movement Press Ltd., London. Excerpts from *The Children of Light and the Children of Darkness* and *The Irony of American History* reprinted by permission also of James Nisbet and Company Limited, London.

pp. 141–142   From Louis J. Halle, *Civilization and Foreign Policy,* New York: Harper & Row, 1952. Reprinted by permission of the author.

pp. 142–144   From Carlton J. H. Hayes, *Essays on Nationalism,* New York: The Macmillan Company, 1926. Reprinted by permission.

pp. 144–145   From Michel Aflaq, "Nationalism and Revolution," in Sylvia Haim, ed., *Arab Nationalism: An Anthology,* Berkeley: University of California Press, 1962. Reprinted by permission.

pp. 183–185   Reprinted from *Capitalism and Freedom* by Milton Friedman by permission of the University of Chicago Press. Copyright 1962, University of Chicago Press.

pp. 185–186   From Benito Mussolini, *The Political and Social Doctrine of Fascism*, translated by Jane Soames, London: The Hogarth Press Ltd., 1933. Reprinted by permission.

pp. 220–224   Reprinted by permission of the publishers from John Kenneth Galbraith, ECONOMIC DEVELOPMENT, Cambridge, Mass.: Harvard University Press, Copyright 1962, 1964 by John Kenneth Galbraith.

pp. 224–226   From Robert Theobald, *The Rich and the Poor*, New York: Mentor Books, 1961. Reprinted by permission of Clarkson N. Potter, Inc., Publisher.

pp. 226–228   From Peter T. Bauer and Basil S. Yamey, *The Economics of Under-Developed Countries*, Chicago: The University of Chicago Press in association with James Nisbet and Company Limited and The Cambridge University Press, 1957. Reprinted by permission.

pp. 228–230   From Bertrand Russell, *Portraits From Memory and Other Essays*, London: George Allen and Unwin Ltd., 1956. Copyright, © 1951, 1952, 1953, 1956 by Bertrand Russell. Reprinted by permission of Simon and Schuster, Inc. and of George Allen and Unwin Ltd.

pp. 274–276   From THE SOVIET ECONOMY: An Introduction by Alec Nove, New York, Frederick A. Praeger, Inc., Publishers, 1961. Reprinted by permission of Frederick A. Praeger, Inc. and George Allen and Unwin Ltd., London.

pp. 276–279   Reprinted by permission of Coward-McCann, Inc. from CHINA AND HER SHADOW by Tibor Mende; © 1960 by Tibor Mende. Reprinted by permission also of Thames and Hudson Ltd., London.

pp. 279–282   From Wilfred Malenbaum and Wolfgang Stolper, "Political Ideology and Economic Progress: The Basic Question," *World Politics*, Vol. XII, No. 3 (April, 1960). Reprinted by permission.

pp. 310–313   From *The New York Times*, February 15, 1956, p. 10. © 1956 by The New York Times Company. Reprinted by permission.

pp. 317–323   Translation from the *Current Digest of the Soviet Press*, published weekly at Columbia University by the Joint Committee on Slavic Studies, appointed by the American Council of Learned Societies and the Social Science Research Council. Copyright 1963, Vol. XV, No. 28, by the Joint Committee on Slavic Studies. Reprinted by permission.

pp. 323–326   From *The New York Times*, July 24, 1955. © 1955 by The New York Times Company. Reprinted by permission of the publisher and of the author.

pp. 327–330   From POLITICS AMONG NATIONS, second edition, by Hans J. Morgenthau. Copyright 1948, 1954 by Alfred A. Knopf, Inc. Reprinted by permission.

pp. 330–332   From "UN: The Decisive Factor for Peace," from UN: THE FIRST TWENTY YEARS by Clark M. Eichelberger. Copyright © 1965 by Clark Mell Eichelberger. Reprinted by permission of Harper & Row, Publishers.

pp. 367–370   From "The War for Europe." Reprinted from *The Economist* (London) of July 10, 1965. By permission.

pp. 330–373   From Ghita Ionescu, *The Break-up of the Soviet Empire in Eastern Europe*, Harmondsworth, Middlesex: Penguin Books Ltd., 1965. Reprinted by permission.

TABLES AND OTHER MATERIAL

pp. 85–86   From William Buchanan, "Stereotypes and Tensions as Revealed by the Unesco International Poll," *International Social Science Bulletin*, Vol. III, No. 3 (1951), pp. 519–520. Reprinted by permission.

p. 258   From Alexander Eckstein, "The Strategy of Economic Development in Communist China," *American Economic Review*, Vol. LI, No. 2 (May, 1961), Table 1, p. 509. Reprinted by permission.

pp. 263–268   Condensed from Jan S. Prybyla, "Communist China's Strategy of Economic Development 1961–1966," *Asian Survey*, October, 1966, pp. 589–603. Reprinted by permission.

PREFACE

INTERNATIONAL CONFLICT AND THE
possibility of global war haunt all of mankind. They are no longer the
problems exclusively of government officials, diplomats, and international
civil servants but are questions which every thinking citizen must face,
whether he likes it or not.

In university and college communities, students and faculty increasingly are showing their concern for these problems. In many instances, it
was the issue of American involvement in Vietnam which galvanized individuals into taking an active position and debating seriously the nature
of American interests in Southeast Asia. In other instances, opportunities
for overseas experience in the Peace Corps or similar programs have suddenly made us aware of how little we really know about the peoples of
Africa, Asia, or Latin America, their aspirations, and their problems. The
possibilities for study and travel abroad have increased significantly in
the past ten years as traveling time to even distant lands has shrunk to a
matter of hours.

But with the world literally at our doorstep, the problems of conflict
and tension have become more acute, not less. Indeed, our very existence
in an age of nuclear weapons depends upon how well we understand
these problems and how effectively we learn to ameliorate them. Whether
international tensions and misunderstandings culminate in war and
wholesale destruction or in mutually satisfactory accommodation will in
no small measure depend upon the public's educated awareness of the
issues involved and its capacity for dispassionate analysis of the causes
and remedies. An educated, as distinct from an indoctrinated, electorate
is a prerequisite for placing restraints on political arbitrariness by a few
leaders. A widespread knowledge of the mechanics, dynamics, and motivating forces of international conflict and accommodation is an indispensable first step toward international sanity.

Seeking to make a modest contribution toward this end, this book
addresses itself not exclusively nor even principally to students in the disciplines most closely associated with international conflict and adjustment, those who aspire to careers in politics, sociology, history, or economics. Its purpose is broader: to reach all students, but especially those
with little or no previous social science training. The book, it is hoped, will
be useful to students in more technical fields who may be called upon to

work in the developing countries, who may combat poverty at home, or who wish simply to place their technical and scientific knowledge in a meaningful social context. It is paradoxical that while the world cannot do without highly and narrowly trained specialists, it can even less afford to rely on specialists who are unaware of the social and political implications of their conduct. The systematic exposure of the scientist and technician to the methods and complexities of the socio-political world is of cardinal importance to the attainment of the human objectives to which men aspire.

Implicit in this work is the assumption that if men open their minds to the many-sidedness of the issues behind international conflict, if they learn to sift the evidence and weigh the alternatives, and if they familiarize themselves with the conditions and techniques of accommodation, they will be wary of rash and easy solutions, less prone to acquiesce in high-sounding, dogmatic phrases, and better prepared to handle complex and delicate controversies. Each chapter in the book is organized to help the reader train himself better in these directions. The first section of each chapter contains a formal analysis of a given problem, with sufficient background information to enable one to come to grips with the central issues. The second section presents three or four different views or positions on the subject in the original words of their authors. These views are usually divergent and often conflicting, thus they provide the basis for much thought-provoking discussion.

Careful consideration of these positions and their implications will make one aware of the many dimensions of each problem and of the unlikelihood of finding simple, pat solutions. International political problems, unlike problems in mathematics, seldom have solutions that are as final or precise as those with which students of the physical sciences are familiar. Yet the impermanent and relative character of political accommodation is instructive, for it indicates the need for constant and continuing adjustment, patience, and study, and above all, a measure of goodwill.

Throughout the book, the importance of the interdisciplinary approach is stressed. Insofar as possible, each major problem is examined in its political, social, economic, psychological, and historical aspects, although in each instance one of these aspects usually emerges as the most insistent and determining.

As a final exercise in developing analytical tools for the study of world affairs, the authors suggest the preparation of a model "position paper" on some foreign policy problem. This would be similar in form to the position papers prepared in the United States Department of State. An outline and guide for preparing a position paper will be found in the appendix of this book. Such a project involves the selection of some current problem of American foreign policy, an examination of its background and of the key issues involved, an analysis of three or four possible courses of action or policies which the United States might follow in dealing with the problem, and a conclusion recommending the policy that one feels the United States should adopt. Preparing such a paper will not only be a useful means of integrating and applying much of the material studied in this book but will also provide a very realistic idea of what is involved in the actual formulation of foreign policy. It will make one more aware of the challenge that constantly confronts every statesman —how to blend what is theoretically and rationally desirable with what is politically possible.

This book is an outgrowth of more than a decade's effort at The Pennsylvania State University to provide an interdisciplinary course in world affairs for students who have had little or no previous university training in the field and otherwise might never undertake systematic, though brief, study of the subject. In preparing it, we should like to acknowledge the stimulation, suggestions, and assistance of our colleagues Professor William Butz of The Pennsylvania State University and Professor Neal Riemer of the University of Wisconsin (Milwaukee) and of others who have taught the course and helped to improve it. We are also indebted for their initial encouragement to the former President and Vice President for Academic Affairs of The Pennsylvania State University, Dr. Milton E. Eisenhower and Mr. Lawrence E. Dennis, respectively, and to the members of the former University Committee on International Understanding.

E.A.
K.F.
J.P.

CONTENTS

1

The Problem of Understanding World Affairs

WAR IN THE NUCLEAR AGE

Today, every inhabitant of this planet must contemplate the day when this planet may no longer be habitable. Every man, woman and child lives under a nuclear sword of Damocles, hanging by the slenderest of threads, capable of being cut at any moment by accident or by miscalculation, or by madness. The weapons of war must be abolished before they abolish us.[1]

THUS SPOKE PRESIDENT JOHN F. KENnedy to the United Nations General Assembly, September 25, 1961, as he emphasized the number one problem of our time—war. Earlier in the same address, he had declared:

Unconditional war can no longer lead to unconditional victory. It can no longer serve to settle disputes. It can no longer concern the great Powers alone. For a nuclear disaster, spread by winds and water and fire, could well engulf the great and the small, the rich and the poor, the committed and the uncommitted alike. Mankind must put an end to war, or war will put an end to mankind.[2]

General Douglas MacArthur expressed the same apprehension when he said, "War has become a Frankenstein to destroy both sides. . . . If you lose, you are annihilated; if you win, you stand only to lose." [3]

Some military strategists [4] have questioned such dire predictions,

[1] United Nations, *General Assembly Official Records*, 16th Session, Plenary Meetings, Vol. 1, 1013th Meeting, par. 50.

[2] *Ibid.*, par. 40.

[3] Douglas MacArthur, "The Abolition of War," in *Vital Speeches*, Vol. XXI, No. 9 (February 15, 1955), pp. 1041–1042.

[4] Herman Kahn, for example, has studied the nature and potential consequences of nuclear war at great length and concludes that with proper preparations, it would be possible for both the United States and the Soviet Union to "cope with all the effects of a thermonuclear war, in the sense of saving most people and restoring something close to the prewar standard of living in a relatively short time." Even if the 53 industrially important metropolitan areas of the United States—ranging from the largest ones like New York City or Los Angeles to the smaller ones like Trenton, New Jersey, and Erie, Pennsylvania—were totally destroyed, Kahn concludes that with

but none have minimized the almost unbelievable destruction which would be wrought by a major nuclear war. The atomic bomb which was dropped on Hiroshima on August 6, 1945, ushering in the age of nuclear war, is already beyond the memory of the most recent generation of Americans. They know of its devastating results only through what they have read or heard. Yet even the statistics of destruction are so awesome as to be scarcely comprehensible to anyone who did not live through that horrendous experience: [5]

> 70,000 to 80,000 killed out of a population of 344,000.
>
> An equal number injured.
>
> 81 percent of the buildings in the city proper destroyed.
>
> 16.7 percent of the buildings severely damaged.
>
> 270 out of 298 doctors killed.
>
> 1,645 out of 1,780 nurses killed.
>
> 42 out of 45 hospitals destroyed or rendered useless.

This was what one single bomb carried by one B-29 plane could do. It destroyed almost as much as did the huge fire raids on Tokyo, March 9–10, 1945, in which 334 B-29 planes dropped some 2,000 tons of bombs, killing nearly 84,000, wounding nearly 41,000 and destroying 267,171 buildings, one-fourth of the total in Tokyo.[6]

Yet the atomic bomb of 1945 was a mere "drop-in-the-bucket" compared with the hydrogen bombs of the past decade. The Hiroshima bomb had an explosive power equal to about 20,000 tons of TNT. This was 1,000 times larger than the biggest "blockbusters" of World War II, which equalled about 20 tons of TNT. Hydrogen bombs of today are usually measured in terms of millions of tons of TNT (1 megaton = 1 million tons), with the "big" ones equal to 20,000,000 tons of TNT (20 megatons) and up.[7] A 20 megaton bomb is 1,000 times bigger in destructive capacity than the Hiroshima bomb, and one million times greater than the largest blockbusters of World War II.

---

reasonable preparations our economic recovery could take place at a rate which would restore most of the prewar gross national product in a relatively few years. Herman Kahn, *On Thermonuclear War* (Princeton, Princeton University Press, 1960), pp. 71, and 75–84.

[5] United States Air Force, Historical Division, *The Army Air Forces in World War II*, Vol. 5 (Chicago, University of Chicago Press, 1953), pp. 722–723.

[6] *Ibid.*, pp. 614–617. For a grim, human account of the reaction and experiences of survivors of the Hiroshima bombing see John Hersey's novel, *Hiroshima* (New York, Knopf, 1946), and Arata Osada, *Children of the A-Bomb, The Testament of the Boys and Girls of Hiroshima* (New York, Putnam's, 1959).

[7] The Soviet Union in 1962 tested bombs in the apparent range of 30 megatons, and Premier Khrushchev on January 16, 1963, boasted before the East German Communist Party Congress that Soviet physicists had developed a 100 megaton bomb. *Current Digest of the Soviet Press*, February 20, 1963, p. 17.

As David Inglis, the well-known nuclear physicist, has observed, it is extremely difficult to understand a factor of one million. The housewife, who normally feeds three or four hungry mouths in her family, would have some idea of what a million means if she contemplated the feeding of a big city like Chicago with three to four million people.[8]

Dr. Inglis goes on to suggest that for anyone who has read of the devastation which took place in Rotterdam, Hamburg, London, Cologne, Coventry, Tokyo, or other cities which suffered the enormous losses from chemical explosives in World War II, the best way to imagine the power of one big H-bomb is to think of all this destructive power dropped on one city in a single explosion. "That is just part of what one H-bomb can do. One single twenty megaton H-Bomb delivers more explosive power than that of all the weapons used by all nations for all purposes during all the years of World War II, for that matter, during all the wars of history." [9]

An even more graphic and awesome estimate of the nature of modern nuclear war comes from no less an authority than United States Secretary of Defense Robert S. McNamara. In a statement submitted to the House Armed Services Committee, February 5, 1965,[10] he said that under even the most favorable foreseeable circumstances of protection,[11] American fatalities in a major nuclear attack on this country in 1970 would total 41 million people out of a total population then of 210 million. Under the worst circumstances (no further fallout shelter program or missile or bomber defenses, and a simultaneous attack on both cities and military targets), fatalities might run as high as 149 million, or approximately 70 percent of the population.

The following table summarizes the estimated fatalities which the United States might expect in a major nuclear attack, depending on an early or delayed attack on our cities and on additional investments in the current program of United States strategic offensive forces.[12]

From this, it can be seen that a nationwide fallout shelter program might reduce fatalities by about 30 million, according to Defense De-

8 David R. Inglis, "The Nature of Nuclear War," in *Nuclear Weapons and the Conflict of Conscience*, edited by John C. Bennett (New York, Scribner, 1962), pp. 42–43. Dr. Inglis is a Senior Physicist at the Argonne National Laboratory, Illinois.

9 *Ibid.*, p. 43.

10 U.S. Congress, House of Representatives, Committee on Armed Services, *Hearings on Military Posture and H.R. 4016*, February 2 through March 22, 1965, 89th Congress, 1st session, pp. 204–209.

11 These would include a $5 billion full fallout shelter program and $20 billion in additional missile and manned bomber defenses. It would also be based on the relatively unlikely contingency that an enemy missile attack on U.S. cities were sufficiently delayed after an attack on U.S. military targets to permit our strategic missiles (which can reach their targets in less than one hour) to retaliate and destroy, prior to launch, a large part of the enemy's forces withheld for use against our cities. *Ibid.*, p. 204.

12 *Ibid.*, p. 205.

partment estimates, while a large additional missile and bomber defense
program costing up to $20 billion might reduce them by another 40 to
50 million, depending on whether there was an early or delayed attack
on American cities. No defense program within this general range of expenditures, according to Secretary McNamara, would reduce fatalities
much below 80 million unless the enemy delayed his attack on our cities
long enough for our missile forces to retaliate and destroy a substantial
portion of the enemy bases.[13]

TABLE 1

Estimate of U.S. Fatalities in a Nuclear Attack on the United States

ADDITIONAL INVESTMENT	MILLIONS OF U.S. FATALITIES	
	Early Urban Attack	*Delayed Urban Attack*
No additional investments	149	122
$5 billion (Fallout shelter program for entire population)	120	90
$15 billion (Above, plus $10 billion for added missile and bomber defenses)	96	59
$25 billion (Above, plus a further $10 billion for missile and bomber defenses)	78	41

SOURCE: United States Secretary of Defense Robert S. McNamara, 1965.

None of these estimates is absolute, Secretary McNamara emphasized, and the enemy could increase the number of American fatalities
by increasing the outlays on his offensive striking forces. No perfect
protection for our population could be assured.

. . . against the forces we expect the Soviets to have during the next decade,
it would be virtually impossible for us . . . to provide anything approaching
perfect protection for our population no matter how large the general nuclear
war forces we were to provide, including even the hypothetical possibility of
striking first. Of course, the number of fatalities would depend on the size and
character of the attack as well as on our own forces. But the Soviets have it
within their technical and economic capacity to prevent us from achieving a
posture that would keep our immediate fatalities below some level. They can
do this, for example, by offsetting any increases in our defenses by increases in
their missile forces. In other words, if we were to try to assure survival of a very
high percent of our population, and if the Soviets were to choose to frustrate this
attempt, . . . the extra cost to them would appear to be substantially less than
the extra cost to us.[14]

13 *Ibid.*, p. 209.
14 *Ibid.*, p. 173.

The Secretary pointed out, however, that this argument was "not conclusive against our undertaking a major new damage-limiting program." He added:

The resources available to the Soviets are more limited than our own and they may not actually react to our initiatives as we have assumed. But it does underscore the fact that beyond a certain level of defense, the cost advantage lies increasingly with the offense, and this fact must be taken into account in any decision to commit ourselves to large outlays for additional defensive measures.[15]

While the United States might suffer these terrific losses if subjected to nuclear attack, McNamara emphasized that even after absorbing a first strike our authorized strategic missile force, if directed against the enemy's urban areas, could cause more than 100 million fatalities and destroy 80 percent of his industrial capacity. If this were then followed by a manned bomber attack on the enemy urban areas, fatalities might be increased by 10 to 15 million and industrial destruction by another 1 or 2 percent.[16]

Nikita Khrushchev, former Soviet Premier, gave an even more terrifying picture of the consequences of a nuclear war to all peoples when he addressed the East German Communist Party Congress in January, 1963: [17]

According to calculations by scientists, 700,000,000 to 800,000,000 people would die in the first strike alone. Not only the large cities of the two leading nuclear powers—the U.S.A. and the U.S.S.R.—but also the cities of France, Britain, Germany, Italy, China, Japan and many other countries would be wiped from the face of the earth and destroyed. The consequences of a nuclear war would have their effect on the life expectancy of many generations of people, would produce disease and death and lead to the most monstrous development of mankind. . . .

There is no doubt that if a thermonuclear war were unleashed by the imperialist maniacs, the capitalist system that gave rise to war would perish in it. *But would the socialist countries and the cause of the struggle for socialism throughout the world gain from a world thermonuclear catastrophe? Only people who deliberately close their eyes to the facts can think this. As far as the Marxist-Leninists are concerned, they cannot think in terms of a communist civilization built upon the ruins of the world's cultural centers, on ravaged earth contaminated by thermonuclear fallout. This is not to mention the fact that for many people there would be no question of socialism at all, since they would have been removed from the face of our planet.* [Italics, the authors'] [18]

15 *Ibid.*, p. 209.
16 *Ibid.*, p. 191.
17 *Pravda*, January 17, 1963. Translation from the *Current Digest of the Soviet Press*, published weekly at Columbia University by the Joint Committee on Slavic Studies, appointed by the American Council of Learned Societies and the Social Science Research Council. Copyright, 1963, Vol. XV, Issue No. 4, p. 17, by the Joint Committee on Slavic Studies.
18 Khrushchev expressed similar opinions in an address before the Supreme Soviet, December 12, 1962. *Pravda*, December 13, 1962. Translation from the *Current Digest*

Similar views have been expressed by the prominent Soviet military theorist Major General Nikolai Talenskii, who in his published writings has accepted many Western estimates of the destructiveness of modern nuclear war and has concluded that war no longer can be used as a satisfactory instrument of foreign policy. He says:

Rocket and nuclear warfare, even without the use of chemical and bacteriological weapons would lead to the annihilation of entire nations and the devastation of their lands. Vast areas would be contaminated by lethal concentrations of radiation.

* * *

Not to see the dangers of rocket and nuclear war is harmful and to underestimate them is criminal. The world wars unleashed by the imperialists seriously undermined capitalism as the previously dominant social system. There is no doubt that in the event of a new war capitalism will succumb completely. But does this mean that the sacrifices of war, however heavy, are justified? This is a harmful, anti-humane point of view.

The world population would be reduced by one-half as a result of a new global war. Moreover, the most active, capable and civilized portion would be wiped out. It should also be borne in mind that the material and technological basis for life would be destroyed. Thermonuclear weapons would destroy plants and factories, devastate fields and orchards, destroy means of transportation and communications, almost all buildings, hospitals, etc. Libraries, institutes and museums would fall into ruin: humanity would be thrown back and its way to Communism would become immensely longer.

* * *

The development of the technique of exterminating people has resulted in a situation that makes it impossible to resort to war to solve political disputes as was done throughout the . . . history of mankind. A rocket and nuclear war is dangerous not only for the side subject to attack, but is at the same time suicidal for the aggressor.

It is our opinion that, in terms of military technology, war as an instrument of policy is outliving itself.[19]

---

of the Soviet Press, published weekly at Columbia University by the Joint Committee on Slavic Studies, appointed by the American Council of Learned Societies and the Social Science Research Council. Copyright, 1963, Vol. XIV, Issue No. 51, pp. 3–4, by the Joint Committee on Slavic Studies. It should also be recalled that in addressing the Supreme Soviet in February, 1956, Khrushchev modified Lenin's classic dictum on the "inevitability" of war between capitalism and communism, and on the necessity of war as a means of advancing towards communism. Khrushchev seems to have been thinking in this connection primarily of major wars between capitalist and communist states. "Limited" wars such as those between "imperialist" powers and their "colonies" or "national liberation wars" initiated by colonial peoples against their rulers seem to occupy a more acceptable status in Soviet military theory.

[19] N. Talenskii, "On the Character of Modern Warfare," *International Affairs* (Moscow), October, 1960, pp. 24–25, 27. General Talenskii expressed similar views in later articles, "The 'Absolute Weapon' and the Problem of Security," *International Affairs* (Moscow), April, 1962, pp. 22–27, and "Anti-Missile Systems and Disarmament," *International Affairs* (Moscow), October, 1964, pp. 15–19.

Alongside such estimates of the potential destructiveness of World War III, the figures on the losses suffered during World War II almost pale into insignificance: [20]

Approximately 22 million military and civilian deaths on all sides.

34 million wounded.

Total monetary losses estimated at $1,348 billion.

From this, one sees that the total military and civilian deaths suffered by all belligerents during the six years of World War II is about one-half the minimum casualties (41 million) which the Defense Department estimates would be suffered by the United States alone in a major nuclear exchange today (see Table I above). No wonder President Kennedy said, "Mankind must put an end to war, or war will put an end to mankind." Or, one might conclude even more strongly, unless we solve the problem of war, nothing much else will matter.

While many Western and Soviet leaders seem to agree that a major nuclear war would be unbelievably destructive and impractical as an instrument of policy, the Chinese Communists do not at present seem to regard it as such a grave threat to themselves or to the future of the Communist revolution. Indeed, their public statements have frequently seemed alarmingly reckless about war in general, and nuclear war in particular. In their view, all wars which are fought "by the people" under the leadership of a "correctly" operated Marxist-Leninist Communist Party (*i.e.,* one which subscribes to Peking's interpretation of Marxism-Leninism) are "just" and "revolutionary."

For example, Lin Piao, Communist Chinese Defense Minister and probably the most powerful figure in the Communist hierarchy in Peking alongside Mao Tse-tung, declared in a major pronouncement of Chinese revolutionary philosophy, in September, 1965:

War can temper the people and push history forward. In this sense war is a great school. . . . Revolutionary people never take a gloomy view of war. . . . The seizure of power by armed force, the settlement of issues by war, is the central task and the highest form of revolution. This Marxist-Leninist principle of revolution holds good universally for China and for all other countries.[21]

Shortly after the atom bombs were dropped on Hiroshima and Nagasaki, Mao Tse-tung wrote:

On the other hand, many Soviet military writers have continued to assert with Marshall Sokolovskii that "the essential nature of war as a continuation of politics does not change with changing technology and armament." See Thomas W. Wolfe, *Soviet Strategy at the Crossroads* (Cambridge, Mass., Harvard University Press, 1964), p. 72, and also chapter VI in this volume, "The Question of War as an Instrument of Policy."

[20] See the articles on "War" and "World War II" in the *Encyclopaedia Britannica* (Chicago, Encyclopaedia Britannica, 1965), Vol. 23, pp. 335 and 793Q.

[21] Lin Piao, "Long Live the Victory of the People's War," *Peking Review,* September 3, 1965. This article was published in all major Chinese Communist newspapers and widely distributed abroad.

Can atom bombs decide wars? No they can't. Atom bombs could not make Japan surrender. Without the struggles waged by the people, atom bombs by themselves would be of no avail. . . . Some of our comrades too believe that the atom bomb is all-powerful; that is a big mistake. . . . What influence has made these comrades look upon the atom bomb as something miraculous? Bourgeois influence.[22]

And a year later, he declared:

The atom bomb is a paper tiger which the U.S. reactionaries use to scare people. It looks terrible, but in fact it isn't. Of course, the atom bomb is a weapon of mass slaughter, but the outcome of war is decided by the people, not by one or two new types of weapons.[23]

In his famous article, "Problems of War and Strategy," Mao Tse-tung used these ominous words:

Some people have ridiculed us as advocates of the "Omnipotence of war"; yes, we are, we are advocates of the omnipotence of revolutionary war which is not bad at all, but is good and is Marxist. . . . We can say that the whole world can be remolded with the gun.[24]

Mao, like other Communist spokesmen, has suggested that if the "imperialists" should launch a Third World War, it would result in the turning of many hundreds of millions of people to socialism and the consequent further weakening of capitalism. Lin Piao, in the important pronouncement referred to above, "Long Live the Victory of the People's War," September, 1965, reiterated this theme:

World War I was followed by the birth of the Socialist Soviet Union. World War II was followed by the emergence of a series of Socialist countries and many nationally independent countries. If the U.S. imperialists should insist on launching a third world war, it can be stated categorically that many more hundreds of millions of people will turn to Socialism; the imperialists will then have little room left on the globe; and it is possible that the whole structure of imperialism will collapse.[25]

This is the situation in the late 1960's when three major powers have fully developed nuclear weapons and two others (France and Communist China) are in the intermediate stages of such development.

[22] "The Situation and Our Policy after the Victory in the War of Resistance against Japan" (August 13, 1945), *Selected Works of Mao Tse-tung*, Vol. IV (Peking, Foreign Languages Press, 1961), pp. 21–22.

[23] "Talk with the American Correspondent Anna Louise Strong" (August, 1946), *Selected Works of Mao Tse-tung*, Vol. IV (Peking, Foreign Languages Press, 1961), p. 100. Lo Ju-ching, who was purged from his post of Chief of Staff of the Chinese "People's Liberation Army" during the so-called "cultural revolution" of 1966, wrote: "The Atom bomb can scare only cowards who have lost their revolutionary will, it cannot scare revolutionary people." *Peking Review*, September 3, 1965, p. 33.

[24] *Selected Works of Mao Tse-tung*, Vol. II (London, Lawrence and Wishart, 1954), pp. 272–273.

[25] *Peking Review*, September 3, 1965, p. 29.

What will it be like if nuclear weapons spread to other countries? Already it has been estimated that a dozen or more countries such as India, Canada, Sweden, Israel, Japan, West Germany, Italy and Yugoslavia could, if they chose, begin programs leading to the explosion of a nuclear device in a few years.[26] Whether the spread of nuclear weapons can be checked before it becomes too late has become one of the most urgent problems of our time.

Not only does the threat of a nuclear war hang over our heads like a sword of Damocles, but the day-to-day costs of military preparations take over 50 percent of our federal administrative budget.[27] Out of administrative budgets of $107–$135 billion a year in 1966, 1967, and 1968, $58–$75 billion each year was devoted to national defense. Another $6 billion on the average was spent each year for veterans benefits, while about $13 billion each year went to pay the interest on the national debt (most of which has resulted from expenditures on war or preparation for war). This means that over two-thirds of our total administrative federal budget, or $75–$96 billion per year at present, goes for wars, past, present, or future. It also means that no large reductions in the total federal expenditures can be expected unless there is significant progress towards general disarmament and the prevention of war.

In contrast, approximately $4.5 billion per year, or about 6 percent of the national defense budget, has been allocated for international affairs and foreign aid, including the State Department, Foreign Service, United States Information Agency, Peace Corps, Food for Peace Program, foreign aid, and United States contributions to the United Nations. Total United States contributions to all United Nations programs in the mid-1960's were about $200 million yearly, including the regular budget assessments and voluntary contributions for special programs such as refugees, technical and economic assistance, and UNICEF. This equals less than three-tenths of one percent of the $70 billion national defense budget, but represents about one-third of the annual United Nations revenues from its more than 120 members.

The impact of the $4 billion spent on international affairs or of the $200 million spent on United Nations activities cannot of course be measured fully in terms of dollars and cents or compared fairly in such terms to the $70 billion spent on national defense. A comparison of these figures, nevertheless, illustrates strikingly the proportionately heavy financial outlays for defense and related activities by the United States. As for the world as a whole, it has been estimated that $200 bil-

26 *The New York Times,* August 1, 1965, Section 4, p. 3.

27 The term "administrative budget" covers the cost of goods, services and operating expenses of all national government agencies. It does not include the so-called "trust fund expenditures" such as social security benefits or federal highway grants which are financed out of special taxes and levies collected for these purposes and deposited in trust funds for subsequent disbursement.

TABLE 2 [28]

Administrative Budget Expenditures of the Federal Government (Major Items)
(Fiscal years. In billions)

	1966 actual	1967 est.	1968 est.
National defense (incl. Vietnam)	57.7	70.2	75.5
Interest on national debt	12.1	13.5	14.2
Veterans benefits	5.0	6.4	6.1
Space research and technology	5.9	5.6	5.3
International affairs and foreign aid	4.2	4.6	4.8
Agriculture and agricultural resources	3.3	3.0	3.2
Natural resources	3.1	3.2	3.5
Commerce and transportation	3.0	3.5	3.1
Health, labor, welfare and housing	7.9	11.3	12.3
Education	2.8	3.3	2.8
General government (legislative, administrative and judicial)	2.5	2.7	2.8
Adjustments	−.5	−.6	+1.4
Total administrative budget	107.0	126.7	135.0

lion is now spent annually by all countries on defense preparations.[29] When one realizes that the combined gross national product of all the underdeveloped countries of Asia (excluding Communist China), Africa and Latin America is only between $300 and $350 billion per year,[30] one sees another confirmation of the relatively heavy burden of military expenditures in the world today.

It is hard for the average individual to comprehend the actual size of $1 billion, accustomed though we are to astronomical budgets and to the ease with which government agencies seem to spend billions for this or that. Some idea might be gained, however, if one realizes that if he were to spend $1,000 a day, seven days a week, year in and year out, he would have had to have begun doing so about 744 B.C. in order to have spent one billion dollars by 1966 A.D. This is 2 percent of what the United States spends annually in the mid-1960's for national defense, and about 1 percent of the total federal budget.

28 United States, Bureau of the Budget, *The Budget of the United States Government for the Fiscal Year Ending June 30, 1968* (Washington, Government Printing Office, 1967), p. 18.

29 *The New York Times,* December 4, 1965, p. 30.

30 See below, chap. 6, p. 192. The Soviet Union spends about the same proportion (10–15 percent) of its annual gross national product on armaments as the United States even though the Soviet GNP is not quite half that of the U.S.

On top of this, one must never forget that the costs of war cannot be fully expressed in terms of casualties and monetary outlays. There are the refugees and displaced persons. There are the long-term economic consequences of devoting major portions of the world's productive capacity to the materials of war rather than to the needs of man. And there are the spiritual and moral effects upon the human spirit of the prolonged use of total violence against other human beings.

Under these circumstances, it seems almost inconceivable that anyone in his right mind would consciously choose the path of war today. Indeed, as the technology of warfare has become increasingly destructive during the twentieth century, this conclusion has long seemed inescapable. The advent of the machine gun, the tank, the airplane, poison gas, the long-range bomber loaded with blockbusters, the atomic bomb, and now the multimegaton hydrogen and cobalt bombs has in each successive period prompted many to conclude that the horrors of the new weapons would in themselves dissuade men from going to war again, at least on a major scale. Such, unfortunately, has not been the case, and despite the rationally compelling reasons for avoiding it, nuclear war with all its catastrophic implications remains an ever-present possibility and the number one problem of today. Why this is the case and what might be done about it are among the central themes of this book.

Adlai E. Stevenson, United States Ambassador to the United Nations, spoke to this point before the United Nations General Assembly when he referred to what he called "the double character of war." [31]

I assume that we are all convinced that the revolutionary advance in destructive capability—and the danger that little wars anywhere can lead to bigger wars everywhere—has made war an obsolete means for the settlement of disputes among nations. Yet World War II, I remind you, occurred after it already was clear to intelligent men that war had become an irrational instrument of national policy—that another way must be found to settle international accounts and to effect needed change.

The reason is not hard to find: the level of destruction does not obliterate the inherently double character of warfare. In our minds we tend to associate war—and correctly so—with the ancient lust for conquest and dominion; we tend—rightly—to identify war as the instrument of conquerors and tyrants.

Yet in every war there is a defender who, however reluctantly, takes up arms in self-defence and calls upon others for aid. And this is the other face of war: war has been the instrument by which lawlessness and rebellion have been suppressed, by which nations have preserved their independence, by which freedom has been defended. War is an instrument of aggression—and also the means by which the aggressors have been turned back and would-be masters have been struck down.

---

[31] United Nations, General Assembly, Official Records, 19th Session, Provisional Verbatim Record of the 1323rd Meeting, 26 January 1965, A/PV. 1323 (mimeographed), pp. 52–53.

All through the years we have been taught again and again that most men value some things more than life itself. And no one has reminded us more eloquently and resolutely that it is better to die on your feet than to live on your knees than the noble spirit that left us the other day in London—Sir Winston Churchill.

As long as there are patriots, aggression will be met with resistance—whatever the cost. And the cost rises higher with the revolution in weaponry. . . .

There, precisely, is the difficulty we are in. Now, in our day, the end result of aggression and defence is Armageddon—for man has stolen the Promethean fire. Yet resistance to aggression is no less inevitable in the second half of the twentieth century than it was 2,500 years ago.

The powers of the atom unleashed by science are too startling, too intoxicating, and at the same time too useful as human tools for any of us to wish to abandon the astonishing new technology. But, if we will not abandon it, we must master it. Unless the United Nations or some other organization develops reliable machinery for dealing with conflicts and violence by peaceful means, Armageddon will continue to haunt the human race; for the nations will—as they must—rely on national armaments until they can confidently rely on international institutions to keep the peace.

UNDERSTANDING THE PROBLEM OF WAR

To understand the problem of war and conflict in the world today is to understand the urges and drives of some 120 sovereign national states as well as the aspirations and the ideologies of their peoples. Ambassador Stevenson has spoken of aggression and defense. But what drives a nation to aggression? This question is not easily or simply answered. Over the years, many theories and explanations of war and aggression have been advanced.[32] The principal ones are outlined briefly below.

Human Nature. War, it is claimed, results from basic aggressive drives within man himself—greed, selfishness, jealousy, lust for power. Just as individuals are drawn into competition and conflict by these aggressive drives, so are nations, as collective groups of individuals, drawn into war. Until "human nature" is radically changed, according to this view, wars and conflicts will be inevitable.

Economic Rivalry. According to this theory, wars result from the uneven distribution of economic and material resources, the struggle for markets and sources of raw materials, and from the pressure of overpopulation and economic underdevelopment. The quest for colonies in Asia and Africa, the rivalry for oil in the Middle East or for control of

[32] For a comprehensive analysis of the problem of war and its causes, see Quincy Wright, *A Study of War* (Chicago, University of Chicago Press, 1942), 2 vols. Chapter XI of Volume I and most of Volume II deal extensively with the causes of war. A stimulating collection of classical and contemporary writings on the causes of war may be found in Leon Bramson and George W. Goethals, *War: Studies from Psychology, Sociology, and Anthropology* (New York, Basic Books, 1964).

the "rice-bowl" of Southeast Asia are cited as examples. The Communist theory of war as a manifestation of the struggle between the capitalist classes and the proletarian working classes also falls into this category.

Ideological Rivalry. The basic cause of war today, it is argued, lies in the ideological struggle between democracy and communism, between the "free world" and the countries governed by the "dictatorship of the proletariat." In Western eyes, the Communist principles of "world revolution" are viewed as the main danger, while in Communist eyes, the forces of "capitalist imperialism" threaten to engulf the world in a new war. Peaceful coexistence between ideological enemies is regarded as a contradiction of terms. Earlier in history, during such periods as the Crusades and the Reformation, "wars of religion" between Christians and Moslems, or Catholics and Protestants bore some resemblance to modern ideological struggles.

Armaments and Military Rivalry. Still another approach explains war primarily as the end-product of armaments races between nations and the quest for superiority in military power. The intense rivalry today between the United States and the Soviet Union for superiority in nuclear weapons greatly aggravates international tensions and, if not checked, may eventually culminate in war. In today's technological world, the dangers of war by accident or miscalculation weigh heavily on our minds. The development of nuclear military power by Communist China has intensified the pressure in countries like India to acquire or develop their own nuclear weapons. If the spread of nuclear weapons is not effectively restricted, and if five, ten or twenty other states acquire a nuclear military capacity in the next few years, the dangers of war, it is held, will quickly multiply. It is this fear which leads many to place high priority on the achievement of effective international agreements on arms control and disarmament.

International Misunderstandings. ". . . since wars begin in the minds of men, it is in the minds of men that the defenses of peace must be constructed; . . . ignorance of each other's ways and lives has been a common cause, throughout the history of mankind, of that suspicion and mistrust between the peoples of the world through which their differences have all too often broken into war." [33] These words from the preamble to the Constitution of UNESCO, the United Nations Educational, Scientific and Cultural Organization, illustrate the belief that international misunderstanding is at the root of war. Implicit in this belief is the assumption that man often suspects and fears that which he does not know, and that, out of this climate of suspicion and mistrust, wars can readily develop. Foreigners are often distrusted because they are different and speak a strange tongue. Under the impact of a strong nationalistic

[33] U.S. Dept of State, *Basic Documents: UN Educational, Scientific and Cultural Organization,* 4th ed., 1956, Dept. of State Publ. 6364, p. 7.

loyalty, a person may come to regard his own country and its institutions as superior. If, in addition, his newspapers and schoolbooks have presented one-sided or grossly biased accounts of the foreign policies of his government and its neighbors, serious misunderstanding may ensue which makes the peaceful adjustment of differences extremely difficult. This viewpoint assumes also a fundamental community of interest among the peoples of all nations which can be recognized through better mutual knowledge and understanding and which is essential to the development of effective institutions of international cooperation.

The Struggle for Power. This view, while not rejecting *in toto* the preceding theories, regards them at best as only partial or incomplete explanations of the phenomenon of war. War, according to this theory, results not from any one of the above factors by itself, but is rather one of the risks and unsought by-products of the continuous and total struggle for power between nations. International politics, it is argued, cannot be based on any assumption of a fundamental community of interests between national states, but reflects instead the struggle for power between these states, each of which is striving to pursue what it regards as its own national interest. Power is viewed in a comprehensive sense as embracing all of the means and resources by which a state can become strong enough to pursue its interests without effective restraints on its freedom of action. Thus, armaments are only one of the elements of national power, like strategic geographic frontiers, possession of or access to natural resources and trade outlets, a dynamically appealing political and economic ideology, or a skillful and resourceful diplomacy. War results when one state or group of states attempts to expand its power position and encounters forcible resistance from another state or group of states unwilling to accept such an upsetting of the existing status quo.[34]

Absence of World Law and Government. According to this theory, war results primarily because there is no effective world law or government to regulate the relations of nation-states. Each of the 120 sovereign states in the world regards itself as a relatively free agent in world affairs, free to pursue its interests as it is able, and free to accumulate the power to do so, including the use of armaments and war. It is this freedom to use military power which distinguishes nation-states in the international community from individual citizens and groups within national communities. Conflict and competition, the struggle for power and advancement—political, economic, psychological, ideological—occur at all levels of society—local, national or international. But, aside from civil war, which in most states is the exception rather than the rule, the struggle for power by military might is found only at the international level.

[34] This theory is set forth vigorously in Hans J. Morgenthau, *Politics Among Nations,* 3rd ed. (New York, Knopf, 1960).

It happens here, according to this theory, because there are no strong governmental institutions at the world level comparable to the state at the national or local level. Through the effective authority of courts, police, and the general rule of law, states at the national and local level can usually keep conflict and competition within peaceful limits. The problem of war is therefore seen as the problem of developing comparable institutions of authority at the international level. The feeble attempts through international law and treaties to restrict the freedom of states to resort to war have been inadequate because they left untouched the framework of national sovereignty which still leaves states free *in practice* (though not always *in law*) to pursue unlimited ends with unlimited means. International society, in many respects, resembles the frontier-type communities regularly seen on the TV Westerns where every man carries a six-shooter on his hip, and the one who can draw fastest and shoot best is able to get what he wants until the sheriff catches up with him. Until states accept the authority of government over their actions, wars between them, it is argued, will be unavoidable.[35]

NO SIMPLE SOLUTIONS

As one begins to analyze these theories of war and conflict and plow through the maze of divergent interpretations and interests, one soon realizes that there are no simple, quick solutions to the world's ills. One also discovers that the sharpest controversies usually arise out of situations in which each party to the dispute sincerely believes he is right. The essence of truly great disputes is that there is something—often much —to be said on both sides.

When confronted with such a complicated variety of views on world issues, the average citizen may at first become bewildered and frustrated. Naturally, he would like to see easy, quick, inexpensive and, if possible, permanent solutions. But they do not seem to exist. Yet the realization that they do not exist is the first step towards wisdom. The next step is the development of a framework of thought or analysis which will help one understand the nature of the international crises which continually plague mankind.

DIFFERENT VANTAGE POINTS ON WORLD AFFAIRS

In developing such a framework of analysis, it is helpful to realize that world affairs can be viewed from at least four different vantage points: the vantage point of a nation-state, the vantage point of an ideological

[35] For a comprehensive presentation of this theory, see Grenville Clark and Louis B. Sohn, *World Peace through World Law*, 2nd ed. rev. (Cambridge, Harvard University Press, 1960).

system, the vantage point of moral or religious idealism, and the vantage point of critical scholarship. The vantage points are not necessarily mutually exclusive but may under certain circumstances blend into a kind of composite vantage point. Thus one should not be surprised to encounter in a single statement a blending of the vantage points of a nation-state and of an ideological system. One is also likely to find from time to time analyses which blend the vantage points of religious idealism and the nation-state. Other combinations are also possible, and the thoughtful student of world affairs will learn how to recognize them and analyze their validity.

THE VANTAGE POINT OF A NATION-STATE

This is the viewpoint most likely to be taken by national governments, foreign offices, and the officials responsible for the conduct of foreign policy. Wide sections of public opinion frequently also take this approach.

Since there are some 120 different nation-states in the world, there could conceivably be 120 different national viewpoints on every major world problem. A good place to observe this is in the debates of the United Nations General Assembly, where most of these states are represented. Each year, for example, the Assembly devotes its first three to four weeks to what is called general debate, during which period every member state is given the opportunity to present its general views on the world situation and on the issues to be considered by the Assembly. Over one hundred states usually make such statements each year, and they provide a quick and useful indication of the wide range of national outlooks which exist.

Each state is concerned basically with the preservation of its national security and the promotion of its general welfare.[36] These are the objectives of the foreign policy of every state. But each state is at the same time differently endowed in terms of geography, population, natural resources, economic development, and other elements of national power. There are also important differences in ideological outlook and religious and cultural systems which will be noted more fully below. These many differences from state to state explain the differences in outlook which the leaders of the various states take regarding world affairs.

Thus the United States government and its allies see the world crisis today largely in terms of the expansion of Communist power and the in-

---

[36] By "national security" is meant the preservation of the independence of a nation-state and the protection of the state and its citizens from external attack or intervention in its domestic affairs. Promotion of the "general welfare" of the state and its people includes the fostering of conditions that add to the economic, social, cultural, educational, scientific and political well-being of the national community. The term "national interest" is used to embrace those objectives and methods which are deemed essential to maintain national security and promote national welfare.

tolerant, totalitarian character of this power. Until recently, it was primarily the expansion of Soviet power which was feared. Today, the expansion of Chinese Communist power in Asia is regarded as the more immediate threat, while Soviet policies are seen as more restrained and more conscious of the potential destructiveness of modern nuclear war. In an attempt to "contain" Russian and Chinese Communist power, the United States and its allies joined together in the North Atlantic Treaty Organization (NATO) and the Southeast Asia Treaty Organization (SEATO). In Korea, the United States vigorously supported the collective security measures of the United Nations to check Communist expansion, while in Vietnam, the United States has assumed the almost exclusive responsibility of attempting to prevent a Communist régime from being established in the South.

These actions reflect the basic assumption of the United States government that its security and welfare would be vitally endangered if a hostile power or group of powers were able to dominate the continent of Europe or Far Eastern Asia. Since Europe is closer geographically, politically, economically and culturally to the United States, most Americans have little difficulty believing that the security and freedom of the European states are extremely important to the United States. The Far East, on the other hand, raises more controversy, especially as to the extent to which United States security requirements necessitate American military action to check the expansion of rival powers. There is no better illustration of this than the doubts and uncertainties over the extent to which the United States should have become militarily involved in the Vietnam crisis of the 1960's. Would United States security be so endangered by a Communist victory in Vietnam as to warrant the large-scale commitment of American lives and resources? More significantly, could the United States bring to bear sufficient power and resources to achieve the desired outcome at a price the American people would be prepared to pay? This latter question emphasizes a point which no responsible official of any government can ignore—are the resources available to my government in this situation commensurate with the objectives or commitments I am trying to execute, and is the price worth paying?

The whole concept of political and military commitments throughout the world is a relatively new one for the United States and reflects the "revolution in American foreign policy" which has occurred since World War II. Prior to this time, one of the most persistent themes in United States foreign policy was noninvolvement in political and military undertakings in Europe and Asia. Neutrality and the avoidance of alliances were regarded as the most appropriate methods for achieving United States security. The concept of "national interest" had much narrower geographical dimensions then than it has today.

The Soviet Union views the world crisis in much different terms. Its quest for security embodies several traditional methods which have been pursued by Czarist and Soviet rulers alike—acquisition of warm-water ports, control of the Dardanelles, and an influential or controlling interest in the strategically important regions of Eastern Europe, the Middle East and the Far East adjacent to or near the Russian frontiers. Having felt the full weight of Germany's military power in two world wars, and lacking any formidable neutral geographic barriers to Germany's eastward expansion, Soviet leaders are deeply concerned about any resurgence of German power today, either within the framework of an independent German state or within a multilateral NATO force. A "friendly," "Communist-oriented" Germany rather than a NATO-oriented Germany and "friendly," "Communist" states in Eastern Europe have, therefore, considerable strategic as well as ideological appeal. NATO and the Western alliance system, together with the network of American military bases around the peripheries of Soviet territory, are viewed as a threat to the Soviet position and power. While the United States considers NATO "defensive," the Soviet Union continually calls it "aggressive." Two more diametrically different national viewpoints can scarcely be imagined.

The Soviet perception of world affairs is also strongly influenced by ideological considerations such as the building of communism and the spread of world revolution. On many occasions, particularly since World War II, the expansion of the Soviet strategic and political positions in Europe, the Middle East and Asia has coincided with the aspiration and effort to spread Communist ideology. In like manner, it should be recognized that the creation of American positions of strength and security throughout the world is often closely linked with the desire to promote freedom and democracy in other lands. One thus sees the blending of the vantage points of the nation-state and of an ideological system into a kind of composite vantage point in which the two approaches may appear indistinguishable. The careful student of world affairs, however, will need to recognize that while the two vantage points are often interrelated, they are not identical. A more accurate comprehension of world problems will result from an awareness of the respective roles and influence of each outlook. This will be treated more fully below.

There is neither time nor space here to set forth the viewpoints of all 120 sovereign nation-states. Yet learning to recognize their divergent concepts of national interest and security is one of the first steps in developing an intelligent understanding of world affairs. The student is encouraged to read widely for himself and to become familiar with as many different nation-state viewpoints as possible.[37]

37 An excellent presentation of the foreign policies of 24 representative nations, written in most cases by leading scholars from each of the countries concerned, is found in Joseph E. Black and Kenneth W. Thompson (editors), *Foreign Policies in a World of Change* (New York, Harper & Row, 1963). A shorter, analytical study of the

The outlook of Communist China, and its conflict of interests with both the Soviet Union and the United States, should be examined, as well as the position of France and its critical views of the United States, Great Britain and the NATO system. Furthermore, it is indispensable today to have some knowledge of the outlook of the newly emerging nations of Asia and Africa, over 60 of which have achieved independent statehood since World War II and which are struggling to overcome their marginal levels of existence and economic development. These countries, for the most part, regard the East-West struggle with great apprehension, and fear that the rival alliance systems will not only drain off capital resources needed by the developing countries but will also precipitate, sooner or later, World War III. Many, like India, feel that their own national security will be best served if they do not join any alliance system and, like the United States during the first 150 years of its history, avoid political and military alignments with the major world powers. To these new countries, the East-West struggle is of less significance than what they call the "North-South" struggle between the ex-colonial powers and themselves, involving the establishment of their own genuine political and economic independence from Europe and North America.

THE VANTAGE POINT OF AN IDEOLOGY

Viewing world affairs primarily from the standpoint of an ideology will produce sharply divergent interpretations of international problems. Is the world crisis today primarily a struggle between "democracy" and "communism," "freedom" and "slavery," or is it essentially a conflict between rival nation-states with ideology only a secondary factor? Did the United States send its troops to Vietnam to defend the "freedom" of the Vietnamese people or to check the expansion of Communist China's power in Asia?

These are troubling questions in a study of world affairs. Many Americans feel that the United States has a mission to further the cause of freedom throughout the world. Often, official American statements reflect this viewpoint. Secretary of State John Foster Dulles, for example, declared in an address entitled "Freedom's New Task" on February 26, 1956:

This nation was conceived with a sense of mission and dedicated to the extension of freedom throughout the world. President Lincoln . . . said of our Declaration of Independence that there was "something in that Declaration giving liberty, not alone to the people of this country, but hope for the world for

policies of 11 states is Roy C. Macridis (editor), *Foreign Policy in World Politics*, 2nd ed. (Englewood Cliffs, N.J., Prentice-Hall, 1962). The student will also find it helpful to read the statements of general debate before the UN General Assembly each year. See United Nations, General Assembly, Official Records, [latest] Session, Plenary Meetings. A convenient summary of these statements may be found in *UN Monthly Chronicle* (issued by the United Nations Office of Public Information).

all future time. It was that which gave promise that in due time the weights should be lifted from the shoulders of all men and that all men should have an equal chance."

That has been the spirit which has animated our people since they came together as a nation. . . .

Let me conclude with the words which Benjamin Franklin wrote from Paris on May 1, 1777:

"It is a common observation here that our cause is the cause of all mankind, and that we are fighting for their liberty in defending our own. It is a glorious task assigned us by Providence; which has, I trust, given us spirit and virtue equal to it, and will at last crown it with success." [38]

President Lyndon B. Johnson, in his State of the Union message to Congress, January 4, 1965, spoke in a similar vein:

Our concern and interest, compassion and vigilance, extend to every corner of a dwindling planet. Yet, it is not merely our concern but the concern of all free men. . . . For in concert with other nations, we shall help men defend their freedom. Our first aim remains the safety and well-being of our own country. . . .

Our own freedom and growth have never been the final goal of the American dream. We were never meant to be an oasis of liberty and abundance in a worldwide desert of disappointed dreams. Our nation was created to help strike away the chains of ignorance and misery and tyranny wherever they keep man less than God means him to be.[39]

Later, in the same message, President Johnson said with reference to United States involvement in Vietnam:

Our goal is peace in Southeast Asia. That will come only when aggressors leave their neighbors in peace.

What is at stake is the cause of freedom, and in that cause America will never be found wanting.

Communists, on the other hand, also have a deep feeling of mission. To them, Western democracy is simply the political ideology of capitalism. They believe that capitalism will inevitably collapse because, they believe, it engenders class struggle and war. They also feel that genuine peace and individual freedom will come only when the class struggle has been ended by the abolition of private ownership of capital and when the new classless society is sufficiently productive to provide goods according to the needs of all its members.

The sincere communist, viewing the world through the vantage point of his own ideology, feels that time is on his side and that the ultimate establishment of communism is certain because the "laws of historical development," as he understands them, are moving in his di-

---

[38] *Department of State Bulletin,* March 5, 1956, p. 367.
[39] *Department of State Bulletin,* January 25, 1965, pp. 95, 96.

rection. He sees confirmation of this in the fact that in 1939 some 170 million people were living under communism, whereas in the 1960's nearly 1 billion people were doing so.

The program of the Communist Party of the Soviet Union, adopted at its 22nd Party Congress in October, 1961, vigorously proclaims this official ideological confidence: [40]

The Great October Socialist Revolution [41] ushered in a new era in the history of mankind, the era of the downfall of capitalism and the establishment of communism. Socialism [42] has triumphed in the Soviet Union and has achieved decisive victories in the People's Democracies; socialism has become the practical cause of hundreds of millions of people, and the banner of the revolutionary movement of the working class throughout the world.

* * *

The gigantic revolutionary exploit accomplished by the Soviet people has roused and inspired the masses in all countries and continents. A mighty purifying thunderstorm marking the spring-time of mankind is raging over the earth. *The socialist revolutions in European and Asian countries have resulted in the establishment of the world socialist system.* A powerful wave of national-liberation revolutions is sweeping away the colonial system of imperialism.

One-third of mankind is building a new life under the banner of scientific communism. The first contingents of the working class to shake off capitalist oppression are facilitating victory for fresh contingents of their class brothers. The Socialist world is expanding; the capitalist world is shrinking. Socialism will inevitably succeed capitalism everywhere. Such is the objective law of social development. Imperialism is powerless to check the irresistible process of emancipation.

Our epoch, whose main content is the transition from capitalism to socialism, is an epoch of struggle between the two opposing social systems, an epoch of socialist and national-liberation revolutions, of the breakdown of imperialism and the abolition of the colonial system, an epoch of the transition of more and more peoples to the socialist path, of the triumph of socialism and communism on a world-wide scale.

With regard to the conflict in Vietnam, Soviet leaders also insist that they too are helping oppressed people uphold their "freedom." An editorial in *Pravda*, October 27, 1965, put it this way:

[40] *Programme of the Communist Party of the Soviet Union,* October 31, 1961 (Moscow, Foreign Languages Publishing House, 1961), pp 5–7.

[41] This refers to the Bolshevik Revolution of November, 1917. According to the old Russian calendar, it was October, 1917.

[42] In communist theory, the term "socialism" refers to the first stage on the road to communism. It is characterized by the existence of the "dictatorship of the proletariat," the forcible abolition of private ownership of capital, and the substitution of public ownership. From this, it can be seen that Soviet leaders use the term "socialism" in a much different way than do the democratic socialist parties in Western Europe.

At the present time, when American imperialism has committed a number of acts of open and naked aggression, when it is waging a dirty war against Vietnam and creating a threat to world peace, it is the obligation of every socialist country and every detachment of the revolutionary movement to concert its actions with those of all the other progressive forces to rebuff imperialism, defend peace, and uphold the just cause of the Vietnamese people and all other peoples who are fighting for their freedom.[43]

If world affairs are viewed exclusively from the vantage point of democratic or communist ideologies, the emerging interpretations are so contradictory and incompatible that permanent peaceful accommodation between the two views seems almost impossible. Neither system, it would appear, can feel secure in the long run unless the other disappears or radically changes its beliefs. The dilemma posed by such sharply conflicting ideologies leads some individuals to justify extreme proposals such as "preventive war," "wars of extermination," or "wars of liberation." [44]

At this point, most government officials and many individual citizens recoil and question whether their country should become involved in war simply to further their ideology in other parts of the world. The potential destructiveness of nuclear war, noted at the beginning of this chapter, seems to be recognized by both Soviet and American leaders and to be responsible for the caution and restraint they have shown towards actions which might lead to war of major or world-wide proportions. The war in Vietnam has been a "limited war," and Soviet and American leaders alike very deliberately tried to keep it this way despite the uncertainties of Communist China's attitudes and actions in the background.

Unless their own national security is directly threatened, responsible government officials and wide sections of public opinion are not usually disposed to resort to war for purely ideological reasons. Ideology may be used to rally public opinion at home or to justify certain actions abroad, and its influence on foreign policy decisions is frequently felt, but it will almost always take second place to national security considerations should there be a conflict between the two.[45]

[43] "The Supreme Internationalist Duty of a Socialist Country." Translated in full in *The Current Digest of the Soviet Press,* November 17, 1965, pp. 6–8, at p. 8.

[44] During the 1950's, "wars of liberation" were thought of by some Americans as efforts to "liberate" the countries of Eastern Europe behind the Iron Curtain. Some writers felt that such a "liberation" policy was preferable to the then official American policy of "containment." See, e.g., James Burnham, *Containment or Liberation?* (New York, John Day, 1953). In more recent years, Communist China and the Soviet Union have encouraged and supported what they describe as "wars of national liberation," which they regard as "just wars" designed to overthrow the rule of an "imperialist" power or its agents. The war in Vietnam is so designated by Communist leaders.

[45] Hans J. Morgenthau, in his *In Defense of the National Interest* (New York, Knopf, 1951), presents a thought-provoking argument that American foreign policy has on many occasions been overly preoccupied with "crusading" on behalf of ideological and moral principles and has been neglectful of what Morgenthau con-

In the Cuban missile crisis of October, 1962, the Soviet Union, despite its ideological sympathies for the Castro government, retreated from a military confrontation with the United States rather than risk a conflict in a distant area where it was relatively weak in relation to the United States and might ultimately expose its home territory to the devastation of a major nuclear war. Likewise, in October, 1956, when the Hungarians rebelled against Soviet domination of their country, the United States did not intervene militarily although most Americans were deeply moved by this struggle for freedom behind the Iron Curtain. Yet the United States government and most of its citizens reluctantly concluded that the cost of trying to uphold the cause of freedom in Hungary in the face of the Soviet army was too great for the interests of American national security and too likely to trigger World War III. Therefore we limited our actions to moral protests and resolutions of condemnation by the United Nations.

THE VANTAGE POINT OF IDEALISM

A third category of views regarding world affairs arises when the situation is considered from the vantage point of the moral or religious principles of idealism. Here the approach is to examine the world scene and the foreign policies of various governments in terms of the extent to which government actions conform to specific principles of religious or moral belief. The effort is frequently made, as was seen also in the case of the ideological outlook, to define the national interest in a way that will seem consistent with certain religious or moral principles. The attempt to put idealist principles first in formulating foreign policy often leads to criticism of government policies which appear to be based primarily on considerations of political or military expediency or strategy. The idealist approach, in turn, is criticized as naive and unrealistic because it subordinates the factors of national power, strategy and expediency to the dictates of moral or religious principles.

There are many different concepts of idealism among the principal religions of the world—Christianity, Judaism, Islam, Hinduism, Buddhism, and Confucianism—and all of them have varying degrees of influence on the outlook of their respective believers towards world affairs. A

---

siders to be American national-security interests. In the zeal to further democratic ideology, American policy, according to Morgenthau, has from time to time made moral or legal commitments which it did not have the power to enforce, and which it could not honor without gravely jeopardizing the security of the United States.

Thomas I. Cook and Malcolm Moos, in a book entitled *Power through Purpose* (Baltimore, The Johns Hopkins Press, 1954), criticize Morgenthau's concept of national interest and suggest that America's strongest asset in world affairs is its reputation as a practitioner and defender of democratic freedom. They contend that the real interest of the United States lies in vigorously furthering these democratic principles throughout the world and in trying to sow seeds of discontent within communist and other undemocratic countries.

good example of this approach is seen in the following quotation from an article, entitled "Foreign Policy and the Law of Charity," by a Jesuit writer, James L. Vizzard:

In this nation founded by men who spelled out clearly the moral basis of our political society, it is strange and discouraging to have to insist that our national interest is a much broader concept and reality than mere military security, political stability or economic advantage. Unless this nation has interests and responsibilities which are rooted in moral principles, how do we differ from the arbitrary "legality" of totalitarian states? Unless "national" interest is based upon moral interest, our objectives can claim no superiority over those of the Communist nations. If our foreign economic policy fails to recognize that the very fact of our abundance creates opportunities and obligations which far transcend any narrowly conceived selfish and temporary interest, then we deserve to be weighed and judged by the world and by God in the same balance as Russia.

In public debate and private discussion a great variety of reasons are given to justify programs of international aid: we have smothering farm surpluses; our expanding industrial economy demands overseas markets and raw materials; we need to win friends and bolster our national security; if *we* don't, the Communists will.

But the moral reasons for these programs, if they are mentioned at all, are brought in only parenthetically, or with embarrassed apology. Patronizing "realists" clearly imply that charity and justice have no pertinence to the issues, that they represent only the sentimental idealism of international "do-gooders."

Yet, in fact, love of neighbor and justice not only have validity, even in terms of national interest, but are motives for programs of aid which are more urgent, more far-reaching, and of greater value than any other motives. Moreover, these motives, if properly explained, could win much more sincere and practical approval here and abroad. Finally, programs undertaken for these motives are more likely to achieve, as by-products, the aims of our foreign policy.[46]

[46] *World Alliance Newsletter,* June, 1956, p. 1. This was published by the World Alliance for International Friendship through Religion. (Since January, 1958, the *Newsletter* has been entitled *Worldview* and is distributed by the Church Peace Union, 170 East 64th St., New York 21, N.Y.) Father Vizzard was then Assistant to the Executive Director of the National Catholic Rural Life Conference. The quotation was part of a policy statement of this organization.

Many Christian spokesmen and theologians would probably not go so far in suggesting that love of neighbor is a workable standard for formulating a government's foreign policy. Reinhold Niebuhr, for example, is an outstanding Christian theologian who regards the Christian ethic of love as not immediately applicable to the problem of securing justice in a sinful and selfish world. Without denying that Jesus' ethic of love and nonviolence is absolute and uncompromising, Niebuhr contends that it represents a form of ultimate perfectionism rather than an immediate alternative to political strategies for achieving justice. He conceives of man as a basically sinful creature, and therefore argues that some form of coercion and power must be exercised in order to restrain man's tendencies to do evil. His argument is that the ethic of love and nonviolence, if applied absolutely in the face of the rise of tyranny, would result in the extension of tyranny rather than its destruction. See, for example, his *Christianity and Power Politics* (New York, Scribner, 1952).

One of the most impressive and authoritative pronouncements of the Catholic Church on world affairs is found in the well-known Encyclical *Pacem in Terris* (Peace on Earth) of Pope John XXIII, April 11, 1963, from which the following representative paragraphs are quoted: [47]

1. Peace on earth, which men of every era have so eagerly yearned for, can be firmly established only if the order laid down by God be dutifully observed. . . .

80. Our Predecessors have constantly maintained, and We join them in reasserting, that political communities are reciprocally subjects of rights and duties. This means that their relationships also must be harmonized in truth, in justice, in a working solidarity, in liberty. For the same natural law, which governs relations between individual human beings, must also regulate the relations of political communities with one another. . . .

93. Not only can it happen, but it actually does happen that the advantages and conveniences which nations strive to acquire for themselves become objects of contention; nevertheless, the resulting disagreements must be settled, not by arms, nor by deceit or trickery, but rather in the only manner which is worthy of the dignity of man, i.e., by a mutual assessment of the reasons on both sides of the dispute, by a mature and objective investigation of the situation, and by an equitable reconciliation of differences of opinion. . . .

113. All must realize that there is no hope of putting an end to the building up of armaments . . . unless the process is complete and thorough and unless it proceeds from inner conviction: unless, that is, everyone sincerely cooperates to banish the fear and anxious expectation of war with which men are oppressed. If this is to come about, the fundamental principle on which our present peace depends must be replaced by another, which declares that the true and solid peace of nations consists not in equality of arms but in mutual trust alone. . . .

114. . . . There can be, or at least there should be, no doubt that relations between States, as between individuals, should be regulated not by force of arms but by the light of reason, by the rule of truth, of justice and of active and sincere cooperation.

Similar views and interpretations of the world situation have come from major Protestant groups in the United States. One of the most active of these is the National Council of the Churches of Christ in the United States, representing a large number of Protestant denominations as well as Orthodox Christian Churches. It was formerly known as the Federal Council of Churches of Christ in America. Through a Department of International Justice and Good Will, the National Council and the Federal Council have for many years encouraged wide study and discussion of the problems of peace and war. Their reports and pronouncements have consistently reflected a religious and moral approach to world affairs, but the policies which they have proposed have usually been justified as serving the national interest of the United States.[48]

[47] A convenient pamphlet edition of *Pacem in Terris*, edited by William J. Gibbons, has been issued by the Paulist Press, 180 Varick Street, New York City.

[48] One of the first studies published by the Federal Council of Churches was Sidney Gulick, *The Christian Crusade for a Warless World* (New York, Macmillan,

On December 3, 1965, the National Council of Churches issued a policy statement on the Vietnam war supporting the search for a negotiated settlement of that conflict and suggesting among other things that the United States halt its bombings of North Vietnam long enough to create more favorable circumstances for negotiations.[49] It also suggested that efforts be made simultaneously to induce North Vietnam to stop sending military personnel and material into South Vietnam. In justifying its various suggestions, the Council said:

In a world revolution, rapid change and sharp conflict of ideologies, Christians have an opportunity and duty to be a reconciling and healing force between nations and people and races where possible.

In a Message to Churches transmitting this policy statement, the Council declared further:

. . . Christians in the United States are failing thus far to make their specific contribution to the maintenance of peace in the world, having been almost silent while our nation's involvement in Vietnam increases step by step. . . .

The reasons Christians have a specific responsibility to speak and to criticize is that they have a loyalty to God which must transcend every other loyalty, and they belong to one family with all other Christians on all six continents. At the same time they seek to be loyal citizens of their nation.[50]

After stating the conviction that unilateral action by the United States in Southeast Asia would not lead to peace and that no conceivable victory achieved on this basis could compensate for the distrust and hatred it would generate among Asians, the Message called upon Christians in the United States:

. . . to maintain our spiritual and ethical sensitivity and keep before us our awareness of the imperatives of the Christian Gospel . . . (which) are clearly written in the New Testament. "Love your enemies and pray for those who persecute you. . . . If your enemy is hungry, feed him. . . . And He made from one every nation of men to live on all the face of the earth. . . . Do not

---

1922). Its purpose was to develop a public opinion that would support international policies of "righteousness and goodwill."

During World War II, the Federal Council created the Commission to Study the Bases of a Just and Durable Peace which prepared a statement of principles it felt should be followed to assure an effective postwar organization of peace. These principles stressed the necessity of bringing national and world political and social institutions into conformity with the basic moral order undergirding human society. See the report, *A Message from the National Study Conference on the Churches and a Just and Durable Peace* (Delaware, Ohio, 1942). The chairman of the commission which prepared this statement was John Foster Dulles, who later became Secretary of State.

Another major report was issued in 1953 by the National Council of the Churches of Christ in the U.S.A. entitled, *Christian Faith and International Responsibility*.

[49] Full text in *The New York Times,* December 4, 1965, p. 6.
[50] *Ibid.*

be conformed to this world but be transformed by the renewal of your mind. . . . Do not be overcome by evil, but overcome evil with good." [51]

Other examples of religious or idealist views of world affairs might be cited, but enough has been said to indicate that certain idealist principles, as a point of departure, may easily lead to a different concept of national interest and welfare than when international problems are considered primarily from the viewpoint of the political or strategic position of the nation-state. As with the vantage point of ideology, questions are often posed: "Do religious, moral and idealist principles play a decisive role in the shaping of foreign policy?" "Can they have real influence if they seem to conflict with the political or strategic requirements of national security?"

While the vantage points of ideology and idealism have been treated separately in the preceding discussion, they have some similarity in their contention that the concept of national interest should not be thought of exclusively in terms of power, but should be based more on ideological or idealist principles. They also are similar in placing greater emphasis on what might be called "principles" rather than "expediency" as determinants of foreign policy. In line with this, some writers prefer to treat ideology and idealism as a single school of political outlook which they call "idealism." They then emphasize the distinction between "idealism" as one main conception of politics and "realism" as a second main conception. The idealist conception considers politics in terms of ideological, ethical, or moral principles of universal validity, while the realist approach regards the political scene as an unending struggle for interests and power between different groups or states. [52]

---

[51] It might be noted, in contrast, that the idealist or religious viewpoint of world affairs does not seem to be held by the leaders of the Soviet Union or Communist China. Mao Tse-tung, for example, has declared: "How different is the logic of the imperialists from that of the people! Make trouble, fail, make trouble again, fail again . . . till their doom; that is the logic of the imperialists and all reactionaries the world over in dealing with the people's cause, and they will never go against this logic. This is a Marxist Law. When we say 'Imperialism is ferocious,' we mean that its nature will never change, that the imperialists will never lay down their butcher knives, that they will never become Buddhas, till their doom." Mao Tse-tung, August 14, 1949, *Selected Works of Mao Tse-tung*, Vol. IV (Peking, Foreign Languages Press, 1961), p. 428. "You are not benevolent! Quite so. We definitely do not apply a policy of benevolence to the reactionaries and towards the reactionary activities of reactionary classes. Our policy of benevolence is applied only within the ranks of the people, not beyond them." Mao Tse-tung, "On the People's Democratic Dictatorship," (June 30, 1949), *Selected Works of Mao Tse-tung*, Vol. IV (Peking, Foreign Languages Press, 1961), pp. 417–418. And this: "We are not Duke Hsiang of Sung and have no use for his stupid scruples about benevolence, righteousness, and morality in war." Mao Tse-tung, *On the Protracted War* (1938) (Peking, Foreign Languages Press, 1960), p. 94.

[52] For excellent presentations of the respective roles of realism and idealism in international politics, see Edward H. Carr, *The Twenty Years' Crisis, 1919–1939* (London, Macmillan, 1946, 1962), Hans J. Morgenthau, *Politics Among Nations*, 3rd ed. (New York, Knopf, 1960), and Kenneth W. Thompson, *Political Realism and the Crisis of World Politics* (Princeton, Princeton University Press, 1960).

THE VANTAGE POINT OF CRITICAL SCHOLARSHIP

The three previous vantage points on world affairs reflect the views of those who are seeking to advance particular interests of certain nation-states, ideologies, or religious principles. The conflicting interpretations arising from these points of view may discourage the reader who is seeking an understanding of all sides of a problem. He may ask: "Is it possible to obtain a 'true' picture of world affairs, a view not vitiated by national, ideological, or religious bias? Can one rise above the interests of his nation, ideology, or religion and obtain an 'objective,' impartial picture of the international situation?"

These very natural questions are much easier to ask than to answer. The physical scientist can approach the problems of the natural world in a relatively detached, objective manner and can often isolate in his laboratory all elements involved in a particular problem. After observing and measuring all pertinent elements in a scientific manner, he may be able to reach certain conclusions which can be verified as "true." That the same approach can be applied to the problems of human and social behavior, and especially to the problems of international relations, seems more questionable. Can the student of world affairs, for example, remain detached and objective when he feels that his country's national security or way of life is threatened or when he is confronted with a sharp challenge to his religious, moral, or ideological loyalties? Unlike the physical scientist who is able to separate himself from the physical phenomena he is studying in his laboratory, the student of world affairs himself is one element in the problem and therefore cannot so easily detach himself from what he is studying.

Although complete objectivity in studying world affairs seems therefore to represent an almost impossible ideal, there may be certain scholarly standards which, if followed, will produce a more complete and accurate picture of world problems than might otherwise be true. This approach might be called the vantage point of critical scholarship.

The critical scholar, for example, can guard against outright falsehoods, clear-cut distortions, and incomplete accounts. Thus he may give the lie to certain atrocity stories which circulated in Europe and the United States during World War I.[53] He may correct the distortion, popular in the 1930's, that the United States was pushed into World War I solely by bankers and munitions-makers concerned primarily with financial profits.[54] He may also give a more complete picture of the origins of

---

[53] See, for example, James M. Read, *Atrocity Propaganda, 1914–1919* (New Haven, Yale University Press, 1941), and James R. Mock and Cedric Larsen, *Words That Won the War* (Princeton, Princeton University Press, 1939).

[54] A convenient summary of the main viewpoints of scholars on America's entrance into World War I may be found in Thomas A. Bailey, *A Diplomatic History of the American People*, 7th ed. (New York, Appleton-Century-Crofts, 1964), Chaps. 38–

World War I by a careful study of the archives of all the major nations involved.[55]

Critical scholarship, furthermore, can make us aware of the ways in which history and other textbooks have often reflected strong nationalist prejudices and have thereby reinforced popular suspicions and antagonisms. German and French textbooks, for example, present different versions of relations between their countries, especially in regard to the major wars fought. German children have been told many times about the burning of the castle at Heidelberg by the French, and French children have been told about the burning of the castle at Saint Cloud by the Germans. In like fashion, American schoolboys are invariably told about the burning of the White House by the British in the War of 1812, but not about the burning of the Canadian Parliament building at Toronto by the Americans.[56]

History textbooks in Western countries still give very superficial and inadequate treatment to Asia and Africa. Although the peoples of Asia comprise over one-half of the world's population, surprisingly few pages of most standard public school textbooks are devoted to this part of the world. The wide variations in Asian cultures have often been submerged in uniform generalities. The great personages of recent Asian history have been virtually ignored. The backwardness of Asians in industrial

---

39. Although economic pressures may have made it easier for the United States to fight Germany rather than the Allies, many scholars do not conclude that these reasons were decisive in the American decision. More influential reasons were: (*a*) Germany's resumption of unrestricted submarine warfare in January, 1917; (*b*) Germany's interest in preventing the United States from continuing as a major base of supplies for the Allies; (*c*) the belief that a German victory would so upset the European balance of power as to threaten the future security of the United States and the freedom of shipping on the Atlantic Ocean.

55 See, for example, Sidney B. Fay's book *The Origins of the World War* (New York, Macmillan, 1928, 1930), which sheds considerable new light on the diplomatic background of World War I through the study of extensive collections of documents released by the German, Austrian, and Russian governments at the end of the war.

56 See D. W. Brogan, "Deodorized History," in *UNESCO Courier*, May, 1956, pp. 20–21. Carlton J. H. Hayes, *France: a Nation of Patriots* (New York, Columbia University Press, 1930), analyzes the impact of nationalism on French textbooks and presents many excerpts from them to illustrate the discussion.

The United Nations Educational, Scientific and Cultural Organization has been much concerned about correcting the biased, inaccurate, and incomplete accounts in public school textbooks. Teachers of various countries have been encouraged to sit down together and examine their respective textbooks with a view to agreeing on how the books might be made more accurate. As a result of discussions among German, French, British, and American historians, for example, progress has been made in agreeing on more accurate accounts of the background of World Wars I and II. See the United Nations Educational, Scientific and Cultural Organization, *A Handbook for the Improvement of Textbooks and Teaching Materials as Aids to International Understanding* (Paris, 1949), and "Bilateral Consultations for the Improvement of History Textbooks," in the series *Educational Studies and Documents*, July, 1953, No. IV.

development is often portrayed as meaning backwardness in every aspect of development. Stereotyped phrases such as "natives," "uncivilized," and "white man's burden" are common.[57] Critical scholarship can obviously do much to provide school children with a more complete and accurate understanding of this vast portion of mankind.

In dealing with the more controversial problems of current international affairs such as disarmament, the reunification of Germany, or the increase of communist influence in the Middle East and Asia, the critical scholar cannot be content simply with the American national viewpoint on these problems, nor with an interpretation based solely upon democratic ideology and hypotheses. He must also examine the Soviet and Chinese national outlooks and the interpretation based upon communist ideology and hypotheses. In addition, the viewpoints of our principal allies, as well as of other interested countries such as India, Pakistan, the United Arab Republic, and Israel, may need to be considered. With such an approach, the critical scholar not only gains a fuller understanding of the central issues of each problem but also lays a better basis for discovering whether or not areas of compromise and agreement are possible among the interested governments. By a critical examination and appraisal of various proposals for meeting each problem, more prudent conclusions can be reached.

Finally, the critical scholar is conscious of his own limitations as an observer and of his own framework of values and methods which to a greater or lesser degree will color his account. Frequently, he will also be aware of the inadequacy of his own store of factual information for drawing valid conclusions. To the extent that he is aware of his own limitations, he ceases to be a blind captive of the view of others, for he realizes that they, too, have their limitations.

CONCLUSION

Four vantage points on world affairs have now been discussed. They help to explain why so many different interpretations of world affairs exist. Undoubtedly, the reader could think of other vantage points to add to the ones already considered. The ability to recognize them should enable him to cut through some of the maze and confusion that often seem to surround international affairs. Such a vast amount of material on all phases of world affairs is now available that the student may find it helpful to classify the various items at his disposal according to the particular vantage point each seems to reflect. Identification of the approaches of various writers or speakers will enable the student better

---

[57] Ronald Fenton, "Asian History through Western Glasses," *UNESCO Courier*, May, 1956, p. 12.

to appraise the usefulness and validity of the different materials and to arrive at a more reasoned judgment and conclusion of his own.

In the next section, four different views or positions regarding the current world crisis will be presented: (1) an official American view; (2) an official Soviet view; (3) a view based primarily on idealism; and (4) an official view of a new independent state in Asia—Indonesia. These will illustrate, more fully than has been done in the preceding discussion, how divergent interpretations of world affairs result from the different vantage points from which world affairs may be viewed. The reader will discover, upon careful study of these positions, that more than one vantage point can sometimes be seen in different sections of the same position. He will find it useful to identify the vantage point or vantage points underlying each of the four positions.

POSITIONS

1. THE UNITED STATES VIEW OF THE CURRENT WORLD CRISIS

The following statement by Secretary of State Dean Rusk, made on September 14, 1964, is a good example of the official view of United States relations with the communist world.[58]

Our foreign policy, in the most fundamental sense, derives from the kind of people we are and hope to be and the shape of the world around us. Neither element, in the longer run, turns upon partisan differences among us. That is why President Truman and Senator Arthur Vandenberg, later President Eisenhower and Senator Lyndon Johnson, found it both possible and necessary to work together in the national interest of us all.

* * *

We as a people have a deep concern about the people in the Communist world. It is partly because we are so deeply attached to the notion that governments derive their just powers from the consent of the governed. It is also because many among us have personal, cultural, and historical ties to areas which are now under Communist control.

Let us begin by recognizing, very simply and very clearly, the nature of communism and the problems it poses for us. During and after World War II, the governments of the world sat down to construct a tolerable world order. They had been chastened by World War II, and all of us were thinking long and hard about the kind of world in which we wanted to live. The result was the United Nations Charter, ratified by our Senate by a vote of 89 to 2.

Unfortunately, we could not say, in the words of the GI, that we "had it made." For Joseph Stalin had taken up the cold war, then refused to join in the

58 *Department of State Bulletin,* October 5, 1964, pp. 463–464.

serious work of the United Nations, and launched the postwar Communist world once again upon a program of world revolution. There then was posed the underlying and continuing crisis of our period of history—the struggle between those who would build a world society on the basis of the charter and those who would brush that world aside and substitute it for a world revolution of coercion. I know of no part of the Communist world which has turned away from this ultimate objective, no part which does not believe that the triumph of communism is inevitable. Those of us who are the heirs of the great drama of freedom, which has been playing for centuries, have no doubt about the outcome of the contest between freedom and coercion, so long as free men remember that freedom is not free but requires continuing dedication, effort, and sacrifice.

Ours is not the first period of history in which men have confronted each other with incompatible objectives. But ours is the first period of history in which man's powers of destruction have reached such unimaginable proportions that all are required to think hard about means as well as ends. There can and will be a victory of freedom, but there is little victory for anyone in a pile of cinders. It is simply too late for man to be governed by his primitive passions. At a time when the arms race is taxing his scientific capacity beyond its limits, his survival depends upon his bringing to bear his highest intelligence to resolve the great issues of war and peace.

ELEMENTS OF U.S. POLICY TOWARD COMMUNIST WORLD

There are those who believe that we ourselves should erect a solid wall between ourselves and the peoples of the Communist world—a wall of implacable hostility and rigidity, a wall through which the winds of freedom cannot blow. I would suggest that if we are seriously concerned about a victory for freedom and if we understand that this victory should come through peaceful process if possible, then no single phrase can describe an imaginative and productive policy toward those countries which call themselves Communist.

Such a policy requires several elements. The first and harsh requirement is that we join with other free peoples to prevent the further expansion of the Communist world by force and violence, whether directly by marching armies or indirectly by terrorism and subversion. I put the emphasis on expansion by violence, because I do not know of any Communist regime which has come to power through the free choice of the peoples concerned, registered in an electoral process. I find no newly independent country, emerging out of colonial status, which has turned to the new colonialism of the Communist bloc. This first requirement of policy means that we must maintain the most powerful aggregation of military strength the world has ever known, a strength which wins the respect of our adversaries. . . .

A second requirement of policy is that we address ourselves, with men and material, to the strengthening of those peoples who have elected freedom and who are prepared to build the world of the charter. When we respond to calls for assistance in settling disputes within the free world, we reduce opportunities for those who would fish in troubled waters. . . .

Third, while there can be no yielding to aggressive violence, we must continue to explore with the Communist world the possibilities of reducing the dangers of conflagration and of finding elements of common interest, whether large or small, on which mutually advantageous agreements can be based. We ourselves should not declare as a matter of doctrine that no such common interests can be found. It would seem elementary, for example, that both sides would wish to avoid a thermonuclear war if possible. We would hope that a common interest can be found in turning the arms race downward in order that vast resources can be freed for the unfinished business of the peoples of both sides.

The following statement by Secretary Rusk on April 23, 1965, adds to the preceding United States view of the world crisis by interpreting the meaning of the Communist concept of wars of national liberation.[59]

What is a "war of national liberation"? It is, in essence, any war which furthers the Communist world revolution—what, in broader terms, the Communists have long referred to as a "just" war. The term "war of national liberation" is used not only to denote armed insurrection by people still under colonial rule— there are not many of those left outside the Communist world. It is used to denote any effort led by Communists to overthrow by force any non-Communist government.

Thus the war in South Viet-Nam is called a "war of national liberation." And those who would overthrow various other non-Communist governments in Asia, Africa, and Latin America are called the "forces of national liberation."

Nobody in his right mind would deny that Venezuela is not only a truly independent nation but that it has a government chosen in a free election. But the leaders of the Communist insurgency in Venezuela are described as leaders of a fight for "national liberation"—not only by themselves and by Castro and the Chinese Communists but by the Soviet Communists.

A recent editorial in *Pravda* spoke of the "peoples of Latin America . . . marching firmly along the path of struggle for their national independence" and said, ". . . the upsurge of the national liberation movement in Latin American countries has been to a great extent a result of the activities of Communist parties." It added: "The Soviet people have regarded and still regard it as their sacred duty to give support to the peoples fighting for their independence. True to their international duty the Soviet people have been and will remain on the side of the Latin American patriots."

In Communist doctrine and practice, a non-Communist government may be labeled and denounced as "colonialist," "reactionary," or a "puppet," and any state so labeled by the Communists automatically becomes fair game—while Communist intervention by force in non-Communist states is justified as "self-defense" or part of the "struggle against colonial domination." "Self-determination" seems to mean that any Communist nation can determine by itself that any non-Communist state is a victim of colonialist domination and therefore a justifiable target for a "war of liberation."

As the risks of overt aggression, whether nuclear or with conventional forces, have become increasingly evident, the Communists have put increasing stress on the "war of national liberation." The Chinese Communists have been more militant in language and behavior than the Soviet Communists. But the

59 *Department of State Bulletin,* May 10, 1965, p. 697.

Soviet Communist leadership also has consistently proclaimed its commitment in principle to support wars of national liberation. . . .

International law does not restrict internal revolution within a state or revolution against colonial authority. But international law does restrict what third powers may lawfully do in support of insurrection. It is these restrictions which are challenged by the doctrine, and violated by the practice, of "wars of liberation."

It is plain that acceptance of the doctrine of "wars of liberation" would amount to scuttling the modern international law of peace which the charter prescribes. And acceptance of the practice of "wars of liberation," as defined by the Communists, would mean the breakdown of peace itself.

2. THE SOVIET VIEW OF THE CURRENT WORLD CRISIS

The following statement is taken from a speech made on May 8, 1965, by L. I. Brezhnev, First Secretary of the Communist Party of the Soviet Union, on the occasion of the twentieth anniversary of the victory over Nazi Germany.[60]

The creation of the anti-Hitler coalition during . . . [World War II] was an example of the cooperation of countries with different social systems in the common struggle against an aggressor. What has happened to this coalition in the intervening years?

After the end of the great battle and the rout of the enemy, the chief participants in the anti-Hitler coalition did not set out on the common road of building a lasting peace but took divergent paths. One might say that the ink on the declaration of the defeat of Hitler's Germany, signed in Berlin by representatives of the U.S.S.R., the U.S.A., Britain and France, was not yet dry before our former allies began to break the ties that united the chief participants in the war against German fascism.

Very soon after the rout of fascism a new imperialist striking force was formed, headed by the U.S.A., which openly claimed "world leadership." As you see, the American imperialists had learned nothing from the fate of the German-fascist pretenders to world supremacy.

The entire course of international events in recent times confirms the conclusion reached by the world's Communist Parties that the chief force of war and aggression in our days is American imperialism.

Having assumed the role of the bulwark of world reaction, the ruling circles of the U.S.A. are grossly interfering in the internal affairs of other countries and peoples, opposing the relaxation of international tension and creating more and more new breeding grounds for conflicts.

No sooner do the people of any country, be it in Latin America, Asia or Africa, rise in struggle for freedom and independence before the international gendarme—American imperialism, with its warships, planes or U.S. marines—

[60] Original in *Pravda*, May 9, 1965, pp. 1–4. Translation from the *Current Digest of the Soviet Press*, published weekly at Columbia University by the Joint Committee on Slavic Studies, appointed by the American Council of Learned Societies and the Social Science Research Council. Copyright, 1965, Vol. XVII, No. 18, pp. 11–12, by the Joint Committee on Slavic Studies. Reprinted by permission.

immediately appears. This is what happened in the Congo. This is what is happening today in the Dominican Republic, where American soldiers by force of arms are suppressing the aspirations of the people of this country for freedom and independence.

Provocations are continuing against heroic Cuba.

The events in Vietnam serve as the most striking manifestation of the gendarme policy of American imperialism.

The American intervention in Vietnam has evoked wrath and indignation throughout the world. The professional bullies of the American military are cold-bloodedly repressing the patriots of Vietnam, who, under the leadership of the National Front for Liberation, are struggling for the freedom and independence of their homeland. For several months now the American imperialists have been carrying out aggressive operations against the D.R.V., raiding the republic's cities and villages from the air and engaging in piratical operations by their naval forces in its territorial waters.

In this situation, it is an affair of honor and the international duty of the socialist countries to give effective support to the fraternal country that is being subjected to attack by the imperialists.

* * *

By its actions aimed at suppressing the liberation struggle of the Vietnamese people, U.S. imperialism is hurling an open challenge to the national-liberation movement of the peoples of the entire world. This is why support for the Vietnamese people, who are fighting against the imperialist aggression of the U.S.A., is a matter of honor, a matter of vital interest for all peoples who are defending their freedom and independence. Everyone who cherishes the preservation of peace on earth has an interest in this.

* * *

Apparently the ruling circles of the United States of America would like— on what grounds it is impossible to say—to assume the role of supreme arbiter over other peoples. They want to prescribe for the peoples of other countries what systems they should have at home and are trying to suppress by armed force those who do not kowtow before them.

What are the generally accepted norms of international law to them, the creators of such a policy! Without giving it a second thought they violate the solemn pledges recorded in the United Nations Charter and other international documents that the United States has also signed. This is a policy of violence and arbitrariness, a policy of aggression. And no pseudo doctrines concocted in Washington can conceal this obvious fact. The course of suppressing the national-liberation movement of the peoples with the help of military adventures and diktat will bring the U.S.A. neither honor nor respect. This course is doomed to ignominious failure, for it conflicts with the will of the peoples who are rising for freedom, independence and social progress.

* * *

The Soviet Union has never intended and does not intend to attack anyone. As is known, our country is engaged in peaceful labor. We are building plants, factories, housing, schools and hospitals, we are doing everything to improve the life of Soviet people. But let no one attempt to confuse our fervent desire to safeguard peace on earth with toothless pacifism. We do not conceal the fact that a substantial part of our national budget goes to building up the combat strength of our armed forces. The Soviet people well understand the need for these expenditures and fully support the measures of the Party and government to strengthen the defense might of our homeland!

We do not want to rattle sabers. This has never been our custom and is not our policy. . . .

* * *

We solemnly proclaim that we do not want war. Peace, freedom and the independence of all peoples—this is policy of our party and the Soviet government, it is to this that we summon all countries and peoples!

3. FALSE VALUES OF EAST AND WEST HAVE LED TO THE PRESENT WORLD CRISIS

The following position, taken from the literature of the American Friends Service Committee and from the writings of India's Prime Minister, Jawaharlal Nehru, illustrates the pacifist philosophy of nonviolence and, to some extent, India's philosophy of noninvolvement in the military alliances of the major powers.

Our Real Enemy: False Values [61]

The real evils that have driven the world to the present impasse, and which we must struggle to overcome, spring from the false values by which man has lived in East and West alike. Man's curse lies in his worship of the work of his hands, in his glorification of material things, in his failure to set any limit on his material needs. This idolatry leads him to lust for power, to disregard human personality, to ignore God, and to accept violence or any other means of achieving his ends. It is not an idolatry of which the communists alone are guilty. All men share it, and when it is examined, the global power struggle is given a new perspective.

1. *Lust for power.* One of the things that the United States fears most about the Soviet Union is its expansionism. The communist revolution proclaims itself as a global revolution, and in its seemingly insatiable lust for power has already brought much of the world within its orbit. Americans see this expansionism as something that must be halted at any cost and by whatever means.

But no less an historian than Arnold Toynbee has pointed out that a dominant factor in world history from about 1450 on was *the expansionism of the West.* It was the peoples of Western Europe, driven by their lust for power and possessions, who pushed out in all directions, subjugating or exterminating those who blocked the path, and resorting in their colonial operations to bloodshed and slavery and humiliation whenever it appeared necessary. Nor can the United States escape responsibility. Our history has also been marked by a dynamic, persistent, and seldom interrupted expansionism.

[61] From *Speak Truth to Power,* American Friends Service Committee Publication, 1955, pp. 28–31. Reprinted by permission.

Less than two centuries ago the nation was a string of colonies along the Atlantic seaboard. Now it straddles the continent, and its military bastions are found in over half of all the nations in the world. Its navies cruise the coasts of Russia and China, and its bombers are based in Germany and Japan. It is easy for Americans to regard this as normal, though they would be outraged and terrified if Russian warships cruised our coasts and Russian bombers were based on Canada or Guatemala. It is also easy for Americans to forget that this expansionism was often as ruthless as that which we fear in others. The Indian was almost exterminated, the Negro and later the flood of European immigrants were cruelly exploited; violence was threatened or provoked with Mexico, with Spain, with Colombia, with Nicaragua—all in the name of expanding the power and influence of the United States.

To point out such things is not to justify either Russian or Western expansionism, nor is it to underestimate the human suffering and the social cost that are involved in new embodiments and contests of power. But it suggests that the disease is not geographical and that to build ever greater instruments of power is not to end the disease but to spread it until it destroys the whole organism of civilization.

2. *Denial of human dignity.* Another of the fundamental evils in modern totalitarian regimes that is often cited is the degradation of the human being into an impersonal object to be manipulated in the interests of the state. Men become mere cogs in the machinery of a monolithic party which recognizes no higher authority than its own. The concept of man as a child of God, possessing dignity and worth, and vested with inalienable rights, is patently denied.

It is clear on the other hand that this noble concept of man, and the limits it imposes on the power of government, still has vitality in the West. But the West has been quick to ignore it when the situation demanded. The tendency toward centralization of power, toward subjugation of men to the demands of an impersonal technology, did not originate in modern Russia or the Orient, or in the minds of Marxist theoreticians. It was, and is, a part of the process of industrialization and technical development of the West. The tragedy of material progress is that nowhere in the world, any more than in Russia today, has enough original capital been accumulated for both industrial development and military expansion without subjecting men to some degree of exploitation and indignity. Indeed, the process of Western Industrialization made virtual slaves of vast multitudes of peasants and laborers in underdeveloped countries and often imposed on them in addition the humiliation of "white supremacy." There is obviously room for much freedom and material well-being to flourish in the more highly developed countries, but . . . even these blessings are endangered as the demands of military preparedness make inroads on liberty and accelerate the drive toward centralized authority.

Again, this is in no sense to condone the invasion of human personality wherever it may occur, but only to indicate that the virus is not localized. The elimination of communism would not eliminate the evil we see in communism. Indeed, it may safely be predicted that the waging of atomic war against the Soviet Union, far from providing a cure, would itself be a virulent, if not final, instrument for the destruction of liberty and the dehumanizing of man.

3. *Atheism.* A third charge against Soviet communism is its atheism. Re-

ligion is rejected as the "opiate of the people" and in its place is put the Marxist doctrine of materialism. However tragic and blasphemous this denial may seem to us, it is relevant to remember that it, too, is a product of the West. Karl Marx denounced religion on the basis of his observation of Western, not Russian, society. Arnold Toynbee, in *The World and the West,* points out that Western culture has become in recent centuries ever more materialistic and secular, and has steadily moved away from its Christian or spiritual origin. More recently the Evanston Assembly of the World Council of Churches recognized the "practical atheism" of much of life in the so-called Christian countries.

Communism has simply carried to its logical conclusion, and expressed in theoretical form, what the West has practiced. "It seems in many ways," says William Hordern, in his *Christianity, Communism, and History,* "to be nothing but one particularly unruly expression of the modern view of life. While condemning communist 'materialism' in theory, the rest of the world has lived by materialistic motives. The communists have been hated primarily because they have dragged the skeleton from the closet of Western culture." This is a harsh judgment, but we believe it is an accurate one, for the power of Hydrogen is clearly trusted among us more than the power of Love. Like the communist East, therefore, the Christian West is secular, and that secularism that unites all men in its bondage will not be ended by the simple expedient of destroying those nations where the disease is most virulent at the moment.

4. *The cult of violence.* Finally, we come to the acceptance of violence as the essential means of social revolution, and the corollary doctrine that the end justifies the means. Here again for many Americans are decisive reasons for citing Soviet communism as an absolute evil, which must at all costs be destroyed.

Violence has, indeed, reached unsurpassed proportions in our time. The outbreak of the first World War marked the beginning of this modern orgy of uncontrolled violence, and it has continued ever since. But no reputable historian has ventured the ideas that either the first or the second World War was spawned by communism. Nor are the Russians responsible for the concept of blitzkrieg, or obliteration bombing, or for the first use of atomic weapons. These have all been loosed upon the world by the very nations which now profess outrage at the cynical Soviet concept of the role of violence and the validity of *any* means. Western theory is indeed outraged, but Western practice has in this area, too, belied Western theory. We have, in fact, been prepared to use any means to achieve *our* ends. Here again, as in so many other points in the exposure of the devil theory, we are reminded of the words Shakespeare put into the mouth of Shylock: "The villainy you teach me, I will execute, and it shall go hard, but I will better the instruction."

Moreover, military leaders are apparently ready now to use any means, even the ultimate immorality of hydrogen bombs, to stop communism. Is it not clear that to resort to immoral means in order to resist what is immoral is not to preserve or vindicate moral values, but only to become collaborators in destroying all moral life among men? Especially if the issue is a moral one, we must renounce modern war. If we say that any means are justified, we adopt a completely amoral position, for there is then no ethical line that can be drawn anywhere. All morality has been discarded. Only if we ourselves reject the doctrine that the achievement of *our* ends justifies any means is there any hope that we may be able to bring healing to a world caught in the fearful dilemma of our time.

The remainder of this position is taken from the writings of Nehru: [62]

In the multitude of crises, political and economic, that face us, perhaps the greatest crisis of all is that of the human spirit. Till this crisis of the spirit is resolved it will be difficult to find a solution for the other crises that afflict us. . . .

In India during the last quarter of a century and more, Mahatma Gandhi made an outstanding contribution not only to the freedom of India but to that of world peace. He taught us the doctrine of non-violence, not as a passive submission to evil, but as an active and positive instrument for the peaceful solution of international differences. He showed us that the human spirit is more powerful than the mightiest of armaments. He applied moral values to political action and pointed out that ends and means can never be separated, for the means ultimately govern the end. If the means are evil, then the end itself becomes distorted and at least partially evil. Any society based on injustice must necessarily have the seeds of conflict and decay within it so long as it does not get rid of that evil.

All this may seem fantastic and impractical in the modern world, used as it is to thinking in set grooves. And yet we have seen repeatedly the failure of other methods and nothing can be less practical than to pursue a method that has failed again and again. We may not perhaps ignore the present limitations of human nature or the immediate perils which face the statesmen. We may not, in the world as it is constituted today, even rule out war absolutely. But I have become more and more convinced that so long as we do not recognize the supremacy of the moral law in our national and international relations, we shall have no enduring peace. So long as we do not adhere to right means, the end will not be right and fresh evil will flow from it. That was the essence of Gandhi's message and mankind will have to appreciate it in order to see and act clearly. . . .

Today fear consumes us all—fear of the future, fear of war, fear of the people of the nations we dislike and who dislike us. That fear may be justified to some extent. But fear is an ignoble emotion and leads to blind strife. Let us try to get rid of this fear and base our thoughts and actions on what is essentially right and moral, and then . . . the dark clouds that surround us may lift and the way to the evolution of world order based on freedom will be clear.

4. THE WORLD CRISIS AS VIEWED BY A NEWLY INDEPENDENT NATION

If the East-West struggle is the main concern of Americans, Russians, and perhaps Chinese, the so-called North-South struggle is the principal concern of the newly independent nations, which now number over sixty. This struggle involves the efforts of these new states, most of which are in Asia and Africa, to establish solid foundations of genuine political and economic independence and to shake off the last vestiges of foreign control and influence by the powers of Europe and America.

[62] Copyright, 1950. Reprinted from *Independence and After*, by Jawaharlal Nehru by permission of the John Day Company, Inc., publisher, and of the Office of the Prime Minister of India.

The following statement was delivered before the United Nations General Assembly on December 11, 1964, by the Foreign Minister of Indonesia. It represents the intense feeling shared by many of the new states of Asia and Africa that the problems of independence are much more vital to them than the cold war.[63]

Since 1945, more than fifty nations of Africa and Asia have gained their independence and become Members of this world organization. As newly independent nations, they have, of course, their own problems, their own needs, their own demands. They have their own problems of security and of peace in their growth and development. Bound together by their common struggle for freedom and justice, for a better life and well-being, they have brought into the United Nations their vital fight against colonialism and imperialism, which has indeed brought into the United Nations more life and purpose for a great part of mankind. In December 1960, they succeeded in having the United Nations adopt the well-known Declaration on the decolonization of all colonial territories. But this was fifteen years after the founding of the United Nations and the proclamation of its Charter.

The struggle for peace and security in the United Nations has so far been dominated by the struggle for peace and security of the great Powers involved in the so-called cold war. I do not say that the peace and security of the great Powers is not of great value to the world as a whole, including the newly independent nations. But very often it is forgotten that these newly emerging nations have their own problems of peace and security.

What are these newly emerging nations really up to? What are their specific and distinct problems, which demand the greatest attention of all those who really care for the well-being of mankind? This is the problem of the greatest part of mankind.

Without ignoring the principles and purposes which the United Nations Charter professes to pursue, these new nations of Africa and Asia have not only vehemently fought for their freedom and independence; they have also been compelled to organize themselves, outside the United Nations, in many organizations and conferences, in order to strengthen themselves, their development and, at the same time, in my view, the actual purposes of the United Nations. The Bandung Conference of 1955, in which all twenty-nine of the then independent Afro-Asian nations participated, was a milestone in that common effort for development and growth. Newly emerging nations who belong to what is called the non-aligned group organized international conferences in Belgrade in 1961 and again, progressing further, in Cairo in September of this year [1964]. Those in Africa have organized themselves in the Organization of African Unity, which has furthered their close co-operation in specific African development. Other important summit meetings have been held regionally to find the right ways and means for solving specific problems concerning the development of the nations concerned. A second Afro-Asian Conference will be held early next year, again to review the common struggle and responsibility for the common growth of the newly independent States in this changing world.

    [63] United Nations, Official Records of the General Assembly, Nineteenth Session, Plenary Meetings, 1300th Meeting, 11 December 1964, A/PV.1300, paragraphs 146–169.

What are now their specific problems which deserve specific attention, also in the United Nations, of which they are all Members?

In this statement I will not deal with the usual issues such as disarmament, specific questions of human rights, economic co-operation and the like, . . .

My intention today is to draw . . . attention . . . to the great and fundamental problem of the growth of newly independent nations, which in number already constitute the greater part of the United Nations membership and in population represent indeed the greater part of humanity. The fight for freedom and independence for those dependent peoples still under colonial domination, such as those in Angola, Mozambique and the like, will of course be continued relentlessly, and my delegation's unambiguous support for this anti-colonial fight within and outside this Assembly is well known.

But the existence of a new phenomenon, which is not always under consideration in this Assembly, should also be recognized fully and tackled without delay. If one looks at this troubled world today, one is struck by the fact that explosive troubles are found in the world of the newly emerging nations in their further struggle to secure their national independence and national freedom, and in the development of their national life. Their problem has little to do with the existing cold war; it has nothing to do with peaceful coexistence between the cold-war Powers, nor has it much to do with disarmament. In fact, while there is now some relaxation in the cold war between Washington and Moscow, the troubles the newly emerging nations must face have not eased. It is a problem in itself; it is a phenomenon to be recognized by itself.

In simple terms, it is the peace and security of the development of the newly independent nations, of the newly sovereign nations of the world representing the greater part of humanity. Whereas from the founding of the United Nations until only a few years ago, peace and security were linked with the relationship between the big Powers, especially in regard to the ideological conflict, it has become clear by now that peace and security, or the relaxation of international tensions, is not merely the absence of hot war or cold war between the big Powers. One might say that this problem of peace and security for the newly developing countries is a continuation of their former struggle for independence, of their previous long and bitter anti-colonialist struggle.

For many countries, the struggle to achieve independence has been very hard indeed. They have had to undergo decades of bitter struggle involving bloodshed and manifold sacrifices. Yet their hard-won independence usually takes the initial form of merely nominal independence. It is internationally recognized and accepted by their membership in the United Nations, but it soon appears that development after the attainment of independence is an equally difficult job, requiring the same sacrifices and endurance, facing the same opponent, the old colonial Power appearing in a new cloak. It is indeed illusory to assume that the attainment of national independence by the once-colonized peoples is the end of the struggle. They cannot be satisfied merely to have their national sovereignty legally and internationally recognized, to have their own government, a parliament, political freedom, even with freedom of speech, without having the real power in national hands. National independence is just a bridge, a golden bridge, for the further achievement of genuine independence, of social justice, of peace and prosperity for their peoples.

This is not an easy task. It is not just a matter of technology. It is a matter of nation-building, which must precede the problem of technical development. Technical development, to be well-suited and really beneficial to a specific country, requires a solid foundation of nation-building. This means the transformation of a medieval society, twisted and deformed by centuries of colonial rule, into a society with self-respect and self-confidence, with the courage and determination to carry on the struggle, and with the readiness to sacrifice. After all, technical development will never flourish in a medieval society full of contradictions and imbued with the sentiments of an inferiority complex. Revolutions and counter-revolutions are rampant.

The reason is the failure to recognize one fact—that for these newly developing countries, the magic word "technology" has two sides: it can be a tool by which to develop these countries technically, or it can be a tool by which the former colonial Powers are able to maintain or even increase their customary exploitation. In this context, it can be used as a means for pursuing the policy of "divide and rule," utilizing this pacific penetration as a basis for intervention and subversion, in addition to the legitimate but unfair competition between the strong and the weak. Even technical aid from the industrial Powers is used as a means of peaceful penetration, in order to force the newly developing countries into the economic system, if not the social philosophy, of the so-called aiding Power.

If the newly developing countries are unprepared for, or unaware of, these implications, the problems they face will become insurmountable even before they embark upon technical and economic development. The systems used are very often quite unsuited to the recipient developing country. Besides, they will make it hard for the developing countries to establish conditions consistent with the social and cultural traditions of their own people. The developing countries will thus be forced to conform to the concepts and traditions of the old dominating Powers. By doing so, they will become easy prey for neo-colonialism, for neo-domination, ready to be guided by proxy, in the political, in the economic and even in the military spheres.

When a newly independent and developing country has tried, in its own right, to devise its own concept of an economic and social system different from that of the old colonial Power, this deviation has quickly been regarded as Communism. In fact, of the more than fifty countries which became independent after the Second World War, and became Members of the United Nations—most of which were supported morally and sometimes materially by the Communist countries—not even 5 percent have become Communist. Nowadays this view no longer prevails, and in fact no establishment of Communism is apparent in the newly independent countries; and still—this is important to note—these newly developing countries remain the target of colonialist or neo-colonialist Powers.

Thus, it is nonsense to contend that the old colonial Powers conduct their policies of interference, of subversion, of establishing military bases and the like, because of their anti-Communist fight. They do so simply because of their desire to maintain their hold, their dominance, their exploitation of their former colonies, and to see to it that these new countries do not develop beyond a comfortable conformity with their own world, dying as it may be. Foreign military bases—usually explained as a means for containing communism—are now in reality used to protect neo-colonialist domination in the newly independent countries. The method is no longer merely peaceful penetration. It becomes violent penetration when opposed; the countries concerned even use mercenaries of unidentified nationality, and do not even shrink from openly using their imperialist regulars.

To serve all these designs, they also create satellites and use them as their so-called legal instruments for their interventionist and subversive activities. These neo-colonialist designs are not unknown to a great many nations of the world. At the recent Cairo Conference, forty-seven non-aligned nations recognized that "Imperialism uses many devices to impose its will on independent nations. Economic pressure and domination, interference, racial discrimination, subversion, intervention and the threat of force are neo-colonialist devices against which the newly independent nations have to defend themselves."

Of course it is not difficult for the big neo-colonialist Powers to carry out this strategy and these tactics. Newly independent countries in the process of consolidation and stabilization still have to face the heritage of forces, whether in terms of persons or of social forces, directly or indirectly planted by the old colonial Power. One need only read the few books published on the subject of how intervention and subversion are skillfully planned and carried out, to understand the problems faced by the newly developing countries. The neo-colonial Powers have all the means of superiority at their disposal: experience, money, economics, military force, publicity, etc.

And indeed, it is not difficult for them to stir up trouble in newly-developing countries which must still heal the wounds left by colonialism. In these new countries, still struggling for stability and a new concept of national and international life, it is not difficult for the old colonial Powers to find sources of contradiction or conflict, both in the sphere of internal development and in that of the development of relations with their neighbors, particularly in Africa and Asia, which were colonized and balkanized for centuries.

In the development of its independence as a new State, each country, be it in the Americas or in Europe, must go through this process of nationhood. If there is no intervention, especially from abroad, no intervention from large, powerful nations, every conflict or contradiction within the new State or between neighboring States can be easily solved. In fact, the question is whether or not the newly-developing country is left alone during the search for its own national development and growth.

Not entirely irrelevant to this idea of being left alone, free from outside interference, there was the doctrine of President Monroe of the United States of America related to the Western hemisphere's own interests. In our fashion, in South-East Asia, we know the Sukarno-Macapagal doctrine, a doctrine declared by our President and the President of the Republic of the Philippines at the beginning of this year. Its aim is to promote our self-confidence, to enable us to run our own national affairs and to free our countries from foreign intervention to the extent that in quarrels or disputes between ourselves in our own region, we ourselves should find the solution by mutual discussion and understanding, without interference from outside Powers.

This concept of national growth and self-confidence, as it is also reflected in the Charter of the Organization of African Unity, which is also being opposed and subverted by the old colonial Powers, has become a vital problem for many newly-independent countries. It may even, because of the opposition and subversion, become a crisis with which the greater part of the world, the world of the newly-developing nations, is confronted.

It is no longer the problem directly recognized in the struggle for world peace and security, as the United Nations knew it in the years immediately after 1945, nor even in 1950 or later, when the acute antagonism of the cold war prevailed. It is not merely the struggle to achieve national independence and sovereignty handled so far by the United Nations. It is now the new emerging problem—no less acute than any other—of the security, of the peace and security of the newly-developing nations, of the newly-emerging forces. More than half the present membership of the United Nations is confronted with this new international problem. It affects the life and future of hundreds of millions of people, and is already causing the eruptions and renewed eruptions of trouble and conflict in many parts of the world, especially in Asia, Africa and Latin America. If the United Nations does not deal with this new international problem, it will have failed to live up to its great international task. The United Nations cannot ignore with impunity this new international phenomenon.

SELECT BIBLIOGRAPHY

BENNETT, JOHN C. (ed.), *Nuclear Weapons and the Conflict of Conscience* (New York, Scribner, 1962). A collection of essays by several well-known political scientists, physical scientists, and theologians dealing with the ethical issues involved in the nuclear arms race and the possibility of nuclear war.

BOULDING, KENNETH E., *The Meaning of the Twentieth Century* (New York, Harper & Row, 1964). An extremely thought-provoking book suggesting that the twentieth century marks the second great transition in the history of mankind. The first transition was that from "precivilized" to "civilized" agricultural and urban society about 5,000 or more years ago, following the development of agriculture and the appearance of settled communities. The present transition is from "civilized" to what the author calls the "postcivilized" society of technology, organized research, and development.

BRAMSON, LEON and GOETHALS, GEORGE W., *War: Studies from Psychology, Sociology, and Anthropology* (New York, Basic Books, 1964). A collection of classical and contemporary writings on the causes of war by psychologists, sociologists, and anthropologists, including Sigmund Freud, William James, William McDougall, Gordon Allport, William Graham Sumner, Margaret Mead, Harold Lasswell, and Raymond Aron.

CARR, EDWARD H., *The Twenty Years' Crisis, 1919–1939* (London, Macmillan, New York, St. Martin's, 1946, 1962). Written originally in 1939, on the eve of World War II, to counteract the neglect of the factor of power in much thinking about international politics, this book remains one of the clearest discussions in print of the respective roles of idealism, utopianism, and realism in foreign policy making. Highly recommended as supplementary reading for this chapter.

HADLEY, ARTHUR T., *The Nation's Safety and Arms Control* (New York, Viking, 1961). An extremely readable, well-informed book on the problems and possibilities of arms control. The publication grew out of the 1960 Arms Control Summer Study held under the auspices of the American Academy of Arts and Sciences with eminent scholars from the physical, technological, and social sciences as participants.

KAHN, HERMAN, *On Thermonuclear War* (Princeton, Princeton University Press, 1960). A provocative analysis of the nature and consequences of nuclear war and strategies of deterrence. Suggests that more thorough preparation for civil defense and shelter protection would substantially reduce the catastrophic effects of nuclear attack and improve the possibilities of national recovery. Applauded by many students of military strategy, the book has also been strongly condemned by other observers who feel it is indifferent to the human values and lives which would be lost if nuclear war were accepted as an instrument of national policy. Kahn's thinking has been continued in a subsequent volume, *On Escalation* (New York, Praeger, 1965).

MORGENTHAU, HANS J., *Politics Among Nations,* 4th ed. (New York, Knopf, 1967). Written as a basic text, this book is an excellent presentation of Morgenthau's "realist" theory of international politics. Very stimulating supplementary reading for this chapter.

RUSSELL, BERTRAND, *Has Man a Future?* (New York, Simon and Schuster, 1962). A short series of essays by the distinguished British philosopher on the dilemma of the survival of life and values in the nuclear age, and also on political steps which the author concludes are necessary to prevent nuclear war.

STOESSINGER, JOHN G., *The Might of Nations,* rev. ed. (New York, Random House, 1965). A very useful study which treats international relations as much more than a struggle for power and emphasizes the struggle for world order as an equally important factor. Also stresses the frequent and significant differences between the way nations perceive one another and the way they really are—the gaps between perception and reality which greatly complicate decision making in world politics.

STONE, JEREMY J., *Containing the Arms Race: Some Specific Proposals* (Cambridge, Mass., The M.I.T. Press, 1966). An analysis of strategic military systems—bombers, missile and antimissile defenses—and the problems of their control. Examines the arguments for and against the principal policy proposals for arms control and presents information essential for the lay citizen to understand the issues in the public debate over arms control.

WRIGHT, QUINCY, *A Study of War* (Chicago, University of Chicago Press, 1942, 1965). A monumental study of the nature and causes of war throughout human history. The latter part deals especially with the causes of war and the problem of controlling and preventing it. An abridged edition by Louise L. Wright was issued in 1964.

2

The Contemporary Sovereign State System

THE HAPPY CIRCUMSTANCES OF THE
nineteenth century which permitted the United States to enjoy relative
international repose were responsible for a peculiar and not wholly realistic American outlook on world affairs. The absence of a major European war, the quiescence of East Asia, and the veto British naval power
placed on any other European power's ambitions to play a major role in
the affairs of the Western Hemisphere encouraged most Americans not
only to accept a golden age of detachment from world politics but to
believe such detachment was a divine blessing available to any people
morally strong enough to refuse engagement in the shoddy game of international power politics. Alteration of the three external conditions outlined above and the great expansion of United States power in the
twentieth century shattered the basis for this belief, but the belief itself
died more slowly. Indeed, the 1950's and 1960's have been a period of
painful adjustment by American thinking to the realities of how the
world is divided into sovereign units whose perpetual conflicts of interests
have made the term peace only relative.

THE HISTORY OF SOVEREIGNTY

No doubt the first sovereign territorial unit was the hunting ground
of some prehistoric family or clan. By dint of that family's exclusion of
others from the area or its reduction to it, a realm was created where the
family acknowledged no higher authority. From such imagined crude beginnings evolved the concept of a more formal community which recognized no power above itself. History records such sovereign states in
ancient Sumeria and in all civilizations since, including, of course, the
city-states of classical Greece.

It was in Roman times that this concept found expression in the

Latin word *superanus,* meaning supreme power (and from this through the French *souveraineté* to the English word used here). But if Roman political scientists invented the word for it, Roman imperialists by extinguishing the sovereignty of so many states also imparted to European political theory the contrary concept of universality and of all communities existing under one law. To this, Christianity added the belief of a single community under God. Thus for the post-Roman Western world a conflict emerged between advocates of local sovereignties and those of a single, all-encompassing society. In the Middle Ages, with their emphasis on Christian unity and defense against Islam, Europeans tended to accept the universal spiritual authority of the medieval Papacy and, somewhat more grudgingly, the theoretical universal temporal authority of Charlemagne and his Holy Roman Emperor successors.

At the end of the Middle Ages in Europe, however, a strong trend back toward multiple sovereign units began. The division of labor and resulting greater exchange of goods led to a need for a breakdown of economic barriers between the medieval baronies. At the same time gunpowder rendered obsolete the baronial castle and enabled more ambitious barons to reduce their weaker neighbors to their will. Soon certain of these barons, styling themselves kings, were able to challenge the always weak universal authority of the Holy Roman Emperor. Fateful schisms in European Christianity, especially the Protestant Reformation of the sixteenth century, further undermined what there remained of medieval universality. The outcome was the rise of such sovereign kingdoms and empires as that of Spain, Portugal, England, and France in western Europe, and of the Romanov and Habsburg empires in eastern Europe. In the sixteenth century, Jean Bodin bolstered the growing authority of such monarchies with his treatise on sovereignty, which he described as residing in the crown.

A new phase in the evolution of the modern state system came with the idea of popular sovereignty as opposed to royal sovereignty. First suggested in the writings of John Locke, the concept that sovereignty resided in the people gained wider acceptance in the American and French revolutions of the late eighteenth century. Thus the United States, the First French Republic, and a number of short-lived other European republics established during the wars of the French Revolution (1792–1801) joined the older monarchies as sovereign states. With the intensification of nationalism (see Chap. 4) there was added the theory that each national group of people had the right to establish its own sovereign government. Fulfilling this ideal in the nineteenth century were the fusion of thirty-odd German states into the German Empire, the unification of Italy's city-states into the sovereign Kingdom of Italy, and the division of the Ottoman Empire into sovereign national constituencies such as Greece, Rumania, Serbia, and Bulgaria. In this same century, it will be recalled, the United States experienced a severe crisis over the issue of whether sovereignty rested with the people of the individual states or with the people of the federal republic as a whole, and only in 1865 was this settled in favor of the latter view.

The First World War saw the further multiplication of sovereign states with the partition of German, Habsburg, and Russian empires into a dozen separate sovereignties, all more or less based on national divisions. Simultaneously, various colonial peoples, such as the Indians and Arabs, demanded their sovereign independence, demands which were to be fulfilled largely after the Second World War.

Thus, in recent times the most common form of sovereignty has become that of the nation-state, of which there are presently twenty-three in Europe alone and over 120 in the world at large. The idea of universality, however, refused to die and manifested itself in such diverse forms as international Marxism, the League of Nations, the United Nations, and the World Federalist movement. Moreover, the U.S.S.R. is a multinational sovereign state containing twenty-two major national groups and scores of lesser ones, while the European Economic Community confronts its six sovereign members with the possibility of fusing into a single larger sovereignty. Just as changing economic conditions made obsolete the tiny baronial units of medieval Europe, the changes of the twentieth century are rendering obsolete the nation-state units of today, with consequent advocacies of larger sovereign units such as the Common Market, Pan-Africa, and a North Atlantic Community, and a return to universality through the United Nations. But for the present we are concerned with a world of many sovereign states.

CONTEMPORARY RELATIONS BETWEEN SOVEREIGN STATES

CONFLICT OF INTERESTS

One of the hallmarks of sovereignty is self-definition of interests. Hence, each sovereign government makes such definition. Foremost among its interests is preservation of its territory, without which, obviously, the sovereign state would no longer exist. A second interest is the promotion of its citizens' welfare. In a democracy the general welfare is somewhat inexactly determined by the political leaders who respond to the various and often conflicting claims of various pressure groups in the country; in a totalitarian state, the political leaders define the public's welfare more arbitrarily. But both kinds of regimes nevertheless stake out their sovereign interests (often called "national interests" because most sovereignties are nation-states today).

In such a system it is at once clear that there will be numerous conflicts of interest between various states. For example, Austria and Italy have disputed the treatment accorded German-speaking inhabitants of the Italian South Tyrol, India and South Africa have been at loggerheads over the latter's racist policies, and Kenya and Somalia have been among the many countries in conflict over mutual frontiers. Moreover, as the world shrinks and interdependence among all peoples increases, there are more clashes. Thus, United States and Russian interests entail not only conflict over the future governments and leadership of a reunited Germany or Congo, but on international exchange, the functioning of UNESCO, control of the Straits at Istanbul, and travel restrictions on each others' diplomatic personnel. Similarly, England and France have areas of conflicting interests in their relations with the United States, reinstituting a version of the gold standard, the Common Market, and a ban on atomic testing in the atmosphere. Overlapping and antagonistic national interests, therefore, are common facts of life among sovereign states. There may be some few exceptions, such as between Chile and Zambia or Nepal and Finland, but even these mutually remote and small countries may well find themselves on different sides of an issue in the United Nations. As for the larger states, they are perpetually bumping into each other and interfering with one another's sovereign rights.

RESOLUTION OF CONFLICTS OF INTERESTS

The noteworthy thing about the many clashes of interest among sovereign states is not that they sometimes produce violent conflict, but that they do not lead to war more often than they do. In fact, the art of adjusting international conflicts of interest without war is highly refined. Every sovereign government distinguishes between its vital and nonvital interests. The latter are generally subject to compromise and even the former may be, under dire circumstances, though this is much less common. The Soviet Union, despite a natural desire to see a pro-Soviet government established in the Congo, in the face of contrary pressures did not press this interest in 1960–1963, presumably because it was not deemed a vital interest at that time. Contrarily, the U.S.S.R. emphatically and bloodily insisted upon a pro-Soviet government in Hungary in 1956 because this was deemed vital to Soviet interests. Such decisions were based upon estimates of what was at stake in each instance by Soviet leaders. How, then, do governments calculate their vital and nonvital interests?

A French diplomat once sagely observed that with nation-states it was not a matter of wanting what they liked, but of liking what they had. In other words, a sovereign government arrives at what its interests are by respecting the power situation. This involves estimating its own power and that of its various rivals and deciding what can be deemed vital and nonvital within that context. Obviously the more powerful state will be more expansive in its definition of its interests than will the small state.

For the latter to do otherwise would be to invite frustration and defeat. Thus, a powerful China might claim and occupy an area in the Himalayas also claimed by a weaker India but forego occupation of Formosa because of the certain opposition of more formidable United States power to such a move. In another case, Yugoslavia in 1948 had sufficient power to defy Russian efforts to make it subordinate to Moscow, while Hungary in 1956 did not have sufficient power to resist similar pressure. These are, however, very simple examples of the role of power in relations between sovereign states. It operates in a far more complex way in bargaining over trade concessions, negotiating alliances, seeking support for a resolution in the United Nations, or opposing a rival seeking influence in a third government. But if the conduct of foreign policy is to be coherent, power cannot be ignored—however moral, ethical, humane, or idealistic one's foreign policy objectives.

THE ELEMENTS OF NATIONAL POWER

Geography, in spite of the missile age, is still a significant influence upon a country's power. The English Channel through centuries afforded a special protective advantage to Great Britain, even saving the country from invasion and probable conquest by Hitler's armies as recently as 1940. It remains today still an element in Britain's defense posture. Russia's expanse made it possible to meet a succession of invaders by trading space for time and the coming of winter. In its early years an otherwise weak United States enjoyed a more favorable power equation because of its relatively isolated location between two vast oceans. Usually access to the sea has been an asset, as have mountain frontiers; contrarily, land-locked states and those with no geographically distinguishable frontiers have often been at a disadvantage. Thus, geographic location, size, and topography have a bearing on power.

Population is another factor. Sheer numbers are sometimes, but not always, a power increment. Today, China's great population must be reckoned with by any government calculating Chinese strength. India and Indonesia, on the other hand, are two examples of heavily populated countries which are not especially powerful. In contrast, Germany with less than 80 million and Britain with only 50 million have played extremely influential roles in world developments. This points up the importance of a people's characteristics as distinct from its numbers. While hazardous to generalize about any large agglomeration of people because of individual differences, one may still describe the Germans as hard-working and disciplined, characteristics which have contributed to German strength and influence. Similarly, the British have evinced considerable ability in political organization and administration, as well as a capacity to sustain defeat without becoming demoralized, both factors helping to explain Britain's exercise of very considerable power over several centuries. The stubborn determination of the Russians contributed to their ability to sustain successive incursions by Poles, Swedes, Frenchmen, and Germans.

Natural resources are also basic to power, although this factor is linked with *economic development* (see Chap. 6). A country well endowed with mineral wealth, arable soil, forests, fish-filled waters, and water-power sites certainly has great potential economic strength. In the case of a Russia or a Sweden such favorable natural endowments do in fact add up to actual power because technology, skilled labor, and astute management have exploited them. Contrarily, the nonexploited riches of a Malawi or a Brazil so far have not contributed to the power of such national communities. There are cases, such as the Swiss and Belgian, where considerable power exists despite a paucity of natural resources because of exceptional skills and economic organization which enable such countries to obtain wealth by trading, processing, and selling someone else's raw materials. But clearly maximum power is obtained when a country has both the resources and the skills to develop them. A nation-state without either must calculate its power in other terms, and in an age when wealth and military competence depend on industrialization, the calculations must inevitably be discouraging for them.

Political cohesion is another contributor to power. A country whose government commands the basic loyalty of most of its citizens is manifestly stronger than one which must cope with disloyal or recalcitrant elements. A classic example of the latter may be observed in the history of the British Isles where the unhappy, restless, southern Irish not only refused to support Great Britain in the latter's foreign policy but used every British international embarrassment to strike for freedom from the British Crown. Thus, there were Irish rebellions when England faced Louis XIV, Napoleon, and Imperial Germany. Only Irish independence after World War I precluded a similar development during England's difficult times in World War II. "England's misfortune is Ireland's opportunity" ran the slogan. On the other hand, Britain derived great strength from the political cohesion of the rest of the inhabitants of the Isles.

Affecting this cohesion may be the intensity of nationalism as well as the ideological bonds of a people. The former operated in Germany's favor during World War II, but divisions among the German people over Nazism's tyranny and racism tended to work in the other direction. Many Soviet citizens fought in World War II for Russia, but not for Stalin's brutal dictatorship; many American Negroes fought in the same contest for America, but not for Alabaman segregation. Lack of unity among the various peoples comprising Czechoslovakia in 1938–1939 played a role in that country's inability to prevent its destruction by Germany. Exceptional cohesion among the Finns, on the other hand, was a major contributor to their ability to survive two wars with the U.S.S.R. (1939–1940, 1941–1944) and retain Finland's national independence.

In this connection some reference to the relative merits of democratic and dictatorial forms of government is pertinent. Though difficult to document, it would appear that democracies are handicapped by their cumbersome methods of arriving at decisions in the international power struggle. Both definition of national interests and prompt action in their defense are more difficult to achieve democratically than by an authoritarian regime where such decisions are made by a few leaders. But for a sustained period of stress, such as in a long war, that government which is viewed by the people as belonging to them will be stronger, other factors being equal, than a government which is not so viewed by the citizens.

A sixth power factor is *military posture*. In the preatomic age this meant the size, readiness, and efficiency of conventional armies, navies, and air forces. In the nineteenth century British power was greatly enhanced by the Royal Navy, the world's largest and most competent fleet. Wherever a warship could go, there Britain possessed a special influence on the course of events and the protection of British interests. The preeminence of its army afforded first Prussia, a small and poor kingdom, and later Germany, with exposed frontiers and rivals on all sides, considerable leverage in their power politics. The United States, on the other hand, counted on other power factors during much of its history and was happily able to minimize the size and expense of a military establishment.

Today, at least for the atomic powers, military posture is a far more complex business including not only the capacity to deliver an effective atomic bombardment in spite of formidable enemy defenses, but also to sustain such an attack by an enemy and then mount a counter atomic attack (the "second strike" in military verbiage) against him. Because the outbreak of such a war would be catastrophic for all humanity, the rationale advanced for such a military posture is that so long as governments are convinced of their rivals' second strike capacity they will refrain from any atomic attack. Differences of opinion exist as to the genuine rationality of this argument, but it is the rationale for the contemporary atomic military posture of the United States and the Soviet Union. It is also the justification for the continued maintenance of more conventional forces to afford a country the power which accrues from the ability to threaten military action short of atomic war.

For most sovereign states, lacking as they do atomic weapons, the older military posture is still important. The Republic of Israel, surrounded by hostile Arab states openly pledged to its destruction, effectively bolstered its modest power potential with a well-organized, ably led, and technically competent standing army. The relatively poor state of the Indian armed forces, by contrast, has placed India at a serious disadvantage in its border crisis with China.

Finally, *diplomacy* must be included as an element of power. In the United States, especially, the potential, as well as the limits, of diplomacy have not been firmly grasped. The American adage that this country "wins all its wars and loses all its peace conferences" so clearly demonstrates such a popular misunderstanding of diplomacy that this factor deserves study in a separate section.

THE ROLE OF DIPLOMACY

Though the word "diplomacy" was used in its modern sense for the first time by Edmund Burke in 1796, its practice dates far back into the past. The word itself derives from the ancient Greek word *diploma,* meaning written copy. But diplomacy was born even earlier—no doubt at the prehistoric moment when two humans perceived the advantage of haggling instead of fighting over their differences. By fighting, both ran the risk of injury. In avoidance of that risk they shared a community of interest. Recognition of that common interest made diplomacy feasible. In essence, *diplomacy is a means of obtaining the maximum possible advantages for one's country from a rival person, tribe, or country without resort to war.*

The principal task of the diplomat is to resolve conflicts of interests among sovereign states over which there is no higher authority to force an accommodation; secondarily he may also engage in negotiating agreements on issues which do not entail conflict of interest. Examples of the latter activity are diplomatic agreements on ocean and air travel regulations, exchange of weather data, the international postal service, and preservation of wild life. But when fulfilling his principal function, the diplomat is engaged in obtaining as much as he can from a reluctant antagonist, in pressing his own government's interests at the possible expense of a rival government, or in persuading his foreign counterpart that what he seeks is to their mutual advantage even though a conflict of interests exists. From this it follows that the diplomat must gauge as accurately as possible the respective power relationships and definitions of national interests of all the countries involved, including, of course, his own.

For a diplomat to miscalculate the power equation in any given situation is to invite possibly fatal consequences in terms either of surrendering unnecessarily his own nation's interests or of overestimating his rival's weakness. It would not be going too far to assert that it was the latter kind of miscalculation which led to the colossal errors in foreign policy of Napoleon and Hitler. As in so many human affairs, the diplomat must not permit success to dull his objectivity.

But if the diplomat is thoroughly aware of the elements of national power and can assess the approximate power equation between his country and every other country and combination of countries, he is prepared to define the goals and aspirations which his government can reasonably seek in the world arena. His is the art of the possible; hence a good diplomat must also be a good statesman.

DIPLOMACY AND POLICY

While great variety exists in the conduct of diplomacy, it is also possible to identify certain broad patterns of policy. When a nation-state is able to exist with almost no contacts with other countries and to avoid involvement in the latters' conflicts, it may be said to be pursuing a policy of noninvolvement. In times past, China, Japan, and Korea pursued such a policy and in a modified form so did the United States in the nineteenth century. Sweden and Switzerland also managed to avoid involvement in both world wars of the twentieth century, but no major state has been able for any appreciable length of time to follow such a pattern in today's interdependent, shrunken world.

At the other extreme from a policy of noninvolvement is a policy of domination. This is a pattern of seeking and exercising overwhelming influence and authority over other sovereign areas. Since such a policy entails major infringement on the sovereignty of others, a policy of domination frequently entails violent resistance by the sovereignty threatened. When Japan in 1931 seized Manchuria and later North China, it was pursuing a policy of domination which China forcibly resisted. Similarly, in 1939 the German policy of domination toward Poland precipitated not only counteraction by the Poles, but World War II. On the other hand, an example of domination executed without war is that of the German destruction of Czechoslovakia (1938–1939) or of Soviet Russia's annexation of the Baltic republics of Estonia, Latvia, and Lithuania (1940).

A third policy pattern is that of balance of power. The most widely practiced of all patterns, the balance of power has come into play as a means of self-preservation when one or more nation-states believe themselves menaced by still another, and join together in a pooling of power against the menace. The classic illustration of this policy is that of Britain. Over the past four centuries successive bids for domination of Europe were made by Spain, France, and Germany. In each instance the British threw their power on the side of the weaker governments menaced by one of these three and thereby helped create coalitions whose combined power was sufficient to prevent sixteenth-century Spain, Napoleonic France, and twentieth-century Germany from pursuing to fruition policies of domination in Europe. Incidentally, United States power was twice thrown into the scales against Germany along with Britain's, and since World War II American policy has sought to create, in the balance of power tradition, blocs against the U.S.S.R. and the People's Republic of China.

For a number of reasons the balance of power is a precarious, ever-changing policy. New weapons, estranged allies, changes in leadership continually alter the aspirations of governments and the means at their disposal to seek their goals. Thus, Soviet acquisition of atomic weapons drastically reduced United States power and obliged this country to adjust to a new balance. Similarly, the Soviet Union's friction with China altered the Soviet power equation. Amidst such changes it is easy for a government to miscalculate the balance of power and, believing it more in its favor than is in fact true, to be tempted into aggressive moves which mobilize enemies determined to frustrate those moves. A test of strength involving war may then ensue, depending on how the leaders calculate the power situation. If one side concludes that the balance has been upset in its favor, it may go ahead in spite of the opposing power build-up; or, through diplomacy, there may be a peaceful accommodation. From this it should be evident why nation-states engaged in a balance of power situation are continually colliding with each other, maneuvering to upset the balance in their own favor, and augmenting their military capabilities in order to increase their own power and deter their rivals from aggressive activity. Almost continual friction and frequent resort to armed force between sovereign states have not been precluded by the balance of power pattern, but it would not be correct to attribute these developments to the pattern itself. It must simply be observed that the pattern has had limited success in checking them. The cold war between the United States and the U.S.S.R. following World War II entailed a mutual probing of each other's positions which was characterized by a balance of power policy on the part of both. On several occasions armed clashes between the two were only narrowly avoided, most notably over Berlin and Cuba.

This inherent instability in the balance of power, as well as the special dangers of a policy of domination in our atomic age, and the impossibility of noninvolvement have led to consideration of a fourth policy pattern called "collective security." In essence this endorsed a return to Europe's historic concept of universalism under which all states would band together to protect one another against aggression and uphold international law. Thus in a collective security system, the principle of "all for one, and one for all" would be the standard of action. This principle, however, proved most difficult to realize in practice both in the League of Nations and in the United Nations. Indeed, such a pattern of international relations will not materialize until the major power centers of the world agree that international peace has a higher priority than any other national objective.

Diplomacy and Democracy

It may come as a surprise to learn that, until very recently, diplomatic activity was not nearly as apparent to the average American as it is today. The public, even in totalitarian states, is now offered a front-row seat in many current diplomatic negotiations. Special conferences are scheduled in an unending stream. Preconference publicity ranges from newspaper reporting of the agendas to televised tours of the conference city. The meetings themselves are blanketed with newsmen, who record the words of everyone and freely interpret what they mean. Photographs of smiling chiefs of state and issuance of communiqués impress the public with its proximity to diplomatic activity. In addition, legislatures investigate, deliberate, and legislate on foreign policy matters. Treaty provisions not immediately revealed, such as parts of the Yalta Agreement, occasion criticism by press and parliaments of secret and, by implication, bad diplomacy. All this is a recent development, which considerably postdates both the arrival of democratic government and free press.

Up to World War I, diplomacy was carried on largely without the knowledge or control of the electorate. Several factors were responsible. First, the prolonged period without a general European war and the abbreviated course of local conflicts created an atmosphere in which foreign relations did not seem very vital to the average man. Second, of all areas of government activity democratization had least affected the foreign service corps. A diplomatic career required education, a private source of income, and not infrequently political connections. As a result, diplomatic personnel was drawn mainly from the leisure class. It maintained an exclusiveness, a dignity, a prestige that permitted it to go about its business without very much prying by legislators, journalists, or politicians. As a matter of fact, the European diplomat before 1914 was a good deal more at home in the company of foreign diplomats than in that of most of his fellow countrymen. He was distinguished by a certain loyalty to his profession, as well as to the international social set which practiced it.

The resultant atmosphere was of considerable significance to diplomatic negotiation. Men of long experience, with confidence in the personal integrity of the foreign diplomats with whom they did business, carried on negotiations in the quiet seclusion of embassies, chateaux, and manor houses. They haggled, compromised, and sometimes lied, but they did so behind closed doors. Their brilliant strokes and their mistakes remained largely unpublished. They answered only to their foreign ministers, who listened attentively to their advice and accorded them considerable freedom of action. Because "secret diplomacy" of this kind came to be associated with the factors behind World War I, considerable criticism of it developed, and the way was paved for certain innovations in the traditional conduct of diplomacy.

The principal charge against prewar secret diplomacy was that it not only had failed to prevent war, but it had actually hastened war's coming. This charge was based on the evidence that, by making alliances with some states against others (Germany and Austria against Russia, France and Russia against Germany), the diplomats had divided Europe into two armed camps. When an international crisis arose, these alliances quickly involved all the major powers of Europe in a conflict which had started as a relatively localized affair. Thus, in the 1914 crisis, Germany allied with Austria supported the latter in an uncompromising policy which produced war with Serbia backed by Russia. Similarly, France, instead of exerting her influence for conciliation, gave priority to her Russian alliance and promised military support to Russia if needed. The actions led to a deepening of the crisis and eventually to general war.

This kind of diplomacy was viewed as bankrupt. Who was responsible for it? Many eyes turned to the professional diplomats and chiefs of state who had authored the alliances and then tragically given them support. Why had their fatal course of action not been arrested? Because, came the answer, the diplomats had been permitted to pursue their trade in secret, without the knowledge or approval of the citizens whose lives were at stake. Had the people known of these secret agreements, they, the ardent advocates of peace, would have insisted upon a different course of diplomatic action. The corrective cited for this dangerous, secret, undemocratic kind of diplomacy was democratic control of foreign policy. Because Woodrow Wilson was the chief exponent of this school of thought, the new twist to diplomacy is often referred to as Wilsonian diplomacy.

In his famous Fourteen Points, defining the World War I aims of the United States, Wilson expressed the criticism of the old diplomacy just noted. Point One called for: "Open covenants of peace, openly arrived at, after which there shall be no private international understandings of any kind but diplomacy shall proceed always frankly and in the public view." Wilson visualized foreign affairs being conducted in the same manner as domestic affairs in a democracy. This implied confidence in the citizenry's interest, knowledge, and judgments of foreign policy, public debate on it, expression of majority opinion on it in the legislative branch of the government, and approval by the legislative branch of all action undertaken in foreign affairs.

With its facilities for publicly recording all treaties and its planned substitution of collective security for alliances, the League of Nations represented a major attempt to inaugurate this new diplomacy.

It is true that, contrary to his precepts, Wilson found it necessary at the Paris Peace Conference (1919) to engage in a certain amount of secret diplomacy. In his very battle to secure the agreement of other nations to his League concept, he was obliged to go into closed sessions with the leaders of Britain, France, Japan, and Italy. Behind those closed doors, certain of the Fourteen Points had to be delicately compromised—to accommodate the territorial gains secretly agreed upon by the Allies during the war. For example, Japanese claims to economic concessions in Chinese Shantung were supported reluctantly by Wilson to secure Japanese adherence to the League of Nations. This dilemma, however, and the way in which Wilson met it did not alter his fundamental endorsement of open diplomacy.

To illustrate the new diplomatic approach upon his return to the United States, Wilson made a speaking tour of the nation in order to win public support for ratification of the Treaty of Versailles. And in the election of 1920, Wilson committed the Democratic Party to a clear-cut stand in favor of United States' membership in the League.

Throughout the world generally, Wilsonian diplomacy was much in evidence during the 1920's. Secret clauses were contained in certain agreements negotiated by the European states, most notably in 1925 between disarmed Germany and ostracized Russia, in which Russia granted Germany the right to carry on military training in Russia where Allied supervisors of German disarmament could not check. Nevertheless, the League of Nations did a "land office" business publishing the texts of "open covenants of peace, openly arrived at."

With the rise of dictatorships, the diplomatic crisis over Fascist Italy's attack upon Ethiopia in 1935, French efforts to build a new alliance against Nazi Germany, and the birth of the Rome-Berlin Axis in 1936, Wilsonian diplomacy went into eclipse everywhere, except perhaps in Britain and the United States. To the bitter end of his "appeasement" policy, Neville Chamberlain, British Prime Minister (1937–1940), dealt with Hitler in conferences whose proceedings and agreements were made public. Both Chamberlain and Roosevelt made public addresses the occasions for appealing to Hitler to abandon aggression; both responded to public opinion in their respective electoral campaigns; and both devoted much attention to persuading public opinion to accept their foreign policies and the diplomatic means of pursuing them.

During World War II, diplomacy was, of course, considerably restricted since it ceased almost entirely between the Axis states and the Allies. However, relations between allies, between belligerents and neutrals, among neutrals, and even between belligerents just before the surrender did afford much room for diplomatic activity. Much of it, in spite of military considerations, was of the Wilsonian variety. Press releases and public announcements accompanied every one of the numerous conferences between the Allies.

Since 1945, democratic diplomacy has also been much in evidence. This does not mean that all diplomatic activity in the United Nations, or in the many postwar bilateral and multilateral conferences, has been carried on in full view of the public or in response to popular wishes. The layman cannot be certain how large a role secret diplomacy may have played since 1945. Certainly, corridor conversations and private "off-the-record" meetings remain a part of diplomatic activity. Nevertheless, Wilsonian diplomacy is very much alive today, as is evidenced by a few examples. The long, persistent search by the various postwar British governments for diplomatic formulas to reduce East-West tension reflects a response to the British public's intense desire for peace. Undoubtedly, one of President Dwight D. Eisenhower's most significant actions was the negotiation of a popularly demanded Korean truce in 1953. Despite the practice of limiting the Soviet public's sources of information, Moscow leaders also reveal an awareness of the Russian public's yearning for peace by their frequent preachments on how the Kremlin labors for international understanding. As Dag Hammarskjold, Secretary-General of the United Nations, commented: "The diplomat who works . . . without recognition—and a proper handling—of the publicity aspect of his work, or without giving to public opinion its proper place in the picture, has little place in our world of today." [1]

Further emphasis upon democratic formulation and implementation of foreign policy has been evinced in the United States Congress' insistence that it exercise more control over the expenditure of funds it has appropriated for foreign affairs. The delayed publication of the complete text of President Franklin D. Roosevelt's Yalta Agreement, in which certain "secret" clauses had been incorporated, added support (in the opinion of many Americans) to the argument that more popular control of diplomacy was needed.

On the other hand, a major objection to Wilsonian diplomacy has been the charge that publicity of the kind now surrounding diplomatic negotiation has a very damaging effect. Such criticism can best be understood if the fundamental objective of negotiations is recalled. Negotiations are often initiated when each side discloses its maximum demands to the other side. This step is then followed by persuasion, bargaining, and pressuring until a compromise line of agreement is reached somewhere between the positions from which each side began. To carry this operation on successfully, in full view of the bargaining states' citizenry, is almost impossible, according to some observers.

When a nation's diplomats pose their maximum demands, the people of their country are inclined to assume that this is what should be obtained from the negotiation. How far to retreat from the maximum toward the minimum demands is a matter of shrewd judgment, based on skillful analysis of the opposition. It is not a matter for the divided and

[1] Dag Hammarskjold, "New Diplomatic Techniques," in *Vital Speeches,* December 1, 1953, pp. 107–108.

more emotional opinion often held by the public. If the public is a partner to the negotiation, its opinion will intrude into the situation with often fatal consequences. The nature of the compromise, or even the issue of whether there should be any compromise, can become hopelessly snarled in debate. Diplomats can hardly help becoming unduly sensitive to what the press is saying and to the sometimes irresponsible charge that they are sacrificing principle in their diplomatic maneuvering. They become rigid so as not to be called weak. As Dag Hammarskjold put it, "Open diplomacy may . . . easily become frozen diplomacy" [2] because it sheds its maneuverability; the maximum conditions, originally intended as a bargaining device, become the minimum terms, and no compromise is ever reached. It is a common temptation of a Western diplomat to return from an international conference as a hero because he has not "yielded" rather than as one who has "made a deal." The public dreads war, but "Heroes, not horse-traders, are the idols of public opinion." [3]

Finally, to admit the citizenry to a share in diplomacy at the negotiating stage means opening the door to participation by people who are not only divided in opinion but who, today at least, are frequently not qualified to deal with foreign policy. The average citizen is not qualified because he lacks accurate and complete information; he lacks information partly because he lacks sustained interest in the course of diplomacy and partly because it is a full-time job to acquire the necessary information. Further, not having a comprehensive outlook, he is more susceptible to short-range rather than to long-range considerations. For example, the public of Britain eventually saw the unwisdom of saddling Germany with the reparations it had demanded in 1919, but by the time it recognized it, the damage had already been done.

Charles B. Marshall, a former member of the Department of State's Policy Planning Staff, summarized these charges against the public speaking as a participant in diplomatic activity: "Popular opinion is not of much, if any, value in helping in the discovery of answers to the problems in this field [diplomacy]. It certainly counts, however, in setting bounds to the area of maneuver available to those charged with the responsibility." [4]

In conclusion, criticism of Wilsonian diplomacy is directed at the limitations that experience has revealed are placed upon diplomatic negotiation by the requirement of "open covenants, openly arrived at." Critics insist that foreign policy cannot be conducted in the same manner as domestic policy. An international conference is not the same as a New England town meeting. Negotiations over international control of atomic

2 *Ibid.,* p. 108.

3 Hans J. Morgenthau, *Politics Among Nations,* 4th ed. (New York, Knopf, 1967), p. 534.

4 Charles Burton Marshall, *The Limits of Foreign Policy* (New York, Holt, Rinehart and Winston, 1954), p. 13.

weapons cannot be approximated to one in which two school districts negotiate a merger.

Responding to democratic ideals, the conduct of diplomacy has changed since World War I, but the democracies have been confronted with a new dilemma. How can the long-established techniques and procedures of diplomats be applied effectively and at the same time subjected to appropriate popular control? Some suggested answers to this as yet unresolved problem are presented later in the chapter, in the section on "Positions." First, however, attention must be directed to the international situation as it has taken shape since the end of World War II.

DIPLOMACY'S NEW DIMENSIONS

Inevitably, the shrinkage in physical distances has presented diplomats with more concerns. As recently as the late 1930's the United States Department of State regarded such places as Vietnam, India, and most of Africa as beyond its area of concern and of little consequence in the formulation of American foreign policy. Similarly, Russia viewed Cuba, Guinea, and Indonesia as remote. As for China, it was wholly preoccupied with reasserting control over its own territory and played a passive role at best beyond its frontiers. Some of the European powers, most notably Britain and France, were more global-minded, but even for them with much of the Afro-Asian world under their colonial rule the geographic scope of their diplomacy was much more limited than in the jet age.

Another new dimension is the greater complexity of international relations. Economic, ideological, psychological, and military considerations weigh much more heavily today in diplomatic calculation—if only because contemporary power equations are so much more complex. The extension of military and economic aid to foreign countries, especially by the United States and the Soviet Union, has obliged both countries' diplomats to enlist the assistance of agricultural, financial, population, educational, and anthropologic experts. For its part, the People's Republic of China has led the way in furthering its diplomacy through political intrigue and aid to certain pro-Communist groups inside various countries, thereby setting a higher premium than before on the diplomat's grasp of subtle political forces in every country.

Added to these burdens has been the revolutionary dissolution of the old European colonial empires and the emergence in their place of over sixty newly independent states. During both the colonial revolts, which largely concluded by 1965, and subsequent clashes of national interests between the new governments there were busy times for the diplomats—not only of the new countries, but of the rest of the world whose power struggles were often transferred to awakened Africa and Asia. The unfamiliar cultures, hypersensitive nationalism, and frequent internal political instability of these new countries added to their demands upon the diplomats. Among the crises in these areas which have had world-wide repercussions were those in Palestine, Kashmir, the Congo, Cyprus, and Vietnam.

Finally, there is the added burden for diplomats in the second half of the twentieth century of atomic war. In the past, war has always been the threatened last recourse by diplomats. But to threaten war between atomically armed governments, even if only in bluff, is so fraught with the risk of initiating a first strike by one's opponent that this becomes a most dangerous device of diplomacy. At the same time, diplomats have the imperative task of preventing small wars begun by conventionally armed countries from involving atomic powers and then escalating into atomic war.

Such altered dimensions of diplomacy help to explain why the United States Department of State, which in 1790 had a staff of eight, now employs over 30,000 people in the United States and 200,000 overseas. Secretary of State Thomas Jefferson was unburdened with foreign-aid programs, allies (the United States has pacts with more than forty countries today), visits by foreign Heads of State, Asian affairs, United Nations diplomacy, atomic test-ban treaties, or any of the other numerous duties of a contemporary Secretary of State. Benjamin Franklin and his hotel room served to represent the American government in eighteenth-century Paris; today the Paris embassy of the United States occupies several massive buildings, employs more than 2,000 people and costs 15 million dollars annually. Thus have expanded the functions of diplomacy. They place an even higher premium on the diplomat's ability to fulfill his function with skill and wisdom.

POSITIONS

1. A REALISTIC USE OF DIPLOMACY IS THE BEST MEANS NOW AVAILABLE FOR PRESERVING PEACE

The following passages are from *Politics Among Nations* by Hans J. Morgenthau, Professor of Political Science and Director of the Center for the Study of American Foreign Policy at The University of Chicago: [5]

We have seen that international peace cannot be preserved through the limitation of national sovereignty, and we found the reasons for this failure in the very nature of the relations among nations. We concluded that international

[5] From POLITICS AMONG NATIONS, second edition, by Hans J. Morgenthau, pp. 505, 511, 516–524, 526, 527–534. Copyright 1948, 1954, by Alfred A. Knopf, Inc. Reprinted by permission. These passages also appear in chapters 31 and 32 of the 4th edition of *Politics Among Nations*.

peace through the transformation of the present society of sovereign nations into a world state is unattainable under the moral, social, and political conditions prevailing in the world in our time. If the world state is unattainable in our world, yet indispensable for the survival of that world, it is necessary to create the conditions under which it will not be impossible from the outset to establish a world state. As the prime requisite for the creation of such conditions we suggested the mitigation and minimization of those political conflicts which in our time pit the two superpowers against each other and evoke the specter of a cataclysmic war. This method of establishing the preconditions for permanent peace we call peace through accommodation. Its instrument is diplomacy.

THE DECLINE OF DIPLOMACY

Today diplomacy no longer performs the role, often spectacular and brilliant and always important, that it performed from the end of the Thirty Years' War to the beginning of the First World War. The decline of diplomacy set in with the end of the First World War. In the twenties, a few outstanding diplomatists were still able to make important contributions to the foreign policies of their countries. In the decade preceding the Second World War the part diplomats took in shaping foreign policy became even smaller, and the decline of diplomacy as a technique of conducting foreign affairs became more and more patent. Since the end of the Second World War, diplomacy has lost its vitality, and its functions have withered away to such an extent as is without precedent in the history of the modern state system. . . .

Imbued with the crusading spirit of the new moral force of nationalistic universalism, and both tempted and frightened by the potentialities of total war, two superpowers, the centers of two gigantic power blocs, face each other in inflexible opposition. They cannot retreat without giving up what they consider vital to them. They cannot advance without risking combat. Persuasion, then, is tantamount to trickery, compromise means treason, and the threat of force spells war.

Given the nature of the power relations between the United States and the Soviet Union, and given the states of mind these two superpowers bring to bear upon their mutual relations, diplomacy has nothing with which to operate and must of necessity become obsolete. Under such moral and political conditions, it is not the sensitive, flexible, and versatile mind of the diplomat, but the rigid, relentless, and one-track mind of the crusader that guides the destiny of nations. The crusading mind knows nothing of persuasion, of compromise, and of threats of force which are meant to make the actual use of force unnecessary. It knows only of victory and of defeat.

If war were inevitable this book might end here. If war is not inevitable, the conditions for the revival of diplomacy and for its successful operation in the service of peace remain to be considered. . . .

The revival of diplomacy requires the elimination of the factors, or at least some of their consequences, responsible for the decline of the traditional diplomatic practices. Priority in this respect belongs to the depreciation of diplomacy and its corollary: diplomacy by parliamentary procedures. In so far as that depreciation is only the result of the depreciation of power politics, what we have said about the latter should suffice for the former. Diplomacy, however morally unattractive its business may seem to many, is nothing but a symptom of the struggle for power among sovereign nations, which try to maintain orderly and peaceful relations among themselves. If there were a way of banning the struggle for power from the international scene, diplomacy would disappear of itself. If order and anarchy, peace and war were matters of no concern to the nations of the world, they could dispense with diplomacy, prepare for war, and hope for the best. If nations who are sovereign, who are supreme within their territories with no superior above them, want to preserve peace and order in their relations, they must try to persuade, negotiate, and exert pressure upon each other. That is to say, they must engage in, cultivate, and rely upon diplomatic procedures.

The new parliamentary diplomacy is no substitute for these procedures. On the contrary, it tends to aggravate rather than mitigate international conflicts and leaves the prospect for peace dimmed rather than brightened. Three essential qualities of the new diplomacy are responsible for these unfortunate results: its publicity, its majority votes, its fragmentation of international issues.

THE VICE OF PUBLICITY

Much of the confusion attending discussion of the problem of secret diplomacy results from the failure to distinguish between two separate aspects of the problem: between "open covenants" and "covenants openly arrived at," between publicity for the results of diplomatic negotiations and publicity for the diplomatic negotiations themselves. Disclosure of the results of diplomatic negotiations is required by the principles of democracy, for without it there can be no democratic control of foreign policy. Yet publicity for the negotiations themselves is not required by democracy and runs counter to the requirements of common sense. It takes only common sense derived from daily experience to realize that it is impossible to negotiate in public on anything in which parties other than the negotiators are interested. This impossibility derives from the very nature of negotiation and from the social context in which negotiations generally operate. . . .

THE VICE OF MAJORITY DECISION

The evil wrought by the public conduct of diplomacy is compounded by the attempt to decide issues by majority vote. In the General Assembly of the United Nations this method has developed into the tradition of at least two thirds of the members voting down at least the Soviet bloc. That this method of conducting the business of diplomacy has strengthened the Western bloc, but has made no direct contribution to the peaceful settlement of a single issue outstanding between East and West, is obvious from the results. . . .

THE VICE OF FRAGMENTATION

The decision by majority vote implies the third of the vices that stand in the way of a revival of the traditional diplomatic practices: the fragmentation of international issues. By its very nature, the majority vote is concerned with an isolated case. The facts of life to be dealt with by the majority decision are artificially separated from the facts that precede, accompany, and follow them, and are transformed into a legal "case" or a political "issue" to be disposed of as such by the majority decision. In the domestic field, this procedure is not necessarily harmful. Here the majority decision of a deliberative body operates within the context of an intricate system of devices for peaceful change, supplementing, supporting, or checking each other as the case may be, but in any case attuned to each other in a certain measure and thus giving the individual decisions coherence with each other and with the whole social system.

On the international scene, no such system of integrating factors exists. Consequently, it is particularly inadequate here to take up one "case" or "issue" after the other and to try to dispose of them by a succession of majority votes. . . .

THE PROMISE OF DIPLOMACY: ITS NINE RULES

Diplomacy could revive itself if it would part with these vices, which in recent years have well-nigh destroyed its usefulness, and if it would restore the techniques which have controlled the mutual relations of states since time immemorial. By doing so, however, diplomacy would realize only one of the preconditions for the preservation of peace. The contribution of a revived diplomacy to the cause of peace would depend upon the methods and purposes of its use. The discussion of these uses is the last task we have set ourselves in this book. . . .

Four Fundamental Rules

Diplomacy must be divested of the crusading spirit. . . .

The objectives of foreign policy must be defined in terms of the national interest and must be supported with adequate power. . . .

Diplomacy must look at the political scene from the point of view of other nations. . . .

Nations must be willing to compromise on all issues that are not vital to them. . . .

Five Prerequisites of Compromise

Give up the shadow of worthless rights for the substance of real advantage. . . .

Never put yourself in a position from which you cannot retreat without losing face and from which you cannot advance without grave risks. . . .

Never allow a weak ally to make decisions for you. . . .

The armed forces are the instrument of foreign policy, not its master. . . .

The government is the leader of public opinion, not its slave.

Those responsible for the conduct of foreign policy will not be able to comply with the foregoing principles of diplomacy if they do not keep this principle constantly in mind. As has been pointed out above in greater detail, the rational requirements of good foreign policy cannot from the outset count upon the support of a public opinion whose preferences are emotional rather than rational. This is bound to be particularly true of a foreign policy whose goal is compromise, and which, therefore, must concede some of the objectives of the other side and give up some of its own. Especially when foreign policy is conducted under conditions of democratic control and is inspired by the crusading zeal of a political religion, statesmen are always tempted to sacrifice the requirements of good foreign policy to the applause of the masses. On the other hand, the statesman who would defend the integrity of these requirements against even the slightest contamination with popular passion would seal his own doom as a political leader and, with it, the doom of his foreign policy for he would lose the popular support which puts and keeps him in power.

The statesman, then, is allowed neither to surrender to popular passions nor to disregard them. He must strike a prudent balance between adapting himself to them and marshaling them to the support of his policies. In one word, he must lead. He must perform that highest feat of statesmanship: trimming his sails to the winds of popular passion while using them to carry the ship of state to the port of good foreign policy, on however roundabout and zigzag a course. . . .

The way toward international peace which we have outlined cannot compete in inspirational qualities with the simple and fascinating formulae that for a century and a half have fired the imagination of a war-weary world. There is something spectacular in the radical simplicity of a formula that with one sweep seems to dispose of the problem of war once and for all. This has been the promise of such solutions as free trade, arbitration, disarmament, collective security, universal socialism, international government, and the world state. There is nothing spectacular, fascinating, or inspiring, at least for the people at large, in the business of diplomacy.

We have made the point, however, that these solutions, in so far as they deal with the real problem and not merely with some of its symptoms, presuppose the existence of an integrated international society, which actually does not exist. To bring into existence such an international society and keep it in being, the accommodating techniques of diplomacy are required. As the integration of domestic society and its peace develop from the unspectacular and almost unnoticed day-by-day operations of the techniques of accommodation and change, so any ultimate ideal of international life must await its realization from the techniques of persuasion, negotiation, and pressure, which are the traditional instruments of diplomacy.

The reader who has followed us to this point may well ask: But has not diplomacy failed in preventing war in the past? To that legitimate question two answers can be given.

Diplomacy has failed many times, and it has succeeded many times, in its peace-preserving task. It has failed sometimes because nobody wanted it to succeed. We have seen how different in their objectives and methods the limited wars of the past have been from the total war of our time. When war was the normal activity of kings, the task of diplomacy was not to prevent it, but to bring it about at the most propitious moment.

On the other hand, when nations have used diplomacy for the purpose of preventing war, they have often succeeded. The outstanding example of a successful war-preventing diplomacy in modern times is the Congress of Berlin of 1878. By the peaceful means of an accommodating diplomacy, that

Congress settled, or at least made susceptible of settlement, the issues that had separated Great Britain and Russia since the end of the Napoleonic Wars. During the better part of the nineteenth century, the conflict between Great Britain and Russia over the Balkans, the Dardanelles, and the Eastern Mediterranean hung like a suspended sword over the peace of the world. Yet, during the fifty years following the Crimean War, though hostilities between Great Britain and Russia threatened to break out time and again, they never actually did break out. The main credit for the preservation of peace must go to the techniques of an accommodating diplomacy which culminated in the Congress of Berlin. When British Prime Minister Disraeli returned from that Congress to London, he declared with pride that he was bringing home "peace . . . with honor." In fact, he had brought peace for later generations, too; for a century there has been no war between Great Britain and Russia. . . .

Diplomacy is the best means of preserving peace which a society of sovereign nations has to offer, but, especially under the conditions of modern world politics and of modern war, it is not good enough. It is only when nations have surrendered to a higher authority the means of destruction which modern technology has put in their hands—when they have given up their sovereignty —that international peace can be made as secure as domestic peace. Diplomacy can make peace more secure than it is today, and the world state can make peace more secure than it would be if nations were to abide by the rules of diplomacy. Yet, as there can be no permanent peace without a world state, there can be no world state without the peace-preserving and community-building processes of diplomacy. For the world state to be more than a dim vision, the accommodating processes of diplomacy, mitigating and minimizing conflicts, must be revived. Whatever one's conception of the ultimate state of international affairs may be, in the recognition of that need and in the demand that it be met all men of good will can join. . . .

2. THE SOUNDEST BASIS FOR FOREIGN POLICY IS THE USE OF POWER IN THE SERVICE OF MORAL PRINCIPLE

The material reprinted here is to be found in Thomas I. Cook and Malcolm Moos, *Power Through Purpose.*[6] The authors are Professors of Political Science.

PREFACE

The United States is the heir and standard-bearer of a culture begotten and bred in Europe. That culture rests on the twin foundations of Graeco-Roman politics and law and Judaeo-Christian ethics and religion. Our own tradition and history give us a unique position as modern champions of those ancient insights. Our constitutional democracy and our industrial technology provide us with unique opportunities to realize the Western promise in the daily practice of our lives and through the sure functioning of free institutions. We are equipped to

6 Thomas I. Cook and Malcolm Moos, *Power Through Purpose* (Baltimore, The Johns Hopkins Press, 1954), Preface, pp. 109–110, 112–113, 203, 212 *passim*. Reprinted by permission.

achieve both citizenship as social and political participation in the shaping of our lives and destinies and the full development of the ultimate and irreducible person. Possessed of vast power and called to leadership in the world, we can, if we will, spread our ideals elsewhere and help others on the road to their realization. Our middle-class society is marked by an increasingly shared amplitude of economic means and by broad enjoyment of leisure for the cultivation of humane ends. It is the true classless society, without benefit of revolution or need for totalitarian discipline. It is the leader in the fight against these needless and soul-destroying ills, and against their spread. Its mission is to persuade those still free that they can with its help profitably and successfully follow its way, and to rescue those who are the victims of tyranny and set them, too, on the right path. To that end it must first strengthen its adherence to its own ideals and institutions at home, and purify its political practice. It must fight without compromise the internal enemies of its method of freedom. It must maintain without compromise the essential rights of those committed to those methods, and must champion the values of creative dissent and personal difference. Its foreign policy must no less clearly and forthrightly distinguish between friend and foe, and must be devised as an integral part of the total politics of a nation whose interest is international and whose ethical principles rightly claim universal validity.

Such are the theses of this book. In propounding them, the authors have sought to clarify the issues in the present "Great Debate," and to fight the extremes of utopian worldism and realistic nationalism. . . .

CRITICISM OF A NEW BALANCE OF POWER SYSTEM

Some of the more moderate among the present proponents of American policy based on realistic calculations of national interest correctly argue that the United States has taken the place as a world power once held by Britain.

. . . . The lesson, the balance-of-power advocates insist, is plain. America, possessed of England's sometime power, must also adopt and adapt its concept of policy. . . . The only real alternative is between a narrowly selfish and expansionist use of power, accompanied by delusions of grandeur whose outcome is apt to be defeat, and an enlightened and responsible promotion of the national interest, directed to the sustained husbanding of American leadership through moderation in objective combined with firmness in action. But the latter choice, these advocates tell us, involves the proper selfishness of minimizing risks which could dissipate power. We must speedily become aware that the United States can by deliberate action create and preserve a balance of power in the rest of the world. On the other hand, it cannot impose its will or its way on that world, or over a major part of it. Likewise, it cannot attain security by a callous or indifferent isolation, provocative of envy and resentment.

. . . The policy of balance of power is today impracticable. Its initiation would immediately necessitate the organization and buttressing, if not the creation, of at least one side of the balance. The force to be counterpoised against the U.S.S.R. would have to be brought into existence. In Europe, an old world would have to be called into being by revivification ere the new world could make itself the balancing force. In the Far East, the radically different problem of organizing a modern system of independent and modernized states would present equal difficulties. From the outset, therefore, it is clear that such a program is artificial. It involves a mechanical attempt to manufacture an equivalent of what was in its day a growth of policy out of living political forces and established conditions of international relations. In the name of reliance on historical experience and use of the teachings of history, it overlooks or fails to understand the reality of history as living and changing situations. These necessitate new techniques to implement our lasting moral objectives. . . .

Those who argue that American national interest necessitates a balance-of-power policy do not seriously contemplate a possible future when we should be required to throw our weight to the Russian side. From such a line of action they would quite properly recoil in horror. Moreover, they are no doubt correct in the assumption that within a foreseeable future it is the anti-Communist powers which will need the support of a make-weight. Yet a policy whose defined conditions and enduring consequences would be unacceptable to its own proponents cannot be a proper formulation of national interest, nor a genuine realism. The nature and degree of support which ought to be given to actual or potential opponents of Communist and of Soviet ambition, East or West, are still open to debate. But bipolar opposition and conflict are lasting and fundamental as long as the Soviet Union adheres to neo-Marxist teaching and promotes it as a world program. Hence debate over policy cannot be conducted, nor American interest furthered, on the theory and practice of balance of power.

A new American balance-of-power system is not, then, a practicable way to further the nation's interests. . . .

A PREFERABLE STRATEGY

Our own strategy, which may indeed lead soon or late to war being thrust upon us by an increasingly insecure Russian regime, must be directed to encouraging germs of discontent within the Soviet Union and its satellites wherever possible, and to the extent possible. We must organize and aid potential revolutionaries there, yet as far as possible restrain them from ill-calculated or premature action. We must persuade the Russian people that we are opposed to a tyranny which at once deprives them of immediately available material well-being, personal security, and freedom, and threatens the peace and prospects of ameliorative prosperity for the rest of the world. We must ourselves develop our own system, including its military power, so that at the ripe moment we may aid them first to throw off their chains with minimum cost and disruption, and then to reconstruct society on their own design and tradition, without undue suffering, and without intervention designed to impose our special dogmas or institutions or to further interests peculiar to ourselves. . . .

For our sway over others will be no imperial rule, but the respected influence of demonstrated success and primacy in devotion to a common humanity. Our arts will be wise assistance and unfailing support towards liberation, towards others sharing in and contributing to a common, yet vastly rich and varied culture. Peace will indeed be our end, and a custom sought for the world, through international law and international institutions founded on principle, to which we ourselves are also willingly subject because [we are] their leading proponents. In search of that law, it will be our ardent mission not simply to spare the humble but to deliver the oppressed. To that end we shall indeed make war *à outrance,* with no compromise, on the proud dictators who pervert all principle and debase men whom they have first oppressed. Thus our moral empire will rest on a freely accepted appeal to the minds and hearts of peoples liberated with our assistance, enjoying our respect on grounds of a common humanity, and welcomed as partners in the human venture who by their efforts and insights enrich the stock of human culture. Only such uncompulsive empire is consonant with our heritage, our insights, our concept of mission, and the moral security of our own institutions. By reason of that heritage and inspiration, we can accept no less, and seek no more.

3. THE DIFFERENCES BETWEEN COLLECTIVE SECURITY AND BALANCE OF POWER

This selection is by the American political scientist, Inis L. Claude, Jr., as it appears in his *Power and International Relations.*[7]

The principle of collective security requires that states identify their national interest so completely with the preservation of the total world order that they stand ready to join in collective action to put down any aggressive threat by any state, against any other state anywhere. By assumption, peace and security are indivisible; the initiation of war anywhere is a challenge to the interest of all states, because it undermines the general order which is central to the security of every state. The balance of power concept, on the other hand, leaves much more latitude for the ad hoc calculation of what the national interest requires in particular circumstances. . . . States applying the balance principle may ignore some conflicts as irrelevant to their interest; they may welcome some conflicts as likely to affect their competitors in a way favorable to their own position in the general configuration of power; they may even regard aggression as a means legitimately available to themselves for improving their situation. Collective security decrees a set response in support of any victim of aggression; balance of power confirms the freedom of the state to pick and choose. Clearly, collective security is more thoroughly anti-war and more deeply committed in principle to supporting the victim of aggression as such.

The difference in this respect is fundamentally a difference regarding the *facts.* The balance principle says that a state should join in resistance to an aggressor only if its own security is affected; the collective security principle says that a state should do so *always because* its interests are affected by any aggression. . . .

This difference points to the fundamental contrast between the two concepts, which has to do with the degree of managerial centralization that they entail. Balance of power is a system only by courtesy; while the accusation that it amounts to anarchy is too strong, it is assuredly a most unsystematic system.

[7] Condensed from POWER AND INTERNATIONAL RELATIONS, By Inis L. Claude, Jr. © copyright, 1962, by Random House, Inc., pp. 146–149. Reprinted by permission.

It depends upon the autonomous, self-directed operations of a multitude of states and particularly of a smaller group of major states, and it therefore produces a continuing series of improvisations. Collective security, on the other hand, represents the urge for systematization, the institutionalization of international relations. It proposes to coordinate the policies of the states in accordance with firmly established general principles and to create institutions capable of providing some degree of centralized supervision and management of the system. The two systems may lead to the same action in a given case, but the balance system leaves this result to the contingencies of diverse calculations and autonomous maneuvers, while the collective security system undertakes to make it the predictable outcome of the operation of international machinery in the application of settled principle. . . .

Typically, the exponent of the balance of power concept is preoccupied with the problem of dealing with a concrete and immediate issue affecting the security of his state—e.g., how the United States can cope with the dynamics of Soviet expansionism—and he is unwilling to be diverted by consideration of the requirements for an adequate general system of international relations. . . . The balance of power system represents an aversion to systematic regulation of international relations; it enshrines the principle of the freedom of states to maneuver at will.

SELECT BIBLIOGRAPHY

ALMOND, GABRIEL A., *The American People and Foreign Policy* (New York, Harcourt, Brace & World, 1950). An appeal for more rational thought and a search for a concensus among "elite" elements in American society on foreign policy formulation. The wide variety of outlook among various social groupings in the United States is seen as a further complication in the determination of this country's foreign policy.

BUTTERFIELD, HERBERT, *Christianity, Diplomacy and War* (Nashville, Tenn., Abington Cokesbury, 1954). A case by a British historian for coupling Christian morality with diplomacy in an effort to bridge the frightening emotional chasms which separate peoples at war and make postwar accommodation so much more difficult.

CLAUDE, INIS L., *Power and International Relations* (New York, Random House, 1962). An evaluation and comparison of balance of power, collective security, and world government as patterns of policy. The author is a political scientist who pleads for grasping every means whereby power can be canalized away from violent, disruptive employment.

FOSDICK, DOROTHY, *Common Sense and World Affairs* (New York, Harcourt, Brace & World, 1955). A primer for Americans who wish to understand the fundamentals of international politics. Principles, not recommendations for specific situations, are clearly and simply set forth for the conduct of foreign policy by a former member of the State Department's Policy Planning Staff.

HALLE, LOUIS J., *Civilization and Foreign Policy* (New York, Harper & Row, 1952). An examination of the nature of the sovereign state system and an exploration of guiding principles for United States foreign policy in such a world. Before turning to research in the field of foreign affairs, the author served ten years with the Department of State.

KENNAN, GEORGE F., *Realities of American Foreign Policy* (Princeton, Princeton University Press, 1954). Americans must learn to accept the inescapable ties between national life generally and foreign policy if their policy is to come of age. A veteran diplomat, United States ambassador to the U.S.S.R. and Yugoslavia, the author is also a respected academician.

MARSHALL, CHARLES B., *The Limits of Foreign Policy* (New York, Holt, Rinehart and Winston, 1954). An explanation of the difficulties and limitations imposed upon United States diplomatic activity by the intrusion of the public. Diplomacy cannot function in a mass-meeting environment, claims this former member of the State Department.

MORGENTHAU, HANS J., *Politics Among Nations*, 4th ed. (New York, Knopf, 1967). Already cited, this work has become a classic on the sovereign state system, both historically and contemporaneously.

NICOLSON, HAROLD, *The Evolution of Diplomatic Method* (London, Constable, 1954). A summary of the growth of diplomacy by a British diplomat and historian. He gives much attention to the problem of diplomatic effectiveness in a democratic age.

THUCYDIDES, *The History of the Peloponnesian War*, Richard Livingston (ed. and trans.) (New York, Oxford University Press, 1943). A classic example of power politics in a civilization divided into sovereign communities and the harm which the civilization inflicted on itself through failure to work out a satisfactory accommodation between those communities. Required reading for statesmen for twenty-four centuries.

3

The Nature of Man, Conflict, and War

IN SERIOUSLY SEEKING FOR THE ROOTS of international conflict and war in our time, one cannot avoid asking the question: Is man by nature warlike? Can certain innate compulsions, or instincts, be identified in man which enable us to assert with assurance that he is by his very nature addicted to making war? Obviously, if an affirmative answer to such a question can be categorically given by those who have studied *Homo sapiens,* then we have already arrived at the final chapter in this book—and at a fundamental conclusion, however gloomy, about international conflict. Fortunately, no such categoric answer is forthcoming from those best qualified to inform us about the nature of man and conflict.

Few of us have not heard our elders observe, "There have always been and there will always be wars." And indeed, historians tell us that the written records upon which they reconstruct our picture of the past confirm that at least in historic times war has been a frequent and pervasive human activity. Yet this is insufficient for our purposes. Popular folklore is not always a sound guide to truth, and the historian is concerned with man only during the brief millennia since man learned to write and began leaving behind the kind of evidence with which the historian works.

Even more popular today is the often expressed belief that wars could be avoided if only the peoples of the world knew one another better. Calling into doubt this observation would seem to be the experience of the post-World War II era, during which peoples have become far more familiar with each other than ever before, yet war—international, civil, brush-fire, guerrilla, by whatever name—has been a constant feature of the world scene. On the other hand, does the fact that there has not been an atomic war since 1945 signify that while man still engages in violent group conflict he is responding to a growing awareness of other men by conducting only limited wars?

In the United States, where psychology has attracted a wider popular following than elsewhere, there has been much loose use of such terms as frustration, fixation, and inferiority complex in attempting to explain all types of human behavior, individual and group. As professional psychologists would be the first to point out, group behavior in particular cannot be accounted for in such simple terms.

The fact of the matter is that no categorical answers about the nature of man and conflict are possible because we know very little about what makes man "tick." History, the oldest of the disciplines concerned with human behavior, is at best fragmentary in its evidence and only descriptive of *how* man behaved. While it seeks also to uncover *why* he behaved as he did in each given experience, history cannot get inside a man to discover his genuine feelings, thoughts, and motivations. Even to arrive at tentative explanations historians fall back on what psychologists and sociologists have found out about contemporary humans and then endeavor to identify similar circumstances and infer similar responses on the part of the persons they are studying in history. Thus, history is of very limited use here. As for the economists, political scientists, sociologists, psychologists, and anthropologists, they perhaps strike out more boldly than historians but are constantly obliged to rehypothesize as their information only now begins to accumulate in significant quantity. It is essential, however, that we avail ourselves of the most authoritative scholarship available in all of these disciplines in attempting to gain some insight into the basic nature of man and conflict, and this is the focus of this chapter. But first, because many scholars hold that any understanding of human nature must begin with a biologic study of man, we turn to a brief summary of what light is shed by recent biology upon the animal character of man and its relevance to the problem of war.

MAN IN BIOLOGIC PERSPECTIVE

For roughly a hundred years after the postulation of Darwin's theory of evolution, Western man, already optimistic and arrogantly confident of his progress toward an ever better state, was receptive to the idea that he was rapidly shedding the last vestiges of his animal ancestry. More recently, however, especially since the spectre of his total annihilation has appeared as a possibility, man has taken a new look at himself with chastening effect. Man is an animal, albeit of a very special kind. While he has capacities for unique activity, he at the same time remains of the animal kingdom.

MAN THE ANIMAL

To the biologist the four billion earth specimens we call men constitute the *Hominidae* family of the primate order. The primates, in turn, are classified as mammals, the highest category in the vertebrate group. Contrary to popular belief, man is not the descendant of the anthropoid

apes, though both man and ape have a common, branch-swinging an-
cestor. Certain it is that man's remote forebears were animals of a less
complex and refined composition than that of present-day *Hominidae*.

In skeletal structure, blood chemistry, general physiology, and repro-
ductive processes man is not so different from many other species of the
animal kingdom. A number of basic behavioral patterns are common to
all the primates. For instance, the ape, like man, may breed at any time,
has a complex family life within which the offspring are protectively
reared for an extended period, and displays considerable capacity for reasoning. Also like man, the ape can walk upright and uses his "hands" for
a variety of purposes, including the manipulation of crude tools such as
rocks and clubs. Indeed, studies of anthropoid apes in their native habitat
by such scholars as Clarence R. Carpenter reveal that man is less unique
among the primates than was formerly believed—deflating as this discovery may be to the human ego.[1]

However closely related as man is to other primates, there are vitally
significant differences to be noted. First, man made a decisive break with
nonhuman primate behavior when he came down out of the trees to live.
When and where this happened is not easily determined, though it is
likely that drastic climatic changes forced adoption of this "unnatural"
habit. Drought, for example, which is known to have been prevalent during the Pleistocene Era (the Great Ice Age from about 1,000,000 to 10,000
years ago), is a possible explanation.[2] In any case this abandonment of his
arboreal life was accompanied by such radical physical changes as the
evolution of the human foot and erect posture. It also appears to have
entailed man, alone among the primates, having acquired carnivorous
eating habits. Logic further suggests that as a hunter of meat, man sharpened his cunning, became more aggressive, roamed further, and pre-
empted territory for himself. Almost certainly, this altered pattern of life
developed a creature whose instincts combined with learned behavior to
produce in time a very complex, predatory animal.[3]

This animal, in turn, became further distinguished by the growth
of his brain, which is indeed man's most unique possession. Evidence
supports the thesis that this growth took place in relatively short geologic
time, man acquiring his present brain size in the early Pleistocene, or

[1] See C. R. Carpenter, *Naturalistic Behavior of Nonhuman Primates* (University
Park, Pa., The Pennsylvania State University Press, 1964). While the author consciously
avoids theomorphism (the attributing of animal characteristics to man) and anthropo-
morphism (the attributing of human characteristics to animals), the reader must be
impressed with the hitherto unknown complexities of nonhuman primate social behavior and their human parallels.

[2] Actual evidence of man's existence in the Pleistocene is established, but anthropologists hypothesize that man may have already appeared in the preceding
geologic era, which would make him considerably older than a million years. See
William Howells, *Mankind in the Making: The Story of Human Evolution* (Garden
City, N.Y., Doubleday, 1959), pp. 137 ff.

[3] For a highly readable and persuasive development of the emergence of predatory
man see Robert Ardrey, *African Genesis* (New York, Atheneum, 1961), pp. 261 ff.

about three-quarters of a million years ago. This brain, in relation to body weight, is three to four times as large as that of nonhuman primates and makes possible a self-awareness and capacity for conceptual thought known only in *Homo sapiens.*

While experiments indicate that chimpanzees, especially, are capable of fairly sophisticated reasoning, it is at a level far below that of healthy adult humans. Using his brain, man became increasingly attached to logic, precision, and the measurement of things. He devoted much thought to his own transitory existence on this earth; the inexplicable and chaotic disturbed him and drove him to seek explanations for the happenings of the world about him. In historic times, particularly, man sought to control and mold nature to his will; in this process he came to accept the expanding realm of knowledge as good and desirable.

No less a human distinction was the visualization of situations without actually experiencing them physically, thereby enabling man to arrive at solutions to his problems often much more quickly and safely. The transmission of his accumulated knowledge to succeeding generations, a process called "time-binding," was still another vital distinction. A dog might master amazing tricks, but it does not teach these tricks to its pups; a chimpanzee has even been known to learn a few "words" and use them properly, but it does not teach them to its offspring. Only man is a time-binder in this sense.

In concluding this section, it should be noted that man's nature is like an iceberg, the bulk of it still remains submerged and, so, unknown. But it does seem clear that he has evolved into a creature of primeval, animal instincts combined with an intellect of unique and enormous importance. As much as, if not more than, other animals, man is predatory and instinctively motivated by an all-powerful drive to survive and reproduce. But he is above and beyond the rest of the animal world in his intelligence. In view of the ambivalent use to which he has put his intelligence—the manufacture of ever more destructive weapons, for example —it is at least questionable whether man's animal instincts or his human mentality is the stronger force for his survival.

ANIMALS AND WAR

Among animals, including man, exists the common phenomenon of physical violence against other members of the same species. Not all species are so characterized, nor is it common to all members within a given species, but among the higher animals it is a biologic constant. Hunger and sex urges, when frustrated, result in clearly identifiable biochemical reactions which prepare the animal for aggressive, violent attacks upon others. The bull moose battles to the death in the northern wilds during the rutting season, hungry lions will battle over a zebra carcass on the veldt, and one needs only to read a newspaper to be aware that human murder for sexual reasons is a common occurrence, too. Indeed, some human behaviorists argue that violence for many members of *Homo sapiens* is pleasurable, hence its emphasis by press, motion pictures, and television. How many attendants at pugilistic contests and automobile races are more engrossed in the art of boxing or driving than in the strange, gripping sensations accompanying the savage pounding of a human body or the observation of flirtation with death on a racetrack? This is a vicarious enjoyment of violence made possible by the human capacity for conceptual thought.

Cannibalism, too, is not uncommon among animals. There exists much evidence of human cannibalism on a large scale in prehistoric times; it is still socially acceptable in contemporary New Guinea; and under dire conditions it has occurred much closer to the home of this book's readers in our own time. Thus, man is not above this kind of animal violence.

Indeed, even when the important distinction is made between aggression by one member against another of the same species and organized mass aggression between groups of the same species, one cannot assert that human behavior is altogether different from that of other animals. Recent studies reveal that rat colonies wage constant and deadly war with other colonies and that bands of nonhuman primates will invade the feeding grounds of others of their species and violently drive the original feeders away. Konrad Lorenz, the internationally known naturalist, has pointed out that these warring rats demonstrate within their groups strong loyalty, faithfulness, hierarchic consciousness, and exceptional concern for their young; and this leads to the hypothesis that such mass aggression is the counterpart to extremely strong bonds of social unity within each rat colony.[4] Certainly nonhuman primate behavior substantiates this hypothesis. Moreover, less aggressive species seem to engage in less complex social behavior.

The student of human behavior must exercise extreme caution in attempting to derive explanations about man from the findings of animal behaviorists, but the parallels are striking and intriguing. Man, like other mammals, engages in conflict with other individuals of his species. And along with some other mammals, man also practices mass aggression against other groups of men. But whereas the former type of conflict seems rooted in elementary drives connected with survival (aggression for food, defense, and reproduction), the latter type appears to correlate with the complexity of social organization. This line of thought suggests, therefore, that the explanation for man's war making must be sought not only in biologic terms, but also in sociologic terms.

[4] Konrad Lorenz, *On Aggression,* trans. Marjorie K. Wilson (New York, Harcourt, Brace & World, 1966), pp. 157 ff.

MAN IN SOCIOLOGICAL PERSPECTIVE

It requires no special perception for any of us to recognize that human beings, with few exceptions, are gregarious. They find it both natural and necessary to associate with other humans in groups which may vary greatly in size but which are distinguished by a particular living pattern. Anthropologists and sociologists refer to such groups as societies and to their living patterns as cultures. Therefore, to avoid confusion, we will accept the following definitions by the American anthropologist M. J. Herskovits: "A culture is a way of life of a people, while a society is the organized aggregate of individuals who follow a given way of life. In simple terms a society is composed of people; the way they behave is their culture." [5]

Why there is a human compulsion to form social groupings need only be passingly noted here. Clearly the helplessness of his newborn and their protracted period of dependency dictate that man, like other higher animals, organizes in families. But *Homo sapiens* was pressed by other considerations into social living so that with one or two rare exceptions he evolved societies and cultures of considerable complexity. All of these cultures, according to anthropologists, possess basic universal traits which emphasize the universality of man as a social being.

Cultural Universals

Division of economic responsibilities is easily identified in all cultures. In some the habits of production, distribution, and consumption are elementary. Methods of production are crude, and goods are produced primarily for the producer's own use. The distributive and exchange functions may exist only between husband, wife, and children, or may entail only barter between families. In contrast, other economic systems are highly organized, specialized, mechanized, and automatized. But in every culture there is economic organization, which is passed on to the next generation.

Another cultural universal is social hierarchy. This may extend no further than the family but is universally present. Monogamy and patriarchy are the most common patterns of family life, but polygamy, polyandry, and matriarchy characterize some others.

Similarly, each society evolves a system of political control or government to regulate certain affairs in the whole group's interests. Systems to meet this need vary from the power of a father over his children, or of a grandfather over his children and grandchildren as was the case in ancient China, to the power of life and death exercised by a modern totalitarian government over a great mass of people. Sometimes, as in modern

---

[5] Melville J. Herskovits, *Man and His Work* (New York, Knopf, 1952), p. 29.

democratic society, political authority and organization may be very extensive, but not intensive. Thus, a member of Swedish society is subjected by Swedish culture to only modest political regulation—he has freedom to worship, speak, travel, and work as he pleases, though he will surely feel the culture's restrictions if he arbitrarily takes life or property away from a fellow member of the society.

The desire for aesthetic satisfaction in various forms of art expression is another cultural universal. Stonehenge, France's Lascaux caves, African wood carvings, European medieval church architecture, and contemporary surrealist painting, as well as literature and music, illustrate this universal aspect of culture.

Finally, every culture formalizes aspirations and goals for its society. Such aspirations may be of the worldly type common in Western culture today where an end to economic poverty and inequality before the law are deemed worthy objectives. More common in history have been aspirations associated with death and the achievement of consolation, if not peace of mind, in the face of this eternal human mystery. Thus the cultures of the American Indian, of Egypt's Old Kingdom, or of contemporary Buddhist communities all offered certain beliefs and rituals focused on the unknowns of life and death. Indeed, until very recent times all cultures have derived their moral sanctions and prohibitions from their religions, thus raising the question whether a religionless culture will not disintegrate because of the collapse of its moral code when the latter is robbed of divine sanction.[6]

CULTURAL VARIATION

Despite such universals as just outlined, cultures do of course vary widely. From its economic organization to its overall goals, each culture is a response to its environment. In our society homosexuality may be a taboo, but in many non-Western societies homosexual activities are deemed normal and socially acceptable.[7] Mediterranean peoples are stamped by a climate which discourages unremitting physical labor; Arctic temperatures obviously affect Eskimos in a quite different manner. And out of these influences emerge all kinds of other cultural features. Mediterraneans evolve eating habits, clothing styles and materials, even courting customs and gods, related indirectly to their climatic environment.

No less important in cultural variation, as well as change, is borrowing by one society from another. Called acculturation by anthropologists,

[6] The French sociologist Henri Bergson maintains that morality, whatever its rational utility in a society, has an indispensable religious basis and thus implies an affirmative answer to this question. See Henri Bergson, *The Two Sources of Morality and Religion,* trans. R. A. Audra and C. Brereton (New York, Holt, Rinehart and Winston, 1935), pp. 88–90.

[7] Clellan S. Ford and Frank A. Beach, *Patterns of Sexual Behavior* (New York, Harper & Row, 1951), p. 130.

this process is especially rapid in this century of shrinking distances. Japanese art motifs have struck a responsive chord in the United States, the Cadillac has become a status symbol in Kuweit, atomic explosions and Western music have become part of the Chinese cultural scene, turbans are worn in Copenhagen and trousers in Calcutta.

Such acculturation would appear to be essentially progressive, since existing ways of meeting situations are altered when substitute patterns are discovered to be more effective. But there are liabilities in cultural alteration. Innovations which prove inapplicable to local situations may serve only to destroy parts of the old culture without replacing them. This is what has occurred on a large scale during the last hundred years where Western cultures were brought into intimate contact with those of Asia and Africa. Ancient religions, tribal political organization, self-sufficient economies, and feudal social hierarchies have been eroded by the Western intrusion, but Afro-Asians have not readily assimilated the culture of the West and are thus left, at least temporarily, in a deeply disturbing condition of cultural flux. The resulting upheaval in the societies of contemporary Afro-Asia is readily observed. This reference to social upheaval leads to an examination of social psychology as a key to explaining war in terms of man's social nature.

Finally, there are cultural differences which no doubt have explanations in terms of either environment or acculturation but which remain undiscovered by students of culture. How does one explain, for example, why many African cultures accord great respect to the aged, but not to females; while in the United States the reverse is almost true? Or why is there a naturalness among Finns toward human nakedness which is matched by strong British inhibitions toward the same subject? Why are fried grasshoppers a delicacy in Mecca, but not in Montgomery, Alabama?

Having cursorily glanced at why and how man is given to social behavior in general, let us now return to our central quest: does *Homo sapiens* engage in mass aggression because he holds membership in a society? And if so, why?

WAR, A FUNCTION OF CIVILIZED CULTURES

Today's Westerner, taking pride in what he deems and labels an advanced society, understandably might well conclude that simpler, more primitive societies must have been and are more warlike. After all, Western man has agreed with General Sherman that "war is hell" and acknowledges the desirability of at least avoiding nuclear war, if not all violent international conflict. His efforts at organizations for peace in the past half century have been admittedly impressive. Moreover, since members of primitive societies in many respects appear to be less remote from the existence of other animals, common sense suggests primitive man must have been given more to violent behavior and thus to war.

But, as Bertrand Russell warns, common sense is not always a reliable guide to sound conclusions. More important, as was noted in the preceding section of this chapter, only a few mammals including *Homo sapiens* engage in mass intraspecific conflict. It should come as no surprise, therefore, to learn that archaeological findings lead to the conclusion that earlier primitive societies were less characterized by war than so-called more advanced societies. Presumably the former remained simple and primitive because they were isolated and therefore experienced little acculturation; this same isolation also afforded little or no opportunity for contact and possible conflict with alien social groups. Further explanation may rest in the hypothesis that simpler societies had elementary economies in which a hand-to-mouth existence was characteristic. Agriculture, if present at all, was secondary to hunting, fishing, and berrying. This meant that food-producing areas were neither stationary nor clearly defined and hence less likely to be bones of contention between alien societies. Such an economy also yielded little in the way of food surpluses which might tempt a hungry group to attack one with food reserves. Finally, it is unlikely that the more simply organized groups possessed either the necessary time free from scrabbling for survival or the weapons and food reserves essential to military expeditions. It is also possible, in taking note of Konrad Lorenz's hypothesis (see p. 77), that the dangers of primitive existence and the very limited size of his groupings afforded early man ample opportunity to work off whatever aggressive inclinations he may have had without channelling them into mass aggression. In any case, all evidence points to war as a prominent, highly organized, frequently practiced function not of Australian bushmen or Eskimos, but of the great, complex societies we call civilizations.[8]

WHY CIVILIZED MAN MAKES WAR

An Economic Explanation. The word civilization derives from the Latin *civita,* a term meaning city. Thus a civilization is a society with an urban element in its culture, which in turn implies production of food surpluses sufficient to maintain that part of the society living in the city and a means for storing those surpluses. As tent cities gave way to stationary settlements, civilized societies became dependent upon nearby food-producing regions for survival; and as urban population expanded, there was an accompanying growing dependence upon more of the city's surrounding agricultural area. From this economic complex arose the need for more political organization both to coordinate life within the community and to enable its inhabitants to add food-producing land. When this process brought the city-states of Sumeria, Middle-Eastern site of the first civilization, into conflict with each other, these political units then assumed the function of war making—either to defend what

---

[8] See Ruth Benedict, *Patterns of Culture* (Boston, Houghton Mifflin, 1934), pp. 30–32; Frederick L. Schuman, *International Politics* (New York, McGraw-Hill, 1958), p. 16.

was already occupied or to expand at another community's expense. History also records cases of nomadic hill peoples raiding the Mesopotamian settlements, but here again it appears that it was the surplus of wealth accumulated by the urbanites which attracted the nomads. As a result, it was these early "civilized" communities which learned how to maintain standing armed forces, refine military equipment and techniques, and conduct war professionally. No civilization since that of Sumeria—Chinese, Hindu, Egyptian, Babylonian, Assyrian, Persian, Greek, Roman, Islamic, or Western—has known this kind of war making as a prominent and important part of its culture. Some, such as the Assyrian, devoted rather more time and energy to it, some like the Chinese suppressed it for extended times over large areas, but none did without it.

However, one must beware of overemphasizing food surpluses and shortages as a root of intergroup conflict. As contemporary India demonstrates, hungry peoples are not necessarily driven to aggression upon less poor neighbors, while it is patently impossible to explain in these narrow terms any of the wars waged by the United States in this century.

It is helpful at this point to turn back to the causes of war listed in Chapter 1 (pp. 12–15) for a better understanding of the many and varied roots of intergroup conflict in our own time. World War II, for example, was the result of all seven causes listed; economic, ideologic, and military rivalries were prominent in the genesis of the Korean War (1950–1953); military, and perhaps other, considerations were involved in the Sino-Indian clash of 1962; a struggle for power would appear to best account for the Algerian War (1954–1963); and religious ideology was certainly one factor in the armed clash between Pakistan and India in 1965. Thus, while some authorities such as Hans J. Morgenthau argue that most wars stem from a struggle for power, which is perpetual between sovereign states, this does not strike the authors here as a complete enough explanation. A multiplicity of impulses to conflict may be present in a society and some further analysis of what forces are at work in such a situation lead to the next considerations of *Homo sapiens* in his social environment.

THE ROLE OF GROUP MEMBERSHIP

In the process of fulfilling his basic needs as a member of a social group, the human being at the same time is subjected to a process of social training, discipline, and integration which social psychologists now believe play a vital role in intergroup conflict. If any society is to survive, then its members must be loyal to it and be willing to uphold it. A basic task in every society is the "taming" of its wild new members, namely, its infants, in order to initiate them into its cultural pattern. Thus, from birth children are taught the values of their parents' culture and are molded into conforming members of their parents' society. For a society not to successfully undertake such training of its infants is to invite social disintegration. The degree of integration, of course, varies. Some societies, usually denoted as open or pluralistic societies, have a variety of institutions to which their members' loyalties are directed. In western Europe and North America, particularly, society channels loyalty toward the family, the local community, the church, the nation-state, and associations such as trade unions, political parties, professional organizations, recreational groups, and educational institutions. Other societies tolerate fewer loyalties. Colonial New England placed loyalty to the Puritan Church above all others, ancient Chinese civilization gave priority to familial loyalty, and German Nazis endeavored to make the German state the supreme object of every German's loyalty. In the latter case and in similar efforts to subordinate all aspects of a culture and all members of a society to a single authority and object of loyalty there is produced what are denoted as totalitarian societies.

But whether in a pluralistic or totalitarian society, membership entails inhibitions for the individual member and, if the social psychologists are correct, complementary tendencies to aggression. Child training usually inculcates willing acceptance of many of these inhibitions and for most members they become unconsciously accepted as the normal pattern of living. In this way man becomes committed to his society and to what it claims it stands for. The actions of his social group become "right" and legitimate in his eyes; actions which challenge his group inevitably and naturally are viewed as "wrong." A nonconformist is charged with being antisocial and may be penalized in various ways, depending upon how seriously the society views his "crime." If such threats come from an alien society, an out-group, then the in-group may well respond aggressively. If the integrity of the in-group is weak, obviously its desire and capacity for violent, mass response will be weak. But if it is to survive and is subject to recurrent threats from out-groups, such an in-group will develop more internal regimentation among its members than would a less threatened society. This would appear to account, at least in part, for the relatively greater pluralism in insular British society after 1066 as compared with the greater degree of totalitarianism in exposed, insecure German society of the last century. In a word, social insecurity breeds more intensive social integration. And the latter, in turn, appears to result in a greater propensity for mass aggression against alien societies. This last point certainly bears some further examination.

As noted above, from infancy a society's members are indoctrinated with the "virtues" of their in-group. From this, according to social psychology, each member acquires a vital self-identity with his society. His status becomes interwoven with what he believes is his society's status. Individual self-respect and ego become inextricably interlaced with the individual's view of his society's prestige among other societies. If his society suffers, the member feels this personally. In a word, social membership is directly linked with each member's ego. Social disintegration, therefore, may mean personality disintegration, for in his society rests the member's whole frame of reference. Without the latter he becomes not only a man without a country, but a man deprived of the values, aspirations, and "truths" he had been taught since birth. It is obvious that humans do accommodate themselves (especially as young adults) to changes in their cultural patterns, but this is never a painless process and when pressure for such cultural alteration is identified as external, the resistance to it greatly intensifies. Thus conflict between different societies is quickly personalized for their constituents and the disposition to fight, if necessary, to preserve "a way of life" grows.

Stereotyping. At this point it is appropriate to turn to the social phenomenon known as stereotyping. As a kind of defense mechanism, all social groups acquire images of both their own group and of the out-groups. Stereotypes are based upon observation, not on imagination or caprice, but they are subjective in the sense that they generalize from selected observations about a whole society. The stereotype of one's own group tends to be, not unexpectedly, favorable and flattering—its art is more refined, its impulses more generous, its endeavors more worthwhile, its women more beautiful. Stereotypes of out-groups, on the other hand, tend to be unfavorable and unflattering. Both become part of the folklore of the society and are maintained by the schools and sources of public information. Indeed, this inculcation of its young with such images is a stupendous task for any society.

According to social psychologists, changes in stereotypes of out-groups tend to vary with the degree of danger the in-group believes is constituted by any particular out-group. A less threatening alien society may be stereotyped as merely "backward" or "decadent," while one with whom there is more conflict and which is powerful more often is stereotyped as "barbarous," if not "bestial." Should open conflict erupt then even clearer, simpler images emerge. The in-group may even endorse extinction of the out-group as a "moral" or "holy" obligation. Obviously, stereotyping is reciprocally mutual and plays a part in not only intensifying hostility between different societies but in imparting to their conflicts a crusading spirit which blocks avenues of possible compromise and accommodation. All of the great conflicts between civilized communities down through history seem to have assumed this kind of emotional overtone. Even today the European has not lost entirely his stereotype of the "cruel" Turk with whom he battled for centuries. There are still Protestants who hold to the Reformation stereotype of the Roman Catholic as "subversive," "intolerant," and "sadistic." Some observers hold that the racial prejudice whites display toward yellow peoples stems from a stereotype evolved from the frightening experience of Europeans with invading Mongols centuries ago.

In our own American experience, one can note the successive stereotyping of such enemies as the Indians, Spaniards, Mexicans, Germans, Japanese, and Russians. The latter, particularly, have enjoyed a series of stereotypes in recent years. In the 1920's and 1930's, many Americans looked upon Russians as repulsive, bomb-throwing, inept bolsheviks; during World War II when the United States and the Soviet Union were allies, the Russians were seen as stalwart, brave, not-so-different comrades; later this stereotype gave way to that of well-organized, secretive, evil, would-be world conquerors; and today still another stereotype appears in the making as new dangers and threats from other directions arise. It is also evident that stereotyping plays a prominent role in American racial tensions.

A study made in 1948 by UNESCO illustrates rather dramatically the wide variety of stereotype-impressions that various nationalities have of one another.[9] The study was based on a public opinion poll in nine countries, in which a representative sample of approximately 1,000 persons in each country was interviewed. Each person interviewed was given a list of twelve adjectives [10] and was asked to indicate which he thought applied to the people of certain countries, including his own. A partial summary of the results of the survey in four countries appears on pages 85–86.

The figures in each table indicate the percentage of respondents who felt that each adjective applied to the nationality being described. The totals do not equal 100 percent because the same adjective could be applied to more than one nationality. It should be remembered that this survey was made in the summer and early fall of 1948, when the Marshall Plan had been in operation for a few months, when the Berlin blockade had started, and when the preliminary negotiations for NATO had just got underway.

Country in which
  survey was made:
  Great Britain   *People Described*

Adjectives:	American	Russian	French	Chinese	Self
Intelligent	38%	12%	32%	17%	52%
Practical	38	21	20	11	47
Generous	52	3	14	7	48
Backward	4	36	9	37	6
Domineering	37	42	11	2	6
Peace-loving	39	6	21	22	77

[9] UNESCO, *International Social Science Bulletin,* Autumn, 1951, Vol. II, No. 3, pp. 515–528.
[10] The twelve adjectives were hard-working, intelligent, practical, conceited, generous, cruel, backward, brave, self-controlled, domineering, progressive, and peace-loving.

Country in which
  survey was made:
  West Germany
  (British Zone)   *People Described*

Adjectives:	American	Russian	French	Chinese	Self
Intelligent	34%	4%	22%	6%	64%
Practical	45	8	5	3	53
Generous	46	2	5	1	11
Backward	1	41	10	12	2
Domineering	10	12	12	1	10
Peace-loving	23	5	12	5	37

Country in which
  survey was made:
  France   *People Described*

Adjectives:	American	Russian	Self
Intelligent	37%	15%	79%
Practical	81	11	17
Generous	34	7	62
Backward	2	56	4
Domineering	46	49	4
Peace-loving	26	10	69

Country in which
  survey was made:
  United States   *People Described*

Adjectives:	Russian	British	Self
Intelligent	12%	49%	72%
Practical	13	32	53
Generous	3	13	76
Backward	40	11	2
Domineering	49	33	9
Peace-loving	7	42	82

SOURCE: William Buchanan, "Stereotypes and Tensions as Revealed by the Unesco International Poll," *International Social Science Bulletin*, Vol. III, No. 3 (1951), pp. 519–520. By permission.

In this section an effort has been made to demonstrate that by virtue of group membership human beings become parties to intergroup conflicts. The individual may have no dispute or quarrel with an individual in another society, but both are integrated into their respective social groups and thereby become enmeshed, unconsciously for the most part, in the enmities, aggressions, and conflicts of those groups. And when a society undertakes violent mass action its members are at war. It still remains, however, for us to explore the psychological and sociological causes of intergroup conflict and war.

INTERGROUP CONFLICT *vs.* INTERGROUP WAR

As noted earlier in this chapter, one explanation of why societies wage war upon one another may be over the issue of food. At least, with only the scanty information available on the earliest wars, this is a reasonable hypothesis. However, our growing awareness of the complexity of *Homo sapiens,* especially as a social being, compels students of human behavior to seek other roots of his violent conflicts.

CONFLICT OVER GROUP GOALS

During and immediately following World War II, it was popular in both academic and journalist circles to generalize from observations about Nazi Germany. This led to ascribing national aggression to the personal frustrations of a large number of citizens in a nation and to national leadership in the grasp of a few deviant individuals. The obvious evidence to support this argument was that many Germans in the years before World War II were indeed frustrated by unemployment, the humiliation of defeat after the First World War, resentment of reparations, and discomfort with a new style of government. It was these frustrations that deviant personalities like Adolf Hitler were able to use as stepping stones to power and then to lead Nazi Germany into a war of conquest.

While conceding some validity to this analysis, today's social behaviorists are chary of concluding that a large number of personal frustrations among a group's individual members automatically results in collective frustration and often, therefore, in collective aggression. We are also warned against the assumption that intergroup conflict, and especially intergroup war, always, or even generally, are determined by the group's most prejudiced, frustrated, and hostile leaders. Two societies may simply and sanely find themselves seeking what each deems a vital goal, but both of which cannot be fulfilled. Thus, control of the water resources of the upper Indus River system or of the Jordan are "bread-and-butter" issues between India and Pakistan and Israel and its Arab neighbors, respectively. Even if the disputants were not alienated by other considerations (as is the situation in both of these cases), agreement on the surrender of part of the resources to the other side in some kind of compromise is the only alternative to a test of raw power. As the world succumbs to technological shrinkage, this kind of conflict will surely multiply. But if conflicts between civilized societies appear to be increasing and inescapable, does this lead to the conclusion that resort to war is also inescapable?

THE ROLE OF GROUP LEADERSHIP

Group leadership can exert considerable influence upon what choice a group may be persuaded to make in resolving its conflicts with other groups. A glance at Nazi Germany's history is helpful here. In Germany's case, real and concrete disputes concerning its eastern frontiers brought it into conflict with its neighbors. An attempt at compromise was made in 1938 when part of Czechoslovakia was ceded to Germany, but Chancellor Hitler, powerful and paranoic, shortly tore up this settlement by seizing all of Czechoslovakia. This then stiffened Polish and British positions against any compromise on the German-Polish frontier, the immediate point over which World War II began. In this case, Germany's leadership in no way sought other than total achievement of its goals and thus headed straight for a test of military strength.

Hitler, however, in his ambitions and willingness to gamble for enormously high stakes, was an unusual group leader. More common are those who make more conservative estimates of the possibilities of total achievement of goals and often negotiate compromises instead of promoting war. Obviously, however, this demands a similar disposition on the part of the other group's leadership. It also depends upon means of communication between the opposing groups' leaders. If permanent diplomatic representatives of each reside in the other community, then negotiations can be initiated with a minimum loss of face. On the other hand, two communities which have long maintained hostile stances toward one another for other reasons, will find it more difficult for their leaders to communicate with each other over any issue of conflict.

Furthermore, no group leader, whether of a civil rights, trade union, or student protest movement, or of a sovereign government, can lead his followers wherever he wishes. The more charismatic the leader, the more influence he may have upon his followers. But whether having usurped power or having been elected to it, a leader's freedom is circumscribed by his in-group's feelings and attitudes concerning any out-group with whose leaders he may wish to deal. If long-standing antagonism and hardened, hostile stereotypes divide the two groups, then the pressure will be stronger for a solution through force rather than negotiated compromise. There have been cases of leaders swimming against such a social current of hostility, but at the risk of surrendering their leadership positions. In our own national history President John Adams failed of reelection, at least in part, because of his firm stand against a popular tide for war with France in the 1790's. President Woodrow Wilson sacrificed his leadership by advocating a policy of overseas involvement at the end of World War I which so many of his countrymen, accustomed to noninvolvement and mistrust of foreign governments, refused to accept.

In conclusion, leadership is a highly variable and important factor in intergroup conflict. Basically, leaders are the product of their society and look out upon the world to a large extent as they have been trained since infancy by that society. They do, however, by virtue of having emerged as leaders, have greater influence on group decisions and actions than their followers. Within limits, therefore, leadership may influence the choice in intergroup conflicts between negotiated compromise or resort to war.

INFLUENCE OF THE ATOMIC AGE

Because of the nature of intergroup relations just reviewed, war preparation and war making have long been wholly legitimate, institutionalized social functions. Given a certain set of circumstances, most civilized communities have been willing to go to war. In recent times the establishment or preservation of national independence has been accepted by most national groups as not subject to compromise and therefore grounds for war. However, there have been some exceptions. In 1940, the Estonian nation, rather than see its whole culture destroyed at once, peacefully accepted absorption into Soviet Russia. Czechs and Danes did the same rather than wage suicidal war against Nazi Germany. Admittedly, this entails an anguished decision and few societies make it. The North American Indians postponed for three hundred years such a surrender and Jewish Zionists refused to make it in the passing of three thousand years. Nonetheless, sheer survival has upon occasion forced a group to reject war as a policy even at great cost in terms of the group's independence and cultural integrity.

Today, atomic weapons constitute a new, more widespread discouragement to war. The latter has been deemed legitimate because it entailed a "pay-off." Not only did societies wage war to gain something, but also to minimize losses (in contrast to the Estonians, the Finns in World War II went to war to prevent a similar fate at Russia's hands and though they were obliged to surrender some territory they preserved their independent republic). But if conflicting groups armed with atomic weapons now go to war, the possibilities of a pay-off are much reduced. At best, one could hope to destroy an alien power, although its incinerated cities and radioactive soils and waters would hardly be worthwhile gains, at the cost of partial incineration of one's own society.

At worst, one might gain the foregoing at the cost of total destruction of one's own society as well. Up to now, recognition of each other's capacity to make this estimate credible has deterred the atomically-armed nations from engaging in atomic war despite the serious conflicts separating them. This international situation is not unlike that in a society where every individual carried a gun. In the latter case practicality dictated disarming the society and constituting a police force in order for the society to function, i.e. to yield a "pay-off." The transition, however, was not easy and depended upon the majority perceiving that its interest would be better served by such a drastic step in altering the limits within which individual conflicts could be settled. This was a long and slow process. Reason suggests that a similar alteration of the limits within which group conflicts could be settled is increasingly desirable in the atomic age, but the means whereby this might be accomplished are anything but clear, especially as we become increasingly aware of the complexities of the nature of human beings.

THE ROLE OF POPULAR EDUCATION

Here we turn to still another variable in this analysis of intergroup conflict and war. Each of us as an individual when confronted with nettling situations has been conditioned by long training to abjure violence. For example, while driving an automobile one is frequently aroused by the actions of another driver, especially when he has violated traffic regulations. We may give vent to loud horn-blowing or emphatic speech, and we may let off further steam in grumpiness toward our families or in knocking down tenpins. But the urge to violence is displaced because of our social training and the awareness of social penalty. Some social psychologists argue that education of whole groups of people could induce similar responses in instances of intergroup conflict.

Such an approach would entail education of group memberships to the futility of war and the desirability of settling conflicts without it. Admittedly, this would also entail the education of a number of groups since this approach to conflict would have to be mutual. But in time, runs this hypothesis, all groups would gain the perception that peaceful resolution of conflict held out more advantages than violence. Accompanying this growing realization would come the establishment of supergroup institutions to facilitate this approach—what today is now called "world government."

Supplementing the foregoing education must come an attack on stereotyping. According to Otto Klineberg, cited at the end of the chapter, "If prejudice can be learned, it can also be unlearned." Therefore, efforts would have to be undertaken to reveal the nature of stereotyping and, more important, simply to alter them. Older Americans will recall the World War II image held of the Japanese as dwarfed, buck-toothed sadists; a stereotype which has given way to one of the Japanese as diligent, clever, sensitive sophisticates. On the other hand, under duress of international tension with China's government, the American stereotype of the Chinese has shifted from friendliness to hostility. Is it not logical to assume, therefore, that if stereotypes are so malleable, they may be drastically altered through popular education and removed as a reenforcement for violent group aggression?

Still a third point is that intergroup hostilities could be afforded release through less harmful channels. Here the argument is for international conflicts to be diverted into competition in such areas as athletics, scientific achievement, education, production of material goods, and even economic aid to the developing world by the richer communities. This again would be a major educational undertaking.

There are, however, great obstacles in this approach. Education concerning the futility of war assumes a rationality in man for which he has not been conspicuous. Moreover, as Adlai Stevenson's speech to the United Nations reminded us (see pp. 11–12), man is also educated to meet aggression with resistance, to die on his feet, if the cause is worthy, rather than to live on his knees. And once intergroup conflict begins, its participants behave even less rationally than in other circumstances—witness the behavior of armies whose individual members in their home group environment would not even dream of acting as they do as a tightly organized group abroad in an alien culture! Furthermore, is it possible to eliminate stereotypes? Or do individuals and societies abandon or modify one hostile stereotype only to seize upon another? Do societies retain their cohesion only by maintaining hostility toward some out-group and so by their very nature cultivate stereotypes? Finally, with reference to substituting other competitive channels between conflicting groups, we cannot lose sight of the fact that conflicts do not begin in the minds of men, but rather are rooted in very real issues—food, water, territory, power, national independence, even religion. It is most difficult, therefore, to educate men to abandon such conflicts in exchange for other competitive activities which might afford emotional release of hostilities but do not remove the basic source of the hostile postures. All of this is not to write off education's role—to do that would have convinced the authors that they should never have attempted this book—but to warn against regarding popular education as a short, or even sure, road to the solution of human conflict and war.

CONCLUSIONS

If this chapter has achieved its purpose, the reader has come to recognize two things: (1) at the root of international politics are human social and psychological factors, and (2) our knowledge about these social and psychological factors is much too limited to afford any firm, uncontroversial answers as to why man makes war. While an anthropologist in the section immediately following asserts that war is inherent in man, other social behaviorists take different views.

But after all, to know what one does not know is an important educational step. One is at least insulated against "popular truths" which are not true. Moreover, the chapter has sketched a broad framework for the study in succeeding chapters of some of the more specific and better understood contributors to human conflict and war.

POSITIONS

1. WAR MUST BE ATTRIBUTED TO MAN'S INBORN FIERCE NATURE

The following passages are from *Evolution & Ethics,* by Sir Arthur Keith.[11] The author, an anthropologist, wrote *Evolution & Ethics* in England during World War II.

There is another very important factor which forms part of the machinery of evolution—namely, man's inborn competitive spirit or nature. Man is by nature competitive, combative, ambitious, jealous, envious, and vengeful. These are the qualities which make men the slaves of evolution. We are all familiar with the rivalry between man and man in civil life; but is not the competition, the rivalry between the nations of Europe even more intense? The "struggle for survival"—I think it would be more accurate to say, the "struggle for integrity"—often reaches such an extremity that decisions can be reached only by the use of force—by resorting to war. Here again I bracket evolution and war together.

I come now to the crucial question put to me by my correspondent: "Is evolution of mankind the correct method of procedure?" No one with a spark of humanity in him could approve of the bloody spectacle which meets his eye in all parts of the earth today. If war be the progeny of evolution—and I am convinced that it is—then evolution has "gone mad," reaching such a height of ferocity as must frustrate its proper role in the world of life—which is the advancement of her competing "units," these being tribes, nations, or races of mankind.

There is no way of getting rid of war save one and that is to rid human nature of the sanctions imposed on it by the law of evolution. Can man, by taking thought, render the law of evolution null and void? . . . I may say that I have discovered no way that is at once possible and practicable. "There is no escape from human nature". . . my main theme [is]—namely, that a double

11 Sir Arthur Keith, *Evolution & Ethics* (New York, Putnam, 1946, original British edition *Essays on Human Evolution*), pp. 105, 109, 113, 116–119, 125, 192, 193. Reprinted by permission of Rationalist Press Association Ltd., London.

code of morals (the ethical and cosmical) are entrenched in man's nature or mentality, and that without this duality there could have been no organized and effective evolution of humanity. . . . There can be no clear thinking about war or any other matter bearing on the relationships of one nation to another until we draw a sharp distinction between the twofold code under which the nations of the world live, move and have their being—the ethical code of civilized behavior and the cosmical code of savage behavior. In war we are under the domination of the cosmical code.

I . . . look on the brain mechanism which subserves the dual code as of extreme antiquity, for it is obeyed instinctively by social animals low in the animal scale; it is deeply entrenched in human nature. Man's emotions, his feelings, and his inherited predispositions are so contrived as to make him responsive to its behests. . . .

We shall obtain some light on the "ethical confusion with which the popular mind is perplexed" if we scan for a moment the writings of those who, applying only the ethical code to the problem of war, denounce it as a crime or as a monstrous vice. "War," said Seneca, "is a glorious crime." Condorcet: "It is a heinous crime." "Great generals," exclaimed Mencius, "are great criminals." All of which verdicts are true, on the basis of an ethical code. When Thomas Hobbes states, in Leviathan (1651), that "in war, force and fraud are cardinal virtues," he is basing his judgment on the cosmical code. When he affirms that "by nature man is both faithful and false," he evinces his belief in the duality of man's mental constitution. The popular saying, "All is fair in love and war," is a recognition of the cosmical code. Napoleon was cosmically minded: "In war," he said, "all things are moral." So was Hindenburg: "War," he declared, "suits me like a visit to a health resort." So was Bismarck. . . . And yet under Hitler, as under Bismarck, Germany was ruled by the dual code; her own folk by the ethical, and all others (save her satellites) by the cosmical code.

Sir Henry Maine, in Ancient Law, writes as a lawyer when he informs us that "sovereign states live in a state of nature." This means that each state is ruled within by the ethical code, and that their external affairs are controlled by the cosmical code. The cosmical code is based on compulsion—on force, and in the last resort, on war. A state applies the cosmical code not only to enemies outside its frontier, but also to enemies—such as criminals and rebels—which are in its midst. . . . The criminal, because of his nefarious activities, has been excluded from the ethical code of his country and has his life or liberty taken from him so that his nation may enjoy internal peace. The soldier, on the other hand, gives his life in order that his country may have security and external peace; the moment he shoulders arms he passes from the ethical to the cosmical code. Under that code it becomes his duty to reverse every item of the ethical code—to kill, to deceive, to lie, to destroy, to damage the enemy by every means in his power. Particularly noticeable is the reversal of his sense of justice: "home" justice is no longer valid. In war, said David Hume, "we recall our sense of justice and sympathy and permit injustice and enmity to take their place." My readers may remember that famous Piraeus party of ancient Greece when Socrates asked his companions for their definition of justice. "Justice," answered Polemarchus, "is helping friends and harming enemies." This answer, which conformed to the cosmical code, was rejected by Socrates; he and his pupil, Plato, were in search of an ideal justice, a justice which had a quality which was both universal and eternal. Yet ancient Greece, like the modern world, was divided into a multitude of political fields, each swayed by the dual code. Justice, under the ethical code, is one thing—under the cosmical code it is quite another. Under the cosmical code justice is that which is enforced by political measures or by the might of arms. Here I take no note of what "ought" to be, but only of what has been and now is.

. . . Later . . . I shall have occasion to deal with the evidence on which Elliot Smith based his conception of human nature as having been originally peaceful. Meantime it may be stated that it is possible to hold this conception of human nature only by concentrating attention on its ethical or peaceful side and overlooking the equally old side—the cosmical or warlike. There is evidence of strife in the world long before civilization came to it. . . .

My readers will have perceived by now that the thesis I am seeking to prove is that fierce war must be attributed to an inborn fierce nature which has developed in tribes long subjected to the rigors of competitive evolution. Such a view will be strenuously opposed by scientists such as Professor W. C. Allee, who regards war as an acquired habit; and by Dr. Carr-Saunders, who traces war, not to the inheritance of warlike qualities, but to the handing on of a warlike tradition. Now, I agree with both of them that if a Mongol child or a German child had been removed from tribal surroundings during infancy and brought up in a home in China, or within the confines of an Indian caste, those children would have grown into peaceful, law-abiding citizens. But this admission does not imply that these children would have lost their warlike aptitudes; only that the conditions which call out such qualities would be lacking. We still have to explain how such a fierce tradition arose along the vast tribal zone of the Old World and endured over thousands of years. I cannot conceive that a tribe, be it Mongolian or German, could tolerate over a long period of time a tradition which was antagonistic to its true nature. Tradition is molded to fit the mentality which fashions it, not the other way around.

2. AGGRESSION IS VITAL TO MAN, BUT IT NEED NOT INEVITABLY LEAD TO WAR

The author [12] of this selection is at once a zoologist, medical doctor, and naturalist. Austrian born, he has studied and taught in Europe and America and some of his published works have appeared in eleven different languages. He holds that aggression is instinctive in man, even vital to man, but on the basis of what we know about aggression it is subject to redirection and control.

. . . I now proceed to summarize the most important inferences from what has been said in this book by formulating simple precepts for preventive measures against that danger. . . .

[12] Abridged from ON AGGRESSION by Konrad Lorenz, pp. 276–281, 282–283, 284–286, copyright, © 1963, by Dr. G. Borotha-Schoeler Verlag, Wien; English translation, copyright © 1966, by Konrad Lorenz. Reprinted by permission of Harcourt, Brace & World, Inc. and Methuen and Co. Ltd., London.

The first, the most obvious . . . precept is . . . , "Know thyself": we must deepen our insight into the causal concatenations governing our own behavior. The lines along which an applied science of human behavior will probably develop are just beginning to appear. One line is the objective, ethological investigation of all the possibilities of discharging aggression in its primal form on substitute objects. . . . The second is the psychoanalytic study of so-called sublimation. We may anticipate that a deeper knowledge of this specifically human form of catharsis will do much toward the relief of undischarged aggressive drives. The third way of avoiding aggression, though an obvious one, is still worth mentioning: it is the promotion of personal acquaintance and, if possible, friendship between individual members of different ideologies or nations. The fourth and perhaps the most important measure to be taken immediately is the intelligent and responsible channeling of militant enthusiasm, in other words helping a younger generation which, on the one hand, is highly critical and even suspicious and, on the other, emotionally starved, to find genuine causes that are worth serving in the modern world. . . .

Even at its present modest stage, our knowledge of the nature of aggression is sufficient to tell us what measures against its damaging effects have no hope of success whatever, and this in itself is of value. To anybody who is unaware of the essential spontaneity of instinctive drives and who is wont to think of behavior exclusively in terms of conditioned and unconditioned responses, it must seem a hopeful undertaking to diminish or even eliminate aggression by shielding mankind from all stimulus situations eliciting aggressive behavior. . . . Another unpromising attempt is to control aggression by putting a moral veto on it. The practical application of both these methods would be about as judicious as trying to counteract the increasing pressure in a continuously heated boiler by screwing down the safety valve more tightly.

A further, theoretically possible but in my opinion highly inadvisable measure would be to attempt to breed out the aggressive drive by eugenic planning. We know . . . that there is intra-specific aggression in the human reaction of enthusiasm and this, though dangerous, is nevertheless indispensable for the achievement of the highest human goals. We know . . . that aggression in very many animals and probably also in man is an essential component of personal friendship. . . . We do not know how many important behavior patterns of man include aggression as a motivating factor, but I believe it occurs in a great many. What is certain is that, with the elimination of aggression, . . . the tackling of a task or problem, the self-respect without which everything that a man does from morning till evening, from the morning shave to the sublimest artistic or scientific creations, would lose all impetus. . . .

A simple and effective way of discharging aggression in an innocuous manner is to redirect it at a substitute object . . . this method has been employed extensively by the great constructors of evolution to prevent combat between members of a group. It is sound reason for optimism that aggression, more easily than most other instincts, can find complete satisfaction with substitute objects. . . . I have found that even highly irascible people who, in a rage, seem to lose all control of their actions, still refrain from smashing really valuable objects, preferring cheaper crockery. Yet it would be a complete error to suspect that they could, if they only tried hard enough, keep from smashing things altogether! . . .

Redirection as a means of controlling the functions of aggression and other undischarged drives has been known to humanity for a long time. The ancient Greeks were familiar with the conception of catharsis, of purifying discharge, and psychoanalysis has shown very convincingly that many patterns of altogether laudable behavior derive their impulses from the "sublimation" of aggressive or sexual drives. Sublimation, however, must not be confounded with simple redirection of an instinctive activity toward a substitute object. There is a substantial difference between the man who bangs the table instead of hitting his antagonist, and the man who discharges the aggression aroused by an irritating family life by writing an enthusiastic pamphlet serving an altogether unconnected cause.

. . . the main function of sport today lies in the cathartic discharge of aggressive urge . . .

The value of sport, however, is much greater than that of a simple outlet of aggression in its coarser and more individualistic behavior patterns. . . . It educates man to a conscious and responsible control of his own fighting behavior. Few lapses of self-control are punished as immediately and severely as loss of temper during a boxing bout. More valuable still is the educational value of the restrictions imposed by the demands for fairness and chivalry which must be respected even in the face of the strongest aggression-eliciting stimuli.

. . .

I have already said that we can learn much from demagogues who . . . make peoples fight. They know very well that personal acquaintance, indeed every kind of brotherly feeling for the people to be attacked, constitutes a strong obstacle to aggression. Every militant ideology in history has propagated the belief that the members of the other party are not quite human, and every strategist is intent on preventing any "fraternization" between the soldiers in confronting trenches. Anonymity of the person to be attacked greatly facilitates the releasing of aggressive behavior. It is an observation familiar to anybody who has travelled in trains that well-bred people can behave atrociously toward strangers in the territorial defense of their compartment. When they discover that the intruder is an acquaintance, however casual, there is an amazing and ridiculous switch in their behavior from extreme rudeness to exaggerated and shamefaced politeness. Similarly, a naive person can feel quite genuine hatred for an anonymous group, against "the" Germans, "the" Catholic foreigners, etc., and may rail against them in public, but he will never dream of being so much as impolite when he comes face to face with an individual member. On closer acquaintance with one or more members of the abhorred group such a person will rarely revise his judgement on it as a whole, but will explain his sympathy for individuals by the assumption that they are exceptions to the rule.

. . . I think we must face the fact that militant enthusiasm has evolved from the hackle-raising and chin-protruding communal defense instinct of our prehuman ancestors and that the key stimulus situations which release it still bear all the earmarks of this origin. Among them, the existence of an enemy, against whom to defend cultural values, is still one of the most effective. Militant enthusiasm, in one particular respect, is dangerously akin to the triumph ceremony of geese and to analogous instinctive behavior patterns of other animals. The social bond embracing a group is closely connected with aggression directed against outsiders. In human beings, too, the feeling of togetherness which is so essential to the serving of a common cause is greatly enhanced by the presence of a definite, threatening enemy whom it is possible to hate. . . . For all these reasons, the teachers of militant ideologies have an enviably easy job in converting young people. We must face the fact that in Russia as well as in China the younger generation knows perfectly well what it is fighting for, while in our culture it is casting about in vain for causes worth embracing. The way in which huge numbers of young Americans have recently identified themselves with the rights of the American negro is a glorious exception, though the fervor with which they have done so tends to accentuate the prevalent lack of militant enthusiasm for other equally just and equally important causes—such as the prevention of war in general. The actual warmonger, of course, has the best chances of arousing militant enthusiasm because he can always work his dummy or fiction of an enemy for all it is worth.

In all these respects, the defender of peace is at a decided disadvantage. Everything he lives and works for, all the high goals at which he aims, are, or should be, determined by moral responsibility which presupposes quite a lot of knowledge and real insight. Nobody can get really enthusiastic about them without considerable erudition. The one and only unquestionable value that can be appreciated independently of rational morality or education is the bond of human love and friendship from which all kindness and charity springs, and which represents the great antithesis to aggression. In fact, love and friendship come far nearer to typifying all that is good, than aggression, which is identified with a destructive death drive only by mistake, comes to exemplifying all that is evil.

3. CAUSES OF WAR ARE TO BE FOUND IN SOCIETY, NOT IN HUMAN NATURE

The following is an extract from *Social Psychology,* by Otto Klineberg,[13] a psychologist at Columbia University. Dr. Klineberg has done extensive research in the sociological and psychological aspects of international affairs, including UNESCO's project, "Tensions Affecting International Understanding," of which he was director.

The problem of the innateness or universality of aggressive behavior is one of obvious practical significance. It would probably be agreed that the occurrence of war and the threat of war in our society represents its worst feature—one which may even contain the germs of the destruction of our whole civilization. The assertion is sometimes made that war will never be abolished because it is rooted in an instinct of pugnacity which is natural to man. Psychology and ethnology have an important contribution to make in connection with this problem.

[13] From SOCIAL PSYCHOLOGY, revised edition, by Otto Klineberg, pp. 89–94, 96. Copyright 1954 by Holt, Rinehart and Winston, Inc. Used by permission of the publishers.

Aggressive behavior is of course found widely in the animal kingdom. It must be borne in mind, however, that it is by no means an invariable rule of behavior. Cases of mutual help and cooperation also occur in abundance, even between members of different species. When aggressiveness is found it is frequently in association with other drives, such as self-preservation, sex, and maternal love, and probably is not to be regarded as an end in itself.

On the physiological side no basis has been discovered for the existence of aggressiveness as such. It has been amply demonstrated by Cannon that in anger there is a whole series of biochemical and physiological changes under the influence of the sympathetic nervous system and the adrenal glands. . . . The general result of these changes is that in the presence of an enemy the organism may respond with an unusual output of energy over an unusually long period of time. These changes do occur in anger, but they occur also in fear and in excitement; they constitute an organic basis for violent emotional behavior in general, rather than for aggressiveness itself.

There are some human groups among whom aggressive behavior was apparently indulged in for its own sake. An Iroquois chief is reported to have proposed to a neighboring ruler that their young men be allowed to have a little war. On the second chief's refusal, he was asked, "With whom then can my children play?" However, this may not be an example of aggressiveness as such, since the Iroquois chief was concerned with the need of his young warriors for practice. Of the Lango it is said—"They are brave and venturesome warriors, who have won the fear and respect of their neighbors, delighting in war not only for the plunder which it brings, but also for its own sake!"

These examples do not necessarily prove that aggressive behavior is innately determined. It may become an end in itself even though it originated as a means to an end. In all cases we have a long previous history of warfare and the possibility therefore that warlike habits have been developed. . . . Much of the warfare of primitive peoples is to be understood as similar to athletic contests or trials of strength, and that may be the primary motivation responsible.

On the other hand, it has been noted that warfare is by no means universal and that there are many societies to which it is foreign. In their survey of the cultural characteristics of a large number of groups, Hobhouse and his associates report that there were at least ten tribes which had no war.

There are many writers who feel that aggressive warfare, far from being native to man, develops only when culture has reached a certain degree of complexity. Letourneau states that at the beginning of society, when men were few in number and did not trouble each other, war was as strange to them as until recently it was among the Eskimo of the far north. Van der Bij also believes that the simplest and most primitive peoples were not warlike; they had no offensive war and were even unwilling to engage in defensive wars. He cites cases from a number of very simple societies in support of this point of view, and believes that war comes only with greater cultural development and an increase in the size of the groups. Elliot Smith is substantially of the same opinion. It may be that these writers tend unduly to glorify the "noble savage" and to attribute all the ills of mankind to an interference with the state of nature, and we must certainly be careful not to exaggerate the purity and nobility of primitive man. There is no doubt, however, that there were many groups who were not at all warlike, and that therefore aggressiveness, at least to the extent that it expresses itself in war, does not satisfy our criterion of universality.

Wars do of course occur with great frequency, but they may usually be understood in terms of certain very definite motives. Obviously, most peoples will defend themselves when attacked. Clearly too, they will fight for food and in many cases for plunder. Examples of this type of warfare are numerous. As Bunzel indicates, war raids for profit are characteristic of many primitive societies; even the peaceable Zuni formerly conducted raids on the sheep of their Navajo neighbors. The Crow raided for horses, as this was their favorite form of wealth, and a stolen horse was the only acceptable bride gift. Among the Kiowa, the whole economic system hinged upon warfare, the objective of which was the acquisition of horses; the enemy was killed only when it was absolutely necessary. In parts of West Africa slave-raiding was one of the main causes of war. Hobhouse and his associates found also that in forty or more peoples, where marriage by capture occurred, the possession of women was the direct object of a warlike raid.

War has often been due to religious causes. Eating a dead man was interpreted by many peoples as giving the conqueror his virtues. Among the Yoruba, hearts were regularly sold in order to give courage, and the procuring of them often led to battle. In Aztec Mexico religious factors were responsible for the major part of the warlike behavior. One of the important beliefs was that the gods, particularly the Sun, would die if deprived of food, and the only satisfying nourishment consisted of human hearts. The victim of the sacrifice was identified with the god, and his killing and eating meant a resurrection of the god and the renewal of his strength. There was a Mexican legend to the effect that the gods themselves had formerly been sacrificed to the Sun in order to endow him with strength to do his work, and they bequeathed the duty to the human representatives, directing them to fight and kill each other to provide the necessary food. There was almost perpetual warfare with the neighboring Tlaxcalans for the sole purpose of obtaining captives to serve as sacrificial victims. . . .

Among the Wyandot Indians it was believed that an increase in the size of the clan would please the animal god from which it was descended. Every effort was made to keep the clan full, that is, to keep in use the complete list of names belonging to it. For this purpose war was carried on in order to secure women and children, and occasionally men, for adoption.

The glory motive, or the quest for prestige, is one of the most frequent causes of aggressive behavior. Head-hunting, for example, although sometimes the result of religious practices, may also be due to the intense desire for a trophy which will elevate its possessor to a higher position in the community. Among the Asaba on the Niger River a man receives the honorary title of Obu if he has done a brave deed, and he most clearly earns this title if he has killed another man. In parts of New Guinea a youth must have "fetched a head" before he may be counted an adult, and the badges of distinction for warriors depend on the number of lives taken. Distinguished Masai warriors had the right to wear bracelets and bells. Among the Bagobo of the Philippines a man's clothing indicated his status, which was determined by the number of deaths for which he was responsible.

It should be pointed out further that when primitive peoples do fight they seem not to be giving expression to a spontaneous and uncontrolled pugnacious drive, but rather to a form of behavior which is regulated and modified by social conventions. In general, primitive warfare was not very destructive of human life, and the casualties were frequently insignificant. When two groups of Australian aborigines fought, the battle was over as soon as one warrior on either side had been killed. Sometimes the first wound ended the combat. Sumner and Keller state that conflicts among primitive people were generally brief and relatively bloodless. "A savage would stand aghast before the wholesale slaughter of civilized warfare, and beside some of its methods his own are those of a gentleman."

As a matter of fact, war was really in many cases a sort of duel or game, and the attitude toward it was frequently sportsmanlike. It is said that the Arkansas Indians once gave a share of their powder to the Chickasaw with whom they were at war; an Algonquin tribe refrained from pressing an attack upon the Iroquois when it was pointed out that night had fallen. Australian tribes have been known to provide unarmed Europeans with a set of weapons before attacking. The Maori are reported to have filled canoes with food for their hungry enemies so that they might fight on more equal terms. On the other hand, sudden raids without any warning are by no means unknown in primitive warfare.

William James once spoke of a "moral equivalent for war." There are many primitive communities which have worked out some such equivalent, particularly in the case of quarrels between individuals. The Indians of the Northwest Coast settle disputes by means of the institution of the potlach. If two men have a quarrel one of them may give a potlach or feast, at which the aim is to give away or destroy as large an amount of property as possible. His rival is humbled as a consequence and regarded as having lost status in the community until he can do likewise. A Kwakiutl chief once said, "The White man fights with his hands, but we fight with property." This fighting with property may also take place under much more informal conditions. There is a story to this effect told of the Tlingit of Alaska. "Two women were quarreling. In a rage one of them said to the other, 'I'll shut you up!' At that she rushed into her house, came out with both hands full of silver money and scattered it to the crowd that was watching the proceedings. This did shut the mouth of her opponent as she could not do likewise." Goldman reports a case among the Alkatcho Carrier Indians in which a man had been insulted by being placed in a position of inferiority at a feast. He went out with his relatives and returned with a number of articles which he presented to his host, thereby humbling him and wiping out the insult.

A particularly interesting method of settling a quarrel is reported for various groups of Eskimos, from the Aleuts at one geographical extreme to the Greenland tribes at the other. An Eskimo who has suffered some injury may compose a satirical song in mockery of his enemy and challenge him to a public singing contest. The village group assembles, and the two contestants take turns mocking each other to the best of their ability. The spectators decide the victor. Sometimes this is not possible until the contestants have been recalled many times.

These examples indicate that aggressiveness, whether or not it has an innate basis, may be modified by the culture in many ways. It may be stimulated in one society and relatively lacking in another. It may arise as the result of any one of a number of different causes. It may express itself in violent physical combat or in a socially regulated contest in which no one is harmed. There is no justification, therefore, for the attempt to explain any specific type of aggressive behavior on the ground that it has a biological basis. To the question as to whether war is inevitable because of the existence of such an aggressive instinct, the ethnologist and the social psychologist have reason to give a categorical negative. War is an institution, and must be explained in relation to the whole social structure in which it occurs. After a somewhat similar survey of the pertinent material, Sumner and Keller came to the conclusion that "There is no 'instinct of pugnacity.' " What there is is a set of life conditions demanding adjustment.

4. GROUP BEHAVIOR IS NOT SUBJECT TO THE SAME RATIONAL OR MORAL PRINCIPLES AS IS INDIVIDUAL BEHAVIOR

The following position is drawn from the writings of Professor Reinhold Niebuhr of Union Theological Seminary. According to Professor Niebuhr, a distinction must be made between the personal morality of individuals and the collective morality of social groups. An individual may observe very high standards of morality in his personal life, but social groups seem incapable of achieving similarly high levels of conduct. Nation-states, which are very complex social groups, cannot, in Niebuhr's opinion, approach the moral and ethical standards that may characterize the behavior of individuals. Since nations often resort to power to advance their interests, power has to be used by other nations to assure some semblance of order and stability.

Professor Niebuhr is consequently very critical of those who feel that international peace and justice depend primarily on the extension of morality, reason, and education. However, as a theologian, he also warns against the dangers of extreme cynicism and egoism which are often associated with the pursuit of power. Finding a balanced relationship between the claims of morality and power is therefore advanced as the most important factor in dealing with world affairs.[14]

The thesis to be elaborated in these pages is that a sharp distinction must be drawn between the moral and social behavior of individuals and of social groups, national, racial, and economic; and that this distinction justifies and necessitates political policies which a purely individualistic ethic must always find embar-

[14] Reprinted with the permission of Charles Scribner's Sons from the following works by Reinhold Niebuhr: MORAL MAN AND IMMORAL SOCIETY, pages xi–xiii, xx, xxii–xxiv (Copyright 1932 Charles Scribner's Sons; renewal copyright © 1960 Reinhold Niebuhr). THE CHILDREN OF LIGHT AND THE CHILDREN OF DARKNESS, pages 173–176 and 186 (Copyright 1944 Charles Scribner's Sons); and THE IRONY OF AMERICAN HISTORY, pages 40–41 and 149–150 (Copyright 1952 Charles Scribner's Sons). Permission for the second and third titles also granted by James Nisbet and Company, Ltd., London.

rassing. The title "Moral Man and Immoral Society" suggests the intended distinction too unqualifiedly, but it is nevertheless a fair indication of the argument to which the following pages are devoted. Individual men may be moral in the sense that they are able to consider interests other than their own in determining problems of conduct, and are capable, on occasion, of preferring the advantages of others to their own. . . . But all these achievements are more difficult, if not impossible, for human societies and social groups. In every human group there is less reason to guide and to check impulse, less capacity for self-transcendence, less ability to comprehend the needs of others and therefore more unrestrained egoism than the individuals, who compose the group, reveal in their personal relationships. . . .

Inasfar as this treatise has a polemic interest it is directed against the moralists, both religious and secular, who imagine that the egoism of individuals is being progressively checked by the development of rationality or the growth of a religiously inspired goodwill and that nothing but the continuance of this process is necessary to establish social harmony between all the human societies and collectives. Social analyses and prophecies made by moralists, sociologists and educators upon the basis of these assumptions lead to a very considerable moral and political confusion in our day. They completely disregard the political necessities in the struggle for justice in human society by failing to recognize those elements in man's collective behavior which belong to the order of nature and can never be brought completely under the dominion of reason or conscience. They do not recognize that when collective power, whether in the form of imperialism or class domination, exploits weakness, it can never be dislodged unless power is raised against it. If conscience and reason can be insinuated into the resulting struggle they can only qualify but not abolish it.

The more persistent error of modern educators and moralists is the assumption that our social difficulties are due to the failure of the social sciences to keep pace with the physical sciences which have created our technological civilisation. The invariable implication of this assumption is that, with a little more time, a little more adequate moral and social pedagogy and a generally higher development of human intelligence, our social problems will approach solution. . . .

What is lacking among all these moralists, whether religious or rational, is an understanding of the brutal character of the behavior of all human collectives, and the power of self-interest and collective egoism in all intergroup relations. Failure to recognize the stubborn resistance of group egoism to all moral and inclusive social objectives inevitably involves them in unrealistic and confused political thought. They regard social conflict either as an impossible method of achieving morally approved ends or as a momentary expedient which a more perfect education or a purer religion will make unnecessary. They do not see that the limitations of the human imagination, the easy subservience of reason to prejudice and passion, and the consequent persistence of irrational egoism, particularly in group behavior, make social conflict an inevitability in human history, probably to its very end. . . .

Teachers of morals who do not see the difference between the problem of charity within the limits of an accepted social system and the problem of justice between economic groups, holding uneven power within modern industrial society, have simply not faced the most obvious differences between the morals of groups and those of individuals. The suggestion that the fight against disease is in the same category with the fight against war reveals the same confusion. Our contemporary culture fails to realise the power, extent and persistence of group egoism in human relations. It may be possible, though it is never easy, to establish just relations between individuals within a group purely by moral and rational suasion and accommodation. In inter-group relations this is practically an impossibility. The relations between groups must therefore always be predominately political rather than ethical, that is, they will be determined by the proportion of power which each group possesses at least as much as by any rational and moral appraisal of the comparative needs and claims of each group. The coercive factors, in distinction to the more purely moral and rational factors, in political relations can never be sharply differentiated and defined. It is not possible to estimate exactly how much a party to a social conflict is influenced by a rational argument or by the threat of force. . . .

Whatever increase in social intelligence and moral goodwill may be achieved in human history, may serve to mitigate the brutalities of social conflict, but they cannot abolish the conflict itself. That could be accomplished only if human groups, whether racial, national or economic, could achieve a degree of reason and sympathy which would permit them to see and to understand the interests of others as vividly as they understand their own, and a moral goodwill which would prompt them to affirm the rights of others as vigorously as they affirm their own. Given the inevitable limitations of human nature and the limits of the human imagination and intelligence, this is an ideal which individuals may approximate but which is beyond the capacities of human societies. Educators who emphasize the pliability of human nature, social and psychological scientists who dream of "socialising" man, and religious idealists who strive to increase the sense of moral responsibility, can serve a very useful function in society in humanising individuals within an established social system and in purging the relations of individuals of as much egoism as possible. In dealing with the problems and necessities of radical social change they are almost invariably confusing in their counsels because they are not conscious of the limitations in human nature which finally frustrate their efforts. . . .

The fact that the coercive factor in society is both necessary and dangerous seriously complicates the whole task of securing both peace and justice. History is a long tale of abortive efforts toward the desired end of social cohesion and justice in which failure was usually due either to the effort to eliminate the factor of force entirely or to an undue reliance upon it. Complete reliance upon it means that new tyrants usurp the places of eminence from which more traditional monarchs are cast down. Tolstoian pacifists and other advocates of nonresistance, noting the evils which force introduces into society, give themselves to the vain illusion that it can be completely eliminated, and society organised upon the basis of anarchistic principles. Their conviction is an illusion, because there are definite limits of moral goodwill and social intelligence beyond which even the most vital religion and the most astute educational programme will not carry a social group, whatever may be possible for individuals in an intimate society. The problem which society faces is clearly one of reducing force by increasing the factors which make for a moral and rational adjustment of life to life; of bringing such force as is still necessary under responsibility of the whole of society; of destroying the kind of power which cannot be made socially responsible . . . ; and of bringing forces of moral self-restraint to bear upon types of power which can never be brought completely under social control. Every one of these methods has its definite limitations. Society will probably never be sufficiently intelligent to bring all power under its control. The stupidity of the average man will permit the oligarch, whether economic or political, to hide his real purposes from the scrutiny of his fellows and to withdraw his activities from effective control. Since it is impossible to count on enough moral goodwill among those who possess irresponsible power to sacrifice it for the good of the whole, it must be destroyed by coercive methods and these will always run the peril of introducing new forms of injustice in place of those abolished. . . .

The future peace and justice of society therefore depend upon, not one but many, social strategies, in all of which moral and coercive factors are compounded in varying degrees. So difficult is it to avoid the Scylla of despotism and the Charybdis of anarchy that it is safe to hazard the prophecy that the dream of perpetual peace and brotherhood for human society is one which will never be fully realised. It is a vision prompted by the conscience and insight of individual man, but incapable of fulfillment by collective man. It is like all true religious visions, possible of approximation but not of realisation in actual history.

Regarding the establishment of international peace and a world community, Niebuhr says:

All these difficulties are sufficiently apparent to prompt the emergence of realistical as well as idealistic interpretations of the global task which faces our age. While America has produced more idealistic plans for world order than realistic ones, the realistic approach has also been attempted in both Britain and America. It is indicative of the spiritual problem of mankind that these realistic approaches are often as close to the abyss of cynicism as the idealistic approaches are to the fog of sentimentality.

The realistic school of international thought believes that world politics cannot rise higher than the balance-of-power principle. The balance-of-power theory of world politics, seeing no possibility of a genuine unity of the nations, seeks to construct the most adequate possible mechanism for equilibrating power on a world scale. Such a policy, which holds all factors in the world situation in the most perfect possible equipoise, can undoubtedly mitigate anarchy. A balance of power is in fact a kind of managed anarchy. But it is a system in which anarchy invariably overcomes the management in the end. Despite its defects, the policy of the balance of power is not as iniquitous as idealists would have us believe. For even the most perfectly organized society must seek for a decent equilibrium of the vitalities and forces under its organization. If this is not done, strong disproportions of power develop; and wherever power is inordinate, injustice results. But an equilibrium of power without the organizing and equilibrating force of government, is potential anarchy which becomes actual anarchy in the long run.

The balance-of-power system may, despite its defects, become the actual consequence of present policies. The peace of the world may be maintained perilously and tentatively, for some decades, by an uneasy equilibrium between the . . . great powers. . . .

While a balance between the great powers may be the actual consequence of present policies, it is quite easy to foreshadow the doom of such a system. No participant in a balance is ever quite satisfied with its own position. Every center of power will seek to improve its position: and every such effort will be regarded by the others as an attempt to disturb the equilibrium. There is sufficient mistrust between the great nations, even while they are still locked in the intimate embrace of a great common effort, to make it quite certain that a mere equilibrium between them will not suffice to preserve the peace.

Thus a purely realistic approach to the problem of world community offers as little hope of escape from anarchy as a purely idealistic one. Clearly it has become necessary for the children of light to borrow some of the wisdom of the children of darkness; and yet be careful not to borrow too much. Pure idealists underestimate the perennial power of particular and parochial loyalties, operating as a counter force against the achievement of a wider community. But the realists are usually so impressed by the power of these perennial forces that they fail to recognize the novel and unique elements in a revolutionary world situation. . . .

A view more sober than that of either idealists or realists must persuade us that,

> "If hopes are dupes,
> Fears may be liars." . . .

The field of politics is not helpfully tilled by pure moralists; and the realm of international politics is particularly filled with complexities which do not yield to the approach of a too simple idealism. On the other hand the moral cynicism and defeatism which easily results from a clear-eyed view of the realities of international politics is even more harmful. The world community must be built by men and nations sufficiently mature and robust to understand that political justice is achieved, not merely by destroying, but also by deflecting, beguiling and harnessing residual self-interest and by finding the greatest possible concurrence between self-interest and the general welfare. They must also be humble enough to understand that the forces of self-interest to be deflected are not always those of the opponent or competitor. They are frequently those of the self, individual or collective, including the interests of the idealist who erroneously imagines himself above the battle.

Professor Niebuhr continues on the question of idealists and realists:

The idealists naturally believe that we could escape the dilemma if we made sufficiently strenuous rational and moral efforts. . . . [However] all the arguments of the idealists finally rest upon a logic which derives the possibility of an achievement from its necessity. . . .

The realists on the other hand are inclined to argue that a good cause will hallow any weapon. They are convinced that the evils of communism are so great that we are justified in using any weapon against them. Thereby they closely approach the communist ruthlessness. The inadequacy of both types of escape from our moral dilemma proves that there is no purely moral solution for the ultimate moral issues of life; but neither is there a viable solution which disregards the moral factors. Men and nations must use their power with the purpose of making it an instrument of justice and a servant of interests broader than their own. Yet they must be ready to use it though they become aware that the power of a particular nation or individual, even when under strong religious and social sanctions, is never so used that there is a perfect coincidence between the value which justifies it and the interest of the wielder of it.

We cannot expect even the wisest of nations to escape every peril of moral and spiritual complacency; for nations have always been constitutionally self-righteous. But it will make a difference whether the culture in which the policies of nations are formed is only as deep and as high as the nation's highest ideals; or whether there is a dimension in the culture from the standpoint of which the element of vanity in all human ambitions and achievements is discerned. But this is a height which can be grasped only by faith; for everything that is related in terms of simple rational coherence with the ideals of a culture or a nation will prove in the end to be a simple justification of its most cherished values. The God before whom "the nations are as a drop in the bucket and are counted as small dust in the balances" is known by faith and not by reason. The realm of mystery and meaning which encloses and finally makes sense out of the baffling configurations of history is not identical with any scheme of rational intelligibility. The faith which appropriates the meaning in the mystery inevitably involves an experience of repentance for the false meanings which the pride of nations and cultures introduces into the pattern. Such repentance is the true source of charity; and we are more desperately in need of genuine charity than of more technocratic skills.

SELECT BIBLIOGRAPHY

CANTRIL, HADLEY, *Human Nature and Political Systems* (New Brunswick, N.J., Rutgers University Press, 1961). A brief, highly readable work on the psychology behind the human compulsion to political organization and the competition between political systems.

DAVIES, JAMES C., *Human Nature in Politics* (New York, Wiley, 1963). Using familiar historical examples, this study develops the theme that despite our paucity of knowledge about human nature, the latter can clearly be identified as the major influence on political behavior. For the layman.

GANDHI, MHATMA, *All Men Are Brothers* (New York, Colorado University Press, 1958). A collection of Gandhi's writings dealing with the possibilities and necessity for man's inhibition of his animal passions. Natural man lives not by destruction, but by self-love and its corollary, the love of others. Herein is found hope for the successful practice of nonviolence in the political sphere.

HERSKOVITS, MELVILLE J., *Man and His Works* (New York, Knopf, 1952). A cultural anthropological classic by one of the leading anthropologists of our times, "moves from a discussion of the nature of culture, its materials, and structure, to a consideration of the processes of change that characterize it, and the general principles that govern cultural change."

KEITH, ARTHUR, *Evolution and Ethics* (New York, Putnam, 1946). An anthropological analysis of man's nature, which is held to be savage and combative toward out-groups, however ethical within in-groups.

KLINEBERG, OTTO, *Social Psychology* (New York, Holt, Rinehart and Winston, 1954). An excellent appraisal of modern developments in the field of social psychology. One of the few psychology textbooks that considers the implications of psychology in international relations.

LOOS, A. WILLIAM (ed.), *The Nature of Man* (New York, The Church Peace Union and the World Alliance for International Friendship through Religion, 1950). A brief text, with a religious orientation, outlining man's world, his spiritual resources, and his destiny.

LORENZ, KONRAD, *On Aggression*, trans. Marjorie K. Wilson (New York, Harcourt, Brace & World, 1966). A popularly written book by a student of animal behavior. Implications of the findings for man's behavior are highly stimulating, if speculative.

MONTAGU, M. F. ASHLEY, *The Direction of Human Development* (New York, Harper & Row, 1955). Addresses itself to the compound question: "What is man's original nature and how is that nature influenced and conditioned to assume a socially functional form?" The central theme is best summarized by a direct quotation: ". . . this evidence indicates that human beings are born good . . . that at birth they are wholly prepared, equipped, to function as creatures who not only want and need to be loved by others, but who also want and need to love others."

MCNEIL, ELTON B. (ed.), *The Nature of Human Conflict* (Englewood Cliffs, N.J., Prentice-Hall, 1965). The editor, a psychologist and author of several of the chapters in this symposium, has collected the works of a number of social scientists on this topic. Here is evidence of our growing knowledge about man and conflict, a growth which is grounds for optimism in the search for a solution to war.

SHERIF, MUZAFER, *In Common Predicament: Social Psychology of Intergroup Conflict and Cooperation* (Boston, Houghton Mifflin, 1966). A probing look by a social psychologist at "intergroup relations" with their accompanying attitudes of love and hate, trust and distrust, goodwill and malice, claims to superiority and claims to equality. The growth of interdependence between groups is viewed as the hopeful way through the contemporary crisis, but the difficulties are formidable.

4

Nationalism

ANY AMERICAN WHO HAS EMOTION-
ally responded to the sight of the Stars and Stripes or the mass singing of
the national anthem, or while abroad and alone has been drawn to seek
the companionship of a total stranger who happens to be the only American present, or has felt his gall unaccountably rise upon hearing a foreigner criticize the United States, that American already has some
familiarity with nationalism. He may not identify his reactions as nationalistic because they were emotional reflexes based on attitudes and
feelings of long, and probably unconscious, standing. But nationalistic
they were. Moreover, such an American would be neither unique among
Americans nor untypical of many other peoples, for nationalism ranks
among the most prevalent and powerful in-group feelings of our age.

THE NATURE OF NATIONALISM

A complex and ever-changing phenomenon, nationalism is not easily
defined. Adding to the difficulty is the general looseness with which its
root word, *nation,* and derivatives are employed. For example, *nation* is
most often used to designate an association of people living together
in a given territory and sharing certain common cultural traits. But the
term is also used to denote a sovereign nation-state. *Nationality,* on the
other hand, has acquired a legal meaning. Thus, a Spanish-speaking Arab
with Moroccan citizenship may be described as of Moroccan *nationality.*
But nationality is also used to denote ethnic identity, in which case the
foregoing Moroccan might be described as having Arab, or possibly
Spanish, nationality.

A DEFINITION

What is meant by nationalism in this study is an in-group consciousness among a people sharing some or all of the following: a physical environment, language, customs, history, religion, political entity, and
view of the future. Obviously, all of these characteristics need not
be present. For more than a century Poles were nationally conscious

though they were politically divided among three alien empires. There is no common religion undergirding American nationalism. The Swiss do not have a common religion or language. Nonetheless there is among Poles, Americans, and Swiss a powerful bond, a feeling by each individual that his fate is linked with the fate of his whole national group.

Finally, there is another vital aspect to nationalism which must be firmly grasped. As Carlton J. H. Hayes, a leading writer on this subject, has put it, nationalism is "A condition of mind among members of a nationality . . . in which loyalty to the ideal or to the fact of one's national state is superior to all other loyalties and of which pride in one's nationality and belief in its intrinsic excellence and in its 'mission' are integral parts." [1]

When this phenomenon first appeared is not easily determined, but that it did not exist much before 1500 is certain. Group loyalties before that time took other forms: to family, church, province, king, or city-state. Moreover, these older loyalties may still survive and to them can be added the modern loyalties to class, race, and ideology. No loyalty in our day, however, has made greater demands: to die for one's country has been inculcated in nationalists as the highest form of human sacrifice, while disloyalty to one's nation is a supreme offense punishable by death. How did such a powerful movement evolve and what does an examination of its various reinforcements explain about it?

Factors Giving Rise to Nationalism

Physical Environment. Probably geography was responsible for several prehistoric families, confined to the same valley or secluded on the same highland, slowly acquiring a community spirit and gradually evolving into larger associations or tribes. Certain it is that the tribes inhabiting the British and Japanese islands developed a larger sense of unity because of detachment from their continental neighbors, whom they knew but did not live with. Similarly, the high, wind-swept plateau of central Iberia afforded the inland tribes of that region a physical unity not shared with coastal Iberian folk. Thus it was much more than coincidental that among the first tribal amalgamations were the British, Japanese, Spanish, and Portuguese. These amalgamations were vital initial steps in the emergence of nationalism among these peoples.

The geographic influence notable in these classic examples cannot, however, be as plainly identified in other growths of nationalism. For this reason, the physical environment, as some authorities suggest, must be cautiously evaluated.

Language. Generally accepted as more important are the factors of man-made environment such as language, customs, history, tradition, and

[1] From Carlton J. H. Hayes, *Essays on Nationalism* (New York, Macmillan, 1926), p. 16.

religion. A common language, for example, is one of the factors most conducive to national consciousness. Anyone who travels in other countries, where his own language is not readily understood, quickly senses the unifying influence of a common tongue. Americans in Paris, Chinese in London, or Frenchmen in Rome feel kinship with other members of their national groups because they can speak the same language.

Historically, the development of national vernacular languages and their increased substitution for Latin toward the end of the Middle Ages contributed considerably to an awareness of national differences. The subsequent invention of printing made the unifying influence of a common language even greater, and the stage was now set for the appearance of truly national literatures. English literature of the Elizabethan Age reflected a distinct national consciousness. Perhaps no better example of early English nationalism may be found than the following passage from Shakespeare's *King Richard II:*

> This royal throne of kings, this scept'red isle,
> This earth of majesty, this seat of Mars,
> This other Eden, demi-paradise,
> This fortress built by Nature for herself
> Against infection and the hand of war,
> This happy breed of men, this little world,
> This precious stone set in the silver sea. . . .
> This blessed plot, this earth, this realm, this England.

French and Spanish literature of this period likewise contributed to a growing national consciousness, and examples could be added from the literatures of other peoples.

Customs. Similarly, customs and mores furnish cultural distinctions which have contributed. Geographic factors have sometimes played an initial role here. Climate and soil, for example, dictated originally the wine-drinking habit of the Frenchman. In time, regardless of his proximity to a vineyard, the Frenchman included wine as a staple in his daily diet—in Dakar as well as in Paris, on the Mississippi as well as on the Loire, in Vietnam as well as in Burgundy. Thus wine-drinking became a distinctive characteristic of French culture. Climate no doubt encouraged the adoption by Indian women of the sari as a comfortable garment, but today Indians may be seen wearing saris in London, at the United Nations headquarters, and in Moscow. The sari has become the Indian woman's national costume.

It is interesting to note that many Russian customs and mores such as adherence to the Eastern Orthodox Church, its architectural distinctions, and until recently the seclusion of women, drew original inspiration from nearby Byzantium and Asia but in time became typically Russian and as such were fundamental to Russia's sense of cultural uniqueness.

Thus, as with language, customs often have roots in the physical environment, but with the passage of time they proliferate, mutate, and make their own contributions to a people's distinctive development.

History. History and heroes are still another influence. Anthropologists have established the fact that most societies evince a longing for immortality that is partly satisfied by consciousness of a past, either historic or legendary. When the historic awareness is shared by a community it has the effect of binding it more closely together. The Saga of the Vikings has done this for the Danes and Norwegians. Germans have derived a common satisfaction from their ancestral tie with the ancient Teutonic tribes who resisted successfully the advance of Roman power across the Rhine. The very fact that China possesses a written history dating not centuries, but millenniums, before the Occident's, affords the Chinese a unique source of national pride and consciousness. Visible remains on the Acropolis of ancient Athens remind Greeks, as those of the Roman Forum remind Italians, of an historic era of which people in the very same place partook. It might be believed, however erroneously, that they were even of the same blood. This the Greeks, and only the Greeks, can collectively sense under the shadow of the Parthenon's Doric columns. And what American of six or more years of age can remain ignorant of America's frontier epoch? Have any people in so brief a time amassed more heroes, legends, and profits than the Americans from their fantastic cult of the "Wild West"?

Religion. A common religion may also be a force welding people together and reinforcing the other factors which have led them to feel unified. The Roman Catholic faith in France and Italy, the Anglican faith in England, Lutheranism in the Scandinavian countries, and the Orthodox Church in Russia have all played an important part in strengthening the nationalism of the respective countries. The Reformation itself, by challenging the universal authority of the Pope in Rome, provided a strong incentive to the rise of national churches in many countries.

Political Entity. This factor more than any other has a chicken-or-the-egg relationship to nationalism. For example, in the cases of France, England, Spain, Portugal, and possibly some other nation-states, political unification preceded the national awakening. Thus, England was a united kingdom under Edward III (d.1377) but became nationally conscious only in the Tudor Period. In contrast are the Germans who became increasingly nationalistic following the Napoleonic wars but established a unified German state only half a century later under Bismarck's leadership. Clear it is, however, that all national movements are marked by a powerful desire to create a nation-state if it does not already exist.

A Sense of Mission. One more aspect is the tendency of national groups to share a common view of their group's future. Such an in-group phenomenon is traceable at least as far back as the Hebrew belief that the ancient Jews were a people chosen by their God for a divine purpose. Among modern nationalists the messianic current runs strong. Each Christian national group has thought of itself as having special relations with God as evidenced in such epithets as God Be With Us, *Gott Mit Uns,* God Save the Queen. In time of war departing soldiers have generally been exhorted in the Western world to go off and fight for God and country, the implication being that their interests were identical. The United States developed a sense of mission in its so-called Manifest Destiny to expand to the Pacific, and more recently, to "Make the World Safe for Democracy." Similarly, Russians and Chinese vie with one another in their world communizing leadership. Sometimes much more modest, the sense of mission is strong in all national communities. Belgians and French justified, not insincerely, their colonial conquests as a civilizing task.

RACISM AND NATIONALISM

A very special relationship is that between racism and nationalism. In Europe where nationalism was born, genuine racial distinctions (those based on biologic inheritance and identifiable in pigmentation and physiognomy) were not prominent and bore little or no relationship to language, religion, or any of the other factors conducive to nationalism. In the nineteenth century, however, a group of writers including Houston Stewart Chamberlain and Count de Gobineau took up the task of establishing racial distinctions between national groups. Unable to mobilize scientific evidence for their theories (there were too many tall and short Germans, swarthy and blond Italians, brown and blue-eyed Englishmen), they claimed to discover racial differences underlying national differences in such unscientific characteristics as "love of the soil," the Germanic "soul," and "Anglo-Saxon genius." Popularized by the German Nazis, this racism had a vogue in Hitler's Europe and expressed itself in the Nazi efforts to place the peoples of their conquered territories in a racial hierarchy with the Germans at the top (*Uebermenschen*) and the Jews at the very bottom and destined for extinction.

Since World War II a strong revulsion against Nazi racism has marked the Western countries, while racism has emerged in Asia and Africa as an important reinforcement of nationalism. Since the white Europeans and North Americans were regarded as the imperialist oppressors and exploiters of these darker skinned peoples, it is readily seen how anticolonial nationalism assumed racial overtones. Intensifying this development was the racial discrimination practiced by certain colonial rulers. Consequently, some contemporary Ghanaians, Togolese, and other black Africans have found an additional sense of national unity in their color.

Just as variable combinations of the factors conducive to nationalism play a part in its rise, so having arisen, nationalism presents different faces. Those people who have long been nationalistically conscious and have had a nation-state of their own appear to be somewhat less sensitive and more poised in their relations with other national groups. Recently established nations, however, are extremely sensitive to what they imagine are national slights or insults. To compare the imperturbable Britisher with an explosive Tanzanian nationalist at a United Nations meeting is to see this difference.

The actual security enjoyed by a nation-state also bears upon its inhabitants' manifestations of nationalism. Like all in-groups threatened from without, the uneasy national community continually generates strong feelings both toward the in-group and toward its real or imagined enemies. This reveals itself in emotional journalism, emphatic stereotyping, and defiant postures.

Both of the above factors in turn influence national governments in their relations with individual citizens. Those governments feeling themselves least insecure can best afford to allow multiple loyalties among their citizenries. Those which are most insecure, either because of foreign threats or acute internal problems, tend to be more authoritarian. This is brought into clear relief in time of war when even the democratic communities abridge individual liberties and stress patriotic conformity. On the other hand, in the newly independent states of Africa and Asia something like the reverse of this trend appeared. Because of the newness and weakness of national consciousness, it proved very difficult to practice partisan politics, since in the absence of a strong, higher national loyalty the elements struggling for political power in these states had no incentive to entrust government to their opponents. In a word, no national in-group existed; each party looked upon the other as an out-group and behaved accordingly with hostility, mistrust, and fear. To create viable, effective government, therefore, leaders in these states tended to abolish the party system as known in the North Atlantic region and organize single, nation-wide parties. In this process (India and the Philippines were exceptions) of seeking national unity the emphasis inevitably was on country before individual and concentration of power in the hands of national leaders (see Chap. 6).

THE HISTORICAL EVOLUTION OF NATIONALISM

The undeniable preeminence of nationalism in contemporary society—in the United States as elsewhere—cultivates the popular notion that nationalism and national loyalty are a permanent feature of civilization, a "natural" part of human society. This legend, for such it is, is vigorously encouraged by national-minded leaders, educators, publicists, and historians. Americans, of course, trace their history only as far back as the seventeenth century and so cannot distort their own national development as much as can others. Modern Greek nationalists would believe that nationalism among the Greeks was a strong force in the Age of Pericles (fifth century B.C.); German Wagnerian nationalism traces its origin to the dim mythological age of Wodin and Thor. Italians include Julius Caesar in their national history; the English, Queen Boetia; and the Russians, Cyrillus—figures dating back a thousand and more years. Actually, nationalism is not nearly so traditional or "natural." It is of recent origin and is man-made. Moreover, most great currents that have shaped human history—the great religions, Chinese and Roman imperialism, feudalism, the Renaissance, the Reformation, scientific advances—were not national and did not teach nationalism, though inadvertently some did foster it. What, then, have been the major steps in the evolution of nationalism?

THE RISE OF EUROPEAN NATIONALISM

It was during the disintegration of Western European medieval society that nationalism first appeared. The disruption of the medieval economy by increased trade and capitalistic enterprise, the inadequacy of decentralized feudal institutions as a proper environment for this growing commerce, the intellectual revolution initiated by the Renaissance, the geographic discoveries of the fifteenth century—all these contributed to a growing fluidity in Europe's Atlantic seaboard communities.

The greatest impetus and fervor for the changes came from the new middle class which arose with them, the town folk or bourgeoisie. This was the element that turned to certain feudal nobles who possessed the power necessary to erect new, much larger political units, within which the bourgeoisie would find the law and order conducive to their economic activities. Thus emerged the unified monarchies of Portugal, Spain, France, and England. On a smaller scale Denmark, Sweden, and the Netherlands also followed this pattern. In each of the enlarged monarchies the bourgeoisie paid taxes and gave personal service to a king whose obligations were to provide internal peace, a court system, protection against outside invasion, and, in some cases, a unified coinage, tariff protection against outside competition, and naval support for overseas commercial undertakings.

It is not surprising that within these states, in all classes, there developed a sense of belonging to the new community. Much of this loyalty had originally found expression in devotion to the person of the king or to heroic figures who had aided the king in the exercise of his power— Joan of Arc of France, the Black Prince in England, and The Cid in Spain.

The unity attendant upon centralization of political power in strong monarchs was further reinforced by other factors that contributed to the rise of national consciousness such as national languages, national literatures, and national churches. People were now more conscious of belonging to English, French, or Spanish states than of belonging to the more universal Christian or European society of the Middle Ages.

By the seventeenth century, the national state, or nation-state, and its sense of national consciousness characterized the political organization of most of Western Europe. Yet, it was not until the French Revolution of the eighteenth century that modern nationalism really came into its own.

THE FRENCH REVOLUTION AND NATIONALISM

It might seem paradoxical that the French Revolution, which included an attack upon the French monarchy, could have fostered nationalism, since the monarchy was one of the forces originally instrumental in creating the nation-state. As a matter of fact, one school of thought maintains that the monarchy was attacked just because it was not sufficiently national. Too many vestiges of feudalism had survived in France, and it was the need to eliminate these, along with the inefficiency and financial mismanagement of the monarchy, which precipitated revolution in 1789. Further lack of sensitivity by French royalty to this emphasis on national politics was evidenced in the royal family's secret negotiations with the Austrian government for aid against the revolutionaries. Revelation of that "unnational" activity brought about the fall of the monarchy in 1792 and the execution of the king.

The most important reason for the impact of the French Revolution on the new, modern nationalism lay in the character of the new political philosophy with which the French challenged the world. With its emphasis on "liberty, equality, and fraternity," it stressed the right of all citizens to have a voice in the control of their government. Popularly controlled government, in theory, was to replace the personal, irresponsible government of absolute monarchs. In the past, the people as a whole had not had an opportunity to influence government in any regular way, and few, if any, had evinced much interest in doing so. Government was the affair of kings and their ministers.

With the philosophy of the French Revolution, however, government was no longer to be the "property" of kings alone. It was to have a broader base in the masses of citizens, and something was now needed to make the latter feel more closely identified with the state than in the past. Something was necessary to win the allegiance of the masses of people, on whose consent government was theoretically to rest. Nationalism, together with popular sovereignty, came to fill this need. Consciously or unconsciously, the leaders of the new French Republic sought to inculcate a loyalty to the new France on the part of all Frenchmen. A comprehensive system of national education, the first of its kind, was launched with the intent of developing in future Frenchmen a loyalty not to any king of France but to the nation-state of France. National military conscription, the first in modern history, was also introduced, and the *Marseillaise* became the French national anthem.

In the next few years, revolutionary France rigorously reorganized many of its institutions along national lines. Provincial tariffs, laws, and boundaries were wiped out. The Roman Catholic Church with its ties to the Papacy was officially disestablished. Even the traditional Western calendar was no longer deemed sufficiently French, and a new one was introduced for a few years, dating not from the birth of the non-French Christ but from that of the French Republic in 1792. Perhaps most significant was the substitution of the single title "Citizen" for all members of the French nation-state in place of the old differentiating titles of the French nobility. Thus the development of French nationalism provided one of the first bases for the subsequent development of French democracy; the latter, on its part, further stimulated nationalism.

The involvement of France in war with her monarchical neighbors in 1792 imparted an even greater impetus to the intensification of nationalism. Now many internal cleavages tended to be dissolved in the new fervor to defend the French nation-state. A nationality was aroused to an unprecedented pitch of emotional devotion and national unity. Members of the French community who did not support the Republic in its war effort were sent to the guillotine. Expressing this emphasis upon national unity are the words of Georges Jacques Danton in 1792: "France must be an indivisible whole: she must have unity of representation. The citizens of Marseilles wish to clasp hands with the citizens of Dunkerque. I, therefore, ask the death penalty against whomsoever wishes to destroy the unity of France." [2]

Before the wars of the French Revolution were concluded, Napoleon had harnessed the French nationalism to his personal ambitions to re-create the empire of Charlemagne or Caesar. This extravagant imperialistic surge not only gave rise to a legend of military prowess that further fed the fires of French nationalism; it also cultivated an anti-French nationalism among Napoleon's victims.

Thus today, while French nationalists recall the era of the French Revolution and Napoleon in terms of the glories of Austerlitz, Jena, and Wagram, Spanish nationalists are inspired by Goya's depictions of Spanish resistance to French occupation; Russian nationalists thrill to Tchaikovsky's portrayal of Napoleon's retreat from Moscow in the *Overture of 1812;* and German nationalists cherish the poetic summons of

[2] From *Nationalism: Its Meaning and History,* by Hans Kohn (Princeton, N.J., Van Nostrand, 1955), p. 27.

Ernst Moritz Arndt to liberation from Napoleon. Quite clearly the French Revolution marks the intensification and spread of European nationalism.

THE GROWTH OF NATIONALISM IN THE NINETEENTH CENTURY

New Impetus. Of great importance to nationalism was the growing industrialization of Europe. Expanding means of production and improved transport facilities enlarged the ranks of the bourgeoisie and confronted it with the need for extending its areas of business activity. Where petty principalities survived, as in Italy and Germany, the bourgeoisie soon were endorsing the creation of larger political units, based on economic grounds. Such units would be of invaluable service to businessmen in the establishment of uniform law codes; standardization of coinage, weights, and measures; elimination of local trade barriers; and raising of national tariffs to reserve the national market for the producers of that nation-state. Powerful economic pressures reinforced the momentum of emergent nationalism.

Another new source of encouragement was the Romantic Movement, with its reaction to the preceding centuries' rationalism and its emphasis upon imagination, intuitive response, and emotionalism. A sentimental review of the past by romanticists uncovered a plethora of folklore, heroes, and exploits which did much to fill the pages of each nationality's history.

More accurate research by historians further aroused interest in events which thus became the ingredients for the picture of a great past for each nationality. As a people's history emerged, so did its consciousness of cultural homogeneity. This, as has been pointed out, is a vital part of nationalism.

New Nation-States. The national movement did not always operate centripetally. Although it pushed Italian- and German-speaking peoples toward unification, it tended to disrupt the great multinational empires of Eastern Europe. In the Austrian Empire, Czechs resented German being the official language in their Bohemia. In the Russian Empire, Poles bitterly complained against limitations placed upon their own, national tongue. Croats burned with indignation when the Hungarian government attempted to force translation of family and street names from Croatian into Magyar equivalents. The only solution for these culturally oppressed folk seemed to be establishment of independent national states.

Greeks and Belgians set off the first tremors after the French Revolution by revolting against their Turkish and Dutch rulers, respectively. When the Turks forcibly endeavored to block Greek secession from the Ottoman Empire, a war broke out. Ten years and ten thousand atrocities later, in 1830, a Kingdom of Greece was recognized. The same year, the Belgians behind Brussels barricades, and with the benediction of France and Britain, secured independence from the Netherlands. The year 1848 saw revolutions from Berlin to Rome and Budapest to Frankfort. Nationalist agitators led Italians, Germans, Czechs, Hungarians, Croats, Serbs, and Rumanians to demonstrate against princes and governments which kept Italians and Germans divided and held the others "prisoners" of vast multinational empires. Although not successful, the 1848 revolutionaries revealed the strength of the rising nationalist tide.

Within a century of Waterloo the map of Europe was redesigned largely in the pattern of this growing nationalistic diversity. Italy in 1861, Hungary in 1867, Germany in 1871, Serbia and Rumania in 1878, Norway in 1905, Bulgaria in 1908, and Albania in 1913 gained sovereignty. Significantly, only the Norwegian detachment from Sweden occurred without violence. Of note, also, is the fact that, except for Norway and Hungary, not a single one of the new states was satisfied with its 1914 borders. Thanks to the mixture of Europe's population, these states could and did point to members of their cultural groups still under foreign rule. Italians were governed by Austria in the Tyrol, Rumanians by Hungary in Transylvania, Serbs by Austria in Bosnia, Bulgars by Rumanians in the Dobruja. The possibility of "redeeming" these brethren dominated foreign policies and choice of sides in World War I. Indeed, it was the problem of nationally restless Serbs living in the Austro-Hungarian Empire which was the immediate cause of the war's outbreak in 1914. Their brother Serbs had successfully expelled their Turkish rulers and created an independent Serbia, with which they wished to be joined. Austro-Serbian tension over this problem reached the breaking point when Serb nationalists assassinated the heir to the Austrian throne in June, 1914.

World War I, rooted partly in nationalism, concluded with a peace conference which was much concerned with this problem. Now the map of Europe was further altered in accord with the distribution of nationalities. This action, referred to as "national self-determination," was vigorously championed by President Woodrow Wilson, who visualized a peaceful Europe emerging from the separation into individual nation-states of each of Europe's nationalities. Undoubtedly this was a rational approach, but in areas where for centuries two or more cultural groups had intermingled, as in many parts of eastern Europe, there could be no national self-determination for all members of every nationality. Nevertheless, Finland, Estonia, Latvia, Lithuania, Poland, Czechoslovakia, and Yugoslavia were recognized as new nation-states. Elsewhere borders were shifted, as between Rumania and Hungary and Austria and Italy, to minimize the number of "unredeemed" members of each nationality. Often other considerations, economic and strategic, interfered, but on the whole Europe was organized largely on a nation-state basis.

Totalitarian Nationalism

Western nationalism in recent years has frequently assumed totalitarian forms. Nationalism has come to demand supreme loyalty from the individual to his nation-state and has come to claim priority over all other human considerations and institutions. In its earlier phases nationalism had been tolerant of or cooperated with other movements which demanded loyalty of the individual. The twentieth century has seen a marked trend in the opposite direction.

The Mass Media. Important in this totalitarian trend was the mushroom growth of mass media of communication. The printed newspaper, rotogravure photography, motion pictures, and radio have proved to be powerful influences in the growth of nationalism among the European masses. Starting with the efforts at mass propaganda by the warring governments of World War I, intellectuals, theatrical artists, and journalists, along with political leaders of nation-states, have employed these media to secure popular endorsement of nationalism. Many educators concerned with instruction in other matters regret that they did not as quickly grasp the tremendous potentialities of these mass media. While they clung to more traditional methods of communicating with students, nationalist proselytizers proved the enormous effectiveness of the newer methods. Unquestionably, the greatest intensification of nationalism as a result of the application of these techniques was to be observed in Nazi Germany. Here, the Hitler forces crudely but successfully manipulated the nationalistic mood to permit the establishment of a dictatorship in the name of national needs. Fascism and Nazism are discussed elsewhere, but it is pertinent to note here that both capitalized in no small measure upon emotional nationalism, aroused through mass-media communication with large segments of the populations in Germany and Italy.

It would be wrong to give the impression that only the fascists cultivated nationalism by means of the press, movies, and radio; other nation-states in the Western world have carried out similar, if perhaps less intense, programs. During World War II, particularly, when war needs demanded cooperation of all citizens, the anti-Axis governments made every effort to remind their peoples of their nations' danger and of their obligation to make sacrifices for their nations' survival. "There'll always be an England," "Remember Pearl Harbor," "Fight for the Soviet Fatherland," are examples of the nonfascist nation-states' appeal to nationalism.

The Spiritual Void. Communication devices may be overemphasized, however. Nationalism became more intense also because the nationalistic appeals fell upon fertile soil. It has been the fate of the twentieth-century European to see the forces transforming his medieval world into a modern one reach a feverish and frightening crescendo. Scientific advances,

industrialization, urbanization, shrinkage of distances, ideological innovations, total war—these and other powerful impacts upon human society
have heightened in this century. The result has been such a pervading
sense of flux, insecurity, and loss of confidence in traditional beliefs that
a great many people in the Western world have found membership and
emotional release in national in-groups. Here, if nowhere else, was something to which the bewildered citizen, whose family, village, and provincial loyalties had disintegrated, could turn. The national group furnished
a means of satisfying man's deep-seated yearning for membership in some
kind of society and for belief in some kind of immortality. Thus, the
time was ripe for nationalism's appeal on a broader, deeper basis than
ever before. Nationalism came to fill the vacuum left by the disintegration of older in-groups.

Aldous Huxley insisted that "nationalism is the religion of the
twentieth century." [3] At first a shocking thought, this interpretation
becomes more creditable in the light of Carlton J. H. Hayes's description
of nationalism.

Nationalism has its parades, processions, and pilgrimages. It has, moreover, its
distinctive holy days. . . . In the United States, for example, the Fourth of July
is substituted for Corpus Christi, and Decoration Day for the commemoration of
All Souls of the faithful departed, whilst in place of the saints' days of the Christian calendar appear the birthdays of national saints and heroes, such as Washington and Lincoln. Nationalism has its temples, and he who would find the
places and the buildings that are held most dear and most sacred by the vast
majority of Americans, should seek not Christian cathedrals but Independence
Hall in Philadelphia, Faneuil Hall in Boston, the shrine to General Lee in Lex-
ington . . . and the city of Washington with . . . its great monuments to Lincoln and Washington.

Moderns, especially Americans, are inclined to regard the medieval venera-
tion of images, icons, and relics as savouring of "superstition," but let them
replace a statue of St. George by a graven image of General George Washington,
an icon of the Blessed Virgin Mary by a lithograph of the brave Molly Pitcher,
and a relic of the Holy Cross by a tattered battle flag, and they display a reverence which they deem beautiful and ennobling.[4]

Walter Sulzbach's sociological analysis leads to the same conclusion.

All religions prescribe certain duties toward the deity and toward other men,
and impose restrictions on normal impulses. In this respect, all of them, primitive or highly developed, place restrictions upon natural egoism. The pursuit of
one's own interest at the expense of others is considered sinful. Because religion
commands men to live socially, some philosophers and sociologists hold that the
chief characteristic of religion is its anti-egoistic social attitude. . . . It may be
said that national consciousness is similar to religion in that it also exalts the

---

[3] Aldous Huxley, *Newsweek,* April 30, 1956, p. 52.
[4] Hayes, *op. cit.,* pp. 108–109.

social group above the individual. The commands of both the nation and religion seem to be considered by their followers as morally justified. But where religion promises some kind of individual reward, the supreme sacrifice which the nation demands of its members may deprive them of life. They die without hope of personal reward in order that the nation may live.[5]

Too much emphasis cannot be placed on this religious aspect of nationalism. The movement did not originate with such demands upon its followers, but they have become very real in the twentieth century and now embrace, as has been indicated, the supreme loyalty of all men. If nationalism becomes the single most important element in the individual's life, it is quite understandable that the nation-state may become an object of worship, with its insistence on prior consideration over all other institutions widely accepted. Impetus has been given to this development by the decline of another bulwark against totalitarianism, liberalism.

The Decline of Liberalism. Liberalism (the body of thought which venerates the individual and advocates that society be organized to assure maximum individual freedom) became an important force in Western civilization about the same time as nationalism. Drawing inspiration from the Renaissance, the Reformation, the birth of modern science, the rise of modern capitalism, and the Enlightenment, liberalism was the ideology of the nationality-oriented bourgeoisie. Because early nationalists also tended to be liberals, the national and democratic movements entered the nineteenth century along complementary lines.

The great Italian nationalist of the last century, Giuseppe Mazzini, was no less an ardent democrat. To him nationalism and liberalism were both aspects of freedom. Nationalism encouraged the creation of free nation-states, and liberalism, freedom for individuals within these nation-states. In this process, Mazzini felt, nationalism would aid and abet liberalism: ". . . The idea of nationality arose at the opportune moment, to multiply the forces of the individual and make known the means by which the labor and sacrifice of each man may be rendered efficacious and beneficial to humanity." [6]

Much the same line of thought influenced Woodrow Wilson and his supporters for national self-determination at the Paris Peace Conference at the end of World War I. Wilson had earlier identified himself with efforts to augment individual freedom in his own free nation-state. Now he led a movement to establish other free nation-states, like Czechoslovakia, Poland, and Finland, inside of which individual freedom could flourish.

However, the difficulty of maintaining individual freedom in an urban, industrial society had challenged Woodrow Wilson's America and

[5] Walter Sulzbach, *National Consciousness* (Washington, American Council on Public Affairs, Public Affairs Press, 1943), p. 119.

[6] Hans Kohn, *Prophets and Peoples* (New York, Macmillan, 1946), p. 93.

Mazzini's Europe even before World War I. How could individual freedom be reconciled with the growing pressures of big factory, big farm, big
government, and big school? Bigness demands cooperation, which in turn
involves some surrender of individualism. The general dislocations within
the Western world after World War I accentuated the need for cooperative attacks upon unemployment, depression, juvenile delinquency, care
of the aged. As a result, whether democratic, Communist, or fascist in
ideology, all Western communities permitted or encouraged the enormous expansion of government functions. Whereas the nation-state had
refrained from government regulation of economic and social life in the
mid-nineteenth century, the twentieth-century state moved in the opposite direction. It became the regulator of the economy, monitor of the
distribution of wealth, and architect of a new social order. Russian Five-
Year Plans, Nazi Four-Year Plans, Britain's National Coalition Government (1931–1937), America's New Deal (1930–1939), Mussolini's Corporate
State, all were aspects of the reaction to the troubles of the time. Liberalism's precious individual surrendered varying portions of his freedom for
greater economic and social security, and liberalism was placed on the
defensive and forced to fight a strategic retreat.

Conversely, nationalism was less out of step with the urban-industrial
pressures for regimentation and collectivization. It emphasized collective
cooperation of millions of citizens of the same nationality. Even in the
Soviet Union, where theoretically the initial steps had been taken toward
an international community run by the proletariat, nationalism made
itself felt. No wonder then that nationalism came to overshadow, and in
some places even to crush, liberalism. The nation-state in the name of
national welfare, health, conservation, population growth, and defense
undertook projects, proposed by national leaders and approved by national majorities, that linked the citizen ever more closely to his nation-
state. Since the citizen's economic security, social well-being, and political
identity emanated from the nation-state, he quite naturally regarded it as
essential to him and therefore entitled to his support and obedience. Only
one step remains to total support and obedience, already increasingly
evident in Western civilization.

Today the Englishman and American, as well as the German and
Russian, run less risk of persecution or prosecution for being a bigamist,
adulterer, libeler, lyncher, or racketeer than for being disloyal to his
nation-state. The hunt for Communists in the United States and the
American public's deep fear of Communists clearly reflect this state of
mind. The American Communist is not regarded as a completely loyal
citizen of the United States, and for this reason he is the object of deep
suspicion in the eyes of many who regard themselves as loyal Americans.

International Repercussions of Twentieth-Century Nationalism. The
impact of this most recent phase of nationalism upon international rela-

tions is readily seen. Where fascists capitalized upon the trend to seize control of nation-states, the repercussions were very disturbing internationally. First Japan in China, then Italy in Ethiopia and Albania, and Germany in central Europe with violence and brutality expanded their territories in the name of national interests. The list of small nation-states swallowed up by their more powerful neighbors was a long one, the Nazis alone between 1938 and 1941 reducing to complete subservence to the German nation-state fourteen previously independent countries. In this process, of course, World War II was ignited.

Expansion of the fascist nation-states was not, however, the only result. Less powerful states confined their expression of nationalism to the persecution of alien elements within their boundaries. As noted previously, the Paris Peace Conference efforts to apply national self-determination to the whole of Europe proved impossible because of the mixed national groupings. Accordingly, many small European nation-states contained national minorities. With the intensification of nationalism, the ruling elements discriminated against those who, because of different language or religion, were suspected of less than 100 percent loyalty to the nation-state. Jews especially were persecuted in Poland, Rumania, and Hungary. Discrimination was also practiced against Ruthenes in Czechoslovakia, Magyars in Rumania, Macedonians in Yugoslavia, and Ukrainians in Poland. Although the harassment did not lead to war, as did the aggressions of the major fascist powers, it generated much unrest and was an invitation to Germany and Russia to "rescue" their ethnic cousins suffering at the hands of non-German and non-Russian nation-states. For example, Soviet Russia's annexations at the end of World War II of eastern Poland, Bessarabia, and Ruthenia were justified on the grounds that these areas contained persecuted White Russian and Ukrainian minorities.

Another outcome was the trend in practically every nation-state to seek solution of its economic problems through unilateral action without regard to the effects upon other nation-states. Economic nationalism will be treated elsewhere, but it should be mentioned at this point, too. United States' tariffs, British investment policy, French currency devaluation, Belgian quotas, and German "dumping" are examples of economic actions taken by governments in their own alleged national interests without regard for their unsettling repercussions on international relations.

Finally, all efforts at international organization such as the League of Nations or the United Nations were affected by twentieth-century nationalism. With supreme loyalty directed to the nation-state, any attempt to subordinate it to some supranational authority was intolerable to the nationalist. Accordingly, members of both the League of Nations and the United Nations carefully preserved their sovereignty. When Japan invaded China in 1931 and Italy bombed Ethiopia in 1935, League attempts to stop them by rebuke or economic sanctions ended with the withdrawal of Japan and Italy from the League in accordance with their sovereign rights. Moreover, the remaining members of the League also asserted their sovereignty by refusing to take further, more effective steps against the aggressors. Although a somewhat different situation ensued in the United Nations when South Korea was invaded in 1950, the outcome of collective action which repelled the invaders probably would not have materialized had not the United States and South Korea been inclined to defend the latter in their own national interests. Despite the presence of international organization, the nation-states, with the fervid endorsement of most of their citizens, have pursued their own local interests. Collective security and the nationalist philosophy of supreme loyalty to the nation-state appear in many respects irreconcilable.

In summary, nationalism became greatly intensified in the Western environment of the twentieth century. The mass media of communication, a growing spiritual malaise, and the weakening of liberalism were among the factors conducive to nationalism's increasing hold after World War I and to its assumption of various totalitarian overtones. Its extreme character in the twentieth century has made it a formidable force militating against all international tendencies, economic, scientific, and organizational. Western civilization has found it impossible to achieve the large measure of international cooperation dictated by the world's growing interdependence, because nationalism has so emphatically buttressed the nation-state system.

Still another indication of nationalism's continuing intensity in Europe was its survival in Eastern Europe where the U.S.S.R., following World War II, made great efforts to create a unified bloc of nations under its dominance. As the Red Army entered Poland, Rumania, Bulgaria, Hungary, Czechoslovakia, and East Germany, it assisted local communists to establish dictatorships in the soviet pattern. In Yugoslavia, without Russian aid, local Communists under Marshal Tito took over there, too. Marxist ideology taught that countries in which private ownership of the means of production was abolished would no longer have conflicting interests. This did not, however, prove to be the case.

The Yugoslavs, having battled Turks, Austrians, and Germans for their national freedom, soon evinced national resistance to Moscow's efforts to dictate policy. Tito was criticized by Stalin for tardy farm collectivization and for seeking special ties with Bulgaria. In a serious miscalculation, Stalin attempted in 1948 to bring down the Tito government with expulsion of the Yugoslav Communist Party from the Cominform and with an economic blockade of Yugoslavia. Strongly endorsed by national sentiment among Communist and non-Communist Yugoslavs, Tito was able to withstand the pressure. Economic assistance from the United States also helped. Thus, Yugoslavia, while remaining Communist, assumed a neutral position between Europe's two power blocs.

By 1956, Polish and Hungarian nationalist chafing at Russian controls led the Polish and Hungarian Communist dictatorships in both countries to demand greater national freedom from Moscow. In Poland this resulted in a shake-up of leaders with Wladyslaw Gomulka, allegedly an anti-Stalinist, becoming the new leader and identified with abandonment of collectivization, accommodation with the Roman Catholic Church, and increased trade with Western Europe.

This modest assertion of Polish nationalism in 1956 encouraged the Hungarian Communists to move in a similar direction. The "Hungarian Gomulka" was Imre Nagy. Coming to power in October, 1956, this man was swept along by nationalist enthusiasm even further than Gomulka. When Nagy announced that a coalition of Communists and non-Communists would take over, Moscow's leaders sought to unseat him. The outcome was an attempt by Nagy to withdraw Hungary from the Soviet bloc's military alliance (the Warsaw Pact), armed resistance to advancing Soviet military forces, and bloody fighting in Budapest which shook the whole world. The Soviets managed to tamp down this Hungarian nationalist outbreak, liquidated Nagy, and established a new Hungarian Communist regime under Janos Kadar. Even Kadar, however, over the next decade cautiously probed toward greater independence for his government, though carefully avoiding the Nagy experiment.

The Hungarian Revolution of 1956 had a number of repercussions. Many Communists were shocked at the spectacle of two Communist countries at war with each other. Russia, quite rightly, was charged with pursuing its own narrow national interests in Hungary and severely soiled thereby its image as the benign center of the Communist supranational brotherhood. If not recognized before, it was now seen by each Communist regime in Eastern Europe that there were definite limits to its national aspirations. At the same time, the Kremlin became more aware of the strong anti-Russian nationalism in its satellites and endeavored to avoid its further aggravation. By 1964, Rumania had opened up commercial relations of considerable extent with the non-Communist West, trade across the Iron Curtain appreciably increased, Yugoslavia continued its neutral policy, and Albania had all but officially withdrawn from the Soviet bloc by aligning with China in its ideological arguments with the U.S.S.R. Thus, nationalism proved a powerful and troublesome force for Soviet policy in Eastern Europe, in spite of the apparent ideological common denominator among those countries.

NATIONALISM, IMPERIALISM, AND ANTICOLONIALISM

Imperialism is a policy of extending one people's or government's authority and control over other peoples and their territory without the consent of the latter. In this sense imperialism is a very old practice dating back to prehistoric times. Certainly the efforts of the first city-states in ancient Sumeria to dominate each other is a clear example, while such names as Meneleus, Alexander of Macedon, Attila, Tamerlane, Saladin, and Ghenghis Khan conjure up more recent illustrations.

Since the fifteenth century, however, Europeans have been imperialism's foremost practitioners. Pressed by economic appetites, religious fervor, and sheer adventurousness and equipped with technical superiority and organizational genius, they began in the Columbian Age to expand into the other continents. By 1800, the Americas had been most thoroughly Europeanized (though in 1776 some of the Europeans in North America had broken free politically), but Asia, Australia, and Africa all had in some measure felt the breath of European merchant, missionary, or marine.

With the rise of European nationalism, however, there was a new impetus behind imperialism. By the latter part of the nineteenth century, the Western scramble for overseas imperial holdings was frequently justified in nationalistic terms. For example, the argument that colonialism was "the white man's burden" left no doubt that Europeans and North Americans believed that the intrusion, by force if necessary, of their national cultures would be beneficial to the "poor, benighted heathens" of the non-West. Certainly there were instances of nationalism being used merely to cloak economic and military motives, but not always. The French plan, fostered by Jules Ferry, of a great band of French-controlled territories across barren, burning, Saharan Africa was essentially nationalist in inspiration. Similarly, the new German Empire found little more than national prestige in its acquisition of semi-arid, rebellious, economically unprofitable Southwest Africa. In the United States Congress in 1898, it was argued that the Philippines should be annexed because to not do so would be to permit some other Western nation to take the islands—and did not the Filipinos deserve the "best," namely exposure to American and not to some other national culture and rule? A Victorian Englishman was hardly apologetic when announcing that the sun never set on the British Empire, though it could be argued whether the economic profits from imperialism to the British people as a whole warranted the cost of empire.

THE BIRTH OF ANTICOLONIAL NATIONALISM

Given the nature of nationalism, it is not difficult to perceive that the unwilling subjects of imperialism evolved a nationalism of their own. We have seen how in-group consciousness plays a role in the birth of nationalism, and what more powerful generator of in-groupism exists than to subject a society to outside domination? Indians discovered for the first time that there was such a thing as India only when they associated with their British conquerors and shared the humiliations of foreign rule. In the same manner, the forcible crashing through China's Closed Door Policy by Westerners lit the fuse of nationalism among the Chinese.

Everywhere, Western imperialism, shot through as it was with Western nationalism, sooner or later awakened a nationalist reaction among the colonial subjects.

At first the reaction was confined, as it still is in much of Africa, to a small literate, travelled, educated elite, for national consciousness is dependent upon not only identification of an out-group but also awareness of the in-group. The latter, of course, depends upon popular consciousness of the national tradition and culture, something highly restricted before the age of radio, motion pictures, and billboards. Thus, the first anticolonial nationalists were educated young lawyers like India's Mahatma Gandhi, doctors like China's Sun Yat-sen, and army officers like Turkey's Mustafa Kemal. Often, as in the above examples, their education was obtained partly in and from the West. It has been said that Indian nationalism was born at Cambridge University, where Gandhi, Nehru, and other Indian leaders studied. In any case, the first task of this elite was to arouse national feelings among their native countrymen.

By 1900, there were ample signs of anticolonial nationalism. Canada, Australia, New Zealand, and South Africa, despite their European culture, had received or were in the process of receiving political self-government as members of the British Commonwealth of Nations. The surviving links between them and Mother Britain were the Crown, economic ties, and family sentiments. But if Britons could look upon this development with pride, their national outlook did not lead them to consider similar concessions to their non-Western colonial charges. Elsewhere, Britain, like the other colonial powers, was confronted with the first indications of native Asian and African anticolonialism.

In India as early as 1885, there appeared the Indian National Congress, a party dedicated to Indian national independence. This movement was to find its greatest leader in the twentieth century in Gandhi.

A revolution in China in 1911 heralded the maturing of anticolonialism there. Although many factors contributed to the overthrow of the Chinese Imperial Government, one was rising resentment against its inability to prevent foreign troops from garrisoning its cities, foreign governments from regulating its tariffs, and foreign gunboats from insisting on extraterritorial privileges for non-Chinese residents and travellers. Sun Yat-sen, the foremost 1911 revolutionist, placed much emphasis on China's need to become nationally conscious and free of foreign encroachment, as well as to modernize its society along politically democratic and economically socialist lines.

At the same time, Arabs manifested restlessness under Turkish and European rule. While Cairo scholars wrote of the Arab origins and custodianship of Islamic culture, Egyptian army officers revolted in 1881 against a government they believed too subservient to foreigners. Though suppressed, this episode was a precursor of things to come.

When Spain ceded the Philippines to the United States in 1898, many

Americans discovered with distress that the $16 million paid to Spain had purchased a nationalist insurrection. Restless under Spanish rule, Filipinos in growing numbers had become sufficiently nationalistic to desire independence, not transfer from Spanish to United States colonial rule. Consequently, Emilio Aguinaldo and his guerrilla band fought for a decade against the incoming Americans, while Manuel Quezon and others attempted to persuade Washington by other means that the Filipinos should be granted independence. "Better a government run like hell by Filipinos than one run like heaven by Americans" was the nationalist reply to the American argument that the islanders were not yet ready for self-government. When President Wilson in 1916 promised independence to the Philippines, he signalled the first major Western concession to Asian anticolonial nationalism.

THE NATURE OF ANTICOLONIAL NATIONALISM

Thus far it has been implied that the awakened nationalism of Asians was like that of Europeans and Americans. Basically, of course, both are explicable in similar terms, but the conditions in which anticolonial nationalism took root gave it distinct character of its own. More than simply resentment against rule by an alien society, anticolonialism had economic and racial overtones.

The "Theory of Exploitation." As Indian, Chinese, Arab, and Filipino elites became nationally conscious, they quickly noted that among the differences between their own cultures and that of the colonial powers was that of living standards. While the Western economy not only already provided a relatively fabulous level of general economic well-being but was constantly and rapidly expanding, it was all too evident to the Gandhis, Suns, and Aguinaldos that their peoples lived not only in poverty but in an undynamic economy which promised no relief. It was but one step from this to the conclusion that Western wealth was partly the result of Eastern poverty and that only an end to colonialism would enable the Asians to improve their economic position.

The resemblance between this "Theory of Exploitation" and Leninist theories of capitalist imperialism was no doubt one of the factors which attracted many anticolonial nationalists to Marxism as the twentieth century advanced. Unquestionably, colonialism did in some ways inhibit economic growth in Asia, but at the same time its investments were responsible for the initial steps toward industrialization. Moreover, as contemporary events demonstrate, national independence by no means removed the most formidable obstacles to economic development in Asia and Africa. Nevertheless, the Asian-African belief in this theory was a vital part of nationalistic outlook.

Racism. While European peoples striving for national independence from other Europeans emphasized their cultural differences, there was no antagonism based on color consciousness. In Asia, as well as in Africa, the opposite was often the case. Although not all Western imperialists were racial-minded, many did practice color discrimination and segregation which inevitably aroused resentment among their colonial subjects.

Rigid segregation of the Indian from the British sahib, and even more so from the sahib's wife, was only one example. The American "colony" in Manila maintained its own exclusive clubs. Curfews, signs reading "Off Limits to Nonwhites," residential zoning, and hotel and transportation segregation constantly reminded the Asian and African that the Westerner not only exercised political power over him without his consent and usually lived better than he did, but also considered him a creature somewhere between the human and animal categories. To Indians, Chinese, Japanese, and other peoples who in all aspects of their civilization except technology believed themselves to be equal or superior to the Westerner, this was an intolerable situation. It was most deeply resented, of course, by the better educated, more well-to-do. Moreover, it generated a counter-racism among them.

Thus, nationalism in time appeared in Asia and Africa, where it assumed an anticolonial emphasis and fused with economic and racial grievances. Though by the time of the First World War (1914–1918) some Western democratic idealists recognized the contradiction between the West's growing commitment to democratic government at home and maintenance of undemocratic colonial rule abroad, Western economic, military, and nationalist pressure groups opposed relinquishment of colonial holdings. The two world wars, however, had the dual effect of weakening the Western will to empire and at the same time stimulating anticolonialism.

THE END OF THE OLD COLONIALISM

As early as the 1860's, the Japanese had recognized that their salvation from Western imperialism rested in rapid adoption of Western technology. As a result, Japan acquired a modern fleet and army and the bureaucratic administration necessary to their functioning. With this power in hand, Japan was successful in negotiating an end to the special privileges the Western powers had wrested from Japan, and then in winning local wars against China, Russia, and Germany which gave Japan recognition by the end of World War I as a great power with an imperialist base of its own on mainland China. Japan thereby became a symbol of successful anticolonialism against the West and a new imperialistic menace which fed the fires of Chinese anticolonial nationalism.

Following World War I, other signs of retreat by the Western imperial nations appeared. Egypt was recognized as independent, though Britain held the Suez Canal. In India a Constitutional Act (1919) pro-

The Nation-States of the World

Europe	The Americas	Asia	Africa
(Independent in 1935): 26	*(Independent in 1935)*: 22	*(Independent in 1935)*: 10	*(Independent in 1935)*: 4
Albania	Argentina	Afghanistan	Egypt (now the United Arab Rep.)
Austria	Bolivia	China	Ethiopia
Belgium	Brazil	Iran	Liberia
Bulgaria	Canada	Iraq	South Africa
Czechoslovakia	Chile	Japan	
Denmark	Colombia	Nepal	
Finland	Costa Rica	Saudi Arabia	*(Independence gained since 1945)*: 35
France	Cuba	Thailand	Algeria
Germany *	Dominican Rep.	Turkey	Botswana
Greece	Ecuador	Yemen	Burundi
Hungary	El Salvador		Cameroon
Iceland	Guatemala	*(Independence gained since 1945)*: 19	Central African Rep.
Ireland	Haiti		Chad
Italy	Honduras	Burma	Congo (Brazzaville)
Luxembourg	Mexico	Cambodia	Congo (Democratic Rep. of Leopoldville)
Netherlands	Nicaragua	Ceylon	Dahomey
Norway	Panama	India	Gabon
Poland	Paraguay	Indonesia	Gambia
Portugal	Peru	Israel	Ghana
Rumania	United States	Jordan	Guinea
Spain	Uruguay	Korea *	Ivory Coast
Sweden	Venezuela	Kuwait	Kenya
Switzerland		Laos	Lesotho
U.S.S.R.	*(Independence gained since 1945)*: 4	Lebanon †	Libya
United Kingdom	Barbados	Malaysia	Madagascar
Yugoslavia	Guyana	Maldive Islands	Malawi
	Jamaica	Mongolia	Mali
(Independence gained since 1945): 2	Trinidad-Tobago	Pakistan	Mauretania
Cyprus		Philippines	Morocco
Malta		Singapore	Niger
		Syria †	Nigeria
		Vietnam *	Rwanda
			Senegal
	Australasia & Oceania		Sierra Leone
	(Independent in 1935): 2		Somalia
	Australia		Sudan
	New Zealand		Tanzania ‡
			Togo
	(Independence gained since 1945)		Tunisia
	Western Samoa		Uganda
			Upper Volta
			Zambia

* Divided into two separate sovereign regimes as of 1 January 1967.

† Syria and Lebanon achieved independence in 1944.

‡ The United Republic of Tanzania was created in 1964 by the union of Tanganyika, which became independent in 1961, and Zanzibar, which became independent in 1963.

vided for the election of provincial assemblies with very limited powers, enough only to stimulate Indian demands for greater autonomy. Opponents of imperialism in Europe and the United States were also sufficiently vocal after World War I to insist that territories taken away from the defeated Central Powers not be annexed by the victors. Accordingly, a mandate system under the League of Nations was established and former German and Turkish territories were assigned mandate status. This entailed annual reports by the mandatory powers to the League, hearings by the League of complaints by the peoples living in the mandates, and promises of independence to those mandated territories created out of the former Turkish areas in the Levant (Iraq, Transjordan, Syria, Lebanon, and Palestine). In actual practice only Iraq became independent (in 1932), but the mandate system was a watershed in the imperial thinking of the West and helped to condition the colonial powers for the total demolition of the old colonial system after World War II.

IN INDIA, CEYLON, AND BURMA

Certainly, in terms of numbers of people involved, the Indian nationalist revolution is the first significant manifestation of this phenomenon since World War II. Awakened to national consciousness only after several decades of agitation by such leaders as Gandhi, the 400 million inhabitants of British-dominated India finally began to stir in the 1920's.

Its distinctive Indian character was reflected in its emphasis upon nonviolent civil disobedience. Indeed, Indian nationalism was almost alone in its remarkable rejection of violent measures to achieve national goals. In 1930, this was dramatized by Gandhi's famous march to the sea, where he and his followers boiled buckets of salt water from which was derived just enough salt to violate the British Government's salt monopoly. Soon other forms of civil disobedience ensued, and Indian nationalists willingly crowded the jails until the authorities had 40,000 prisoners to care for and no room for new violators of the civil laws. Faced with this impasse, Britain opened new negotiations with Gandhi which dragged on through World War II and were concluded finally by the action of Britain's Labor Government in 1947. That year Parliament passed the Indian Independence Act after an agreement had been reached among Indian leaders on the separation of the predominantly Moslem areas from Hindu India and their constitution as the separate state of Pakistan.

At the same time Burma and Ceylon were granted independence, the former opting for complete disassociation from Britain, the latter joining India and Pakistan as members of the newly titled Commonwealth of Nations under which the ex-colonies maintained cultural and economic ties with the United Kingdom but enjoyed complete independence.

In East Asia

The Philippines. Promised independence by an act of Congress, the Philippines became involved in World War II before the 1944 fulfillment date of that promise was reached. The mutual sufferings of Filipinos and Americans during the war brought relations between the islands and the United States to an all-time high. Consequently, on July 4, 1946, the Philippine Republic was recognized. In return for American economic aid, the United States retained certain military and economic privileges in the islands, but Filipino nationalism was largely gratified.

Indonesia. After over three centuries of colonial rule, the Indonesians took advantage of the withdrawal of the Japanese invaders in 1945 and resisted forcibly efforts to reestablish Netherlands' control. With the help of United Nations mediation, the Republic of Indonesia was finally recognized by the Dutch in 1949. Under its fiery, unpredictable, and emotional national leader, President Sukarno, Indonesia's government soon gained a reputation for aggressive nationalism. Not unexpectedly, property seizures soon forced the remaining Dutch settlers to evacuate Indonesia. Demands were then made for annexation of Dutch New Guinea (West Irian), which was transferred under United Nations auspices to Indonesia in 1963. This was followed by an undeclared guerrilla war against the Federation of Malaysia to prevent its integration with North Borneo. When Malaysia was elected to a United Nations Security Council seat in 1965, Sukarno electrified the world by announcing Indonesia's withdrawal from the United Nations, an action later rescinded.

Vietnam. This wealthier, more populous, coastal part of French Indochina resisted French reoccupation after Japan's defeat in 1945. Here, however, significant differences from the Philippines and Indonesia are to be noted. First, the Vietnamese leaders, headed by Ho Chi Minh, were Communists who fused the nationalist and Communist movements. Second, the French were successful in reoccupying parts of Vietnam and holding it for some years after 1945. Ho Chi Minh's forces surged dramatically toward victory only in 1953 when Communist China, free from its Korean War commitments, made aid available to the nationalists-Communists. In 1954, at Dien Bien Phu, an interior village in northern Vietnam, a significant part of the French army was besieged and finally destroyed. Armistice negotiations at Geneva in July, 1954, led to establishment of two provisional regimes: one under non-Communists in South Vietnam, another under Ho Chi Minh in North Vietnam. It was further agreed that a plebiscite to determine the nature of a government for all Vietnam would be held in 1956, but this was not honored. Instead, a new conflict developed between the two sections with the United States gradually being drawn into the role of protector of the South Vietnamese government, while China aided the North Vietnamese.

Korea. Promised independence from Japan by the victors in World War II, the Koreans at the end of the conflict found the north of their country occupied by Soviet armies and the south by American. When the Soviet forces withdrew in 1949, they left behind a Communist government; in the south the Americans endorsed the anti-Communist regime of Syngman Rhee. The United Nations proposed free elections for all Korea, but North Korean leaders and the Russians objected. An abortive attempt by the North Koreans to unite forcibly the country resulted in the bitter three years of the Korean War (1950–1953) before the two Korean states were again to turn to more peaceful pursuits—separated by a demilitarized, internationally patrolled corridor.

China. By far the most significant Asian nationalist movement was that of China, where the Communists were most successful in identifying themselves with nationalism and where the very size of the country made it potentially the foremost nationalist movement in the world.

Unwilling or unable to carry out promised reforms, Chiang Kai-shek, successor to the mantle of Sun Yat-sen, faced mountainous problems after China's exhausting struggle in World War II. Rivalling Chiang was the Chinese Communist Party, militant, boldly led, and able to point to reforms in the northwest region of China under its control. In the ensuing civil war (1945–1949) Chiang and the rump of his forces were driven to the island of Formosa where, in Communist eyes, the Chiang regime survived as the puppet of "imperialist," "capitalist" America.

Mao Tse-tung and other Chinese Communist leaders lost no time in appealing to nationalism. The West in general and the United States in particular became objects of national antipathy. Chinese intervention in the Korean War when the UN troops neared China's frontiers was an overt demonstration of Peking's determination to enter the realm of national power politics. So also were abolition of Tibetan autonomy and the announced intention of reuniting Formosa with the rest of China. Forceful assertion of its own interpretations of Marxism and criticism of Soviet Russia's signalled the Chinese bid for leadership of the world Communist movement (see Chap. 5). To miss the prominent element of nationalism in Red China's relations with the rest of the world is to misjudge its nature, even though communism, too, is a major force.

In the Middle East. At the other end of Asia the Second World War saw the independence of all the former mandates. Syria and Lebanon broke away from France, and Britain surrendered her mandates in Transjordan and Palestine. The latter became the scene of some of the most violent nationalistic outbursts of recent times.

While a mandate, Palestine had become the home of large numbers of Jewish refugees from Europe and was visualized by the Zionist movement as a national home for the Jews. To this concept the Arabs, both in and outside of Palestine, took violent exception. After more than a decade of trying to maintain order, Britain was happy to surrender this nettle to the United Nations.

Unable to satisfy both Jews and Arabs, the United Nations in December, 1947, recommended the partition of Palestine. Reluctantly the Jews accepted the United Nations partition plan and announced that an independent Israeli state would be set up within the boundaries recommended by the United Nations. The Arabs, who had constituted the preponderant population of Palestine for over 1,000 years, regarded the creation of a Jewish state there as a violation of their own national aspirations and rights.[7] They declared they would fight to prevent the establishment of an independent Jewish state on land that they believed belonged rightfully to them. Hence, when British forces finally withdrew in May, 1948, and Israeli independence was formally proclaimed, the Arab forces launched a full-scale invasion in an effort to wipe out the new state. By 1949, the Israelis had repulsed the Arab forces and even occupied some 2,200 square miles of land that the United Nations had originally allocated to the Arabs. An armistice was signed in 1949, based on the existing battle lines.

The constant state of tension along the armistice line flared into open warfare again when Israel joined France and Britain in the 1956 invasion of Egypt. Only the most persistent pressure by the United States and the United Nations forced Israel to evacuate the areas seized and occupied by her armed forces during the Suez incident. An international military patrol under the United Nations (UNEF) policed some of the disputed strips lying between the Israelis and the Arabs, but the latter left no doubt of their determination to crush Israel at the first opportunity.

At this point it should be noted that the rapidly shifting relationships between the Arab states, between Arabs and Israelis, and between the Arabs and the Anglo-French opened the door to an extension of the cold war to the Middle East. The United States attempted to win favor with the Arab nationalists by insisting upon the evacuation of Suez in 1956 by the invading forces, and in 1957 by announcing the Eisenhower Doctrine to strengthen the Middle East against Communist threats. The Soviet Union also became more active in the area. A strongly anti-Western regime in Syria in 1957 was approved and supported by Moscow. An abortive attempt the same year to bring about revolution against Jordan's King Hussein produced charges by the king of Soviet assistance and in turn prompted the extension of United States aid to Hussein's

[7] The population of Palestine in 1922, 1931, and 1946 was distributed as follows:

	Arabs	Jews	Christians	Others	Total
1922	486,177	83,790	71,464	7,617	649,048
1931	693,147	174,606	88,907	10,101	966,761
1946	1,076,783	608,225	145,063	15,448	1,845,559

SOURCE: United Nations Special Committee on Palestine, *Report to the General Assembly*, Vol. I, p. 11 (United Nations General Assembly, 2nd sess., 1947, Suppl. 11).

government. During this period, the Soviet bloc, too, concluded a number of aid and trade agreements with many Arab states.

In the face of Arab nationalism both the U.S.A. and the U.S.S.R. felt it necessary to disclaim all intent of interfering with the independence of the Arab states. Hussein made it clear that he had accepted American aid without commitments to Washington. The Arab countries that signed agreements with the Soviet Union boasted that no "strings" were attached. The presence of Soviet and American agents in the Middle East and the obvious Russo-American competition for influence there should not obscure the fact that nationalism has been, and is, the dominant force at work in the Middle East, as it is in North Africa. The almost universal claims by the Arab states that they are neutral in the cold war underline this fact.

In North Africa

North Africa's Arab and Islamic ties with the Middle East meant that nationalist tremors at the eastern end of the Mediterranean were also felt all along its northern shore.

As noted above, Egyptians had first raised the banner of nationalism against their pre-World War I Turkish rulers. After that conflict Egypt was declared independent, but Britain retained control of the Suez Canal. Agitation by Egyptian nationalists against this "alien presence" on Egyptian soil reached violent proportions when in 1951 Cairo abrogated the Canal treaty arrangements and violent attacks upon British soldiers began. Finally, in 1953, London agreed to the evacuation of all her armed forces. In 1956, when the United States and Britain withdrew an offer of economic aid to Premier Nasser's government, Nasser nationalized the company operating the Suez Canal and declared that the proceeds from the Canal tolls would be used for Egyptian economic development.

A contributing factor in the Anglo-American decision to withdraw their offer of assistance in the construction of a giant dam on the Nile at Aswan had been Nasser's bartering of cotton for military equipment with Communist-dominated Czechoslovakia earlier in 1956. The flow of Czech arms into Egypt, coupled with nationalization of the Suez Canal Co., goaded France, Israel, and Britain into armed invasion of Egypt in late 1956, in an effort to unseat Nasser and regain control of the Canal lifeline to Arabian oil sources. When the United States not only refused tacitly to support the invasion but, along with an overwhelming majority of the other members of the United Nations, insisted on a cease-fire, the three invaders complied and withdrew their forces. Despite the woefully weak showing of the Egyptian armed forces, the Nasser regime hailed the withdrawal as a "victory" and was wildly cheered by Egyptian nationalists.

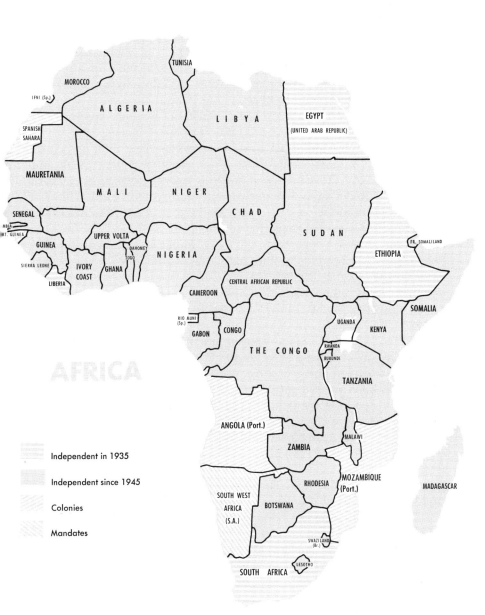

TUNISIA

MOROCCO

IFNI (Sp.)

ALGERIA

SPANISH
SAHARA

LIBYA

EGYPT
(UNITED ARAB REPUBLIC)

MAURETANIA

MALI

NIGER

CHAD

SUDAN

SENEGAL

MBIA
RT. GUINEA

GUINEA

UPPER VOLTA

DAHOMEY
TOGO

NIGERIA

FR. SOMALILAND

ETHIOPIA

SIERRA LEONE

IVORY
COAST

GHANA

LIBERIA

CENTRAL AFRICAN REPUBLIC

SOMALIA

CAMEROON

RIO MUNI
(Sp.)

GABON

CONGO

UGANDA

KENYA

THE CONGO

RWANDA
BURUNDI

AFRICA

TANZANIA

ANGOLA (Port.)

MALAWI

ZAMBIA

MOZAMBIQUE
(Port.)

MADAGASCAR

Independent in 1935

Independent since 1945

Colonies

Mandates

RHODESIA

SOUTH WEST
AFRICA
(S.A.)

BOTSWANA

SWAZILAND
(Br.)

LESOTHO

SOUTH   AFRICA

Adjoining Egypt is the newly independent state of Libya. An Italian colony before World War II and occupied by the British after the war, Libya was the scene of nationalist demands for independence. In 1951 this independence was granted. That the transition was accomplished without violence, in contrast with much of the rest of North Africa, is attributable to Italy's defeat and the reluctance of any other European state to defy rising nationalism in Libya by attempting to impress a new colonial regime upon it.

To the west of Libya is the great expanse of territory known as the Maghreb. Here in Tunisia, Algeria, and Morocco, following 1951, a very serious situation was produced by nationalism. In these three territories, totaling over 1 million square miles, lived nearly 20 million Arabs and Berbers with over 2 million non-Moslems, mostly Frenchmen. Algeria was brought under French domination a century ago; Tunisia became a French protectorate in 1881, and Morocco in 1912. Resentment of French control mounted sharply first among Paris-educated Arabs, then among the masses. Local Arab chieftains found it expedient to place themselves at the head of the nationalist movements. The more moderate Arab leaders, fearing the repercussions of violence, attempted negotiation with Paris; others encouraged coercion, especially after the success of the Egyptians and the forcible expulsion of the French from Indochina.

Unlike the Egyptian and Libyan situations, however, this one was complicated by the presence of many French settlers in the area. Reluctant to abandon them to Arab domination and highly sensitive to any further lowering of French national prestige, especially after military, diplomatic, and political defeat in Indochina, Paris resorted to limited concessions, combined with armed suppression of civil disturbances. The outcome was greater violence. The dispatch of over 300,000 troops, including most of France's NATO contingents, failed to stem the nationalist tide.

In March, 1956, France formally agreed to the termination of the protectorate status of Tunisia and Morocco and recognized their independence (Spain followed suit with her Moroccan protectorate). Although this put an end to violence in the two states, Algerian unrest intensified. Both Tunisians and Moroccans expressed sympathy with their fellow Arabs in Algeria, the new Tunisian president, Habib Bourgiba, stating that his people could not "be truly happy until their sister nation Algeria regains her sovereignty." [8]

The sympathy was expressed in a material way as well, the two new nation-states tolerating the smuggling of arms across their frontiers to the Algerian nationalists. This flow of aid and French efforts to halt it made even more acute the critical state of affairs in North Africa and in

8 *The New York Times,* March 23, 1956, p. 10.

France itself. Eventually French military and civilian elements in Algeria revolted against the vacillating authority of the Fourth Republic and helped bring Charles de Gaulle, himself the greatest living French national figure, to power. After several more years of bitter fighting, France conceded independence to Algeria (1962).

IN NEGRO AFRICA

From the North nationalism swept down over the rest of Africa in the 1950's. Beginning with the granting of independence in 1956 to the Sudan, which had formerly been under joint Anglo-Egyptian rule, thirty former mandates and colonies within the next nine years undertook to govern themselves as sovereign nations. This tremendous political revolution was not accomplished without serious problems which affected the whole world. When the Belgians relinquished control of the Congo in 1960, for example, the civil wars and race riots which wracked that land invited intervention and assistance to different Congolese factions by rival outside governments. For several years the presence of a United Nations force maintained a semblance of order but it was obliged to withdraw in 1964 for lack of financial support by France, the U.S.S.R., and certain other UN members. The Congo then plunged back into civil strife. Nigeria, on the other hand, with the largest population in Africa (34 million), managed the transition to self-government with relative ease, though even this state experienced a military *coup d'état* in 1966.

Complicating problems in most of these African states was the nature of the nationalist tide. The educated elites and urban populations, already divorced from their older African cultures, seemed to embrace nationalism feverishly. The rural and nomadic back-country folk, however, neither felt the need for nor understood the new nationalism in the same way. Consequently, leaders of the new African nations, not unlike European nationalists in the nineteenth century, were obliged to create heroes, images, flags, songs, costumes, and enemies in order to kindle nationalist responses to their leadership. Some enmity was directed against former colonial powers, some against African neighbors, but most against the Republic of South Africa where 2,500,000 whites of European descent politically dominated and socially segregated 10,000,000 people of color. Having resided in South Africa for generations, this white minority with a strong national consciousness of its own (called Afrikaanism) announced its determination to remain in the land, maintain *apartheid* (racial separation), and continue its political power. Protesting outbursts by Negro South Africans were harshly dealt with and strengthened the conviction of the whites that any concessions would open the door to further unrest, violence, and chaos for all. Here, surely, was one of the world's potentially most explosive conflicts and its ingredients were a combination of nationalism and racism.

Elsewhere in Africa, Portugal and Spain continued to hold remnants of their early empires. In each, however, there were local nationalist movements, abetted from neighboring independent Negro republics, which promised soon to render the Portuguese and Spanish positions untenable, thereby nearly completing the end of the old colonialism.

Whether nationalism, which has been dubbed by one authority as the "measles of mankind," will cause the same manifestations in Asia and Africa that it has in Europe and America is not altogether clear yet. The common struggles for independence and the outlooks of the Afro-Asian peoples and their leaders afforded them a sense of solidarity which transcends national boundaries. In 1955, twenty-nine African and Asian governments met to discuss their common problems to the exclusion of all Westerners. In the United Nations, the Afro-Asians coalesced periodically on the issues of colonialism and racism. In 1963, twenty-eight African nations gave substance to pan-Africanism by holding a conference at Addis Ababa. But there were also many indications of the same intense in-groupism, with accompanying out-group hostilities, which bedevilled the nationalist movement in other parts of the world.

CONCLUSION

Although a recent development in human society, nationalism appears to be rooted in very natural yearnings by human beings for social membership. In the past century it has led to the restructuring of much of the world into over 120 sovereign units based roughly upon national consciousness. This has been especially true for Europe, where nationalism first manifested itself, but more recently for all of the continents. In addition to having stimulated this trend toward national self-determination, nationalism has also been responsible for two other highly significant developments: the reluctance of nation-states to subordinate their national sovereignty and freedom to international interests and authority,[9] and their penchant for economic nationalism.[10] It is, of course, important to recognize that nationalism has contributed much to intragroup cooperation, harmony, viability, and satisfaction and may be viewed as a progression away from earlier clan and tribal groupings. But in its insistence upon supreme loyalty, its assertion of national sovereignty, and its tendency to isolate each community economically, polit-

[9] The basic reason for the limited authority of the League of Nations and the United Nations, as evidenced in the unanimity voting rule in the League and the veto in the U.N. Security Council, is rooted in this reluctance of sovereign nation-states to surrender their freedom of action.

[10] Economic nationalism may be defined as the conduct of foreign economic policy in such a way as to (1) protect a nation's domestic producers from foreign competition, (2) reduce the nation-state's dependence on the economy of the outside world, (3) increase its relative economic self-sufficiency, and (4) supplement or bolster the political or economic requirements of national security.

ically, and psychologically, it looms as a major factor in intergroup conflict and is regarded increasingly as a questionable political organization for the shrunken planet upon which we live. The following selections offer several views on whether nationalism has a place in the twentieth-century world and if not, what might be done about it.

POSITIONS

1. NATIONALISM AS ONE OF THE FACTS OF LIFE

The following passages have been taken from Louis J. Halle's *Civilization and Foreign Policy*.[11] The author, a former member of the State Department Policy Planning Staff, has in recent years been on the faculty of the Graduate Institute of International Studies, Geneva, Switzerland.

A prime fact about this world is that it is largely composed of nation-states. We tend to take this political composition of mankind for granted as if it were part of the order of nature, like the divisions of the animal kingdom. But nothing quite like it was known up to five hundred years ago, and in its brief history it has achieved little stability. . . .

There is, however, another grouping of population in the world today that transcends our nation-states as the Hellenic civilization transcended the Greek city-states. This is what we call Christendom or Western Civilization—or even European civilization, although it has now spread far beyond the boundaries of Europe. This larger grouping originally took the form of a single state: The Christianized Roman Empire. It persisted through the chaos of the Dark Ages and through medieval times in the vague form of the Holy Roman Empire. The concept of the universal civilization of Christendom . . . was a vivid reality all through the centuries . . . when . . . Christendom . . . was under assault by the rival civilization of Islam. The cohesion of Christendom was promoted by Islamic pressure as the cohesion of Hellas had been promoted by the hostile pressure of the Persian civilization. And as Hellas broke apart into mutually warring city-states after the defeat of Persia, so the final expulsion of the Saracens from Spain and the successful containment of the Turks coincided with the fragmentation of Christendom into nation-states. . . . In political affairs no binding agent can compare with a common enemy. That agent was generally lacking during the centuries after the fifteenth. . . .

The image of the present world, then, is of one that engages the loyalties of the individual in widening circles. In some isolated societies the people may identify themselves only with their village communities. Other people feel a particular allegiance to their native subnational state, like many inhabitants of California; or to a general section of national territory like our own South or the Welsh corner of England. Beyond this comes identification with the nation-

[11] Louis J. Halle, *Civilization and Foreign Policy* (New York, Harper & Row, 1952), pp. 10, 12–17, 19–20. Reprinted by permission of the author.

state . . . (or) to the civilization that our nations have inherited in common.

These several allegiances may be competing. Their relative values vary with different individuals and groups. A salient characteristic of our times, however, is the extent to which national loyalty tends to predominate over all other loyalties. . . .

Impulses of rivalry and the search for security . . . are involved here. . . . In each nation-state there is a common sense of community in success or failure, in prosperity or affliction. The sense of common welfare is related to the intentions, the successes, and the failures of other nation-states which, in the extreme of nationalism, are all regarded as rivals.

But the perfection of nationalism is qualified still by the wider circle of association which a common civilization represents, and often by the practical necessity of organizing associations among the nation-states. So the way is open for the entrance of complexity into the hearts and minds of men, who hardly know with whom or what to identify themselves and in what degree.

One may ask at this point, whether these associations, these separations, and these rivalries are inherent in the situation of mankind, or whether they represent, rather, an unnecessary indulgence of the Old Adam in us. . . .

It seems to me impossible to imagine a world evolving out of our present in which dynamic opposing forces are unknown, in which an unchanging, static equilibrium has consequently been achieved. . . . We must suppose that as long as we men survive we shall be moved by our aspirations and shall collide with one another in our movements, for this is the nature of life.

. . . This historic world is one of constant transformation in which civilizations, nations, empires, and principalities rise, flourish, and decay in ever-changing relationships of rivalry and association among one another. This is our environment, to which we belong. We are one nation-state among others, not exempt from the influence of change, the impact of competition, and the inroads of decay. Our virtue is uninsured and our survival without guarantee. We cannot say that by living as long as we have we have proved ourselves immortal. We cannot say that our demonstrations of past strength make us forever invincible. We cannot, in this world, claim a right to any degree of security that is not of our own constant making. It would be useless to complain that this environment of ours, with its demands, is improper and should change itself, that other nations and other civilizations should desist from challenging our position in the world or ought not to compete with us except on our own terms. Our foreign policy has to address itself to the world as it is.

2. NATIONALISM DEFENDED

The following excerpts are from Carlton J. H. Hayes's *Essays on Nationalism*.[12] Annotations on the author may be found in the chapter bibliography. Although Hayes's work presents both pro and con arguments, only those in defense of nationalism are quoted here.

According to most contemporary students of the subject, national consciousness is not only natural and instinctive but valuable and useful, and should

[12] From Carlton J. H. Hayes, *Essays on Nationalism* (New York, Macmillan, 1926), pp. 248–252. Reprinted by permission of the publisher.

be fostered rather than repressed. We shouldn't wish to get rid of it, even if we could. In the words of Mr. John Oakesmith, national patriotism "is not only explicable as national sentiment, but justifiable as a reasonable faith." The numerous champions of nationality and national consciousness advance two major arguments in support of their position; first, that nationality possesses great spiritual value in that it is a safeguard against materialistic cosmopolitanism; and, second, that nationality possesses high cultural value. The most eloquent and convincing exponent of the first point is undoubtedly Mr. Alfred Zimmern, and we may properly set forth this argument in his own words:

"Nationality, in fact, rightly regarded, is not a political but an educational conception. It is a safeguard of self-respect against the insidious onslaughts of materialistic cosmopolitanism. It is the sling in the hands of the weak underdeveloped peoples against the Goliath of material progress. . . . The vice of nationalism is jingoism, and there are always good Liberals amongst us ready to point a warning finger against its manifestations. The vice of internationalism is decadence and the complete eclipse of personality, ending in a type of character and social life which good Conservatives instinctively detest, but have seldom sufficient patience to describe. . . . English Readers can find . . . examples . . . of the spiritual degradation which befalls men who have pursued 'Progress' and cosmopolitanism and lost contact with their own national spiritual heritage. . . . No task is more urgent among backward and weaker peoples than the wise fostering of nationality and the maintenance of national traditions and corporate life as a school of character and self-respect."

"It is for this problem of the man without roots that nationality provides a solution. Nationality is the one social force capable of maintaining, for these people, their links with the past and keeping alive in them that spark of the higher life and that irreplaceable sentiment of self-respect. . . . Nationality is more than a creed or a doctrine or a code of conduct, it is an instinctive attachment; it recalls an atmosphere of precious memories, of vanished parents and friends, of old customs, of reverence, of home, and a sense of the brief span of human life as a link between immemorial generations, spreading backwards and forwards. 'Men may change their clothes, their politics, their wives, their religions, their philosophies,' says a Jewish-American writer, 'they cannot change their grandfathers. Jews or Poles or Anglo-Saxons, in order to cease being Jews or Poles or Anglo-Saxons, would have to cease to be.' "

. . . We have reason to distrust the person who loves man in general and despises individual men, who prates so much about his duties to humanity that he has no time to serve his next-door neighbor. Nationality may well be a sufficiently definite, limited field in which the individual can school himself in the exercise of those virtues which are directly serviceable to his immediate fellows, but which in the long run inure to the advantages of the race. Likewise it may well be . . . that nationality is a spiritual protection against material aggression, that more and more as time goes on it will inspire and enable socalled "backward" peoples to put an end to the economic exploitation from which they suffer, and will eventually save the whole world from being turned into a cockpit for capital and labour.

. . . We must . . . acknowledge that nationality has [also] been throughout the ages a great conserver of human differences in architecture, in literature, in the plastic and pictorial arts, in music, in dancing, in all aesthetic manifestations of man's civilisation, and also in modes of thought which enrich his being and in customs and manners which embellish his life. . . .

. . . I, for one, sympathise cordially with those who rebel at the prospect of a drab uniformity of manners, customs, and arts from New York to Singapore, and from Helsingfors to Valparaiso. I do not look forward with pleasure to seeing each mark of civilisation to which I am accustomed at home photographically reproduced in every town in France, Holland, Russia, Turkey . . . and Japan. . . . More than ever today, when the Industrial Revolution is devastating localism everywhere, and piling up the same sort of brick and steel girder in Asia and Africa as in Europe and America, when hotels the world over serve in the same way from *hors d'oeuvres* to coffee the same kind of dinner, when men universally array themselves in like ugly habiliments, at this very time it is a comfort that nationality still endures and still performs its delightful and wholesome function of encouraging at least minor differences in civilisation and culture.

In the light of the cultural and spiritual worth of nationality as well as in the light of its instinctive and universal character, it would seem not only utopian and idle but downright wrong-headed and mistaken to advocate a supersession of nationality by cosmopolitanism or imperialism. Some type of internationalism may be desirable and obtainable, but we shall be reasonable and practical if we accept the dictum of the friends of nationality and construct our internationalism of the future from the building blocks of existing nationalities and even of existing nationalisms.

3. AN ARAB DEFINITION OF NATIONALISM

Following is a definition offered by Michel Aflaq in an essay dated 1940, a time at which, thanks to World War II, the author's fellow Arabs in Lebanon and Syria were about to throw off French control and become politically fully independent.[13]

I fear that nationalism might fall, among us, to the level of mere intellectual knowledge and verbal discussion, and thus lose effective power and warmth of feeling. Often I hear students asking for a definition of the nationalism for which we call! Is it racialism founded on blood, or a spiritual quality drawn from history and a common culture, and does it banish religion or make a place for it?

It seems as though their belief in nationalism depends on the extent to which its definition is true and has power to convince, in spite of the fact that faith must precede knowledge and mocks at definitions, and that, indeed, it is faith that leads to knowledge and lights its way.

The nationalism for which we call is love before everything else. It is the very same feeling that binds the individual to his family, because the fatherland is only a large household, and the nation a large family. Nationalism, like every kind

[13] Michel Aflaq, "Nationalism and Revolution," in *Arab Nationalism: An Anthology*, ed. Sylvia G. Haim (Berkeley, University of California Press, 1962), pp. 242–243. Reprinted by permission of the publisher.

of love, fills the heart with joy and spreads hope in the soul; he who feels it would wish to share with all people this joy which raises him above narrow egoism, draws him nearer to goodness and perfection. Such a joy is therefore beyond human will and as far removed from hatred as possible, because he who feels its sanctity is led at the same time to venerate it in all people. It is, then, the best way to a true humanity. And as love is always found linked to sacrifice, so is nationalism. Sacrifice for the sake of nationalism leads to heroism, for he who sacrifices everything for his people, in defense of its past glory and future welfare, is more elevated in spirit and richer in his life than he who makes a sacrifice for the sake of one person.

He who loves does not seek reasons for his love. If asked to explain it, he cannot account for it clearly. He who cannot love except for some clear reason shows that love has either weakened or died within him.

How, then, can some young men allow themselves to require those incontrovertible arguments which would convince them that their love for their own Arab nationality ought to have the better of their love for the Russians, for example, or ought to be preferred to any partiality they may have for a particular sect or tribe or region? How can they allow themselves to ask whether the Arabs have virtues worthy of being loved? He who does not love his nation unless it is free from blemishes does not know real love. In my view, the only question which young men ought to ask themselves and their teachers is the following: Since we love our nation, with all its good and bad points, how can we transform this love into useful service, and in what manner?

Love, O young man, before everything. Love comes first and the definition follows. If love is the soil in which your nationalism is nourished, then there is no scope for different views on how it ought to be defined and delimited. Nationalism is racial in the sense that we hold sacred this Arab race which has, since the earliest historical epochs, carried within itself a vitality and a nobility which have enabled it to go on renewing and perfecting itself, taking advantage of triumphs and defeats alike. Nationalism is spiritual and all-embracing, in the sense that it opens its arms and spreads its wings over all those who have shared with the Arabs their history and have lived in the environment of their language and culture for generations, so that they have become Arab in thought and feeling. There is no fear that nationalism will clash with religion, for, like religion, it flows from the heart and issues from the will of God; they will walk arm in arm, supporting each other, especially when religion represents the genius of the nationality and is in harmony with its nature.

4. A GAULLIST DEFENSE OF FRENCH NATIONAL INDEPENDENCE

The following remarks were made by President Charles de Gaulle at a press conference held in Paris at the Elysée Palace on September 9, 1965.[14] To further clarify the context of the President's statement, it should be

[14] France, Ambassade de France, Service de Presse et d'Information, "President de Gaulle Holds Twelfth Press Conference," *Speeches and Press Conferences,* No. 228 (September 9, 1965), pp. 6–10.

noted that it was made in response to the question: "Mr. President, France's diplomacy is based on the principle of national independence. The opponents of this principle say that it is outdated. Can this policy of national independence be reconciled with the aspirations of the peoples for greater unity in Europe?"

We are in a century that has reached the two-thirds mark in its course. . . . However, since the turn of the century, the world has undergone changes unprecedented in their pace and scope. Everything leads one to think that the trend is going to continue. For a whole series of facts of far-reaching significance is in the making to reshape the world.

In this series of facts, there is: the accession to sovereignty of a large number of States that have been created or restored since the war and, simultaneously, the unfolding of their reciprocal quarrels; the preponderant power acquired by two countries, America and Russia, which induces them to compete with each other and to align under their respective hegemonies the peoples within their reach; the extremely profound gestation that is taking place in enormous China and that destines her for a leading role in the world; the existence and increase in nuclear weapons capable of destroying great nations suddenly and utterly; finally and above all, the general driving force for progress that the opportunities of the modern industrial age are opening up in each region of the earth. In short, the world, in full evolution, is filled both with almost infinite hopes and gigantic dangers.

Confronted with this situation, what can France's role be? But first, must France have a role? There is no lack of people . . . who think not. According to them, we—no longer being able to act by ourselves politically, economically, technically and militarily—should henceforth allow ourselves to be led by others. Moreover, the ideologies are there to cover up this renouncement. Thus some in our country, employing the screen of the International would like to submit us to Moscow's obedience. Others, invoking either arbitrary theories or the convenience of interests, profess that our country should efface its personality in international organizations made in such a way that the United States can exercise in them, from within or without, a preponderant action with which . . . we have only to conform. It is in this way that those people conceive of our participation in the United Nations or NATO and desire that we see ourselves dissolved in a federation called "European" which would actually be "Atlantic."

I do not think . . . that this sort of national abdication would be justified. I do not think that it would be useful to the others, even to Russia or America. I do not think that the French people, in its overwhelming majority, holds this as consistent with the awareness it has of its own worth, nor even with simple good sense. Doubtless, France no longer appears to be the gigantic nation that she was in the times of Louis XIV or of Napoleon I. Doubtless also, the brutal collapse of 1940—although it was preceded, during the First World War, by an admirable deployment of the capacities and merits of our country, and although it was followed, during the Second [World War], by the impetus of the Resistance, the success of the Liberation and the presence upon victory—this collapse left, in many minds, the imprint of doubt, if not of despair. Doubtless, the unsubstantiality of yesterday's regime had thwarted the national recovery. But this recovery is now evident, even impressive. We are a people that is rising, as are rising the curves of our population, our production, our foreign trade, our monetary reserves, our standard of living, the spread of our language and our culture, the might of our arms, our achievements in sports, and so on. Our government shows evidence of a stability and an effectiveness that, for so very long, had not been known to it. Lastly, throughout the world, France's capabilities, what she does, what she wants to do, are at this time arousing an attention and a consideration that sharply contrast with the indifference or the commiseration which, in the past, too often surrounded her. In short, we can, and consequently we must, have a policy of our own.

Which policy? Above all, it is a question of keeping ourselves free of any vassalage. It is true that, in many areas, we have the best reasons for associating with others. But on condition of retaining our self-determination. Thus, so long as the solidarity of the Western peoples appears to us necessary for the eventual defense of Europe, our country will remain the ally of her allies but, upon the expiration of the commitments formerly taken—that is, in 1969 by the latest—the subordination known as "integration" which is provided for by NATO and which hands our fate over to foreign authority shall cease, as far as we are concerned. Thus, while working to unite States on both sides of the Rhine and the Alps, from the economic, political, cultural and strategic viewpoints, we are making sure that this organization does not deprive us of our free will. Thus, believing it right for an international system to regulate monetary relations, we do not recognize that the currency of any particular State has any automatic and privileged value in relation to gold, which is, which remains and which must remain, under the circumstances, the only real standard. Thus, having been, with four other powers, the founders of the United Nations, and desiring that it continue to be the meeting place of the delegations of all peoples and the open forum for their debates, we do not accept being bound, be it in the financial area, by armed interventions which contradict the Charter and to which we have not given our approval.

Moreover, it is by being this way that we believe we can, in the final analysis, best serve the alliance of free peoples, the European Community, the monetary institutions and the United Nations.

Indeed, the independence thus regained is enabling France to become, despite the ideologies and hegemonies of the colossi, for all the racial passions and prejudices, above and beyond the rivalries and ambitions of nations, a champion of cooperation, failing which the troubles, the interventions, the conflicts that lead to world war would go on spreading. Now, France is, *par excellence*, qualified to act in this way. . . . She is so through the opinion that has historically been held of her and that opens to her a sort of latent credit when the universal is involved. She is so by the fact that she has freed herself of all the colonial holds she formerly exercised over other peoples. She is so, finally, because she appears to be a nation with free hands whose policy is not being determined by any pressure from without.

Moreover, we do not limit ourselves to extolling cooperation in principle.

We put it into practice everywhere we can under conditions that are naturally appropriate. . . . This is true for almost all the nations of Africa that were formerly linked to us, as well as for Rwanda and the Congo (Leopoldville) and, in Asia, for Cambodia and Laos—each of these States having become independent and having determined its relations with us through special agreements for its development, agreements among which the most recent, but not the least important, governs French-Algerian petroleum relations. Our goal is that this also be true for the various countries of Latin America. . . . We hope that this will be true . . . for the peoples of the Orient, from Istanbul to Addis Ababa and from Cairo to Kabul, in accordance with the human and natural reasons that have woven between them and us a traditional friendship.

. . .

Under very different conditions, but guided by the same inspiration, we believe that in Asia the end of the fighting now going on, then the satisfactory development of peoples, can be attained only by establishing relations, by opening negotiations and by achieving a *modus vivendi* among the powers whose direct and indirect responsibility has since the end of World War II been committed to the events of the southeast of that continent, that is, China, France, America, Russia and Britain.

. . . At present, [France] has nothing else to do but reserve herself for . . . the possibility of being useful, particularly in Peking, Washington, Moscow and London, with regard to the contacts which would be necessary to reach a solution. . . .

Moreover, the same entente of the same powers that have the means for war and peace is, for the historic period in which we are living, indispensable to the understanding and cooperation that the world must establish among all its races, all its forms of government and all its peoples, without which it will sooner or later head for its own destruction. It happens, actually, that the five States on which the destiny of Southeast Asia depends . . . and which, moreover, are those that possess atomic weapons, together founded twenty years ago the United Nations Organization and are the permanent members of its Security Council. They could tomorrow . . . see to it that this institution, instead of being the theatre of the vain rivalry of two hegemonies, becomes the framework in which the development of the whole world would be considered and in which the conscience of the human community would thereby grow stronger. It is obvious that at this time such a project has no chance of coming into being. But if . . . agreement of the leading nations responsible for the world should ever appear possible toward this end, France for her part would be quite prepared to cooperate in it.

This is, as a whole, the policy of our country. Assuredly the goals which it has set are long-range. This is due to the dimension of the problems which face the world of our times. But this is also due to the fact that France, no longer caught up in fruitless undertakings, nor dependent on what others do, nor induced to run at any moment in all directions behind passing fancies, is henceforth capable of pursuing extensive and continuous designs. This is what she is doing abroad, while working at home to build her new power.

SELECT BIBLIOGRAPHY

CARR, EDWARD H., *Nationalism and After* (New York, Macmillan, 1945). A British political scientist, professor at the University College of Wales and an authority on international affairs with a world-wide reputation, maintains that the importance of nationalism is declining and yielding to conflict over variant forms of supernationalism.

EMERSON, RUPERT, *From Empire to Nation: The Rise to Self-Assertion of Asian and African Peoples* (Cambridge, Mass.: Harvard University Press, 1960). A penetrating examination of the rise of Afro-Asian nationalism and its revolutionary influence 'upon the cultures of this part of the world. It concludes that nationalism among the non-Western peoples is inevitably a source of international trouble but also points out certain positive aspects.

HAYES, CARLTON J. H., *Essays on Nationalism* (New York, Macmillan, 1926). An American historian, formerly professor at Columbia University, one-time U.S. Ambassador to Spain, examines militant nationalism, its nature, rise, and inherent dangers for the mid-twentieth century.

———— *The Historical Evolution of Modern Nationalism* (New York, Richard R. Smith, 1931). Nationalism is here developed as a body of doctrines, a political philosophy, an "ism," with special emphasis upon the leaders of nationalist thought in the past 150 years.

KOHN, HANS, *The Idea of Nationalism* (New York, Macmillan, 1944). Chapter I is recommended for its definition and description of the character of nationalism. The author, Czech-born, grew up in the midst of one of Europe's most acute nationalistic dilemmas, the Austro-Hungarian Empire. He was a professor of history at the College of the City of New York and a well-known writer on nationalism.

———— *Nationalism, Its Meaning and History* (Princeton, Van Nostrand, 1955). In addition to an analysis of nationalism and its relation to other movements in the modern world, the book contains readings from over twenty writers, from Machiavelli to Nehru, on nationalism. Anvil Original ed., pocket size.

———— *The Twentieth Century* (New York, Macmillan, 1949). A bold attempt to comprehensively view the critical state of Western civilization particularly. Chapter II, "Nationalism and the Open Society," explores the unique problem of nationalism intensifying in a world with shrinking distances between peoples. Author concludes that unrepressed, rampant nationalism can only lead to tragedy.

SHAFER, BOYD C., *Nationalism: Myth and Reality* (New York, Harcourt, Brace & World, 1955). Portrayal of nationalism as an historical process, concluding that there is no basis, historical, biological, or psychological, for believing that nationalism will or must be permanent. Author, an historian, endorses internationalism as antidote to dangers of nationalism.

SULZBACH, WALTER, *National Consciousness* (Washington, American Council on

Public Affairs, 1943). A social economist sets out to disprove the thesis that rational economic considerations are the major impetus behind modern nationalism as a problem in human society.

WRIGHT, QUINCY, *A Study of War* (Chicago, University of Chicago Press, 1942), 2 vols. An imposing analysis by a former professor of international law at the University of Chicago. Vol. II, Chapter XXVIII, "Nationalism and War," emphasizes that nationalism weakens rational action, cultivates mass docility, and venerates militarism, thereby contributing to war.

5

Ideology and World Conflict

PEOPLE ARE BESET TODAY BY MANY demands and pressures for their loyalty. The nation-state, in the name of national interest and security, demands supreme loyalty and obedience from its citizens, reinforcing its demands with the emotional appeals of nationalism. Religious faiths or systems of moral idealism may also demand equally total commitments from their followers and believers. Sometimes the demands of the state conflict with the demands of religious and moral principles, thus creating profound dilemmas for those who are torn between loyalty to their state and loyalty to their religious or moral beliefs.

Ideologies are still another source from which come demands for deep commitment and loyalty on the part of their adherents. Today ideological conflict is deeply imbedded in world affairs and is a major source of tension. The exact extent to which ideologies influence or determine foreign policies and lead to international conflict is a matter of debate and will be frequently raised in subsequent sections of this book.

In many respects, ideologies may be described as secular religions. They claim to embody the "most effective" or "desirable" or "just" systems for organizing society, and in the supreme confidence or faith that their way of life is "best" for all men, they are frequently intolerant of one another. Like religion, they have their scriptures, creeds, rituals, and priests, and they seek the same type of dedicated followers. The conflict between nazism, fascism and democracy, so evident in the 1930's, and the continuing conflict between communism and democracy since the Bolshevik Revolution of 1917 are reminiscent of the religious wars of the past during the periods of the Crusades and the Protestant Reformation.

As systems for organizing society, ideologies represent different ways of looking at the world, of organizing and interpreting the apparently incoherent and jostling mass of historical facts. They are colored mental glasses through which different groups of people peer at world events. As was pointed out in Chapter 1,[1] looking at the same facts from two different vantage points, men will see different patterns of things. The difference is in the organization of the disjointed facts and in the conclusions

[1] See above, p. 15 ff.

151

drawn therefrom. And these differences are terribly important, more so at certain times than at others.

At the present time, one readily thinks of two major ideological systems competing for the loyalties of mankind—the Western democratic system and the Soviet communist system. Closer examination, however, quickly leads one to realize that the battle for men's minds is not so simply divided into two camps and that each of the two camps has significant divisions within it, some of which are sharply antagonistic to one another. Thus within the Western democratic system there are (1) the devotees of private enterprise economics where state regulation is more or less limited, as in the United States or West Germany; and (2) the advocates of various forms of democratic socialism where state ownership or management of important sections of the economy is attempted within the political framework of democratic institutions, free speech, and free elections. The philosophy of the British Labour Party or the government of India is illustrative of this second school of thought.

Similarly, within the communist ideological system there are rival and sometimes intensely hostile divisions, as, for example, between the Soviet, the Chinese, and the Yugoslav versions of communism.[2] Each of these is bidding strongly for the support of other members of the communist group of nations, as well as for that of the newly developing nations of Africa and Asia (see Chap. 7).

Four of these major contemporary ideological systems (Western democracy, Soviet communism, Chinese communism, and Indian democratic socialism) will be introduced in the pages that follow. In addition, there will be a treatment of fascism, a major ideological force in the 1930's and during World War II. Although the principal fascist states were defeated in World War II, the ideology of fascism has not completely disappeared and therefore needs to be understood.

THE WESTERN DEMOCRATIC SYSTEM

In this system are embraced the basic principles of Western political democracy, together with the economic principles of the maximum level of individual economic freedom consistent with the economic welfare of the entire community. By "Western political democracy" is meant the existence of institutions and attitudes which assure (1) the highest degree

[2] The term "communism" is used here in a very broad sense only for purposes of identification. None of these systems actually claims to be "communist" yet, but only to be in different stages of preparation for communism. This preparatory period is usually referred to as "socialism," and the group of states practicing it describe themselves as the "socialist group of nations." But this concept of "socialism" rests on the Marxist principle of the "dictatorship of the proletariat" and hence is fundamentally different from Western "democratic socialism" which recognizes civil liberties, free elections, and opposition parties. See also above, pp. 21–22.

of individual freedom consistent with public welfare, safety, and health; (2) civil liberties and protection of individuals and groups from the arbitrary use of government power; and (3) representative government broadly responsible to public opinion through free elections and the right of opposition parties to criticize the government in power and seek to replace it in a constitutional manner. These are the principles of the American and French revolutions, the political systems of Great Britain and most members of the British Commonwealth, the countries of Western Europe (except Spain and Portugal), and several others scattered throughout Latin America and other parts of the world.

While democracy may take different forms in various countries (e.g., the republican, presidential system of the United States or the constitutional monarchy-parliamentary systems of Great Britain and the Scandinavian countries), there are certain fundamental principles and practices which are found in all states included in the Western democratic system. These principles may be usefully set forth in a series of questions which can also serve as a gauge in determining the extent to which a country may be classified as belonging to the Western democratic system.[3]

1. Do most of the people really have an opportunity, by means of genuinely free elections, to select the men and policies that will govern the nation? In other words, is the government truly based on the consent of the governed?

2. Do the people enjoy the right freely to speak, write, publish, and assemble in order to criticize the government and leaders in power? Have they the right to turn them out peacefully at the ballot box?

3. Is there in existence at least one free, independent, strong, and functioning opposition political party or coalition ready, willing, and able to supplant the governing political party, if the people in a free election turn the government in power out of office?

4. Do the people enjoy the right to worship as their consciences dictate, to participate in religious life through a free church of their own choice, and to pay allegiance to a higher power than that of the secular state?

5. Are they protected against arbitrary and unreasonable action by government which would deprive them of their life, liberty, and property without due process of law? (Due process is here understood to forbid two kinds of governmental action: first, action such as the systematic destruction of a religious group, race, or class; second, "legal" action such

---

[3] Elton Atwater, William Butz, Kent Forster, and Neal Riemer, *World Affairs: Problems and Prospects* (New York, Appleton-Century-Crofts, 1958), pp. 266–267. These points are also discussed in Neal Riemer, *The Revival of Democratic Theory* (New York, Appleton-Century-Crofts, 1962), p. 103. Other aspects of the problem of developing political democracy in the newly independent states are treated in Neal Riemer, "Democratic Theory and the New States: the Dilemma of Transition," *Bucknell Review*, Vol. III, No. 1, March, 1965, pp. 1–16.

as a trial based on false evidence or coerced confession. The first action should be beyond the power of government. The second action is within the power of government but, so far as it is an improper trial, it is contrary to proper legal conduct.)

6. Is the role of the state limited to such necessary public functions as maintenance of internal peace and order, protection from foreign invasion, taxation, providing a stable and uniform currency? Or does the state invade, dominate, and absorb the private, voluntary cultural and social life of the community—our books, plays, radio and television programs, the clubs and organizations to which we belong?

7. If the state attempts to promote the economic and social welfare of its people through ownership or regulation of various segments of the economy, does it use its economic power to nullify political freedom and dominate other institutions such as the church, schools, press and radio?

Economically, most Western democracies, although frequently labeled "capitalistic," would be more accurately classified as "mixed economies" embodying elements of both "market-type" decision making and "command" decisions, with private enterprise more in evidence than publicly owned enterprise, and with a greater leaning towards "market" rather than "command" decisions.[4] "Laissez-faire" capitalism has long been a thing of the past, and government regulation (but not ownership) of wide areas of economic life is commonplace. This is done, however, within the framework of democratic political processes and free criticism of all public policy.

Many of the political principles of Western democracy—especially those relating to individual freedom—have world-wide appeal, although there are differences over how best to implement them. There is also deep resentment among many Africans and Asians over what they regard as the slowness of the Western European powers to grant independence to their colonial peoples. Indeed, the heritage of colonialism in Asia and Africa has been a great disadvantage to the Western democracies in seeking close and cordial relations with the new developing states of those continents.

The economic institutions of Western democracy—especially those associated with private enterprise capitalism—are frequently viewed with doubts and fears in the emerging countries. In a great many cases, the experience of these countries with capitalism has been in the form of colonial domination in which the people of the colonial territories were given little voice in the utilization of their natural resources or wealth, and in which a large share of the proceeds went to the foreign stock-

---

[4] The British Labour Party, although committed in principle to the idea of public ownership or control of the key sectors of the economy, has, when in power, not extended actual nationalization of industry beyond approximately 25 percent to 30 percent of the economy.

holders rather than to the improvement of the economic well-being of the colonial territories themselves. In their reaction to "colonial exploitation," as they frequently call it, many of the new states are insisting upon a wide degree of government control of industry, mining, and other sectors of economic activity to assure that national economic well-being will receive first priority and to prevent the continuation or repetition of "domination" by private capital (see Chap. 7). This in turn often discourages potential foreign investors, complicates the negotiation of foreign economic-aid agreements, and sometimes leads to foreign pressure on the developing countries to modify their economic policies and attitudes towards the regulation of capital investment. Tension results from this, and cries of "interference in domestic affairs," "aid with strings attached," and "neocolonialism" are frequently heard.

Moreover, the obvious difference between the well-developed economies of the United States or of Western Europe on the one hand, and the underdeveloped economies of the new states of Asia and Africa on the other, must raise real doubts in the minds of many Asian and African leaders as to whether Western economic models are practicable for them or even remotely attainable in the foreseeable future.[5] The Western industrialized economies have been in the process of development for about one hundred years and have reached levels of productivity which may seem far beyond the most optimistic hopes of the developing countries for the next two or three generations. If economic development along Western lines takes this long, perhaps other methods would be more rapid. It might well be politically suicidal for an Asian or African leader to take the position that a century, or even half a century, would be required before his country could realize significant gains in the "revolution of rising expectations."

It is precisely at this point that the potential appeal of the Soviet or Chinese economic models is most felt. As will be more fully shown in Chapter 7, the Soviet Union and Communist China are examples of countries starting within the past generation or two from economic levels not greatly different from the underdeveloped countries of today and achieving impressive economic growth in a relatively short period.

THE SOVIET SYSTEM

In sharp contrast to the Western democratic system, the Soviet system is based upon a highly centralized control of political, economic, and

---

[5] In 1962, the average annual per capita income in the economically advanced countries of North America and Western Europe averaged $2,845 and $1,033 respectively, while averaging only $136 in the underdeveloped areas. *The New York Times,* July 6, 1965, p. 9. See below, Chap. 6, p. 192.

social life.[6] Private ownership of capital has been replaced by state and collective ownership, and private property is restricted to those articles of consumption which a person or family chooses to buy, together with a limited supply of tools, equipment, or livestock with which individuals or families by their own efforts (i.e., with no hired labor) can produce their own food, household necessities, and possibly a small surplus which may be sold on the open market. The economy rests on a "command-type" of decision making, rather than on the "market-oriented" methods of Western democracies, and although Soviet leaders continually speak of their system as "democratic," it is obvious that "democracy" means something very different to them than to the peoples of the Western democracies.

To Soviet leaders, as to communist followers in general, Western democracy is the political shell of capitalism—the government structure through which the dominant capitalist class exercises its power and fends off encroachments on the institutions of private property and capital. The working classes, in the eyes of communist thinkers, do not in practice enjoy anything like equal political power to that enjoyed by the leaders of industry and finance. True democracy, in the communist view, is possible only when the class struggle has been ended, when economic classes have disappeared as a result of the substitution of public, socialized ownership of capital for private ownership,[7] and when an economy of abundance has been brought into being which will ultimately enable all men to satisfy their material needs in full. ("From each according to his ability, to each according to his need," as Marx put it.)

The first transitional stage in the development of this ultimate communist dream is the period of the "dictatorship of the proletariat"—the period of "socialism"—during which capital will be socialized and the productive capacity of the country increased by government planning, direction, and mobilization of all available resources. The state, which during the period of "capitalist hegemony" was the tool of capitalism, is now the tool of the working classes. Since the working classes (including the peasantry) constitute the overwhelming majority of the population, the "dictatorship of the proletariat" is, in communist theory, more "democratic" than the capitalist state could ever be.

---

[6] In recent years, some efforts have been made in the Soviet Union towards decentralization of administrative operations as the inefficiencies and complexities of an increasingly top-heavy bureaucracy in Moscow have become apparent. But there has been no significant decentralization in the processes of making basic decisions of public policy.

[7] Communists believe that classes have their origin in the economic structure of society, and particularly in the ownership and nonownership of the means of producing wealth (capital). The concept of the class struggle between the economically dominant and the economically dominated groups flows from this belief. A society in which capital is owned publicly by all members is, therefore, regarded as one in which there will be no classes. The elimination of the class struggle is viewed as one of the prerequisites for "genuine peace" and "democracy."

The idea of a state-directed, command-oriented economic system may have considerable appeal to the leaders of a new underdeveloped country who wish to show quick, dramatic signs of economic growth. The attractiveness of the Soviet or other communist models may be further reinforced by the repeated emphasis of communist leaders on the identification of imperialism with capitalism and on the theory that capitalism cannot survive the class struggle without resorting to imperial expansion and war.

Drawing on Lenin's famous theory of imperialism,[8] communist spokesmen contend that capitalist states, in their effort to preserve their economic system at home and to divert the attention of their people from the hardships of the class struggle, are driven to seek colonies abroad as sources of cheap raw materials and markets and as opportunities for profitable investment of surplus domestic capital. The resulting rivalry between capitalist states for profitable overseas territories leads sooner or later to imperialist wars. Imperialism also extends the class struggle, in communist eyes, on a world-wide scale in the form of the "exploitation" of colonial peoples. The latter, therefore, become the natural "allies" of the proletariats in the industrialized states, and the stage is set for the conversion of imperialist wars into international civil wars against the "world capitalist system." Thus, imperialism is viewed as "capitalism on its last legs," striving through colonial domination and war to prevent itself from being engulfed by the rising tide of world-wide proletarian-colonial revolution. "Imperialism," in Lenin's words, was "capitalism on the eve of proletarian revolution."

Despite the incomplete and distorted character of this communist version of imperialism,[9] it coincides closely enough with what many African and Asian peoples have experienced under Western control to make it seem to them reasonably plausible. To the extent that it is so regarded, and to the extent that the Afro-Asian states have never directly experienced Soviet control or domination, the Soviet Union has had an advantage over the Western democracies in the competition for men's minds in Asia and Africa. This advantage is further buttressed by the fact that the Soviet Union has consistently supported the Afro-Asian states in the United Nations in their efforts to oppose colonialism and speed up the processes of extending independence to all remaining non-self-governing

---

[8] See his *Imperialism: The Highest Stage of Capitalism,* written in 1916 to argue that World War I was an imperialist war on both sides.

[9] Most noncommunist observers would define "imperialism" as the extension of control (military, political, economic) by one state over another with the consequent loss of independence and sovereignty by the latter to the former. In this sense, imperialism is not unique to capitalism but can be observed throughout history in such widely differing systems as the Roman Empire of ancient times, the Mongol Empire of the thirteenth and fourteenth centuries, the nineteenth- and twentieth-century empires of the European states, the United States, and Japan which are now largely liquidated, the Soviet domination of Eastern Europe since 1945, and the Communist Chinese domination of Tibet since the early 1950's.

territories. The moderate or slow pace which the Western European powers have usually taken in this direction, on the other hand, has often been a source of embarrassment to the United States in its relations with the new states of Africa and Asia.

In the eyes of communist leaders, any advantages which they now have in appealing to the uncommitted nations simply confirm those elements of communist theory which hold that capitalism is inevitably going to collapse and that, first, socialism (the dictatorship of the proletariat) and eventually, communism, will triumph throughout the world. Their belief in the inevitable collapse of capitalism grows out of their assumption that historical evolution, as pointed out by Marx, proceeds in accordance with scientific and inexorable laws—that the conflict between economic classes is the most persistent and influential force in historical evolution, that it determines the characteristics of each historical period, and that this struggle is inevitable so long as means of production remain in the hands of a small segment of society rather than in the hands of society as a whole.

During previous historical epochs, the class struggle has taken such forms as the exploitation of slave classes by slave-owners or of serfs and peasants by feudal landlords. In more recent times, the power of the dominant feudal aristocracies was challenged by the growth of an urban commercial and industrial entrepreneur class which eventually culminated in the establishment of industrial capitalism as the dominant economic system. Today, according to communist theory, the capitalist classes are opposed by the industrial and rural proletariats, and the outcome of this struggle will be the replacement of capitalism by socialism and the transfer of power from the capitalist class to the proletariat.[10]

A unique and unprecedented development will now occur, according to communist theory, for by socializing the ownership of capital and transferring it from private hands to society as a whole, the basis of exploitation of one class by another will be removed. The class struggle will thus come to an end, a classless society will emerge, a vast upsurge of productivity determined by social need rather than private profit will become possible,[11] and the "communist millenium" will come into view. All this, in communist eyes, is not simply a matter of hope or desire, but a result of scientifically observable laws of historical development which are as

[10] The classic statement of the class struggle appears in the *Communist Manifesto*, written by Karl Marx and Friedrich Engels in 1848.

[11] Communist theory holds that an economy of abundance sufficient to meet all social needs will not be possible so long as private profit is the main motivation of the economic system. Since the maximum level of profit is likely to be greater under limited production, private enterprise will not produce at the level of abundance required to meet all possible social needs and consumption. For this, a socialized system of production is felt to be essential in which the criteria of social needs will be placed ahead of private profit.

inescapable as the laws of the physical universe.[12] Western democracy therefore finds itself in competition with a system which not only feels it has a better solution to man's ills but is also convinced that its ultimate triumph is determined by the "laws of history."

The triumph envisaged by communist theory is not simply a triumph in a single state or region of the world, but one which is eventually to encompass the entire world. Since capitalism and imperialism exist on a world-wide basis, the class struggle is also international in character and will, so argue the communists, culminate in the establishment of a world socialist system and eventually a world communist society. It is conceded, however, that this will come at different times in different countries because of the "uneven economic and political development" of different capitalist societies throughout the world.[13] Thus, it achieved its first success in Russia, which Lenin characterized as the "weakest link" in the system of world imperialism. After World War II, it gained power in the countries of Eastern Europe, North Korea, and China. In more recent times, it has triumphed in North Vietnam and Cuba and has been trying to make headway elsewhere in Asia, Africa, and Latin America (notably in South Vietnam, Indonesia, and the Republic of the Congo during the leadership of Patrice Lumumba).

In no case as yet, however, has a communist régime come to power except by violent revolution, civil war, or the presence of Soviet armies. Whatever ideological appeal it may have, communism has never up to now been able to win enough votes in any nation-wide free election to gain control of any national government.[14] Whether this will continue to be true in the future competition between democracy and communism is one of the burning questions of our time.[15] It has created deep divisions

[12] These are the central ideas of the communist theory of "dialectical and historical materialism."

[13] These words of Lenin, written in 1915, have been frequently cited by Soviet leaders to explain why there have been delays in the spread of communism throughout the world.

[14] In a number of countries, individual communist party candidates have been elected to national parliaments or other public offices, but their number has not been sufficient to permit the formation of a communist government at the national level. In France and Italy, for example, the Communist parties have normally polled 25 percent to 30 percent of the popular vote in all major elections since World War II.

[15] There is agreement among many specialists on Southeast Asia that Ho Chi Minh's communist-oriented movement would have won any free elections held in North and South Vietnam in 1956 as called for in the 1954 Geneva Agreements on Vietnam. See Dwight D. Eisenhower, *Mandate for Change: the White House Years, 1953–1956* (Garden City, New York, Doubleday, 1963), p. 372. This estimate also seems to have been shared by the governments of South Vietnam and the United States. The former, which had not been a party to the 1954 agreements and was therefore not legally bound by them, refused to arrange for such elections. The United States, which also had not signed the 1954 agreements, supported the South Vietnam Government in this position, and the elections were never held. This is one of the important factors contributing to the renewal of guerrilla fighting by the Vietcong later in the 1950's.

within the ranks of both democrats and communists as to the most effective strategies of action. Within the communist world, there is deep controversy over whether the proletariat can gain political power peacefully and lawfully or whether armed force, violent revolution, and war will be necessary. Within the democratic societies, the question is how far governments can go in the direction of socialized enterprise and government direction of economic life (i.e., the command-oriented type of economic system) without sacrificing the fundamental principles of democratic freedom.[16] Insofar as the competition of different political and economic systems among the new countries of Asia and Africa is concerned, the efforts and examples of Communist China and India bring out most clearly the divergent strategies of action.

THE CHINESE COMMUNIST SYSTEM

This system starts from many of the same Marxist-Leninist ideological principles as does the Soviet system, such as the theory of the class struggle, the theory of imperialism, and the belief in the inevitable collapse of capitalism and the triumph of socialism-communism on a worldwide scale. In operational terms, the Chinese system, like the Soviet, is based on the dictatorship of the proletariat, or "the people's democratic dictatorship" as Mao Tse-tung calls it,[17] and on a "command-oriented" economy. From 1949 to about 1957, the Chinese Communist leadership followed rather closely the Soviet model of economic development. But from 1958 on, as will be pointed out in more detail in Chapter 7, the Chinese broke sharply with their Soviet mentors and, through launching the so-called "Great Leap Forward," began to develop an approach of their own based on the overwhelmingly rural character of their population and on the total mobilization of rural labor for a dramatic assault on the poverty of their country.

Since 1958, the split between the Soviet Union and Communist China has grown to such proportions that scarcely a day passes in which the leaders of the two "proletarian" states do not refer to one another in the most abusive language. Apart from the differences in economic method between the two systems, there exists behind the Soviet-Chinese rift an acute struggle for power in the political, military, and ideological realms and a genuine competition for the leadership of the world communist movement. China with its population of over 700,000,000 was no great threat to the Soviet Union so long as China was economically weak and underdeveloped. But the picture will be quite different as China be-

[16] See Position 3 at the close of this chapter for a presentation of this view.

[17] Mao Tse-tung, "On the People's Democratic Dictatorship," written in 1949. Text may be found in Conrad Brandt, Benjamin Schwartz, and John K. Fairbank, *A Documentary History of Chinese Communism* (Cambridge, Harvard University Press, 1952), p. 449 ff.

comes economically stronger and acquires the full capabilities of a nuclear power.

As Communist China seeks to extend its influence in Asia, it has the advantage of speaking as a completely Asian power, claiming to be a better voice for communism in Asia than the Soviet Union which is primarily a Slavic power, rooted in European culture, with only a minority of its peoples of Asian stock. Marxism-Leninism in its original content appealed primarily to the urban proletariats of the industrial societies of Europe and North America. It sought support from the numerically larger rural peasantry in Russia only when this became tactically necessary to achieve power. Communist China, on the other hand, has placed much greater emphasis on adapting Marxism-Leninism to the conditions of the countryside and the needs of the peasantry. To the predominantly poor, rural populations of most Asian countries (as likewise to those in Africa and Latin America), Mao Tse-tung may well seem to be speaking out of a background much more like that of their own societies than even the leaders of the more industrialized and developed Soviet Union.

Furthermore, the Chinese Communists make a distinction between proletarian revolutions against capitalist-imperialist regimes, such as occurred in Russia, and revolutions in colonial and semicolonial countries like China. Whereas the classic type of revolution in imperialist countries is the Bolshevik Revolution of 1917, the classic type of revolution in colonial and semicolonial countries is the Chinese Revolution.[18] On such grounds as these, Mao Tse-tung regards himself as the most logical exponent and interpreter of Marxism-Leninism in Asia.

In addition, the effectiveness of the Chinese appeal may be enhanced by the fact that their leaders talk in very practical, down-to-earth terms. They use the language of the poor, the underprivileged, and the oppressed even more than do their Soviet counterparts. If the peasants have no tools, they are urged to use their hands—to turn their disabilities to their advantage, and to employ anything which is useful. Chinese leaders also seem to have been particularly successful in combining traditional, national elements in their culture with communist doctrine. Like Soviet leaders, the Chinese Communists have lost no opportunities to attack imperialism and colonialism, only they have done so in more extreme and bitter terms. Having successfully dislodged Western domination politically, militarily, and economically from mainland China, they offer their support to other Asian peoples who have not yet completely divested themselves of Western influence. "Wars of national liberation," as in Vietnam, are supported in this light.

Finally, they contend that armed struggle and violent revolution are

[18] These ideas are well expressed in "The World Significance of the Chinese United Democratic Front of China," an article by Lu Ting-yi, a member of the Central Committee of the Communist Party of China, written in 1951, and reprinted in Devere E. Pentony, *China, The Emerging Red Giant* (San Francisco, Chandler Publishing Company, 1962), pp. 11–15.

the most effective means of bringing socialism and communism to power and that Soviet leaders are guilty of treacherous "revisionism" in suggesting of late that the proletariat could gain effective control of society peacefully and lawfully. In this respect, Chinese Communist leaders are closer to the traditional position of Lenin, Stalin, and other Soviet leaders of the pre-Khrushchev era who argued that a thoroughgoing revolution could never be achieved peacefully, that the dominant capitalist classes would never yield power willingly, and that it was naive to think otherwise. Lenin and Stalin also felt that international wars were inevitable until capitalist imperialism was overthrown since war was the most tempting process by which capitalism might save itself.

The advent of thermonuclear weapons in the 1950's brought a significant modification by Khrushchev in the Leninist-Stalinist position that violent revolution and international wars were inevitable. Violent revolution might still be necessary in some countries where the resistance of the ruling capitalist classes was stubborn. But it was not inevitable, and in some countries (presumably the new ex-colonial ones), conditions might be sufficiently open to the working classes, rallying under the banners of nationalism, anticolonialism, and economic development, to gain legal majorities and establish socialism peacefully. Likewise, there would always be the danger of international war so long as imperialism still existed, but this did not make war inevitable. "Coexistence" between different economic and political systems was, in Khrushchev's view, a much more realistic position.[19] The Chinese disagree vigorously with the Soviet leaders in the emphasis which the latter place on the necessity and correctness of "coexistence."

While emphasizing their desire for "peace," the Chinese Communists hold that peace is possible only when imperialism and the class struggle have been ended and when the socialist-communist system has replaced capitalism. They argue, as did Lenin, that these ends cannot be accomplished by compromise or accommodation with capitalism, but only through genuine proletarian revolution. The imperialist powers, in their eyes, will never accept the "peaceful transformation" of capitalism into socialism, and the concepts of "peaceful competition" between socialist and communist countries are therefore misleading illusions which can only serve the interests of capitalist imperialism. To seek general disarmament, or the control of nuclear testing, for example, before achieving the overthrow of imperialism is to misread the course of historical development.[20]

---

[19] See Khrushchev's speech to the 20th Congress of the Communist Party of the Soviet Union, February, 1956. Text may be found in Position 1 at the close of Chapter 8, pp. 310–313 below.

[20] See the Letter of June 14, 1963, of the Central Committee of the Communist Party of China, *Peking Review*, June 21, 1963, pp. 6–22; also reprinted in full in *Current Digest of the Soviet Press*, August 7, 1963, pp. 3–15. Text may be found in Position 2 at the close of Chapter 8, pp. 313–317 below.

Thus, Soviet leaders who recognize that they would lose much in a major nuclear war have made significant modifications in their interpretation of Marxist-Leninism and today seem to be relying on more moderate methods of peaceful competition. The survival of their state has taken precedence over any doctrinaire application of their ideology. They do acknowledge that local wars and colonial "wars of national liberation" carry less risk of world-wide conflict but feel that the former should be avoided and the latter resorted to only with caution lest they escalate into major wars.

The Chinese, on the other hand, feel that the chances of a major world war are slight in view of the strengthened position of the socialist powers and the fear of nuclear war by the capitalist states themselves. They also feel that greater risks can be taken in supporting local revolutionary wars and wars of national liberation. To approach the latter as cautiously as do the Soviet leaders is, in Chinese eyes, to restrict the opportunities to bring about the downfall of capitalism and thus to water down traditional revolutionary Marxism-Leninism.

This more militant approach of the Chinese to world problems has alarmed many Asian-African leaders who are already apprehensive about the East-West power struggle and who feel that peaceful coexistence may offer some possibilities of averting violent conflict. Peking's refusal to sign the Nuclear Test Ban Treaty of August, 1963, and its determination to become a nuclear power have only intensified these apprehensions. To the extent that Communist China seems inclined to take greater risks with the peace of the world in pursuing its objectives, it is likely to forfeit some of the advantages it might otherwise have in appealing to the peoples of Asia and Africa.

THE SOCIAL DEMOCRATIC SYSTEM OF INDIA

The Indian system stands somewhat midway between the democratic systems of Western Europe and the United States and the communist systems of the Soviet Union and China. On the one hand, it is firmly committed to the political principles of individual freedom and civil liberty which characterize the Western democratic systems. Freedom of speech, assembly, and elections, along with the right of political opposition within the framework of constitutional order, are assured all citizens, both in theory and practice.

At the same time, India has accepted many of the principles and goals of economic socialism, although it has not yet progressed so far towards the establishment of socialized enterprise and central decision making as it apparently intends to go. Considerable portions of the economy still remain in private hands, while in the realm of economic decision making, there is a mixture of "market-type" and "command-oriented" methods. The Constitution of India, portions of which are quoted in Position 2 at the close of this chapter,[21] well illustrates the attempt to blend the goals of political democracy and economic socialism into "democratic socialism," in contrast to the "dictatorial socialism" of the Soviet Union.

India's experiment with democratic socialism is particularly significant because of its attempt to extend economic reforms in the realm of agriculture. In European countries such as Great Britain and the Scandinavian powers, where democratic socialist parties have held political power at various times, socialist principles have been applied mainly to certain segments of industry, transportation, and utilities, but not to agriculture. The communist states, on the other hand, have applied their doctrines to both industry and agriculture, though with considerable variation in form and extent in the different countries. China, as has been observed, has since the late 1950's endeavored to adapt Marxism-Leninism as much as possible to the conditions and needs of its rural population and, in this respect, may speak the language of the Asian peasants more effectively than the Soviet Union. But dictatorial methods have been employed by the communist states, and forced collectivization of land, together with state direction of major agricultural enterprises, have been typical patterns of communist policy.[22]

In democratic India, land reform has also been attempted, but on a much more moderate scale, without the instruments of state coercion seen in the communist countries. The essentials of the Indian agricultural reforms involve improvement of techniques without drastic alteration of the ownership of private property. There is interest in breaking up large estates, with compensation to the owners, but the major concern is with education of the mass of poor farmers in the direction of improved agricultural methods. They have been given better seed, aided in undertaking cooperative irrigation projects, and instructed in the advantages of crop diversification. Although this does involve extensive activity by the Indian state, it has encouraged Indians to improve their lot as individual entrepreneurs, not as members of giant collective farms.

Indian social democrats also have an industrial program, the details of which will be outlined in Chapter 7. Here, as with European democratic socialism, the role of the state looms large, but the similarity ends at this point. In Europe, social democrats faced the problem of establishing collective ownership over industries already established. In India, they face the very different problem of collectively creating new industries, and here the need for huge sums of capital is the major problem. While some foreign private capital may be attracted, India's sensitivity to

---

21 See below, pp. 180–183.

22 Collectivization aroused such hostility among the peasants of the East European states that much of it was subsequently dropped in order to mollify the peasants and secure greater agricultural output.

imperialism and her preference for state-owned or state-directed industry are barriers to large amounts of private investment. Therefore, much of the capital for Indian industrialization must come from India itself, and such capital can be secured only by the government. The crucial question is whether this capital can be raised in sufficient amounts by democratic methods of government, with general popular assent, or whether more coercive methods such as forced savings or reduction of consumer goods production will be needed.

In order to help the Indian government with its industrialization program, the United States government has extended it substantial amounts of economic aid. The World Bank and its affiliated agencies have also made extensive loans to India. These funds from abroad have had a crucial significance for India, for they have supplied capital which in all probability could never have been raised within India without drastic methods of government coercion comparable to those employed by the Soviet Union and China.

It is because India stands before other Asian countries as an example of a democratically motivated political and economic system that the outcome of its efforts is so important to the United States and to other countries in the Western democratic tradition. Indian democracy seems more likely to become a socialist or social welfare type democracy rather than one along the lines of most Western industrialized democratic states, and it is in this role that its appeal to other underdeveloped states of Asia and Africa is likely to be greatest. Although it has not achieved the more spectacular rates of economic growth that have been achieved by the stronger coercive methods of Communist China, the progress of India has not involved the heavy costs in terms of individual sacrifice and suffering inherent in the totalitarian system of China.

The rivalry between the Indian and the Chinese patterns of political and economic development is epitomized in the following statement by an Indian development officer engaged in a continent-wide program of agricultural reform: "My immediate fight is with poverty and apathy. My rivals are the Chinese—not the rich. We shall have failed, if we do not prove that we can accomplish more by democratic persuasion than the Communists by coercion." [23]

FASCISM

While democracy and communism in their various forms are the principal ideological rivals today, it should not be forgotten that fascism and democracy were the chief contenders a generation ago during the period leading up to World War II. Communism, then a weaker force

[23] Quoted in Jawaharlal Nehru, *Visit to America* (New York, John Day, 1950), p. 53.

in world affairs, and holding the reins of government in only one country, the Soviet Union, occupied an anomalous position between Western democracy and fascism. In principle, it was opposed to both, but in practice it shifted back and forth from time to time in its relationship to the two systems, depending on the dictates of political expediency and more particularly the requirements of Soviet national security.[24]

Fascism, in power in Germany, Italy, and Japan in the 1930's, was then challenging the Western democracies in a major struggle for world power, much as is communism today in the Soviet Union and China. Although the three major fascist states were defeated in World War II and obliged as a consequence to renounce their respective fascist institutions and principles, the ideology of fascism has not disappeared from the face of the earth.

Today, Spain and Portugal are the homes of regimes most accurately described as fascist, and Argentina in 1955 came to the end of a decade of fascist rule under Juan Perón. Fascist parties today survive on a small scale under new names in postwar Italy and Germany, and movements with pronounced fascist inclinations can be identified in many countries. Indeed, many of the extremely conservative, right-wing protest groups today exhibit fascist tendencies. Although overshadowed by the East-West ideological cleavage, fascism continues to attract adherents, and should conditions recur similar to those which gave it birth in the 1920's and 1930's, it might again become a major ideological force.

ORIGINS

Fascism's debut took place in Italy where, by 1922, the first fascist leader, Benito Mussolini, had become Prime Minister after his fascist squads had marched on Rome. Eleven years later the "Bavarian Mussolini," Adolf Hitler, headed a fascist regime in Germany.

Sympathizers with democracy have on occasion denounced fascism as simply communism under another name. It is true that certain characteristics have been common to both: a totalitarian ideology, dictatorship by a single party usually dominated by one man, a police state, and a centrally directed economy.[25]

[24] Thus in the mid-1930's, as Nazi Germany was becoming a formidable military power, the Soviet Union sought to strengthen the League of Nations and to reach agreement with the Western European democracies on the formation of a strong anti-Nazi coalition and a system of security guarantees for Eastern Europe. When these efforts came to naught in the wake of the Munich Pact of 1938, the Soviet Union turned to Nazi Germany and concluded a nonaggression pact plus a secret sphere-of-influence agreement covering Eastern Europe. Within less than two years, Stalin was thrown back into the arms of the Western democracies when Hitler attacked the Soviet Union in June, 1941.

[25] C. J. Friedrich and Z. K. Brzezinski, *Totalitarian Dictatorship and Autocracy* (Cambridge, Harvard University Press, 1956), pp. 9-10. Note the identification of both fascism and communism with the six characteristics of totalitarianism as defined by Friedrich and Brzezinski:

Both communism and fascism, then, are committed in practice to fostering the power of the state rather than the freedom of the individual. Communism and fascism, however, are not identical in their more precise ideology, appeal, or environmental history. For example, communism generally has been identified with societies that have known neither democracy nor extensive industrialization—Russia, China, Eastern Europe. Fascism, on the other hand, has been identified most often with technologically advanced, industrial-urban societies which, in addition, have had some experience with parliamentary democracy—Germany, Italy, Japan.

The identification suggests that the origins of fascism should be sought in a type of response to problems associated with industrialization and/or democratic government. Moreover, fascism's attraction proved much greater for some elements in society than for others.

The circumstances leading to fascism invariably included serious national economic maladjustments, with attendant personal insecurity for large numbers of people, combined with a growing lack of confidence in the ability of parliamentary government leadership to find a satisfactory solution to the economic crisis. Fascism was spawned in the post-1918 economic derangements, in the form of foreign trade difficulties, inflation, and unemployment. Conditions in Italy were acute immediately after World War I. In Portugal, Germany, Spain, and Japan the great depression of the 1930's brought severe distress. In Argentina, post-World War II inflation and foreign-trade contraction were factors. In each of these countries, democratic regimes of recent origin bore the brunt of

---

1. an official ideology, consisting of an official body of doctrine covering all vital aspects of man's existence to which everyone living in that society is supposed to adhere, at least passively; this ideology is characteristically focused and projected toward a perfect final state of mankind, that is to say, it contains a chiliastic claim, based upon a radical rejection of the existing society and conquest of the world for the new one;

2. a single mass party led typically by one man, the "dictator," and consisting of a relatively small percentage of the total population (up to 10 percent) of men and women, a hard core of them passionately and unquestioningly dedicated to the ideology and prepared to assist in every way in promoting its general acceptance, such a party being hierarchically, oligarchically organized, and typically either superior to, or completely intertwined with, the bureaucratic government organization;

3. a system of terroristic police control, supporting but also supervising the party for its leaders, and characteristically directed not only against demonstrable "enemies" of the regime, but against arbitrarily selected classes of the population; the terror of the secret police systematically exploiting modern science, and more especially scientific psychology;

4. a technologically conditioned near-complete monopoly of control, in the hands of the party and its subservient cadres, of all means of effective mass communication, such as the press, radio, motion pictures;

5. a similarly technologically conditioned near-complete monopoly of control (in the same hands) of all means of effective armed combat;

6. a central control and direction of the entire economy through the bureaucratic coordination of its formerly independent corporate entities, typically including most other associations and group activities.

the unrest. Italy's parliamentary government was the oldest, dating back to the nineteenth century, but it had not yet gained wide support and endorsement. Portugal had had a shaky parliamentary regime since 1910, Germany's Weimar Republic was established in 1919, Japan's twentieth-century democratic facade hid a feudal oligarchy, and Spain had escaped royal dictatorship in 1931. Like most Latin American states, Argentina had had only spasmodic experiments with democracy. Thus, experience with democratic institutions had been too brief for democratic roots to penetrate deeply, but long enough for democracy to be held responsible for economic distress and the ominous rumblings accompanying it. In these circumstances political upheaval could be anticipated, but the reason why the unrest acquired a fascist complexion must be sought in the reactions of the peoples and their leaders. After all, communism, too, showed increased strength in the same countries in these critical times and failed to achieve power.

Sociological analysis of the groups of people who supported fascism in these countries throws considerable light on the movements' origins. Although there were some people from all classes, the predominant social group represented the middle class—businessmen, property-owners, white-collar workers. A notable exception to this was Perón's enlistment of support among the urban proletariat, the *descamidos*. Generally speaking, however, fascism has been a middle-class movement. Large landowners and professional military officers also were profascist, whereas intellectuals and the laboring classes were not conspicuous in their support. As communists, socialists, and democrats, the workers were more often found in opposition to fascism, although there were important exceptions. Thus, in addition to economic distress, fascism depended upon the reaction of certain social strata to the situation.

Fascism, however, cannot be explained only in deterministic terms, for it also had a very wide appeal on psychological grounds. Claiming to produce the leaders who would lead the nation out of its troubles, fascism appeared as a panacea to distraught people. Not only did it promise to free the nation of its trials, but the only demand it made was obedience from most people in finding the escape. Those who craved leadership and reform found it a welcome relief.

If these were the circumstances in which fascism originated, what were the doctrines accompanying it and providing grounds for describing it as an ideology? The reply requires an approach to fascism from two points of view: as a defensive ideology, and as a dynamic, revolutionary ideology.

FASCISM AS A DEFENSIVE IDEOLOGY

Since fascism appeals primarily to social elements with something to lose rather than to gain, and therefore fundamentally conservative in orientation, it is not surprising to discover much in fascism that is defensive and negative.

Against Communism. The Russian Revolution of 1917, the open schism between communists and social democrats at the end of World War I, and abortive communist revolutions in Germany and Hungary in 1919 suddenly brought into clear relief the actuality and imminence of communism. Though a welcome development to many, it was terribly frightening to the middle and upper classes of European society. Democratic governments, which because of their nature permitted communist activity, appeared to many anticommunists to be too weak for successful resistance to communism. Some stronger anticommunist force was sought. Fascism provided an answer, for it took the stand that the bolshevist evil could be dealt with only as a malignant cancer is treated—with radical surgery.

Mussolini and the original *fasci* of Milan in 1919 battled in the streets with communist demonstrators, and every fascist movement since has taken a vigorous anticommunist stand. Indeed, fascism adopted the position that only two ideologic choices faced the world: communism and fascism. When evidence was not sufficiently convincing, fascists were not above dramatizing the communist threat by any means available. Hitler's Nazis pointed to the burning of the Reichstag building in Berlin as an example of communist arson. Francisco Franco, leader of the Spanish fascists, denounced the Republic of Spain as a communist regime which was preparing to liquidate private property and Christianity. That communists later played an important role in the Republic does not validate Franco's charges, but the accusations served their purpose of alerting propertied and clerical interests to support Franco. Anticommunism is not, of course, unique to fascism, although communists apply the word *fascist* to all their opponents. Nevertheless, opposition to communism is a cardinal precept of fascism.

Against Equality. Since all humans are not equal in strength, stamina, imagination, intelligence, and in other ways, it has been held in some cultures that equality in the political, social, and economic realms is an unsound ideal. Fascism strongly endorses this position. On the one hand, it designates as followers all those who are not capable of leadership. Although fascist doctrine readily admits that this element will be the majority, it takes the view that most humans are more content and satisfied when freed of the responsibility of making important decisions. Therefore, the majority should and will take orders. On the other hand, it proposes vesting authority over all matters in an "elite," those who will give the orders.

The crucial task is that of finding this authority-wielding elite. The initial elite, in both theory and practice, were those who exhibited the courage, leadership, and will-to-power in establishing fascist regimes.

Thus, Nazi Germany's elite were those who captured control of the German government in 1933 and proceeded to establish and operate the Nazi dictatorship. In Spain, it was Franco and his civil war supporters, organized in the Falange Española Tradicionalista (Spanish Traditional Phalanx), a group of army officers and political adventurers. The National Union Party of Antonio de Oliveira Salazar became Portugal's elite, and in Japan the Young Officers Association so viewed itself. It was the duty of the elite, in addition to its exercise of authority over all national matters, to train a second generation of leaders. For this purpose, fascist regimes organized youth indoctrination corps—the Hitler Jugend being perhaps the best known—from which would come recruits for the nation's future leadership. Such ideological training of youth is, of course, also a feature of communist practice.

Against Democracy. Not surprising, in view of fascism's rejection of the principle that all individuals have a right to share in the great decisions of a government, was its rejection of democracy. A system of government which, like democracy, accords equality to the ignorant and weak, as well as to the intelligent and strong, in fascist eyes was certain to lead to disastrous confusion and negativism. Italian fascists emphasized Italy's deplorable economic situation; the Nazis attacked the Weimar Republic as responsible for unemployment; Japanese parliamentarians were charged with failing to seek escape from Japan's economic dilemma in a dynamic East Asia "Co-Prosperity Sphere"; Salazar, Franco, Perón, all could point to the undeniable shortcomings of democracies, though they failed to point out that nondemocracies had equally serious problems.

In place of the democratic regimes which, in both concept and practice, were unacceptable to them, the fascists proposed to establish what they openly called totalitarianism. As Mussolini first explained:

Anti-individualistic, the Fascist conception of life stresses the importance of the State and accepts the individual only in so far as his interests coincide with those of the State, which stands for the conscience and the universal will of man as a historic entity. . . . And if liberty is to be the attribute of living men and not of abstract dummies invented by individualistic liberalism, then Fascism stands for liberty, and for the only liberty worth having, the liberty of the State. The Fascist conception of the State is all-embracing; outside of it no human or spiritual values can exist, much less have value. Thus understood, Fascism is totalitarian.[26]

The implementation of a policy to liquidate democratic institutions varied considerably in actual fascist experience. Within fifteen years Italian fascism had abolished parties, parliament, free press, and the right of association. In a much briefer time Nazism had "accomplished" more

[26] *Enciclopedia Italiana* (Milano, Treves-Treccani-Tumminelli, 1932), Vol. XIV, pp. 847–848.

—most notably in its denial of citizenship and frequently the right to property and life to German Jews. In Spain, curtailment of political parties, elections, a free press, public meetings, and safeguards against arbitrary imprisonment, exile, and execution testified to Falangist Spain's extirpation of democracy.

Against Internationalism. In this attitude will be recognized a corollary of totalitarianism. If the state is the focal point of civilization, allegiance to anything above or outside the nation-state is rejected. Not only was membership in the League of Nations scorned (Fascist Germany, Italy, and Japan left it demonstratively), but fascists also stood for a more vigorous defense of their nations' interests.

The fascist appeal to nationalism was particularly effective in Germany, saddled with the Treaty of Versailles, in Italy, denied some of its claims at the Paris Peace Conference (1919), and in Japan, the victim of racial discrimination in the immigration policies of the United States and the British Commonwealth.

Fascist emphasis upon the national group as removed from, and even antagonistic to, the rest of the international community fitted into the ideologic mosaic in other ways. It appealed to the natural prejudices and in-group feelings of its adherents. It afforded an outlet for external resentment generated by internal repression. Above all, it encouraged the growth of a doctrine of national superiority. In Germany, the Nazis went beyond Mussolini's reminder to the Italians that they were descended from the Romans. Germans were told that their superior capacity for great ventures and conquests was biologically ordained.

Nationalism is, of course, no monopoly of the fascists, but they, perhaps more effectively than supporters of other ideologies, incorporated it in their doctrinal appeal.

Against Pacifism. In view of the doctrines already discussed, it is understandable that strong antipacifism would characterize the movement. Fascism was born in a turbulent, critical, disjointed atmosphere. Concentrating on the emotional side of man, it deliberately encouraged the perpetuation of the restless, agitated mood in which it had its origin.

The vocabulary of fascism early acquired words and slogans suggesting this antipacifism. *Struggle, conflict, war, battle,* and *survival* remind men that life is not a tea party and that preparation for violence is conducive to survival. Hitler called his autobiography not "My Life" but "My Battle" (*Mein Kampf*). Mussolini called upon Italians to recognize that it was "Better to live an hour as a lion, than one hundred years as a lamb." The fascist ideal has been the warrior, the man of action, the Nietzschean superman. Certainly, the violent means employed by fascists to seize and maintain power did not contradict in deed what it taught as a theory—the pacific are trampled underfoot.

The foregoing attitudes do not afford a total picture of the fascist ideology. They do serve to emphasize its response to the fears and in-security of the middle and upper classes, of people who had something to lose—wealth, social status, political power—and dreaded the loss amid the confusion and unrest of the times. Fascism has not, however, been exclusively negative or defensive. It also proclaimed itself the pioneer of a new era, a great revolution.

FASCISM AS A PERMANENT REVOLUTION

It has been said that, in its emotional and conflicting appeals, fascism is peculiarly suited to the frustrations encountered by modern man as he gropes for adjustment to the present dynamic age. It can even be as-serted that fascism has had its greatest popularity where it has been most irrational and emotionally disturbing. Salazar and Franco, compelled to compromise with older, vested interests (Church, landowners, army, big business), have fallen considerably short of the fascist totalitarian ideal approximated by the fanatic Hitler in Germany. Nonetheless, fascist regimes everywhere have been characterized by a much-heralded revolu-tionary program.

Italian "corporativism" and German four-year plans, along with their smaller editions elsewhere, set out to solve economic problems in the interest of the whole nation by state planning and elimination of in-dustrial strife. Yet, whereas both socialists and communists have en-dorsed state ownership of private property in their programs of economic reorganization, fascism did not officially reject the institution of private property. Through extensive government control, however, it effectively subordinated the entire economy to the interests of the state. Extension of social services also marked the fascist practice, its distinguishing feature being their denial to those the state designated as "unworthy": Jews in Germany, liberals in Argentina, anarchists in Spain.

Having found mass emotionalism conducive to its rise, fascism tended to continue stoking the fires of antagonism and aggression. Franco's assaults on communists, republicans, and anarchists, and Perón's attack upon the Roman Catholic Church were feeble echoes of the Nazi efforts to deepen religious and racial antagonisms. The brutali-ties of the Nazis and the fanaticism of the Japanese suicide pilots in World War II reveal the extremes to which fascism's constant emotional stimulation sometimes led. But such emotional engineering served to harness much of the restless energy of the masses to the purposes of the elite.

Finally, fascists proclaimed the great future of their specific nation-state. Italy could anticipate, according to her elite, domination of the Mediterranean. Germany was encouraged to prepare for the acquisition of *Lebensraum*. A great empire in Asia was the expectancy cultivated among the Japanese. Even Franco hoped that from the murky waters of international tensions Spain might gain Gibraltar and French Morocco. Perón was obliged to confine his goals to the more nebulous "high destiny which God has seen fit to assign our country." He added, "the day cannot be far off when all humanity . . . will fix its eyes on the flag of the Argentines." [27] In a word, fascism has been dynamic and aggressive in the kind of foreign policy it preferred. Circumstances have not always permitted pursuit of such a policy, as in Spain and Portugal, but fascism manifested an affinity for it.

THE CORE OF FASCISM

Recognizing man as irrational and emotional, fascism made little pretense of being a rational, logical ideology. It openly reveled in expediency and opportunism and focused more on means than on ends. Accordingly, a summary of its concepts is difficult.

If one ideal stands out, it has been the frank glorification of the state as the undying representative of a nation. It even went so far as to endow that state with mystical biological characteristics. Human beings are cells of very limited life which of themselves are unimportant, but coordinated in the body politic of the fascist society, they become part of something meaningful and immortal. Here, then, is a new meaning to life and an escape from the crass, shallow, frustrating materialism that both communism and democracy foster. These were the pronouncements made by fascists when they had time to interrupt their careers of action and pontificate upon philosophy.

Fascism's critics have charged that it was a patchwork of double talk serving as a cloak for political gangsterism. Reduced to its bare essentials, say its enemies, it sought only augmentation of the power of the state. But power for power's sake represents no scale of values, no goals, no awareness of ends, no meaningful pattern of human existence. Man does not live by bread alone, but he also does not live by power alone. Fascism, therefore, has been described by both communists and democrats as essentially nihilistic, an ideology without a core.

Whether or not there is a central matrix of ideas in fascism, it becomes an academic question when it is realized that some of the world's largest nation-states have had fascist regimes within the last generation and that an appreciable number of people have lived under, and profess to believe in, fascist doctrine in the years since the defeat of the Axis powers in World War II. In this sense, fascism remains an ideological force which cannot be discounted in the struggle for the minds of men. The future of the fascist states today cannot, of course, be foretold. It is not unlikely, for instance, that with the disappearance of Franco, Spain may once again become an ideological battlefield. Its aged fascism seems

[27] Quoted in George I. Blanksten, *Perón's Argentina* (Chicago, The University of Chicago Press, copyright, 1953 by The University of Chicago), p. 293.

no longer to fit the intellectual temper of the new generations of Spaniards, nor does it have the necessary flexibility to accommodate the economic expansion which it has launched in the last few years. Beneath a deceptively smooth and calm surface, there is a ferment of ideas which may one day seek expression in novel forms of political, social, and economic organization.

In the next part of this chapter, four of the ideological viewpoints discussed in the preceding pages will be presented: (1) Chinese Communism; (2) Indian Democratic Socialism; (3) a "free-enterprise" criticism of democratic socialism; and (4) Italian Fascism. A careful evaluation and comparison of these positions will lead to a deeper appreciation of the role of ideology in world affairs today. A more detailed analysis of the economic institutions and programs of the Soviet, Chinese Communist, and Indian systems will be presented later in Chapter 7.

POSITIONS

1. A CHINESE COMMUNIST INTERPRETATION OF THE CONTEMPORARY IDEOLOGICAL WAR

In no country today does ideological commitment appear to be more intense and fanatical than in turbulent, changing China. In the following passage Lin Piao, Vice-Chairman of the Central Committee of the Chinese Communist Party and Vice-Premier and Minister of National Defense in the Peking Government, vigorously sets forth the official outlook of his party and government. Lin Piao in 1966 emerged as one of the top-ranking Chinese leaders next to Mao Tse-tung.[28]

THE INTERNATIONAL SIGNIFICANCE OF COMRADE MAO TSE-TUNG'S THEORY OF PEOPLE'S WAR

The Chinese revolution is a continuation of the Great October Revolution.[29] The road of the October Revolution is the common road for all people's revolutions. The Chinese revolution and the October Revolution have in common the following basic characteristics: (1) Both were led by the working class with a Marxist-Leninist party as its nucleus. (2) Both were based on the worker-peasant alliance. (3) In both cases state power was seized through violent revolution and the dictatorship of the proletariat was established. (4) In both cases the socialist system was built after victory in the revolution. (5) Both were component parts of the proletarian world revolution.

[28] Lin Piao, "Long Live the Victory of People's War," *The Peking Review*, September 3, 1965 (No. 36), p. 9 ff., at pp. 22–25.
[29] The Bolshevik Revolution in Russia in 1917. (ed.)

Naturally, the Chinese revolution had its own peculiar characteristics. The October Revolution took place in imperialist Russia, but the Chinese revolution broke out in a semi-colonial and semi-feudal country. The former was a proletarian socialist revolution, while the latter developed into a socialist revolution after the complete victory of the new-democratic revolution. The October Revolution began with armed uprisings in the cities and then spread to the countryside, while the Chinese revolution won nation-wide victory through the encirclement of the cities from the rural areas and the final capture of the cities.

Comrade Mao Tse-tung's great merit lies in the fact that he has succeeded in integrating the universal truth of Marxism-Leninism with the concrete practice of the Chinese revolution and has enriched and developed Marxism-Leninism by his masterly generalization and summation of the experience gained during the Chinese people's protracted revolutionary struggle.

Comrade Mao Tse-tung's theory of people's war has been proved by the long practice of the Chinese revolution to be in accord with the objective laws of such wars and to be invincible. It has not only been valid for China, it is a great contribution to the revolutionary struggles of the oppressed nations and peoples throughout the world.

The people's war led by the Chinese Communist Party, comprising the War of Resistance and the Revolutionary Civil Wars, lasted for twenty-two years.[30] It constitutes the most drawn-out and most complex people's war led by the proletariat in modern history, and it has been the richest in experience.

In the last analysis, the Marxist-Leninist theory of proletarian revolution is the theory of the seizure of state power by revolutionary violence, the theory of countering war against the people by people's war. As Marx so aptly put it, "Force is the midwife of every old society pregnant with a new one." [31]

It was on the basis of the lessons derived from the people's wars in China that Comrade Mao Tse-tung, using the simplest and the most vivid language, advanced the famous thesis that "political power grows out of the barrel of a gun." [32]

He clearly pointed out: "The seizure of power by armed force, the settlement of the issue by war, is the central task and the highest form of revolution. This Marxist-Leninist principle of revolution holds good universally, for China and for all other countries."

War is the product of imperialism and the system of exploitation of man by man. Lenin said that "war is always everywhere begun by the exploiters themselves, by the ruling and oppressing classes." So long as imperialism and the system of exploitation of man by man exist, the imperialists and reactionaries will invariably rely on armed force to maintain their reactionary rule and impose war on the oppressed nations and peoples. This is an objective law independent of man's will.

In the world today, all the imperialists headed by the United States and

[30] This refers to the period from 1927, when Chiang Kai-shek broke with the Chinese Communists, to 1949 when the Communists won control of mainland China. (ed.)

[31] Karl Marx, *Capital* (Moscow, Foreign Languages Publishing House, 1954), Vol. I, p. 751.

[32] Mao Tse-tung, "Problems of War and Strategy," in *Selected Works of Mao Tsetung* (London, Lawrence and Wishart Ltd., 1954), Vol. II, p. 272.

their lackeys, without exception, are strengthening their state machinery, and especially their armed forces. U.S. imperialism, in particular, is carrying out armed aggression and suppression everywhere.

What should the oppressed nations and the oppressed people do in the face of wars of aggression and armed suppression by the imperialists and their lackeys? Should they submit and remain slaves in perpetuity? Or should they rise in resistance and fight for their liberation?

Comrade Mao Tse-tung answered this question in vivid terms. He said that after long investigation and study the Chinese people discovered that all the imperialists and their lackeys "have swords in their hands and are out to kill. The people have come to understand this and so act after the same fashion." This is called doing unto them what they do unto us.

In the last analysis, whether one dares to wage a tit-for-tat struggle against armed aggression and suppression by the imperialists and their lackeys, whether one dares to fight a people's war against them, is tantamount to whether one dares to embark on revolution. This is the most effective touchstone for distinguishing genuine from fake revolutionaries and Marxist-Leninists.

In view of the fact that some people were afflicted with the fear of the imperialists and reactionaries, Comrade Mao Tse-tung put forward his famous thesis that "the imperialists and all reactionaries are paper tigers." He said: "All reactionaries are paper tigers. In appearance, the reactionaries are terrifying, but in reality they are not so powerful. From a long-term point of view, it is not the reactionaries but the people who are really powerful."

The history of people's war in China and other countries provides conclusive evidence that the growth of the people's revolutionary forces from weak and small beginnings into strong and large forces is a universal law of development of class struggle, a universal law of development of people's war. A people's war inevitably meets with many difficulties, with ups and downs and setbacks in the course of its development, but no force can alter its general trend towards inevitable triumph.

Comrade Mao Tse-tung points out that we must despise the enemy strategically and take full account of him tactically.

To despise the enemy strategically is an elementary requirement for a revolutionary. Without the courage to despise the enemy and without daring to win, it will be simply impossible to make revolution and wage a people's war, let alone to achieve victory.

It is also very important for revolutionaries to take full account of the enemy tactically. It is likewise impossible to win victory in a people's war without taking full account of the enemy tactically, and without examining the concrete conditions, without being prudent and giving great attention to the study of the art of struggle, and without adopting appropriate forms of struggle in the concrete practice of the revolution in each country and with regard to each concrete problem of struggle.

Dialectical and historical materialism teaches us that what is important primarily is not that which at the given moment seems to be durable and yet is already beginning to die away, but that which is arising and developing, even though at the given moment it may not appear to be durable, for only that which is arising and developing is invincible.

Why can the apparently weak new-born forces always triumph over the decadent forces which appear so powerful? The reason is that truth is on their side and that the masses are on their side, while the reactionary classes are always divorced from the masses and set themselves against the masses.

This has been borne out by the victory of the Chinese revolution, by the history of all revolutions, the whole history of class struggle and the entire history of mankind.

The imperialists are extremely afraid of Comrade Mao Tse-tung's thesis that "imperialism and all reactionaries are paper tigers," and the revisionists [33] are extremely hostile to it. They all oppose and attack this thesis and the philistines follow suit by ridiculing it. But all this cannot in the least diminish its importance. The light of truth cannot be dimmed by anybody.

Comrade Mao Tse-tung's theory of people's war solves not only the problem of daring to fight a people's war, but also that of how to wage it.

Comrade Mao Tse-tung is a great statesman and military scientist, proficient at directing war in accordance with its laws. By the line and policies, strategy and tactics he formulated for the people's war, he led the Chinese people in steering the ship of the people's war past all hidden reefs to the shores of victory in most complicated and difficult conditions.

It must be emphasized that Comrade Mao Tse-tung's theory of the establishment of rural revolutionary base areas and the encirclement of the cities from the countryside is of outstanding and universal practical importance for the present revolutionary struggles of all the oppressed nations and peoples, and particularly for the revolutionary struggles of the oppressed nations and peoples in Asia, Africa and Latin America against imperialism and its lackeys.

Many countries and peoples in Asia, Africa and Latin America are now being subjected to aggression and enslavement on a serious scale by the imperialists headed by the United States and their lackeys. The basic political and economic conditions in many of these countries have many similarities to those that prevailed in old China. As in China, the peasant question is extremely important in these regions. The peasants constitute the main force of the national-democratic revolution against the imperialists and their lackeys. In committing aggression against these countries, the imperialists usually begin by seizing the big cities and the main lines of communication, but they are unable to bring the vast countryside completely under their control. The countryside, and the countryside alone, can provide the broad areas in which the revolutionaries can manoeuvre freely. The countryside, and the countryside alone, can provide the revolutionary bases from which the revolutionaries can go forward to final victory. Precisely for this reason, Comrade Mao Tse-tung's theory of establishing revolutionary base areas in the rural districts and encircling the cities from the countryside is attracting more and more attention among the people in these regions.

Taking the entire globe, if North America and Western Europe can be called "the cities of the world," then Asia, Africa and Latin America constitute "the rural areas of the world." Since World War II, the proletarian revolutionary movement has for various reasons been temporarily held back in the North

[33] When Chinese Communist spokesmen speak of "revisionists," they usually have the Soviet leaders and their allies in mind. (ed.)

American and West European capitalist countries, while the people's revolutionary movement in Asia, Africa and Latin America has been growing vigorously. In a sense, the contemporary world revolution also presents a picture of the encirclement of cities by the rural areas. In the final analysis, the whole cause of world revolution hinges on the revolutionary struggles of the Asian, African and Latin American peoples who make up the overwhelming majority of the world's population. The socialist countries should regard it as their internationalist duty to support the people's revolutionary struggles in Asia, Africa and Latin America.

The October Revolution opened up a new era in the revolution of the oppressed nations. The victory of the October Revolution built a bridge between the socialist revolution of the proletariat of the West and the national-democratic revolution of the colonial and semi-colonial countries of the East.[34] The Chinese revolution has successfully solved the problem of how to link up the national-democratic with the socialist revolution in the colonial and semi-colonial countries.

Comrade Mao Tse-tung has pointed out that, in the epoch since the October Revolution, anti-imperialist revolution in any colonial or semi-colonial country is no longer part of the old bourgeois, or capitalist world revolution, but is part of the new world revolution, the proletarian-socialist world revolution.

Comrade Mao Tse-tung has formulated a complete theory of the new-democratic revolution. He indicated that this revolution, which is different from all others, can only be, nay must be, a revolution against imperialism, feudalism and bureaucrat-capitalism waged by the broad masses of the people under the leadership of the proletariat.

This means that the revolution can only be, nay must be, led by the proletariat and the genuinely revolutionary party armed with Marxism-Leninism, and by no other class or party.

This means that the revolution embraces in its ranks not only the workers, peasants and the urban petty bourgeoisie, but also the national bourgeoisie and other patriotic and anti-imperialist democrats.

This means, finally, that the revolution is directed against imperialism, feudalism and bureaucrat-capitalism.

The new-democratic revolution leads to socialism, and not to capitalism.

Comrade Mao Tse-tung's theory of the new-democratic revolution is the Marxist-Leninist theory of revolution by stages as well as the Marxist-Leninist theory of uninterrupted revolution.

Comrade Mao Tse-tung made a correct distinction between the two revolutionary stages, *i.e.,* the national-democratic and the socialist revolutions; at the same time he correctly and closely linked the two. The national-democratic revolution is the necessary preparation for the socialist revolution, and the socialist revolution is the inevitable sequel to the national-democratic revolution. There is no Great Wall between the two revolutionary stages. But the socialist revolution is only possible after the completion of the national-democratic revolution.

---

[34] The term "national-democratic revolution" refers to the struggle for national independence and freedom from foreign imperialist rule. (ed.)

The more thorough the national-democratic revolution, the better the conditions for the socialist revolution.

The experience of the Chinese revolution shows that the tasks of the national-democratic revolution can be fulfilled only through long and tortuous struggles. In this stage of revolution, imperialism and its lackeys are the principal enemy. In the struggle against imperialism and its lackeys, it is necessary to rally all anti-imperialist patriotic forces, including the national bourgeoisie and all patriotic personages. All those patriotic personages from among the bourgeoisie and other exploiting classes who join the anti-imperialist struggle play a progressive historical role; they are not tolerated by imperialism but welcomed by the proletariat.

It is very harmful to confuse the two stages, that is, the national-democratic and the socialist revolutions. Comrade Mao Tse-tung criticized the wrong idea of "accomplishing both at one stroke," and pointed out that this utopian idea could only weaken the struggle against imperialism and its lackeys, the most urgent task at that time. The Kuomintang reactionaries and the Trotskyites they hired during the War of Resistance deliberately confused these two stages of the Chinese revolution, proclaiming the "theory of a single revolution" and preaching so-called "socialism" without any Communist Party. With this preposterous theory they attempted to swallow up the Communist Party, wipe out any revolution and prevent the advance of the national-democratic revolution, and they used it as a pretext for their non-resistance and capitulation to imperialism. This reactionary theory was buried long ago by the history of the Chinese revolution.

The Khrushchov revisionists are now actively preaching that socialism can be built without the proletariat and without a genuinely revolutionary party armed with the advanced proletarian ideology, and they have cast the fundamental tenets of Marxism-Leninism to the four winds. The revisionists' purpose is solely to divert the oppressed nations from their struggle against imperialism and sabotage their national-democratic revolution, all in the service of imperialism.

The Chinese revolution provides a successful lesson for making a thoroughgoing national-democratic revolution under the leadership of the proletariat; it likewise provides a successful lesson for the timely transition from the national-democratic revolution to the socialist revolution under the leadership of the proletariat.

Mao Tse-tung's thought has been the guide to the victory of the Chinese revolution. It has integrated the universal truth of Marxism-Leninism with the concrete practice of the Chinese revolution and creatively developed Marxism-Leninism, thus adding new weapons to the arsenal of Marxism-Leninism.

Ours is the epoch in which world capitalism and imperialism are heading for their doom and socialism and communism are marching to victory. Comrade Mao Tse-tung's theory of people's war is not only a product of the Chinese revolution, but has also the characteristics of our epoch. The new experience gained in the people's revolutionary struggles in various countries since World War II has provided continuous evidence that Mao Tse-tung's thought is a common asset of the revolutionary people of the whole world. This is the great international significance of the thought of Mao Tse-tung.

2. AN INDIAN INTERPRETATION OF DEMOCRATIC SOCIALISM

The following selections from the Constitution of India (1949) reflect the confluence of democracy and socialism. The provisions through Article 31 generally reflect Western ideals of individual political, civil, and economic liberties. The provisions from Article 38 on generally reflect socialist principles that the state assume an extensive and positive role in the economy of the country.[35]

Part III

FUNDAMENTAL RIGHTS

. . .

Right of Equality

14. The State shall not deny to any person equality before the law or the equal protection of the laws within the territory of India.

15. (1) The State shall not discriminate against any citizen on grounds only of religion, race, caste, sex, place of birth or any of them.

(2) No citizen shall, on grounds only of religion, race, caste, sex, place of birth or any of them, be subject to any disability, liability, restriction or condition with regard to—

(a) access to shops, public restaurants, hotels and places of public entertainment; or

(b) the use of wells, tanks, bathing *ghats,* roads and places of public resort maintained wholly or partly out of State funds or dedicated to the use of the general public.

. . .

16. (1) There shall be equality of opportunity for all citizens in matters relating to employment or appointment to any office under the State.

. . .

17. "Untouchability" is abolished and its practice in any form is forbidden. . . .

18. (1) No title, not being a military or academic distinction, shall be conferred by the State.

(2) No citizen of India shall accept any title from any foreign State.

. . .

(4) No person holding any office or profit or trust under the State shall, without the consent of the President, accept any present, emolument or office of any kind from or under any foreign State.

Right to Freedom

19. (1) All citizens shall have the right

(a) to freedom of speech and expression;

[35] *British and Foreign State Papers,* 1950, Part II (London, Her Majesty's Stationery Office, 1959), pp. 37–43, 46–47.

      (b) to assemble peaceably and without arms;

      (c) to form associations or unions;

      (d) to move freely throughout the territory of India;

      (e) to reside and settle in any part of the territory of India;

      (f) to acquire, hold and dispose of property; and

      (g) to practise any profession, or carry on any occupation, trade or business.

. . .

20. (1) No person shall be convicted of any offence except for violation of a law in force at the time of the commission of the act charged as an offence, nor be subjected to a penalty greater than that which might have been inflicted under the law in force at the time of the commission of the offence.

(2) No person shall be prosecuted and punished for the same offence more than once.

(3) No person accused of any offence shall be compelled to be a witness against himself.

21. No person shall be deprived of his life or personal liberty except according to procedure established by law.

22. (1) No person who is arrested shall be detained in custody without being informed, as soon as may be, of the grounds for such arrest nor shall he be denied the right to consult, and to be defended by, a legal practitioner of his choice.

(2) Every person who is arrested and detained in custody shall be produced before the nearest magistrate within a period of twenty-four hours of such arrest. . . .

Right against Exploitation

23. (1) Traffic in human beings . . . and other similar forms of forced labour are prohibited and any contravention of this provision shall be an offence punishable in accordance with law.

(2) Nothing in this Article shall prevent the State from imposing compulsory service for public purposes, and in imposing such service the State shall not make any discrimination on grounds of religion, race, caste or class or any of them.

24. No child below the age of fourteen years shall be employed to work in any factory or mine or engaged in any other hazardous employment.

Right to Freedom of Religion

25. (1) Subject to public order, morality and health and to the other provisions of this Part, all persons are equally entitled to freedom of conscience and the right freely to profess, practise and propagate religion.

. . .

27. No person shall be compelled to pay any taxes, the proceeds of which are specifically appropriated in payment of expenses for the promotion or maintenance of any particular religion or religious denomination.

28. (1) No religious instruction shall be provided in any educational institution wholly maintained out of State funds.

. . .

Right of Property

31. (1) No person shall be deprived of his property save by authority of law.

. . .

Part IV

DIRECTIVE PRINCIPLES OF STATE POLICY

. . .

38. The State shall strive to promote the welfare of the people by securing and protecting as effectively as it may a social order in which justice, social, economic and political, shall inform all the institutions of the national life.

39. The State shall, in particular, direct its policy toward securing—

(a) that the citizens, men and women equally, have the right to an adequate means of livelihood;

(b) that the ownership and control of the material resources of the community are so distributed as best to subserve the common good;

(c) that the operation of the economic system does not result in the concentration of wealth and means of production to the common detriment;

(d) that there is equal pay for equal work for both men and women;

(e) that the health and strength of workers, men and women, and the tender age of children are not abused and that citizens are not forced by economic necessity to enter avocations unsuited to their age or strength;

(f) that childhood and youth are protected against exploitation and against moral and material abandonment.

. . .

41. The State shall, within the limits of its economic capacity and development, make effective provision for securing the right to work, to education and to public assistance in cases of unemployment, old age, sickness and disablement, and in other cases of undeserved want.

42. The State shall make provision for securing just and humane conditions of work and for maternity relief.

43. The State shall endeavour to secure, by suitable legislation or economic organisation or in any other way, to all workers, agricultural, industrial or otherwise, work, a living wage, conditions of work ensuring a decent standard of life and full enjoyment of leisure and social and cultural opportunities and, in particular, the State shall endeavour to promote cottage industries on an individual or co-operative basis in rural areas.

. . .

45. The State shall endeavour to provide, within a period of ten years from the commencement of this Constitution, for free and compulsory education for all children until they complete the age of fourteen years.

. . .

47. The State shall regard the raising of the level of nutrition and the standard of living of its people and the improvement of public health as among

its primary duties and, in particular, the State shall endeavour to bring about prohibition of the consumption except for medicinal purposes of intoxicating drinks and of drugs which are injurious to health.

3. A "FREE ENTERPRISE" CRITICISM OF DEMOCRATIC SOCIALISM

In the following selection from his book *Capitalism and Freedom,* Milton Friedman, Professor of Economics at the University of Chicago, argues that democratic political freedom cannot be maintained unless individual economic freedom is also present. He implies, therefore, that the principles of democracy and socialism are incompatible and that an attempt to blend them, as in the Constitution of India, can only lead to failure.[36]

One feature of a free society is surely the freedom of individuals to advocate and propagandize openly for a radical change in the structure of the society—so long as the advocacy is restricted to persuasion and does not include force or other forms of coercion. It is a mark of the political freedom of a capitalist society that men can openly advocate and work for socialism. Equally, political freedom in a socialist society would require that men be free to advocate the introduction of capitalism. How could the freedom to advocate capitalism be preserved and protected in a socialist society?

In order for men to advocate anything, they must in the first place be able to earn a living. This already raises a problem in a socialist society, since all jobs are under the direct control of political authorities. It would take an act of self-denial whose difficulty is underlined by experience in the United States after World War II with the problem of "security" among Federal employees, for a socialist government to permit its employees to advocate policies directly contrary to official doctrine.

But let us suppose this act of self-denial to be achieved. For advocacy of capitalism to mean anything, the proponents must be able to finance their cause —to hold public meetings, publish pamphlets, buy radio time, issue newspapers and magazines, and so on. How could they raise the funds? There might and probably would be men in the socialist society with large incomes, perhaps even large capital sums in the form of government bonds and the like, but these would of necessity be high public officials. It is possible to conceive of a minor socialist official retaining his job although openly advocating capitalism. It strains credulity to imagine the socialist top brass financing such "subversive" activities.

The only recourse for funds would be to raise small amounts from a large number of minor officials. But this is no real answer. To tap these sources, many people would already have to be persuaded, and our whole problem is how to initiate and finance a campaign to do so. Radical movements in capitalist societies have never been financed this way. They have typically been supported by a few wealthy individuals who have become persuaded—by a Frederick Van-

[36] Reprinted from *Capitalism and Freedom* by Milton Friedman (Chicago, University of Chicago Press, 1962), pp. 16–19, by permission of The University of Chicago Press.

derbilt Field, or an Anita McCormick Blaine, or a Corliss Lamont, to mention a
few names recently prominent, or by a Friedrich Engels, to go farther back. This
is a role of inequality of wealth in preserving political freedom that is seldom
noted—the role of the patron.

In a capitalist society, it is only necessary to convince a few wealthy people
to get funds to launch any idea, however strange, and there are many such persons, many independent foci of support. And, indeed, it is not even necessary to
persuade people or financial institutions with available funds of the soundness
of the ideas to be propagated. It is only necessary to persuade them that the
propagation can be financially successful; that the newspaper or magazine or
book or other venture will be profitable. The competitive publisher, for example, cannot afford to publish only writing with which he personally agrees; his
touchstone must be the likelihood that the market will be large enough to yield
a satisfactory return on his investment.

In this way, the market breaks the vicious circle and makes it possible ultimately to finance such ventures by small amounts from many people without
first persuading them. There are no such possibilities in the socialist society;
there is only the all-powerful state.

Let us stretch our imagination and suppose that a socialist government is
aware of this problem and is composed of people anxious to preserve freedom.
Could it provide the funds? Perhaps, but it is difficult to see how. It could establish a bureau for subsidizing subversive propaganda. But how could it choose
whom to support? If it gave to all who asked, it would shortly find itself out of
funds, for socialism cannot repeal the elementary economic law that a sufficiently high price will call forth a large supply. Make the advocacy of radical
causes sufficiently remunerative, and the supply of advocates will be unlimited.

Moreover, freedom to advocate unpopular causes does not require that such
advocacy be without cost. On the contrary, no society could be stable if advocacy
of radical change were costless, much less subsidized. It is entirely appropriate
that men make sacrifices to advocate causes in which they deeply believe. Indeed, it is important to preserve freedom only for people who are willing to
practice self-denial, for otherwise freedom degenerates into license and irre-
sponsibility. What is essential is that the cost of advocating unpopular causes be
tolerable and not prohibitive.

But we are not yet through. In a free market society, it is enough to have
the funds. The suppliers of paper are as willing to sell it to the *Daily Worker* as
to the *Wall Street Journal*. In a socialist society, it would not be enough to have
the funds. The hypothetical supporter of capitalism would have to persuade a
government factory making paper to sell to him, the government printing press
to print his pamphlets, a government post office to distribute them among the
people, a government agency to rent him a hall in which to talk, and so on.

Perhaps there is some way in which one could overcome these difficulties
and preserve freedom in a socialist society. One cannot say it is utterly impossible. What is clear, however, is that there are very real difficulties in establishing
institutions that will effectively preserve the possibility of dissent. So far as I
know, none of the people who have been in favor of socialism and also in favor
of freedom have really faced up to this issue, or made even a respectable start

at developing the institutional arrangements that would permit freedom under socialism. By contrast, it is clear how a free market capitalist society fosters freedom.

4. MUSSOLINI'S FASCISM

There has probably been no more clear and vigorous exponent of the doctrines of fascism than Benito Mussolini (1883–1945). The following are selections from his contributions on fascism to the *Enciclopedia Italiana* in 1932.[37]

Fascism is now a completely individual thing, not only as a regime but as a doctrine. And this means that to-day Fascism exercising its critical sense upon itself and upon others, has formed its own distinct and peculiar point of view, to which it can refer and upon which, therefore, it can act in the face of all problems. . . .

And above all, Fascism, the more it considers and observes the future and the development of humanity quite apart from political considerations of the moment, believes neither in the possibility nor the utility of perpetual peace. It thus repudiates the doctrine of Pacifism—born of a renunciation of the struggle and an act of cowardice in the face of sacrifice. War alone brings up to its highest tension all human energy and puts the stamp of nobility upon the peoples who have the courage to meet it. All other trials are substitutes, which never really put men into the position where they have to make the great decision— the alternative of life or death. Thus a doctrine which is founded upon this harmful postulate of peace is hostile to Fascism. And thus hostile to the spirit of Fascism . . . are all the international leagues and societies which, as history will show, can be scattered to the winds when once strong national feeling is aroused. . . . Thus the Fascist accepts life and loves it, knowing nothing of and despising suicide: he rather conceives of life as duty and struggle and conquest, life which should be high and full, lived for oneself, but above all for others—those who are at hand and those who are far distant, contemporaries, and those who will come after.

Such a conception of life makes Fascism the complete opposite of that doctrine, the base of so-called scientific and Marxian socialism, the materialist conception of history; according to which the history of human civilization can be explained simply through the conflict of interests among the various social groups and by the change and development in the means and instruments of production. . . .

After Socialism, Fascism combats the whole complex system of democratic ideology, and repudiates it, whether in its theoretical premises or in its practical application. Fascism denies that the majority, by the simple fact that it is a majority, can direct human society; it denies that numbers alone can govern by

[37] From Benito Mussolini, *The Political and Social Doctrine of Fascism,* translated by Jane Soames (London, The Hogarth Press, 1933). Reprinted by permission of the publishers.

means of a periodical consultation, and it affirms the immutable, beneficial, and fruitful inequality of mankind. . . .

But the Fascist negation of Socialism, Democracy, and Liberalism must not be taken to mean that Fascism desires to lead the world back to the state of affairs before 1789 . . . we do not desire to turn back.

. . . Given that the nineteenth century was the century of Socialism, of Liberalism, and of Democracy, it does not necessarily follow that the twentieth century must also be a century of Socialism, Liberalism, and Democracy: political doctrines pass, but humanity remains; and it may rather be expected that this will be a century of authority, a century of the Left, a century of Fascism. For if the nineteenth century was a century of individualism . . . it may be expected that this will be the century of collectivism, and hence the century of the State. . . .

The foundation of Fascism is the conception of the State, its character, its duty, and its aim. Fascism conceives of the State as an absolute, in comparison with which all individuals or groups are relative, only to be conceived of in their relation to the State. The conception of the Liberal State is not that of a directing force, guiding the play and development, both material and spiritual, of a collective body, but merely a force limited to the function of recording results: on the other hand, the Fascist State is itself conscious, and has itself a will and a personality—thus it may be called the "ethical" State.

. . . For Fascism, the growth of empire, that is to say the expansion of the nation, is an essential manifestation of vitality, and its opposite a sign of decadence. Peoples which are rising, or rising again after a period of decadence, are always imperialist; any renunciation is a sign of decay and of death. Fascism is the doctrine best adapted to represent the tendencies and the aspirations of a people . . . who are rising again after many centuries of abasement and foreign servitude. But empire demands discipline, the coordination of all forces and a deeply felt sense of duty and sacrifice: this fact explains many aspects of the practical working of the regime, the character of many forces in the State, and the necessarily severe measures which must be taken against those who would oppose this spontaneous and inevitable movement. . . . If every age has its own characteristic doctrine, there are a thousand signs which point to Fascism as the characteristic doctrine of our time. [That Fascism is a "living thing"] is proved by the fact that Fascism has created a living faith; and that this faith is very powerful in the minds of men, is demonstrated by those who have suffered and died for it.

SELECT BIBLIOGRAPHY

DEAN, VERA MICHELES, *New Patterns of Democracy in India* (Cambridge, Mass., Harvard University Press, 1959). An introduction to the ingredients and patterns of Indian democratic behavior by a perceptive American student of the non-West.

CH'EN, JEROME, *Mao and the Chinese Revolution* (New York, Oxford University

Press, 1965). A very readable biography of Mao against a usefully sketched background of the Chinese Revolution.

GAY, PETER, *The Dilemma of Democratic Socialism* (New York, Columbia University Press, 1952). A critical history of democratic socialism built about a biographical sketch of one of its foremost founders, Eduard Bernstein. It poses the perplexing query of how a social revolution can be accomplished without a political revolution and analyzes the democratic socialist's response.

HUNT, R. N. CAREW, *The Theory and Practice of Communism* (London, Geoffrey Bles, 1950; 5th rev. American ed., Macmillan, 1957). Probably still the best introduction to communism. Its short, annotated bibliography is also helpful.

MENDEL, ARTHUR P. (ed.), *Essential Works of Marxism* (New York, Bantam, 1965). A collection of basic documents including the *Communist Manifesto,* Lenin's *State and Revolution,* and writings by Stalin and Mao Tse-tung. The Chinese interpretation of Marxism-Leninism is contained in "Long Live Leninism," the article generally credited with opening the Sino-Soviet ideological dispute. Also included are selections from such dissenters as Milovan Djilas and Leszek Kolakowski, author of "The Conspiracy of Ivory Tower Intellectuals." Finally, note "The New Program of the Communist Party of the Soviet Union," which in 1961 outlined in more specific detail the vision of full communism.

MILL, JOHN STUART, *On Liberty* (New York, Appleton-Century-Crofts, 1947). One of the best statements of the principles of Western democracy by the great nineteenth-century English essayist. Published in 1859, this constitutes a documentary complement to Marx's *Communist Manifesto,* which appeared only a decade earlier.

MROZEK, SLAWOMIR, *The Elephant* (New York, Grove Press, 1965). Short essays written by a Pole after the Polish political and literary "thaw" of 1956. Cast in Aesopian mold, the fables penetratingly and satirically attack the closed system of thought invented by Marx and developed by his successors. Underneath the fantasy of words is a spirit independent and coldly analytical, an intelligence free of the shackles of an *a priori* view of the world. An important document for our time and a literary delight.

Peking Review. A weekly magazine published in Peking, this affords the English-reading world some insight into contemporary public pronouncements on both the ideology and policies of the Chinese Communist Party. This must be used with care.

RIEMER, NEAL, *The Revival of Democratic Theory* (New York, Appleton-Century-Crofts, 1962). A critical examination of the problem of adapting the principles of classical democratic theory to the conditions of today and of making this theory a meaningful framework for integrating the various components of political life and behavior. Also analyzes the concepts of conflict and accommodation as seen in both national and international affairs.

SCHRAM, STUART, *The Political Thought of Mao Tse-Tung* (New York, Praeger, 1963). A wide selection of Mao's writings from his pre-Marxist days into the period of the Sino-Soviet ideological controversy.

SCHUMPETER, JOSEPH A., *Capitalism, Socialism, and Democracy,* 2nd ed. (New York, Harper & Row, 1947). A classic analysis of capitalism by the famous

Austrian-born economist. It concludes that capitalism must give way to socialism, but not for the reasons advanced by the Marxists.

SHONFIELD, ANDREW, *Modern Capitalism: The Changing Balance of Public and Private Power* (New York, Oxford University Press, 1965). An excellent account of the evolution of capitalism and its accommodation with state planning. Discusses the various approaches to planning in the West and illustrates them with French, German, and British experiences. United States capitalism is compared with its namesake in various West European countries. It reminds that "capitalism" means much more than has ever been considered in Marxist philosophy as well as in the thinking of some conservative Americans.

TANG, PETER S. H., *Communist China Today*, Vol. I: *Domestic and Foreign Policies*, 2d ed. rev. (Washington, Research Institute on the Sino-Soviet Bloc, 1961). A standard work dealing with all aspects of Communist China, including ideological background, party organization, the machinery of the state, and policies. Historically oriented, it does not cover the Sino-Soviet schism.

YEVTUSHENKO, YEVGENY, *A Precocious Autobiography* (New York, Dutton, 1964). An expression by the *enfant terrible* of contemporary Soviet letters of the yearnings and aspirations of the young Soviet generation brought up under what the author calls the "papier-mâché city of lies." The death of Stalin and the subsequent de-Stalinization came as a profound shock to Yevtushenko's generation and he reveals his own unpreparedness to plunge into this great adventure. In his mind, Lenin has replaced Stalin; thus some thought is dominated by a sage whose death in 1924 shelters him from "de-Leninization." For further understanding of Yevtushenko, refer to his *Selected Poems*, published by Penguin Books, Baltimore, Maryland.

6

Economic Underdevelopment and Competing Economic Systems

No AREAS OF THE WORLD OFFER greater scope for the ideological competition discussed in Chapter 5 than do the economically developing countries of Asia, Africa, and Latin America. Democracy, socialism, and communism, in a variety of ways, have made their respective appeals and have been adopted in different degrees and ways by many of these countries. Fascism, too, has appeared in some areas as rightist dictatorships have tried to arrest movements for land redistribution and other economic and social reforms. Since the developing countries (approximately 80 at the present time) have within the past decade come to occupy such a significant place in world affairs, a detailed examination of their economic conditions and needs will be presented in this chapter. An analysis will also be made of the various methods and institutional patterns being used to promote their economic development.

INCOME INEQUALITIES OF THE DEVELOPING COUNTRIES

No more striking features of the emerging countries are likely to be found than those arising out of income inequality—the glaring and growing difference in wealth between the few economically developed states and the many, poor, underdeveloped ones. A parallel source of tension is the difference in wealth within the poor countries between a small number of leading, educated, and influential people and the mass of the citizens. Income inequality has been at all times a social irritant and an important cause of political conflict. Until recently, however, this cause operated mainly on the domestic, national level. In our own times, income inequality has additionally become a fruitful source of international misunderstanding. This is not to say that in past ages differences

189

in wealth on the international level did not produce clashes and aggressions: the invasion and destruction of Rome by hordes of relatively backward peoples, the spread of British, Spanish, Portuguese, French, Dutch, German, and Belgian influence over vast areas of the underdeveloped world, the dismemberment of Poland by Russia, Prussia, and Austria-Hungary, and Imperial Japan's incursions into China argue eloquently against an overly strict and narrow drawing of historical lines. It remains nonetheless true that international income inequalities have in recent times assumed a position of importance they did not have in a more remote past.

There are two reasons for this. First, there is the technical fact of closer, more rapid, comprehensive, and intimate communications between the most distant parts of the world. Second, there is the fact of a spiritual awakening that since World War II has swept the nations of this planet. Technically the world has become one; spiritually it is more fragmented in all but its aspirations. An acute tension thus exists between the technical reality of a single world and the multiplicity of conditions under which the peoples of the world live, and between aspirations and what can actually be done. The fact of the one world through communications need not be belabored: events in the jungles of the Congo and Vietnam become known within hours all over the globe and have a direct impact on the lives of people tens of thousands of miles distant from the scene of events. The fact of spiritual awakening is more elusive, if no less significant. This second revolution has two aspects. On the one hand, it means a sudden rise in the expectations of the poor; on the other, it is the growing realization on the part of the rich that these expectations must not be disappointed. The problem, however, is more easily stated than solved. Economists are aware of the gulf between desires, and desires backed by purchasing power. In their theorizing they solve the disparity by ignoring those wishes not actually backed by resources and get out of it by leaving fond hopes and aspirations to the psychologist or the psychiatrist, as the case may be. But aspirations deeply felt by whole nations cannot be so ignored if only because they tend to become the fuel of revolutions.

Before examining the content of this upsurge of expectations, a closer look must be taken at the existing income inequalities among nations.

MEASURES OF INCOME INEQUALITY

Gross National Product

The term "standard of living" is used frequently, if somewhat loosely, to denote the material conditions under which a given people live. The Americans, for example, are reputed to have a high standard of living;

the Indians, a low one. One measure of living standards is gross national product (GNP): the market value of the annual output of goods and services produced by an economy. If depreciation of the existing capital is taken into account, this concept becomes that of net national product (NNP).

Gross and net national product can be estimated fairly easily for any given economy, provided the tools of statistical analysis are available. But here, precisely, is the rub. Many underdeveloped countries do not have the needed statisticians and know-how and often cannot afford the expense of comprehensive fact-gathering. Moreover, much of the output is consumed directly by the households which produce it and, thus, never reaches the marketable stage at which it can be counted. To make matters more complicated, there exist wide differences in the very concept of GNP, in the way, that is, in which different nations estimate what they have produced.

None of these problems is insuperable. Since the end of World War II, the United Nations Organization as well as independent scholars in the United States and elsewhere have addressed themselves to this question. The results of their efforts have been creditable. The figures, of course, are approximations and should not be taken to express more than the addition of goods and services produced and exchanged in the various countries in a given period of time. There is no implication here of high or low levels of welfare, nor are any aspersions being cast on the various nations' cultural achievements. It is, however, an observable fact that under conditions of extreme material destitution, welfare and culture do tend to suffer, even though contrary evidence based on isolated cases could be adduced to counter this.

Calculations of "real GNP" made in a study edited by Max F. Millikan and Donald L. M. Blackmer[1] show that in 1961, the developed countries of Western Europe, North America, and Oceania, as well as Japan and South Africa, accounted for 58.7 percent of the total world real gross national product, or some $1,029 billion. The communist nations (U.S.S.R., Eastern Europe, China, North Korea, and North Vietnam) represented 23.7 percent of the world's real GNP, or some $415 billion, while the underdeveloped countries of Africa, Asia, Latin America, Europe, and the Middle East accounted for only 17.5 percent of the world's real GNP, or some $306 billion. Interestingly enough, the United States alone accounted for 29.4 percent of the world's real GNP, and the Soviet Union for another 12.1 percent.

International comparisons of absolute levels of GNP give only part of the story. Per capita figures are more instructive. In a study published in 1961, Professor P. N. Rosenstein-Rodan brought out the striking con-

[1] Max F. Millikan and Donald L. M. Blackmer, eds., *The Emerging Nations: Their Growth and United States Policy* (Boston and Toronto, Little, Brown and Company, 1961), Appendix, Table 1, pp. 150–151. Derived from P. N. Rosenstein-Rodan, *infra*, Note 2.

trasts in gross national product per head of population in a number of countries.[2] At that time there were only two countries in the world whose per capita GNP exceeded $2,000—the United States with $2,790 and Canada with $2,048. Australia, New Zealand, and the countries of Western Europe (except the Netherlands, Italy, Ireland, Greece, Spain, and Portugal) fell in the $1,000 to $2,000 range. Only three communist countries, the U.S.S.R., East Germany, and Czechoslovakia, were in the $500 to $1,000 range ($818 for the U.S.S.R.). Only three Latin American countries (Venezuela, Puerto Rico, and Argentina) were in that category, but none exceeded $700. With the exception of Albania, the other Eastern European countries under communist rule were in the $250 to $500 range, that is in the range of Spain and Greece and of such Latin American countries as Uruguay, Cuba, Chile, Mexico, Colombia, Panama, Costa Rica, Brazil, and the Dominican Republic. No Asian country had a per capita GNP of more than $383 (Japan). In fact, most of them ranged from $47 (Nepal) to $123 (Ceylon). The highest figure in Africa was $161 (the then Rhodesia and Nyasaland), but the bulk of African countries were well below $100. At that time the per capita GNP was $83 in Communist China and $70 in India. It is clear that, other things being equal, a per capita GNP ratio of 2,790:70 can become an important source of international tensions. Although other causes were also present, much of the misunderstanding between the Soviets and the Chinese can be attributed to divergent perspectives summed up in the ratio 818:83. It takes nothing short of a tremendous wrench of the imagination for a country whose per capita product is well in excess of $2,000 to comprehend the feelings and aspirations of peoples whose per capita product does not even reach $100. Inversely, it is almost impossible for the poor nations to view dispassionately and with objectivity the actions of, to them, the fabulously rich. Man's capacity for self-destruction makes such an understanding indispensable for survival.

According to the Millikan-Blackmer study already referred to, the countries with a per capita GNP of over $1,200 represented, in 1961, 6.8 percent of the world's population and 40 percent of the world's money GNP. Countries with a per capita GNP of $100 or less had 50.1 percent of the world's population and accounted for only 8.5 percent of the world's money GNP.[3] Whichever way one looks at it, about half the world's people dispose of less than $100 worth of goods and services per head per year. These, it must be remembered, are averages. The actual

[2] P. N. Rosenstein-Rodan, "International Aid for Underdeveloped Countries," *Review of Economics and Statistics,* Vol. XLIII (1961), pp. 107–138. According to a report presented by the Secretary-General of the United Nations to the U.N. Economic and Social Council (July 5, 1965), in 1962 annual per capita income in the underdeveloped areas averaged $136 while in the economically advanced countries of North America and Western Europe it averaged $2,845 and $1,033 respectively. See "Thant Presents Report," *The New York Times,* July 6, 1965, p. 9.

[3] Max F. Millikan and Donald L. M. Blackmer, eds., *op. cit.,* Appendix, Table 2, p. 152.

TABLE 3

Percentage Distribution of Sectoral Origin of GNP

	1	2	3	4	5	6	7	8
Country	Agri-culture, Forestry, and Fishing	Mining	Manu-facture	Con-struction	Elec-tricity, Gas, Water	Trans-port	Trade	Other
U.S.A.	4	1	29	5	2	6	16	27
Britain	4	3	35	7	3	8	12	30
France	9	2	36	8	2	5	13	27
Japan	13	1	31	7	...10...		16	22
U.S.S.R.	22	...52...		10	*	5	...11...	
Hungary	21	...61...		10	*	4	3	1
Poland	26	...50...		9	*	3	10	2
Rumania	30	...47...		8	*	4	8	3
Greece	29	1	18	5	2	8	11	26
India	45	1		...........19...		...16....		19
Indonesia	56	2	8	...........34..................				
China	48	...26...		6	*	4	16	..
Pakistan	53	..	14	3	..	3	9	18
Nigeria	62	1	5	3	..	8	13	8
Tanzania	60	2	4	3	1	4	12	14
Uganda	61	2	7	2	2	3	10	13
Ecuador	38	2	15	4	1	4	12	24
Colombia	32	3	17	5	1	7	12	23

SOURCE: United Nations, *Statistical Yearbook 1964*, Table 172. Note: The figures for the U.S.S.R. are for the year 1962; those for Poland for 1960; India: 1962; Indonesia: 1959; China: 1956; Pakistan: 1962.
* Figures included in Column 2.

distribution of income within most underdeveloped countries is about as lopsided as the distribution of income among nations. Moreover, in some instances in which the total and per capita product appears relatively respectable (e.g., Venezuela, South Africa), the actual situation is far from satisfactory. The great bulk of the product is in such instances generated in one major industry (e.g., petroleum, gold, and diamond mining) and both totals and per capita figures tend to lose their meaning in a social and political sense.

This leads to another significant topic. Developed countries not only have a much larger total and per capita GNP than the underdeveloped ones but the sectoral origin of the product is also different. In general, the greater part of the GNP of an underdeveloped economy is generated in the agricultural sector. This sector is usually plagued by hidden unemployment or underemployment, low productivity, nonviable distribution of the cultivable area, scarcity of capital, and primitive techniques. The manufacturing sector in such cases plays a relatively minor role. Table 3 illustrates this condition.

What Table 3 says in effect is that in the underdeveloped countries, a small national product is produced overwhelmingly by agriculture. The implication is also that this agriculture is not very efficient. Naturally, the exports of such countries will be mainly the products of agriculture, and in many cases one product (e.g., cotton, rubber, coffee, sugar) will form the greater part of the exports. Heavy dependence on agriculture and on agricultural exports may be a serious cause of instability for the economies concerned. Natural disasters (floods, drought) can cause wide variations in output from year to year. Since under normal conditions there is hardly any margin between minimal consumption and famine, such variations can result in widespread destitution and the spread of disease. Also, excessive dependence on agricultural exports, especially the export of a single crop, makes the underdeveloped economies subject to the ups and downs of international commodity prices. A drop of a cent or two in the price of coffee, for example, is capable of wiping out years of hard-won progress and billions of dollars in foreign assistance. Since most people find it difficult to understand the complex workings of the international price mechanism, they tend to interpret the calamities consequent on the fluctuations of international prices as the dark scheming of foreign, "imperialist" powers and as a new form of exploitation. Such interpretations, though somewhat simplistic, are encouraged by Peking and by a long tradition of shifting the blame for almost every national and private woe onto the shoulders of the former colonial powers. It remains nevertheless true that political independence is no panacea for deep-seated economic problems and that from an economic standpoint the next worst thing to being exploited is not to be exploited at all.[4]

Table 3 also suggests that in the underdeveloped countries, the industrial sector is relatively unimportant but that a rather sizeable amount of trading (especially at the retail level) goes on. A comparison of the first group of countries with the last suggests, moreover, that development involves a movement from agriculture, through industry, to the proliferation of all kinds of consumer services (or from the primary, through the secondary, to the tertiary sectors).

In general, the communist countries of Eastern Europe have moved far along the road to industrialization. The table seems to show, however, that this movement has been relatively lopsided and uneven. Agricultural productivity has lagged seriously behind, and there is a distinct neglect of trade and other services. With about 6 percent of its labor force employed in agriculture, the United States produces more food (and of a high quality) than it needs. In the Soviet Union agriculture ties down

---

[4] Joan Robinson, *Economic Philosophy* (New York, Oxford University Press, 1963).

about 45 percent of the labor force, and the results are anything but brilliant. Imbalanced growth, as will be shown in Chapter 7, is in fact the distinguishing characteristic of the communist strategy of development in its Soviet-sponsored version.

We shall return later to the concept of GNP in a somewhat different connection. Before doing so, however, it may be well to take a look at a number of other measures of relative living standards. Most of them are in some way related to the income level.

INFANT MORTALITY AND LIFE EXPECTANCY AT BIRTH

Low income levels for the mass of the population is a fancy name for poverty, and poverty implies malnutrition, unbalanced and irregular diets, endemic disease, high infant mortality, and low life expectancy rates.

TABLE 4

Infant Mortality Rates, 1954 and 1963
(Number of deaths of infants under one
year of age per 1,000 live births)

Country	1954 (except where shown)	1963 (except where shown)
U.S.A.	26.6	25.2
Sweden	18.7	15.0
West Germany	42.9	26.9
Japan	44.6	26.5
U.S.S.R.	68.0	32.0
Poland	82.6	49.1
Albania	97.5	92.1 (1962)
India (registration areas)	100.2 (1958)	83.1 (1962)
Indonesia	150.0	125.0 (1962)
Burma (towns)	198.6	139.3 (1962)
Brazil	170.0 (1954–59)	89.6 (1962)
Haiti	. . .	180.4 (1962)
El Salvador	82.4	67.9
U.A.R.	137.9	133.9 (1962)
Uganda	. . .	160.0 (1959)

SOURCE: United Nations, *Demographic Yearbook 1963*, Table 22. Most of the figures for underdeveloped countries are estimates.

The figures all but speak for themselves.

In the underdeveloped countries life expectancy rates are deplorable. An American baby born in 1962 had a good chance of living to the age of

TABLE 5

Life Expectancy at Birth

Country	Date of Latest Returns	Years	
U.S.A.	1963	Male	66.6
		Female	73.4
Sweden	1962	Male	71.32
		Female	75.39
Britain (England and Wales)	1961–63	Male	68.0
		Female	73.9
France	1963	Male	67.2
		Female	74.1
Japan	1963	Male	67.21
		Female	72.34
U.S.S.R.	1960–61	Both sexes	70.0
Poland	1960–61	Male	64.8
		Female	70.5
Australia	1953–55	Male	67.14
		Female	72.75
India	1951–60	Male	41.89
		Female	40.55
Burma	1954	Male	40.8
		Female	43.8
Cambodia	1958–59	Male	44.2
		Female	43.3
Brazil	1940–50	Male	39.30
		Female	45.50
Haiti	1950	Both sexes	32.61
Colombia	1950–52	Male	44.18
		Female	45.95
Morocco	1960	Both sexes	49.60
U.A.R.	1960	Male	51.6
		Female	53.8
Guinea	1954–55	Both sexes	30.50
Mali	1957	Both sexes	27.00
Upper Volta	1960–61	Male	32.1
		Female	31.1

SOURCE: United Nations, *Demographic Yearbook 1963*, Table 26; *1964*, Table 23.

67 if a boy, and 73 if a girl. In the former Belgian Congo (according to the 1950–1952 returns) the corresponding figures were about 38 and 40. Table 5 gives a number of examples.

MALNUTRITION

Malnutrition, general neglect, overcrowding, and the lack of proper public health and medical services are, of course, among the major contributory causes. The annual milk consumption per capita in the United States and Canada as well as in Western Europe (Spain and Portugal excepted) is in the region of 200 quarts. It is about 75 quarts in most of Latin America and less than 50 quarts in most of Asia. Annual meat consumption in most underdeveloped countries of Asia is about one-sixteenth of that in the United States and Canada. Table 6 gives some representative nutritional data.

TABLE 6

Calorie and Protein Intake per Capita per Day

Country	Year	Calories	% of Animal Origin	Proteins (grammes)
U.S.A.	1964	3,120	40	92
Britain	1963–64	3,280	44	90
Switzerland	1963–64	3,150	35	89
Australia	1963–64	3,160	42	92
India	1962–63	1,940	6	50
Pakistan	1963–64	2,220	. . .	51
Philippines	1963	2,000	12	46
Venezuela	1961	2,340	14	60
Colombia	1961	2,080	18	46
Brazil	1962	2,920	15	69
Dominican Republic	1959	2,080	14	49

SOURCE: United Nations, *Statistical Yearbook 1965*, Table 166.

PUBLIC HEALTH

Table 7 shows the number of inhabitants per physician in a number of countries. It should be pointed out that the figures do not reflect the degree of the physician's training or the equipment and drugs available to the doctors.

In South Vietnam, which has figured prominently in the news in recent years, the situation is desperate. In an address to the Association of American Editorial Cartoonists, President Lyndon B. Johnson summed up the problem in the following terms:

Disease and epidemic brood over every Vietnamese village. In a country of more than 16 million people with a life expectancy of only 35 years, there are only 200 civilian doctors. If the Vietnamese had doctors in the same ratio as the United States has doctors, they would have not the 200 that they do have but they would have more than 5,000 doctors.[5]

In 1960, there were 71 dentists in South Vietnam, most of them in the army. There were no dentists in Yemen (and only 32 doctors) and 161 in Pakistan. In 1962, Laos had 49 physicians, 5 dentists, and 4 mid-

TABLE 7

Inhabitants per Physician

Year	Country	Number
1963	Israel	430
1963	U.S.S.R.	510
1963	Czechoslovakia	570
1961	Italy	610
1963	Hungary	650
1962	West Germany	670
1964	New Zealand	670
1963	U.S.A.	690
1963	Rumania	730
1963	Britain (England and Wales)	840
1963	France	870
1963	Sweden	960
1963	Cuba	1,200
1963	Albania	2,500
1963	Bolivia	3,700
1962	India	5,800
1963	Pakistan	7,000
1963	Thailand	7,600
1963	Burma	9,300
1962	Ghana	12,000
1963	South Vietnam	29,000
1960	Somalia	30,000
1963	Laos	37,000
1964	Upper Volta	63,000
1961	Ethiopia	96,000
1964	Rwanda	144,000

SOURCE: United Nations, *Statistical Yearbook 1965*, Table 193.

[5] Excerpts from an address by President Lyndon B. Johnson to the Association of American Editorial Cartoonists at the White House, May 13, 1965. Agency for International Development, *The Third Face of War* (Washington, D.C., 1965), p. 4.

wives in the public health service, and a grand total of 6 pharmacists. The Dominican Republic (population over 3 million) had 442 doctors (mostly in the bigger towns) and 21 dentists in the public health service.

The big killers in almost every underdeveloped country are the very diseases that have been brought under control by modern medical science elsewhere. Pneumonia, typhus, tuberculosis, smallpox, measles, and other infective and parasitic diseases lead the way, with anaemias, senility, and diseases peculiar to early infancy as close seconds. In many parts of Central and South America, yellow fever is endemic. Cholera, smallpox, and yellow fever are endemic in most parts of Asia, and diseases caused by worms in blood vessels are prevalent over vast areas of the African continent. The main causes of mortality in the developed countries are, in descending order, arteriosclerotic and degenerative heart disease, malignant enoplasms (cancer), and vascular lesions affecting the central nervous system. The incidence of these diseases is relatively small in the economically retarded areas of the world. Deaths from suicide and homicide are much more frequent in the developed countries than elsewhere. For example, suicide is twenty-one times as frequent in the United States as in India and homicide over twice as frequent. It should, however, be noted that some of the discrepancy may be due to statistical distortion due to the more thorough law enforcement and crime detection in the advanced countries.

ILLITERACY

Extreme poverty goes hand in hand with substandard education and illiteracy. Ignorance, in turn, breeds traditionalist attitudes inimical to the kind of progress associated with economic development. Table 8 gives some instances.

It should be pointed out that most communist systems upon coming to power make a determined and in many ways spectacular attack on the twin problems of substandard health and substandard education, especially on the dire absence of scientific and technical training without which no economic progress is possible. Like it or not, this is communism's real achievement and an important cause of attraction for peoples living in conditions of extreme destitution and privation. The fact is brought out to some extent by Tables 7 and 8. No European communist country, with the exception of Albania, has more than 1,000 inhabitants per physician, and most of these countries are in the 500–700 range. It should be remembered that communism so far has been implanted in relatively underdeveloped regions and that the figures, with all their shortcomings, represent a real improvement over conditions that had prevailed in the past. At the same time it must be noted that spectacular breakthroughs of this kind are usually achieved only at the price of quality of service. The Soviet definition of a "doctor," for instance, is not as rigorous as the American or British. Moreover, as will be shown in more detail later, the communist method of economic development involves a serious neglect of housing for the population and implies low consumption levels. Much of the increase in public health services consequently goes to combat the effects of this type of industrialization drive. All the same, the social welfare aspect of communism cannot be dismissed as the ravings of a few propaganda bureaucrats.

The most spectacular attack on the problems of public health and education in recent decades has been made by the Chinese Communists. The drive for good health habits and against flies, rats, and other pests has been pursued with a zeal and fervor and on a scale never before attempted anywhere. Traditional Chinese folk medicine has been nationalized and harnessed to the task of filling the gaps left by the insufficiency of modern medical personnel and equipment. At the same time, the experience so gained has been used with good effect abroad. Chinese experts have taught the Guineans and the inhabitants of Mali how to combine the practice of native "medicine" with such limited resources as modern medical science has been able to furnish. The nearest approach to this kind of method that the West has so far been able to muster has been the work of the American Peace Corps volunteers, a modest, but one of the

TABLE 8

Illiteracy Rates Among Population 15 Years or Over

Date of Census			Country	Rates percent
I	15	1959	U.S.S.R.	1.5
XII	6	1960	Poland	4.7
IX	30	1960	Argentina	8.6
XI	1	1956	Bulgaria	14.7
III	19	1961	Greece	19.6
III	31	1961	Yugoslavia	19.7
II	26	1961	Venezuela	34.2
VI	8	1960	Mexico	34.6
VII	2	1961	Peru	39.4
X	31	1961	Indonesia	57.1
III	1	1961	India	72.2
IX	20	1960	U.A.R.	73.7
II	1	1961	Pakistan	81.2
II	1	1956	Morocco	86.2
IX	1–15	1956	Iran	87.2
I	17	1956	Sudan	95.6

Source: United Nations, *Demographic Yearbook 1963*, Table 13; *1964*, Table 34.

most far-sighted and inspired efforts of Western man in the field of economic development. In the decade 1950–1960, the Chinese Communists had fought illiteracy with a single-minded determination and ruthless resolve unknown to Chinese educational history, and the attack goes on to this day. At a rough guess, China at the time of the communist takeover had about 490 million illiterates out of a population of some 550 million. In the first ten years, more than 25 million people had been taught to read and write. Illiteracy is a recurring disease. It is not enough to teach a man to read—it is not like teaching him to ride a bicycle or to swim. If reading material is not supplied, illiteracy will once again take over. For ideological reasons, if for no other, in the spirit of missionaries who put out below-cost copies of the Bible, the Chinese Communists, like communist regimes everywhere, have flooded the land with Marxist literature of the Maoist creed. Since 1949, more than 250 million Chinese have been born (and another 19 million are being born every year), and 200 million more have reached mental maturity. All of them know how to read the prescribed texts and what to write. It is "blinkered literacy," but literacy all the same. Moreover, great stress is put on the acquisition of technical and scientific expertise (formation of human capital, as the economists call it). All travellers in China witness to this revolution in the desire and thirst for technical knowledge. At the time of the communist takeover, China had only about 100,000 scientists and highly qualified technicians and fewer than 4 million skilled workers of foreman-type standing. For a population nearing 600 million with a 4,000 year history that was, indeed, meager pickings.

Data on book production in the developed countries and in the developing nations under communist rule throw a good deal of light on the preoccupations of the literate leaders of those countries and on the way in which that part of leisure time devoted to study is being used. In both cases, book titles in the pure and the applied sciences and dissertations on economics form an important part of the total number of new titles published each year. A comparison of the relevant data for Cuba and Cambodia is of interest in this connection.

TABLE 9

Books Published by Titles

(Units)

Country	Tot.	Genrl.	Philos-ophy	Reli-gion	Soc. Sci.	Pure Sci.	Applied Science	Philol-ogy	Arts	Geog. Hist.	Lit.
					YEAR: 1963						
Cambodia	193	84	. .	32	29	. .	6	5	14	13	10
Cuba	509	8	5	4	126	12	90	3	24	70	164

SOURCE: United Nations, *Statistical Yearbook 1965*, Table 197.

CAPITAL ENDOWMENT

In a very much simplified way, the crux of economic underdevelopment could be summed up in the phrase "shortage of capital." In other words, people in the developing countries have very little machinery and other equipment to work with. What equipment they do have is simple and antiquated. A Texas farmer, for example, has on the average 1.1 tractors, 0.2 combines, 0.07 hay balers, 0.05 corn pickers, 0.8 trucks, and 0.9 automobiles. His home is equipped with 0.6 telephones and 0.6 food freezers. He applies to the soil about 3 tons of commercial fertilizer a year. The Soviet farmer has, on the average, 0.4 tractors, 0.2 grain combines, and 0.03 motor trucks. He applies to the land 0.1 tons of commercial fertilizer a year. An average farmer in Communist China has 0.0001 tractors, 0.00001 combines, and uses 0.005 tons of commercial fertilizer in the year.[6] Except for a few sectors of the economy, production in the underdeveloped countries is highly labor-intensive and physically demanding. Table 10 shows the consumption of chemical fertilizers in a selected number of countries.

TABLE 10

Consumption of Chemical Fertilizer, 1964/65
(Thousand metric tons)

Country	Phosphatic	Nitrogenous	Potash
U.S.A. (incl. Puerto Rico)	3,175.1	4,286.4	2,639.9
West Germany	790.1	784.6	1,184.0
Britain	468.0	582.7	436.7
Japan	518.5	727.1	593.5
India	150.3	517.5	62.6
Indonesia *	46.2	98.6	4.6
Ceylon	1.4	38.7	26.4
Colombia **	17.5	53.1	52.4

SOURCE: United Nations, *Statistical Yearbook 1965*, Tables 172, 173, 174.
      Measured in terms of phosphoric acid, nitrogen, and K_2O
   ° 1962–63
   °° Phosphatic fertilizer: 1958–59

When in 1949 the Chinese Communists came to power, the use of chemical fertilizer was almost unknown to Chinese agricultural practice. Through deforestation and poor farming practices, Haiti is losing soil

[6] James D. Gordon, "Three States of Farming: Texas, Russia and China," *Texas Business Review*, Bureau of Business Research, The University of Texas, Vol. XXXVI, No. 4, April, 1962, pp. 84–87.

every year. The same is true of large tracts of Brazil and other Latin American countries.

Capital equipment in industry and transportation is also scarce in almost every underdeveloped country. Table 11 gives some telling examples.

TABLE 11

Capital Endowment, 1964

Country	1 Electric Energy (Installed Capacity) Thous. KW	2 Kilometers Railways (Millions) Passenger	3 Net Ton	4 Motor Vehicles (Passenger) Thousand Units	5 Trucks Thousand Units	6 Merchant ships Thous. GRT (1965)
U.S.A.	239,814	29,408	966,633	71,635.7	12,470.6	21,527
Britain	45,236	31,984	26,168	8,264.0	1,662.2	21,530
France	26,729	37,910	65,260	8,800.0	2,032.2	5,198
W. Germany	36,145	37,218	59,037	8,014.3	956.6	5,279
E. Germany	9,525	17,378	39,113	. . . .	. . . .	591
Portugal	1,607	2,780	763	195.0	68.5	698
U.S.S.R.	103,584	195,100	1,854,100	. . . .	. . . .	8,238
Rumania	2,866	13,331	29,386	. . . .	31.2	. . . .
Czechoslovakia	8,120	19,232	55,391	. . . .	. . . .	. . . .
Poland	9,203	33,270	79,059	211.2	173.5	1,040
Spain	9,766	11,820	8,557	633.7	298.0	2,132
Algeria (1)	434	556	960	207.0	92.5	. . . .
Ghana (1)	143.4	392	353	27.4	17.0	. . . .
Ethiopia (2)	111.1	65	202	14.0	6.6	. . . .
Venezuela (3)	1,977	37	26	352.4	145.6	313
Paraguay (5)	29	38	18	6.5	3.8	. . . .
Brazil (4)	6,840	17,315	18,411	906.4	898.2	1,253
Japan	38,063	238,701	59,627	1,672.6	3,554.8	11,171
India (2)	7,645	88,943	88,689	384.0	342.0	1,523
Thailand (1)	361.7	2,798	1,396	66.8	87.0	. . . .
S. Vietnam (1)	116	125	133	32.6	30.6	. . . .
Comm. China (6)	. . . .	45,670	265,260	. . . .	. . . .	551
Australia	7,983	3,552	17,094	2,710.9	864.6	727

SOURCE: United Nations, *Statistical Yearbook 1965*, Tables 143, 153, 154, 155.
(1) Col. 1—1963
(2) Col. 1, 2, 3—1963
(3) Col. 1—1962
(4) Col. 2, 3—1963
(5) Col. 2, 3—1963 Col. 4, 5—1962
(6) Col. 2, 3—1959

Notice the relatively high number of passenger automobiles in such countries as Venezuela, Brazil, India, and Algeria. Though small in comparison with the number of passenger automobiles in the developed countries, it merits mention in view of the retarded state of highways in the underdeveloped areas. It would be correct to assume that these represent town passenger traffic by a small segment of the population (including government officials) given to at least some semblance of conspicuous consumption.

China at the time of the communist takeover may again be used as a good illustration. According to the Chinese Communists, only 21,740 kilometers of railroad lines were in operation on July 1, 1950. This compares with Tsarist Russia's 73,000 kilometers in 1913. Moreover, many of the Chinese lines were single track, and most of them clustered in the eastern and northeastern part of the country. There were few roads. Before 1950, China had no shipbuilding industry and only a few rather backward and inefficient ship-repair facilities. All this, remember, with 14,000 kilometers of sea coast, 1,600 rivers, and some of the best natural ports in Asia. Inland navigation was the most important form of transport. Yet, through war and neglect, only 75,000 kilometers were navigable by small boats in 1949. China, before 1949, was one of the world's leading exporters of tungsten but produced no light bulbs of its own. Two hundred different types of foreign-made locomotives were used on the country's railroads, but none were produced at home. The industrial labor force represented in 1936 about 0.25 percent of the population. Such heavy industries as the country did have were, for the most part, built by the Japanese invader in Manchuria. To protect the cultivator from floods and to conserve scarce water, there were only 42,000 kilometers of dykes, most of them in poor shape. Arable land per head worked out at about 0.45 acres, hardly conducive to good agricultural practices. Most farmers were tenants and tenants in debt. The landlords, if one is to believe on-the-spot reports, were not overly oppressive; they just let the uniformities of free enterprise economics do the job of rent collection and eviction.[7]

POPULATION EXPLOSION

At the turn of the eighteenth century, a young English economist, Thomas Robert Malthus, formulated a theory of population which shocked his contemporaries and has been the source of fruitful and often bitter controversy ever since. The nub of Malthus' Principle of Population was that population had a "natural" (or biological) tendency to increase at a rate well in excess of the rate of increase in food output. In the first flush of discovery, Malthus reduced the two rates to arithmetic (food) and geometric (population) progressions, an impressive if somewhat dubious bit of mathematics which he later abandoned. Whatever one may think of Malthus' theory, there can be no doubt that he focused the attention of social scientists on a problem which first emerged in his time and has continued to worry many well-informed people ever since. If there is a flaw in the Malthusian argument, it is that it underestimated the countervailing effects of technical progress. More precisely, he ig-

---

[7] A. Doak Barnett, *China on the Eve of Communist Takeover* (New York, Praeger, 1963), Part II, Chap. 10, pp. 103–154.

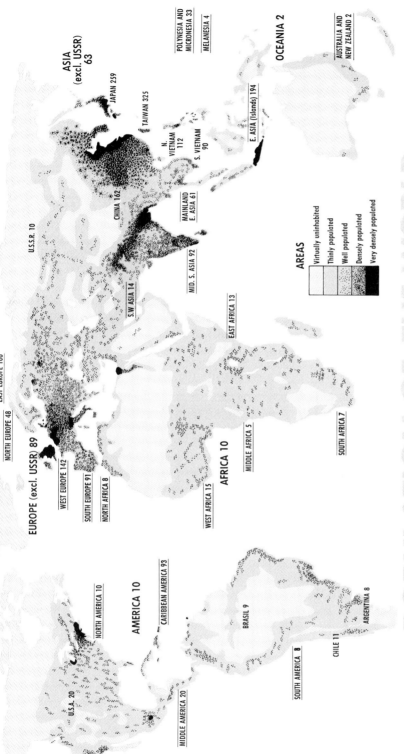

EAST EUROPE 100

NORTH EUROPE 48

EUROPE (excl. USSR) 89

WEST EUROPE 142

SOUTH EUROPE 91

NORTH AFRICA 8

U.S.S.R. 10

ASIA
(excl. USSR)
63

JAPAN 259

TAIWAN 325

N.
VIETNAM
112

S. VIETNAM
90

CHINA 162

MAINLAND
E. ASIA 61

MID. S. ASIA 92

S.W ASIA 14

E. ASIA (Islands) 194

POLYNESIA AND
MICRONESIA 33

MELANESIA 4

OCEANIA 2

AUSTRALIA AND
NEW ZEALAND 2

AFRICA 10

WEST AFRICA 15

MIDDLE AFRICA 5

EAST AFRICA 13

SOUTH AFRICA 7

AREAS

Virtually uninhabited

Thinly populated

Well populated

Densely populated

Very densely populated

U.S.A. 20

NORTH AMERICA 10

AMERICA 10

CARIBBEAN AMERICA 93

MIDDLE AMERICA 20

BRASIL 9

SOUTH AMERICA 8

CHILE 11

ARGENTINA 8

POPULATION OF THE WORLD

The figures, which refer to population density per square kilometre in 1963, are taken from United Nations, *Statistical Yearbook*, 1964, Tables 2 and 3. They are slightly different from the figures in Table 12 on page 206 which are for 1964 and come from the *Statistical Yearbook*, 1965. The latter edition, however, does not contain detailed figures for individual countries and regions as does the 1964 edition and therefore could not be used in preparing this map.

nored them in the context of economies which, incidentally, were nearest to him, and which, under his very eyes, were undergoing an income revolution. The rapid rise in gross and per capita product in England, Western Europe, and America during Malthus' own lifetime and for decades thereafter, showed that the birth rate tended to fluctuate with changed social conditions. Even though it would be rash to formulate this in terms of a "law," there does seem to be a strong tendency for the birth rate to decline with a rise in income and educational levels. Even if this tendency does not operate automatically, rising educational standards and a greater diffusion of learning make arguments in favor of family planning plausible to many people. "Artificial" demographic restraint thus comes to complement the rise in agricultural productivity to make the problem more manageable than Malthus had ever thought it possible. Before 1492, the North American continent with just 2 million Indians was overpopulated. At the present time it provides over 200 million people with the world's highest standard of life. Overpopulation is, therefore, a relative concept; relative, that is, to a given economy's ability to

TABLE 12

Annual Rate of Population Increase 1960–64
(percent) and Population Density 1964 (per sq. kilometer)

	Population Increase Rate	Density
World	1.8	24
Africa	2.4	10
North	2.4	13
West	2.2	16
North America	1.6	10
South America	2.8	12
Tropical	2.8	9
Central	3.2	21
Caribbean	2.5	95
East Asia	1.4	72
Japan	1.0	262
South Asia	2.2	59
Europe	0.9	89
West	1.3	143
East	0.7	100
South	1.3	92
Oceania	2.2	2
U.S.S.R.	1.5	10

Source: United Nations, *Statistical Yearbook 1965*, Table 2.

supply, through rising productivity, an increasing quantity and variety of food to increasing numbers of people and to ensure that this swelling supply of food can be purchased by all.

The Malthusian thesis appears, however, to be applicable to many parts of the underdeveloped world. Planned parenthood campaigns are in such regions hampered by the weight of tradition, lack of knowledge, religious precepts, and guilt feelings. A rapidly rising population which presses on a limited amount of land that had been for centuries farmed by primitive methods can make the vicious circles of poverty all the tighter and render the task of breaking out of them exceedingly difficult. In spite of high mortality rates (which Malthus had once described as "positive checks"), annual rates of population increase tend to be substantially higher in the underdeveloped regions of the world than in the economically advanced countries. Table 12 illustrates this trend.

In short, from the standpoint of sheer numbers, the underdeveloped world is expanding faster than that which is economically advanced. In many countries the rate of population growth exceeds by a substantial margin the rate of growth in GNP.

THE GROWING ECONOMIC GAP

It has been pointed out before that the gap between the developed and the developing countries of the world is a source of tension and possible conflict due to differing perspectives and aspirations, memories of past glories, and recollections of past grudges. It will be shown later (Chap. 7) that the competition for the loyalty of the vast numbers of people who inhabit the underdeveloped world and the divergent solutions to their problems offered by competing economic systems add fuel to a smoldering fire.

In recent decades, the gap has grown wider. In the 1950's, the average annual rate of GNP growth was 9.3 percent for Japan, 7.5 percent for West Germany, 5.9 percent for Italy, 4.5 percent for France, and 3.9 percent for Canada. Among the less developed countries of Asia, Communist China led the way with an estimated average annual growth rate of about 7 percent. The Philippines growth rate was 5.6 percent, and that of India 3.5 percent. In 1960–1963, growth in the underdeveloped countries as a whole slowed to an average rate of 4 percent from 4.5 percent in 1955–1960. The average growth rate in the developed countries in 1960–1963 was 4.4 percent as compared to 3.4 percent in 1955–1960. Two points must be noted in this connection. First, any gains in material welfare resulting from growth will be wiped out if population increases faster than total output. This has certainly been the case in much of Asia and Africa in the last ten years. Thus, for example, South Korea's 1962 GNP increased by 2.6 percent and population by 2.9 percent. In 1964, the 6.8 percent growth rate in GNP was reduced more than 40 percent by the population increase. In absolute figures, South Korea's population increases by about 720,000 every year. Second, the rate of growth says nothing about the absolute size of the addition to output. In order for the developing countries to catch up with the advanced, their growth rates should be substantially higher than those registered by the industrialized nations. Thus, for instance, during the 1950's, in addition to South Korea, the relative posi-

TABLE 13

Index Numbers of Total and Per Capita Product
at Constant Prices. 1958 = 100

Country		A: Total	B: Per Capita
		Years	
		1950	*1963*
Belgium	A	89	122
	B	92	119
Poland	A	53	129
	B	61	121
Japan	A	73	182
	B	77	174
Argentina	A	75	101
	B	88	94
Brazil	A	65	131
	B	83	114
Colombia	A	71	122
	B	85	112
India	A	76	115
	B	87	105
Indonesia	A	84	102
	B	93	99

SOURCE: United Nations, *Statistical Yearbook 1964*, Table 174.

tion of Egypt and Pakistan (to mention only two out of a possible host of other examples) on the international income ladder actually worsened on a per capita basis. From 1960 to 1962, average annual per capita income in the developed countries rose by almost $100, while that in the underdeveloped countries increased by just under $5.

THE LOW LEVEL EQUILIBRIUM TRAP

Countries in the infancy of economic development are usually caught in what economists call a "low level equilibrium trap." In less technical language the phenomenon is sometimes referred to as the "vicious circle of poverty" although, in fact, there are two circles on both sides of the key problem of capital formation. Some of the symptoms of that trap have been revealed in the preceding discussion on income inequality, life expectancy, literacy, and so on. The starting point is the simple proposition that for a country to get out of the morass and stagnation of underdevelopment, capital has to be accumulated. On the supply side, capital formation depends on the willingness and ability to save resources out of current income. Because there is little capital, productivity is low and so, therefore, is real income. A low real income means a small capacity to save, which means little capital accumulation. On the demand side, capital formation depends on the inducement to invest, but this may be low because the purchasing power of the people is small. Small purchasing power is due to the people's low real income, which is due to low productivity, which is the result of too little capital, which in turn, is due to the small inducement to invest.[8] The underlying assumption, of course, is that people in general, however small their income, have some say in the resource allocation (saving, investment, consumption) process. An economic solution to underdevelopment which does not propose to take this decision-making power away from the mass of producers and consumers, must find ways to persuade or induce the millions of decision makers to save and invest their resources in growth-promoting employments. This may be difficult to accomplish—persuasion and gradualism always are. There may thus be strong temptations to concentrate in a few entrepreneurial hands the power of decision over the allocation of scarce resources, and to use more compulsion than is warranted by methods which assume that men participate in the economic process not merely as commandeered impersonal inputs but as makers of meaningful decisions about production and consumption, the composition and pricing of output, and the mix of saving and investment. This is as much as to say that underdeveloped countries tend to be subject to strong centralist pressures and to the lures of dictatorial economic models.

To break out of the low level equilibrium trap three things are needed: (1) an appropriate growth mentality, (2) a method, and (3) an organization for implementing the outlook and method.

GROWTH MENTALITY

For the vicious circles of poverty to be broken and for the economy to emerge from the low level equilibrium trap, there must first be a willingness, indeed a determination, to break them. Second, those who pos-

---

[8] Ragnar Nurkse, *Problems of Capital Formation in Underdeveloped Countries* (New York, Oxford University Press, 1953), pp. 4–5.

sess the requisite outlook must have a method or strategy which would translate the growth impulses into economically meaningful action. Finally, there must be an organization, the institutional arrangements of which facilitate rather than block such action. In short, the problem is one of motivation, method, and system.

The motivation is most important. Traditionalism, apathy, fear of change, excessive preoccupation with immediate consumption, the love of arms and flashy uniforms, political ambitions, and social conceit have been the undoing of many regimes. Whether economic development is desirable or not is a valid, interesting, if increasingly academic, question. What economists call the "demonstration effect" has taken care of that. Travel and communications in all directions have opened the eyes of the citizens of the underdeveloped countries to the glitter and surface glamor as well as to the more lasting benefits of industrialization and, by the same token, have raised their propensity to consume. Their level of aspirations has outstripped what they and their countries are able to afford in the existing constellation of economic forces. They believe, and are repeatedly told by Moscow and Peking, that given the right kind of leadership and political consciousness, these forces can be made to vanish. Under such bombardment and out of a deeply felt conviction that the developed world in some way owes them something for the centuries of economic and political domination and national humiliation, the peoples of the developing countries are often unaware that industrialization exacts a heavy toll from the generations locked in its embrace. They want right now the end product of years of industrial construction without, if at all possible, having to pay the cost of early growth. In fact, they may not be aware that such a cost exists. Years of national liberation movements have led them to believe that the primary, if not the only, reason for their poverty has been the greediness and rapacity of foreign colonial powers. Now that these powers are gone, there is a sense of frustration, a lingering resentment about real and imagined wrongs suffered in a more or less distant past, and a watchful suspicion, carefully nurtured by Peking, of "new colonialism" that allegedly comes in the guise of foreign aid or the Peace Corps. Even if the leaders of the so-called "newly emergent" countries have not always caught up with the idea of economic growth, their people have in a vague, confused, and dangerously impatient way. The nub of the problem is that it is easier to want more than it is to adopt better methods of production and bear the heavy, if temporary, costs of the long march to the paradise of neon signs, throughways, and slot machines.

The mentality called for is not very pretty, at least not in the eyes of twentieth-century democracies. But twentieth-century democracies were not very pretty either, back in the late 1700's and the first half of the nineteenth century. The name often given to the outlook that built Manchester and the steel mills of Pittsburgh is the "Protestant Ethic." [9] It calls to mind visions of hard-working, self-denying, ascetic, puritanical men who found spiritual satisfaction and demure distraction in watching their profits grow into factory chimneys and blast furnaces. Marxism, while deploring the social effects of this state of mind, in fact counsels something very similar. But the "Protestant Ethic," the identification of investment with the virtuous life and the virtuous life with bountiful rewards in the life hereafter, is too narrow a concept. It can hardly explain the economic upsurge of Japan or that of the distinctly non-Protestant Soviet Union. The "Ethic of Economic Asceticism," or as the Chinese Communists put it, the virtue of "Self-Reliance," seems to be more apt. It is the outlook of the lover of black ink on the profit-and-loss account, the mentality of the nineteenth-century British and American entrepreneur, of the Japanese businessman back in the nineteen-twenties and of the Soviet economic commissars in the thirties and forties. In a speech to the National People's Congress, Chou En-lai summed up the problem as he saw it through Maoist glasses: "Diligence, thrift, plain living, and hard work constitute the good proletarian style, while extravagance, waste, and the pursuit of personal enjoyment constitute the degenerate bourgeois style." [10]

This is nothing but the old hymn in praise of investment and the marginal propensity to save that had been sung throughout the "bourgeois" West a hundred years ago. To compose such a hymn may take centuries, as it in fact did in Western Europe. The constitution of the modern Indian state has in it a provision designed to protect the sacred cow: "The State shall endeavor to organize agriculture and animal husbandry on modern and scientific lines and shall in particular, take steps for preserving and improving the breeds, and prohibiting the slaughter of cows and calves and other milch and draught cattle."

GROWTH METHODS

An outlook that welcomes change is, however, not enough. It must be systematized into a technique for breaking out of the low level equilibrium trap. The basic techniques are in many respects similar largely because of the similarity of the problems to be tackled. There do exist, however, important differences in emphasis.

For a country to start on the long road of economic development several things must be done:

[9] Max Weber, *The Protestant Ethic and the Spirit of Capitalism*, trans. by T. Parsons (New York, Scribner, 1958). See also R. H. Tawney, *Religion and the Rise of Capitalism* (London, J. Murray, 1936).

[10] Report by Comrade Chou En-lai on the work of the government to the First Session of the Third National People's Congress, December 21–22, 1964, *Peking Review*, January 1, 1965, p. 9.

(1) *Human and physical capital must be formed.*

The formation of human capital means the expenditure of resources on the development of attitudes, aptitudes, knowledge, and skills conducive to the process of modern production. In a word, it means education. It also implies public health. This aspect of investment has often been neglected in studies of techniques of economic growth largely because of the difficulty inherent in quantifying the return on this type of expenditure. To this day, statistical data on growth tend to ignore investment in human capital, a fact which distorts our understanding of the contributory causes of economic growth.

The formation of physical capital means the construction of buildings and durable equipment, the development of land, and the building up of commodity stocks.

(2) *Resources must be saved out of current income.*

The process of saving, i.e., abstaining from immediate consumption, is indispensable to capital formation. Saving may be voluntary or forced. Voluntary saving depends on a person's marginal propensity to save, which tends to be low for people whose income stream is modest. Involuntary saving depends on the ability of the state to extract tax revenues from the income earners which, in turn, depends to a considerable extent on the income earners' willingness to cooperate.

(3) *Resources saved must be invested in growth-generating employments.*

If the investment function is vested in individuals, it will depend on the inducement to invest. One such inducement is the expected yield from a new unit of capital (the marginal efficiency of capital) which is related to the rate of interest. The expected yield on a new unit of capital depends in the short run on such factors as the size of the existing stock of capital assets and the strength of consumer demand for goods which require much capital for their production. In the long run, the state of expectations depends upon the prospective investor's estimate of future changes in the size of the capital stock and in the size of effective demand during the future life of the asset the prospective yield of which is being calculated. Since long-run estimates are at best guesses, they will tend to be influenced by the investor's confidence or lack of it about what will happen in the future. In underdeveloped countries, such confidence is often influenced by the present unsatisfactory state of affairs which usually includes political instability and monetary inflation. This means that the inducement to invest may often be weak. It also means that savings may be channelled into land, real estate, gold, or foreign exchange (i.e., repatriation or flight of capital abroad).

A second, related aspect of the investment process must also be noted. The relation between investment and growth depends most importantly on the incremental capital-output ratio (ICOR). This means the ratio between additions to investment and the resulting additions to output. ICOR varies geographically, over time, and by industries. It may give rise to varying emphases on the priorities to be assigned among possible investment projects. In general, a dollar invested in the "heavy" industries (e.g., steel) will tend to produce more statistically measurable growth (though not necessarily more consumer welfare) than a dollar invested in, say, the textile industry. In the first case, there is a multiplier effect lacking in the second. The dollar produces steel which goes into the making of a machine tool component, which is used to fix a machine, which produces wheel rims, which are used in locomotives, which haul merchandise, and so on. In the second instance the same dollar produces a shirt which goes on the back of one consumer. The consumer may feel warmer and, therefore, happier, but the statistician measuring growth (and, as yet, unable to precisely measure welfare) is unhappy about the whole thing. The example is, of course, oversimplified and needs a great deal of qualification. But in general, it points to the problem of choice involved in directing scarce investible resources to various competing uses.

In short, capital formation means that resources must be drummed up from a relatively modest resource base and that they must be invested in growth-promoting employments.

In the absence of a sufficient marginal propensity to save, a weak inducement to invest, and a tendency to channel savings into employments which give little growth per additional unit of capital, and given the presence of an outlook which includes growth as a high priority objective, there will be a strong inducement to use force in order to negotiate the three steps to development. Forced savings and commanded investment may, in those circumstances, come to play a leading role in getting the economy out of its low equilibrium trap. The use of constraint in economic policy may have to be backed by unrepresentative political arrangements including a one-party system, the platform of which mirrors the economic philosophy of those whose outlook favors growth as a first priority.

Such a course of action involves what may be called the "confiscation effect." In the widest sense, the confiscation effect means the transfer of the power over the allocation of resources from those who would presumably use it less productively to those who intend to use it more productively. Such a transfer may involve political upheaval as those whose rights are being confiscated begin bitterly to resist the process. In regard to savings, the confiscation effect will usually imply the use of methods to fetter the marginal propensity to consume (i.e., keep consumption at relatively low levels) and effectively to extract the unconsumed portion of current income from the mass of income earners. In regard to investment, the confiscation effect will usually imply the concentration of savings in the hands of those who plan to invest them in conformity with their ICOR estimates.

It should perhaps be pointed out that the use of force to effect the savings and investment process, though it involves institutional arrangements, is not necessarily restricted to any one kind of organizational form. The enclosures of common pastures in the England of the eighteenth century and the collectivization of agriculture in the Soviet Union of the twentieth may be cited as examples of the use of two very different types of economic institutions to implement similar economic objectives. There is nothing in the very nature of the institution of private property to guarantee that it not be used to achieve the confiscation effect. Similarly, the collective form of organization need not always be used to squeeze surplus resources from the members of the collective. Whether these institutions will or will not be used as tools of confiscation depends very largely on the developmental age of the economy in question.

ECONOMIC ORGANIZATION

An economic system is simply the combination of ways in which the job of allocating scarce resources among the many competing, alternative uses gets done. The ways themselves are called institutions as, for example, the institution of private property or that of the profit motive. Traditionally, contemporary economic systems have been classified as capitalist, socialist, communist, and fascist. This classification leaves much to be desired, mainly because it pays too little heed to the changing nature of economic systems. It is also extremely ambiguous and charged with all kinds of emotional irrelevances. More recently an attempt has been made to reclassify economic systems according to whether resources are allocated among the various uses and the allocation decisions coordinated by the market mechanism or by planned command. The result has been a new listing of systems under the names of market-oriented, command-oriented, and mixed market-command.

In a market-oriented economy the allocation of resources is determined by the actions of individual buyers and sellers in free markets. These actions express themselves in market signals called prices, and the prices, in turn, act as rationing and allocating devices by which the actions of individual buyers and sellers are guided.[11]

In a command economy the allocation of resources is decided upon by a centralized supreme authority usually on the basis of political and

[11] In technical terms, the system comprises consumer demand functions, the transformation functions of producers, and the supply functions of productive factors, and combines these in a mathematical equation system which is solved by the market through a constant process of reshuffling production and consumption until an efficient resource utilization equilibrium is reached. See, Bela A. Balassa, *The Hungarian Experience in Economic Planning* (New Haven, Yale University Press, 1959).

administrative criteria. The concentration of key economic decision-making powers in the supreme authority will usually be supplemented by the concentration of political decision-making powers in that authority. The economic preferences expressed and acted upon by such a system are the preferences of the authority. Whether they do or do not correspond to those of the other participants in the economic process depends on the extent to which the authority consults in some extra-economic way the other members of the system, as well as on the extent to which it decides to act on the information so obtained. The institutions of such a system are set up not to reveal the preferences of the individual consumers and producers, but rather to communicate to these consumers and producers the preferences of the authority and to enforce compliance. Thus, for example, prices in a command system do not act as rationing and signaling devices—rationing the demand for goods and signaling the cost—but as accounting and control mechanisms used to accomplish the aims of the decision-making authority.

The essential difference between the two systems consists in the location of economic decision-making power. In a market-oriented system the power tends to be diffused; in a command-oriented economy it tends to be concentrated. The one system emphasizes individualism; the other, collectivism.

Most economies lie somewhere in between. They are usually referred to as "mixed" economies. They contain varying proportions of individual and collective decision making over the allocation of resources, a varying mix, that is, of market and command decisions. As one moves from the one extreme (market) to the other (command), differences in the degree of the mix tend to become differences in kind. The border line is hazy, but it exists. There is a world of difference, for example, between a market economy with a large ingredient of command, such as France, and a command economy with a large ingredient of the market, such as Yugoslavia. The political difference between the two, is, of course, even more striking.

Strictly speaking there is no such thing as a pure market system and a pure command system. Leakages of all kinds are bound to occur even though the intention to keep the system pure may be there. The United States is the nearest approach to the market model, but even here considerable elements of governmental decision making are present in the economic process. The nearest approach to a pure command economy is Communist China, but even there some elements of the market persist. Examples of market-oriented economies are Canada, Australia, Belgium, the Netherlands, West Germany, Switzerland, Brazil, Argentina, Mexico, and Japan. Examples of command-oriented economies are the Soviet Union, Communist China, and the communist countries of Europe and Southeast Asia, Cuba, and increasingly, Egypt. Mixed market-command systems include Britain, France, Italy, India, and Pakistan, in which the market element predominates in spite of considerable command elements, and Yugoslavia, in which the command element dwarfs that of the market. In recent years the Soviet Union, Poland, Hungary, East Germany, and Czechoslovakia have been timidly experimenting with some market features.[12] At the same time, the scope of command has been expanding in some of the market-oriented systems. The major reasons for this shift may be summed up as follows. Command decisions are essentially political and administrative. Usually they are not based on any precise calculation of relative resource scarcities (on microeconomic considerations, the economists call them). This may involve waste. When the decisions to be taken are few and bulky, when it is a question of whether to build the nation's only steel mill or not, such rough-and-ready methods can be absorbed if they result in an increase in measurable output. When, however, the nation is already well equipped with steel mills, the question as to whether another mill should be built and of what kind becomes more subtle. In such a context administrative fiat tends to become increasingly intolerable. In recent years retail stores in Moscow have been complaining about rapidly accumulating stocks of unwanted clothing and food. When each consumer had only one well-worn suit and precious little in his stomach, such problems did not arise, even though the goods might not have been any more attractive than they are now. The introduction of market elements in a command setting is, therefore, motivated by the need and the desire of the decision-making authority to reduce the waste motion in an increasingly complex economy in which the range of choice has vastly expanded. On the other side, the market mechanism takes care only of those wants which are backed by purchasing power. It may, thus, supply tion whether the market should be supplemented by command, or completely the needs of those who by reason of advanced age or infirmity are not in a position to exert any appreciable pull on the market. In short, the market-oriented system usually takes excellent care of the private wants of income earners and largely ignores collective or social wants. Hence the twin movement toward and away from the market. The question whether the market should be supplemented by command, or command by the market, remains, however, a real one; and the answer given makes the difference between democracy and totalitarianism. To obtain just the right mix of market and command without sliding into bureaucratism and economic (and usually political) dictatorship is as difficult as to arrive at the right mix of command and the market without abandoning economic (and political) *Diktat*. It is a question which preoccupies Americans as much as the Soviets. In both the United States and the communist world strong and vociferous forces are opposed to

---

[12] Jan S. Prybyla, "The Quest for Economic Rationality in the Soviet Bloc," *Social Research*, Vol. 30, No. 3, Autumn, 1963, pp. 343–366; "The Economic Strengths and Weaknesses of Communism in Eastern Europe," *Business Topics*, Michigan State University, Vol. 12, No. 1, Winter, 1964, pp. 35–42.

such experiments. In an interview printed in 1965 by the Egyptian monthly *At-Taliya,* Cuba's Érnesto 'Che' Guevara was quoted as saying: "Where the law of value reigns, it directs the economy toward capitalism. In other words, there is in Yugoslavia the danger of an alignment toward capitalism." [13]

MARKET, COMMAND, AND ECONOMIC UNDERDEVELOPMENT

In a sense, most of the underdeveloped economies are systemless. Once the decision has been taken to attempt a break from the low level equilibrium trap, the question arises as to what methods and which of the several forms of economic organization should be adopted. This problem is rendered more difficult by outside pressures on the leaders of the developing countries to follow this or that method and implant these or those organizational forms. As responsible men in these countries are never tired of repeating, much of the foreign aid flowing into their economies is "tied" in one way or another to the givers' urgent request that the recipients refrain from certain courses of action and follow others. The United States Congress is reluctant to extend loans to the Indian government for the construction of state-owned steel mills which would compete with the private steel industry, and the Soviets, for their part, will not lend to private interests.

In this competition both sides may claim certain advantages. The market-oriented solution is advocated by countries that have at their disposal a greater quantity and variety of resources than the countries which encourage the adoption of command systems. Both sides can point to impressive achievements in climbing out of the low level equilibrium trap. From what had been said before about the prevalence of constraint in the early stages of development, it would appear that the command solution has an extra appeal to countries embarking on the long and rough path of economic growth. The command economy is capable of concentrating and directing resources for the sake of growth more readily than market-oriented systems. Such direction will, of course, be purchased at the price of individual rights, especially the right to exercise meaningful economic decisions. But here again, the difficulty is more apparent than real, for it cannot be said that in conditions of acute poverty and in the context of systemless economies, the decision-making function is ever real. To put it bluntly, things cannot be worse than they were before. The appeal of command to the leaders of the underdeveloped countries arises from a negative source. Their experience of markets is limited to the workings of international commodity markets which, on the whole, have not been

13 Harry Schwartz, "Ultra-Reds See Perils in Profits," *The New York Times,* July 4, 1965, p. 2.

favorable to rapid domestic growth. The market solution, therefore, appears to them fraught with the kind of dangers they had experienced in the past. Added to this is the ideological opprobrium which in the eyes of many attaches to the market-oriented solution, sponsored as that solution is by the former colonial powers. In short, the odds are stacked against a combination of economic takeoff and the wide diffusion of decision-making power, and the likelihood of a considerable element of command is ever present. The trend toward command is observable in many countries of Africa, and, programmatically at least, exists in such countries as Burma, India, and Pakistan. In the absence of voluntary saving of any sizeable volume and because of a weak inducement to invest such resources as are available in growth-yielding employment, the entrepreneurial function tends, in much of the underdeveloped world, to be taken over by the state.

THE ROLE OF FOREIGN ASSISTANCE

Does all this mean that underdeveloped countries have to pass through the painful teenage of compulsion of either the early "capitalist" or early "socialist" variety? Are minor versions of the United States, Britain, and France of the nineteen-sixties impossible and minor versions of the Soviet Union of the thirties ineluctable? It is impossible to answer these questions by a simple yes or no. The ideal situation, of course, would be to somehow combine political freedom of even a timid kind, or at least the more relaxed atmosphere of the emerging nations, with rapid takeoff from poverty. India is valiantly trying to do this, and its efforts should not only be watched with interest, but aided. But, still, the odds seem to be against such a possibility. The purgatory of systems of economic constraint on the way to development is not an objective, irreversible, social law. It is merely a distinct possibility. One can always hope for the one exception that will disprove the rule. Moreover, the hypothesis that age and economic fatness always bring with them parliamentary democracy and freedom of thought and expression needs much careful hedging and much more thorough study than has hitherto been devoted to it. It is true, however, that the range of choice in industrial societies as well as the complexity of that choice militate against the kind of simplistic faith that Stalinist Marxism, Maoist Leninism, and Ricardian Classicism preach. Convergence of economic systems through growth, the coming together of certain key attitudes and forms of behavior, remains an interesting hypothesis and one worthy of attention.

The constraint prevalent in many economies embarking on economic development may be softened by foreign assistance. If all, or nearly all, the resources needed for the takeoff have to be generated internally (as is presently the lot of Communist China), constraint may reach mammoth proportions. Some of the burden of development which would have had to be borne by the Indian farmer is actually carried by the American, West German, and increasingly, the Soviet taxpayer. The first Indian Five-Year Plan (1951–1955) was financed to the extent of 10 percent by external financial assistance. Foreign aid paid for well over one quarter of the second Five-Year Plan (1956–1960) and for about 30 percent of the third Five-Year Plan (1961–1966).[14] If the hypothesis of convergence really holds, international cooperation in the task of aid to developing countries would prove to be an important step in the direction of attaining a calmer and saner world.

CONCLUSIONS

The greater part of the world and over two-thirds of the world's people are today in the grips of poverty. In most of these lands the gross national product is small and its distribution is lopsided both as regards the sectors of origin and those of final use. In the underdeveloped countries some 90 percent of the people are engaged in agriculture. This agriculture is primitive, capital-deficient, and highly labor-intensive. Less than 5 percent of the gross national product is saved, and investments tend to be dissipated in acquisitions of land and real estate. The inducement to invest is low and the inducement to expatriate what capital there is tends to be high. Eighty or more percent of the people are illiterate and subject to endemic disease caused by malnutrition and neglect or nonexistence of public health services. Mortality rates are high and life expectancy rates low. Per capita output over much of the world does not exceed $100. Little attempt has been made to explore natural resources or to provide the countries with social overheads such as roads, railroads, and canals, Technical skills are rare, and entrepreneurial ability limited. What industry there is tends to be owned and operated by foreigners. Monoculture and heavy dependence on the export of a single crop or mineral are common. This dependence may be one cause of instability and a serious impediment to sustained growth. For instance, between 1955 and 1962 the unit value of exports from the underdeveloped countries fell by 12 percent. During the same period, the unit value of exports from the industrialized nations rose by 16 percent. In other words, the terms of trade, on the yield from which many developing countries rely heavily to finance their development, have deteriorated in recent years.

Escape from this condition presupposes capital accumulation. This means that the underdeveloped countries must generate domestic savings and invest those savings in growth-promoting projects. But saving and investment are extremely difficult in conditions of material poverty be-

[14] Richard T. Gill, *Economic Development: Past and Present* (Englewood Cliffs, N.J., Prentice-Hall, Foundations of Modern Economics Series, 1963), p. 102.

cause of the low marginal propensity to save and the equally low inducement to invest.

In such circumstances, strong forces will manifest themselves in favor of compulsion. There will be strong inducements to generate forced savings where voluntary savings fail to materialize and to direct investment where private investment fails to do the job. In short, economic models which advocate a command system will tend to have an appeal to the underdeveloped countries that models advocating a market solution do not possess.

The degree of compulsion may be significantly reduced by international efforts to channel resources from the more to the less developed regions. Such efforts would tend to lessen tensions which the present gap between the rich nations and the poor creates.

Some of the difficult and perplexing choices involved in this task are set forth in the following positions.

POSITIONS

1. WHAT ARE THE STRENGTHS OF THE WESTERN ALTERNATIVE FOR ECONOMIC DEVELOPMENT?

The chances of underdeveloped countries' adopting the Western-type strategy of development are good provided the West places itself solidly on the side of reform and movements toward reform. This view is eloquently presented in the following extract from John Kenneth Galbraith's *Economic Development*.[15]

Two major advantages lie with the Western or non-Marxian alternative. There is, according to ancient physical law, a certain difficulty in extracting blood from a stone. This is, in all respects, comparable with the problem of getting savings out of a poor society. When people do not have enough to eat, they are loath to forego any part of their meal that they may eat better in the future. Pleas on behalf of a better life for children and grandchildren leave the man of simple, uncomplicated intelligence unmoved; he reflects that starvation will prevent him from having any viable children and, *pro tanto,* grandchildren either. But Marxian no less than non-Marxian societies must have savings; without them there can be no growth. Accordingly, the Western pattern of development, with its prospect of assistance from outside the country, eases one of the most painful problems of development. This is why economic aid has become such an important feature of Western foreign policy. It is the process by which savings are transferred from countries where saving is comparatively unpainful to those where it is very painful. It exploits one of the major advantages of our system.

[15] Reprinted by permission of the publishers from John Kenneth Galbraith, ECONOMIC DEVELOPMENT, Cambridge, Mass.: Harvard University Press. Copyright, 1962, 1964, by John Kenneth Galbraith, pp. 28–36.

To be sure, the Communist countries are not without resources in this respect. The Soviet Union, though its capacity has been far less than ours, has spared some savings for other countries. Communist economic and political organization deals more effectively—or ruthlessly—with unproductive and excessively luxurious consumption. Such consumption by a small minority is, as I have noted, a common feature of the poor country. And Communist organization can, within limits, squeeze blood from its turnip.

The penalty is the pain, and this cannot be avoided. The rioting in Poland in 1956 which brought Gomulka to power was occasioned in large measure by the enforcement of a rate of savings that was too stern for the people to bear. These last years on the Chinese mainland have evidently been years of serious trouble and tension. Part of the problem is related to the socialist organization of agriculture. But some has certainly been inherent in the effort to extract a large volume of savings from a very poor population.

The larger consequence is that the process of Marxian development risks, as non-Marxian development does not, the alienation of the people. One doubts that past governments of China are remembered with affection. But it is also the expert consensus that a majority of the Chinese people are scarcely pleased with their present rulers. They would not vote for them in an uninhibited poll. By contrast, India, after a decade of development, gave an overwhelming vote to the government that led the task. Had that government found it necessary to subtract the $7.3 billion it received in loans and grants from Western sources (as of 1963) from the meager incomes—an average of about $70 per year—of its own people, its popularity would certainly have suffered. One sees in India, in remarkably clear relief, the importance in the Western design of help in providing capital.

The second and equally substantial advantage of Western development is in the matter of agriculture. Industry, on the record at least, is fairly tolerant as to forms of economic and political organization. American industry works moderately well under private ownership. The most reluctant free-enterpriser must agree that the Soviets have made great industrial progress under socialism. So no decisive contrast can be registered in this sector of the economy. But the undeveloped country is, by definition, a pastoral or agrarian country. Its agricultural policy is, accordingly, vital. And it is still far from clear, as a practical matter, whether it is possible to socialize successfully a small-scale, densely populated, peasant agriculture.

In the Soviet Union, after nearly half a century, the agricultural problem has not been wholly solved. And in this area of economic activity at least, there is no serious talk by the Soviets of catching up with the United States. On the contrary, in agriculture each year we insouciantly extend our advantage in man-hour productivity without effort and rather to our regret. Outside the Soviet Union, agriculture has been even more of a problem. Poland and Yugoslavia have had to revert to private ownership. In China, by all external evidence, the effort to socialize agriculture brought a drastic crisis and considerable modification of the original design. Along with bad weather, it forced the Chinese to turn to the West for some of the largest food imports in history.

There are good reasons for this difficulty with agriculture. Farmers, when they are small and numerous, can, if they choose, defeat any system that is available for their control. The employees of a factory, like the men of an army, are subject to external discipline. Failure in performance can be detected, judged and penalized. The same rule holds for certain types of plantation agriculture. A scattered peasantry, carrying on the diverse tasks of crop and especially of livestock husbandry, cannot be so controlled and managed. Certainly it cannot be controlled if it disapproves of the system. And farmers have rarely, if ever, approved of any economic system which denied them ownership of land. The farmer has it within his powers, when working for others or for the state, to work at the minimum rather than the maximum, and the difference between the two is enormous. He can be made to work at his maximum by giving him land and rewarding him with the fruits of his labor or some substantial share to consume or exchange as he wishes. But this is to restore individual proprietorship— private capitalism—which doctrine excludes.

One day the Marxian economies may succeed in socializing agriculture. Certainly no effort is being spared. And the ability of the small man in agriculture to sabotage a system he dislikes or which treats him badly is not confined to Communism. It is the reason for the low productivity and backwardness of the latifundia of Latin America and the feudal villages of the Middle East. But the fact that independent agricultural proprietorship is accepted is the second clear advantage of Western development.

I come now to the principal disadvantage of Western development. The Marxian alternative, I have noted, emphasizes the destruction of the bonds that tie the economy to the past. Our emphasis is on capital, education, technical assistance, and the other instruments that promote change. Until recently, at least, we have been tempted to suppose that any society is a platform on which, given these missing elements, development can be built.

In fact, institutions do chain economies to the past, and the breaking of these chains is essential for progress. The promise of drastic reform is a valid and an appealing part of the Marxian case. There is no chance of agricultural development in the under-developed (and hence agricultural) country under systems of absentee landlordism where the workers or sharecroppers are confined by law and tradition to a minor share of a meager product. These feudal agricultural systems, moreover, extend their corrupting influence to government, to the provision of public or military sinecures to those who lack a claim on the land, to the milking of industrial enterprise, and to the destruction of the moral fiber of the society itself. "In our country," a guide in Lima once told me, "those who do the least work get the most money. I hear that in the United States it is the other way around. I believe it is a better system." Progress requires the radical elimination of retarding institutions. If elimination can be had from no other source, the Marxian alternative will sooner or later be tried. The revolution that is required here, we should remind ourselves, is less the Russian Revolution than the French Revolution.

There is one further and different point of comparison between the two systems, one which, unfortunately, has been much damaged by bad rhetoric. From the earliest days of their development, personal liberty, equal justice under law, and constitutional government have been important to Englishmen and to Americans. These things have not been the concern of everyone, but we have never supposed them to be a foible of an esoteric and privileged minority.

And so it is in the undeveloped country today. The Andean tenant and the landless worker in an Orissa village do have a preoccupying concern with keeping themselves fed. But a widespread yearning for the dignity of democratic and constitutional government is more common than is usually imagined. No people who live under a dictatorship ever feel themselves to be really first-class citizens.

And it is widely agreed that liberty and constitutional process are safer with the Western than with the Marxian alternative. We have not been nearly as consistent in our support of these as wisdom would have required. A curious inversion of intelligence has regularly caused those who regard themselves as the most learned and subtle in matters of foreign policy to urge the support of the most nauseous dictators. The consequences have been uniformly disastrous.*

On first assessment, then, the advantages of the non-Marxian alternative for the developing country are considerable. It promises at least a partial avoidance of the pain that for the poor country is inherent in finding savings for investment and growth. It promises an acceptable and viable system of agriculture rather than a certainly unpalatable and possibly unworkable one. And it offers personal liberty and constitutional process. Against this, the Marxian alternative promises a rigorous and effective attack on the institutions—the unproductive claims on revenue, and especially the feudal control of land—which exclude change.

But this is not a game where one can count the cards and decide the winner. Some cards count for more than others, and there is the unfortunate possibility, in our case, that some valuable cards will not get played.

The Marxian promise can be decisive. That is because the things we offer are effective and attractive only after the retarding institutions are eliminated. In a country where land and other productive resources are held by and operated for the benefit of a slight minority, and where the apparatus of government serves principally to reinforce such privilege, aid is of no use. It will benefit not the many but the few. And the Western promise of independent proprietorship in agriculture is obviously nullified so long as land remains in the hands of the few. And personal liberty and constitutional government have little meaning in countries where government is of the privileged, by the corrupt, for the rich.

We have no alternative, in short, but to meet the Marxian promise to be rid of archaic and retarding institutions. I doubt that we can organize revolution. But we can place our influence solidly on the side of reform and movements toward reform. We can close our ears to the pleas of vested interest. If we do so, and reform follows, our cards give us a clear advantage. To be sure, we must play them all. We must make good on our promise of a less painful savings and investment process. We must give firm support to the small farmer. We must be clear in our commitment to constitutional process and personal liberty and we cannot suppose that these are wanted only by people of Anglo-Saxon origin of good income. We must not excuse dictatorship on grounds of anti-Communism or convenience or the absence of visible alternatives. This, to repeat, is one of the oldest and certainly the most myopic habit of our foreign policy, and its price we now know is disaster magnified by postponement.

* Except, I am led to add by way of amendment, to the architects of the policy. They are promoted and eventually retire with a high reputation for subtlety of view.

These are highly practical matters. The first resort to the Marxian alternative in this hemisphere in Cuba was in a country where the concentration of wealth and land ownership was extreme, where these had extended a corrupting influence to economic life and to government, and where dictatorship had been endemic. This being the experience of Cubans with the Western model, it was not remarkable that so many were so little perturbed by the alternative. India, in face of formidable difficulties, is strongly committed to development on the Western model. That is because even in British India, and over the whole country at the time of independence, there was a strong attack on retarding institutions—on the feudal claims of princes, zamindars, and great landlords, and on a system of government which was in part an extension of this landed power. A substantial measure of peasant ownership replaced the old system, aid from outside eased the problem of supply capital, and people felt secure in the protection of constitutional guarantees and representative government.

Given the same advantages, we may reasonably assume that people elsewhere will opt for them.

2. ARE WESTERN-TYPE POLITICAL DEMOCRACY AND ECONOMIC TAKEOFF COMPATIBLE AT THE PRESENT TIME?

"Very often, no," answers Robert Theobald in his challenging essay: *The Rich and the Poor: A Study of the Economics of Rising Expectations.* The author, born in India, one time member of the *Economist* Intelligence Unit, argues that the specific conditions of the newly emergent countries may frequently militate against the introduction of Western-type political institutions early in the process of economic development.[16]

Will Western Forms of Democracy Be Workable?

In recent years some newly independent nations that firmly proclaim their adherence to democratic beliefs have temporarily abandoned the institutions of democracy as they are understood in the West; others, who on assuming their independence adopted democratic beliefs, have publicly stated their doubts about the applicability of these principles to the problems they face; still others have refused from the beginning to accept Western democracy as appropriate to their existing problems. These developments have led to much discussion in the West; some suggest that, if the forms of Western democracy are not followed, countries will necessarily fail in their task; others argue that Western democracy cannot be expected to be suitable and that any attempt to apply it will necessarily lead to waste of resources and lack of governmental control.

. . .

The type of government adopted must be designed to deal with the particular problems the poor countries face. Three issues will dominate in coming years. First, the attempt to secure economic growth; this is essential if the in-

[16] Robert Theobald, *The Rich and the Poor: A Study of the Economics of Rising Expectations* (New York, Mentor Books, 1961), pp. 47, 50, 52, 54, 55–56, 57. Reprinted by permission of Clarkson N. Potter, Inc., Publisher.

crease in population is not to lead to a decline in the standard of living and if "the revolution of rising expectations" is to be satisfied. Second, the need to change the attitudes of these countries to bring them into accord with modern conditions; while work and saving must not be worshiped as they have sometimes been in the West, more attention must be given to them. The attempt to meet these two aims will be complicated in many areas by a third requirement, the need to destroy existing social organizations, such as the caste system in India and tribal enmity in Africa, and to weld separate and often traditionally hostile groups into a nation.

These problems are far more complex than those faced by the rich countries in their early stages of economic growth. Adam Smith's influence was at its height and it was believed that he had shown that the self-interested decisions of each individual would lead to the maximum possible rate of growth in the economy and in the welfare of society. Governments did not interfere with the supply of foreign exchange and the level of employment. The "economic system" was presumed to deal with these matters, and if there *was* unemployment and suffering it was thought that any government action could only worsen the situation, for it would interfere with the "immutable" laws of economics.

· · ·

Dictatorial power can build this sense of national purpose; policies are then imposed by a single ruler or a ruling clique. Such a solution has always been condemned in the West, but it is the *goal* of good government that is important not solely the form of the institutions by which it is attained. There is some evidence that the governments of the countries that have changed in recent years from Western democracy to a form of dictatorship have become less corrupt and more efficient, while the rights of the inhabitants of the country often appear to be more secure. The West has always argued that dictatorship, however efficient it may be in the short run, must inevitably fail. Its view is clearly expressed in one of the most famous political aphorisms of all time: "Power corrupts, absolute power corrupts absolutely." This belief, however, is based on the existence of Western values and is not necessarily appropriate in other areas where power is not sought but only accepted. Despite the problems they raise, it would appear that dictatorships, either overt or covert, will remain a common form of government in the poor countries for many years.

· · ·

The amount of power delegated to the central government will need to be far greater than in the early stages of industrial growth in the countries that are now rich. It is, however, possible that the governments of the poor countries can limit their responsibilities by allowing considerable autonomy in the rural areas.

· · ·

The policies developed by the central government must be presented so that they will be seen to be acceptable. As they will often conflict with traditional beliefs, a method must be found of "educating" the population to accept them. Such a suggestion raises specters the West has sought to exorcise—it raises the prospect that governments will "propagandize" their populations to accept new ideas. However, the need for changed values is so urgent that only deliberate planned action can bring it about rapidly enough. The presently accepted goals of the poor countries are no longer adequate to provide for the survival of the community or of the people within it; new values are necessary and these must be taught.

. . .

But who can decide exactly what should be taught? It is certain that unanimity cannot be reached easily, for the values imparted will be one of the major factors in determining the speed and direction of progress. However, the result of too much discussion will be to make it impossible for teachers to discern the goals toward which the country is aiming. Frequent changes in ideas can only result in a sense of flux and frustration in those who are attempting to implement the resulting policies. Decisions will often have to be made by the central authorities and in certain countries it may be necessary to impose some limitations to criticism.

. . .

The stereotypes of the West about the "right" form of government are no longer adequate; each situation in the poor countries will need to be evaluated on its merits. There can be little doubt that the rulers of the great majority of the poor countries are now concerned to give their populations the maximum of freedom, combined with the most rapid, feasible rate of economic growth— despite this they will often be forced to take steps that curtail the amount of civil liberties. The rich countries must understand that these steps are the results of pressures unknown to them and that the policies followed are normally the *least unpleasant* available to the rulers of the poor countries—not those they would ideally adopt if conditions permitted.

3. IS COMPULSORY SAVING INDISPENSABLE TO ECONOMIC GROWTH?

The authors of the lines quoted below answer in the negative, unless, that is, economic growth is understood in a narrow sense, being identified with certain political objectives.[17]

The advocacy of compulsory saving is, as a rule, based on three propositions: economic growth as such is desirable; economic growth is in large measure a function of capital accumulation; and compulsory saving necessarily increases capital accumulation. These propositions do not have general or incontrovertible validity.

. . .

The argument may be put in this way. Private savings make possible a series of continuous and marginal economic adjustments and adaptations which are conducive to growth. These are the kinds of adjustments with which economic analysis has largely been concerned during the last half-century, and they can be left safely to individual and dispersed decision-making. But this approach is

[17] From Peter T. Bauer and Basil S. Yamey, *The Economics of Under-Developed Countries*, Chicago, The University of Chicago Press in association with James Nisbet & Co., Ltd. and the Cambridge University Press, 1957, pp. 190, 191–192, 193–194.

not sufficient for dealing with the initiation of growth itself or with other large, discontinuous strides forward. Large and discontinuous changes are sometimes necessary to overcome obstacles or humps in the way of further economic growth. The problem is one of surmounting an abrupt threshold, and not of making a continuous series of a large number of individually small adjustments to marginal changes in economic variables. To get over the threshold on to a higher plateau of economic activity and well-being calls for an especially large expenditure of capital either on a single indivisible project or on a number of projects which have to be undertaken in combination or not at all. Individual savers or investors cannot comprehend or assess the productivity of such discontinuous and indivisible increments of investment, and hence are unwilling to make savings available for these investments although the benefits to them of the changes would be greater (even in their estimation) than the benefits to be derived from private investments or from current consumption. Compulsion, that is taxation in this context, is necessary to maximise the desirable flow of resources. It is true that individual preferences are overridden, but this in time enables individuals to have a wider and more effective range of choice and an increased command over resources. In other words, the case for compulsion would then be essentially the case for an educative restraint on the disposal of personal incomes.

. . .

Those who advocate compulsory saving usually take a narrow view of economic growth, and identify it with particular forms or directions of change, for example rapid industrialisation. This strengthens the conclusion that we are dealing with questions of political objectives and not with self-contained problems of economic analysis. Recognition that economic change can take place at varying rates and along various routes, and that advocates of compulsory saving favour a rate of change (usually in particular sectors) greater than the current rate of change, points in the same direction. In the sphere of economic growth, as in other spheres of economic decision-making, there are problems of choice. These problems have economic aspects. But economics does not prescribe the choices which ought to be made. Advocates of compulsory saving prefer that important decisions be made by the government rather than by dispersed individuals, and that decisions go one way rather than another. Our own preference is for arrangements in which decision-making is dispersed and individual preferences are given full expression.

In our view, therefore, the clearest case for economic activity by the state is where this is indispensable, in one form or another, to secure a supply of a good or service for which there is a current demand, and of which the cost of production could be recovered if it were possible to charge individual beneficiaries. Expenditures or activities yielding benefits indiscriminately are analytically the least ambiguous examples. However, since the intensity of demand for such services cannot be measured or tested in the market, the volume of such services to be provided or sponsored by the state is a matter of judgment.

Compulsory saving for development generally encompasses activities other than those yielding benefits indiscriminately, for example programmes of accelerated industrialisation. Our discussion is also relevant for over-expanded schemes of expenditure on investments yielding benefits indiscriminately, though, as has been explained, it is a matter of judgment at which point such expenditures are considered to be over-expanded.

The general conclusion is that the assessment of compulsory saving for development is based largely on political grounds. We have stated our reasons for rejecting compulsory saving as an instrument of economic policy.

4. MORE ORGANIZATION, LESS LIBERTY?

As against the assumption implicit in the convergence argument that greater economic development somehow widens choice and broadens the area of freedom, British philosopher Bertrand Russell contends in the paragraphs which follow that there is, on the whole, much less liberty in the world today than there was a hundred years ago, and that this is due in large measure to the great increase in organization.[18]

[John Stuart] Mill's book *On Liberty* is more important to us in the present day than his book *On the Subjection of Women*. It is more important because the cause which it advocates has been less successful. There is, on the whole, much less liberty in the world now than there was a hundred years ago; and there is no reason to suppose that restrictions on liberty are likely to grow less in any foreseeable future. Mill points to Russia as a country so dominated by bureaucracy that no one, not even the individual bureaucrat, has any personal liberty. But the Russia of his day, after the emancipation of the serfs, had a thousand times more freedom than the Russia of our day. The Russia of his day produced great writers who opposed the autocracy, courageous revolutionaries who were able to carry on their propaganda in spite of prison and exile, even liberals among those in power, as the abolition of serfdom proved. There was every reason to hope that Russia would in time develop into a constitutional monarchy, marching by stages towards the degree of political freedom that existed in England. The growth of liberty was also apparent in other countries. In the United States, slavery was abolished a few years after the publication of Mill's book. In France, the monarchy of Napoleon III, which Mill passionately hated, came to an end eleven years after his book was published; and, at the same time, manhood suffrage was introduced in Germany. On such grounds I do not think that Mr. Packe is right in saying that the general movement of the time was against liberty, and I do not think that Mill's optimism was irrational.

With Mill's values, I for my part find myself in complete agreement. I think he is entirely right in emphasizing the importance of the individual in so far as values are concerned. I think, moreover, that it is even more desirable in our day than it was in his to uphold the kind of outlook for which he stands. But those who care for liberty in our day have to fight different battles from those of the nineteenth century, and have to devise new expedients if liberty is not to perish. From the seventeenth century to the end of the nineteenth, "Liberty" was the watchword of the radicals and revolutionaries; but in our day the

[18] From *Portraits from Memory and Other Essays*, pp. 123–127. Copyright 1951, 1952, 1953, 1956 by Bertrand Russell. Reprinted by permission of Simon & Schuster, Inc., New York, and George Allen & Unwin Ltd., London.

word has been usurped by reactionaries, and those who think themselves most progressive are inclined to despise it. It is labelled as part of "rotten bourgeois idealism" and is regarded as a middle-class fad, important only to those who already enjoy the elegant leisure of the well-to-do. So far as any one person is responsible for this change, the blame must fall on Marx, who substituted Prussian discipline for freedom as both the means and the end of revolutionary action. But Marx would not have had the success which he has had if there had not been large changes in social organization and in technique which furthered his ideals as opposed to those of earlier reformers.

What has changed the situation since Mill's day is, as I remarked before, the great increase of organization. Every organization is a combination of individuals for a purpose; and, if this purpose is to be achieved, it requires a certain subordination of the individuals to the whole. If the purpose is one in which all the individuals feel a keen interest, and if the executive of the organization commands confidence, the sacrifice of liberty may be very small. But if the purpose for which the organization exists inspires only its executive, to which the other members submit for extraneous reasons, the loss of liberty involved may grow until it becomes almost total. The larger the organization, the greater becomes the gap in power between those at the top and those at the bottom, and the more likelihood there is of oppression. The modern world, for technical reasons, is very much more organized than the world of a hundred years ago: there are very many fewer acts which a man does simply from his own impulse, and very many more which he is compelled or induced to perform by some authority. The advantages that spring from organization are so great and so obvious that it would be absurd to wish to return to an earlier condition, but those who are conscious only of the advantages are apt to overlook the dangers, which are very real and very menacing.

As a first example, let us take agriculture. In the years immediately succeeding the publication of Mill's *Liberty,* there was an immense development of pioneering in the Middle West of the United States. The pioneers prided themselves upon their "rugged individualism." They settled in regions which were well wooded, well watered, and of great natural fertility. Without excessive labour, they felled the trees, thereby securing log cabins and fuel, and when the soil was cleared, they procured a rich harvest of grain. There was, however, a serpent in this individualist paradise: the serpent was the railroad, without which the grain could not be got to market. The railroad represented a vast accumulation of capital, an enormous expenditure of labour, and a combination of very many persons, hardly any of them agriculturists. The pioneers were indignant at their loss of independence, and their indignation gave rise to the Populist movement, which, in spite of much heat, never achieved any success. In this case, however, there was only one enemy of personal independence. I was struck by the difference when I came in contact with pioneers in Australia. The conquering of new land for agriculture in Australia depends upon enormously expensive schemes of irrigation, too vast for the separate States and only practicable by the Federal Government. Even then, when a man has acquired a tract of land, it contains no timber, and all his building materials and his fuel have to be brought from a distance. Medical attention for himself and his family is only rendered possible by an elaborate organization of aeroplanes and wireless. His livelihood depends upon the export trade, which prospers or suffers according to the vagaries of distant Governments. His mentality, his tastes and his feelings, are still those of the rugged individualist pioneer of a hundred years ago, but his circumstances are totally different. However he may wish to rebel, he is tightly controlled by forces that are entirely external to himself. Intellectual liberty he may still have; but economic liberty has become a dream.

But the life of the Australian pioneer is one of heavenly bliss when compared with that of the peasant in communist countries, who has become more completely a serf than he was in the worst days of the Czardom. He owns no land, he has no right to the produce of his own labour, the authorities permit him only a bare subsistence, and any complaint may land him in a forced-labour camp. The totalitarian State is the last term of organization, the goal towards which, if we are not careful, we shall find all developed countries tending. Socialists have thought that the power hitherto vested in capitalists would become beneficient if vested in the State. To some degree this is true, so long as the State is democratic. Communists, unfortunately, forgot this proviso. By transferring economic power to an oligarchic State, they produced an engine of tyranny more dreadful, more vast, and at the same time more minute than any that had existed in previous history. I do not think this was the intention of those who made the Russian Revolution, but it was the effect of their actions. Their actions had this effect because they failed to realize the need of liberty and the inevitable evils of despotic power.

But the evils, of which the extreme form is seen in communist countries, exists in a lesser degree, and may easily increase, in many countries belonging to what is somewhat humorously called the "Free World." Vavilov, the most distinguished geneticist that Russia has produced in recent times, was sent to perish miserably in the Arctic because he would not subscribe to Stalin's ignorant belief in the inheritance of acquired characters. Oppenheimer is disgraced and prevented from pursuing his work largely because he doubted the practicability of the hydrogen bomb at a time when this doubt was entirely rational. The F.B.I., which has only the level of education to be expected among policemen, considers itself competent to withhold visas from the most learned men in Europe on grounds which every person capable of understanding the matters at issue knows to be absurd. This evil has reached such a point that international conferences of learned men in the United States have become impossible. It is curious that Mill makes very little mention of the police as a danger to liberty. In our day, they are its worst enemy in most civilized countries.

SELECT BIBLIOGRAPHY

GALBRAITH, JOHN KENNETH, *Economic Development* (Boston, Houghton Mifflin, Sentry Edition, 1964). An excellent introduction to the problem. The author, Professor of Economics at Harvard, former U.S. Ambassador to India, and author of *The Affluent Society*, analyzes the purpose of economic development, the causes of poverty, the choices facing developing countries, the process of development, its planning, and practice, and the role of education. There is an interesting postscript on population.

GILL, RICHARD T., *Economic Development Past and Present* (Englewood Cliffs, N.J., Prentice-Hall, Foundations of Modern Economics Series, 1963). A concise account of the problem of economic development. It raises such questions as: What are the factors which make for development? How is the progress of certain countries over the last century or two to be explained? Why is it that during this same period certain other countries have stagnated or decayed? Note especially Chapter 4, "The Growth of the American Economy," Chapter 5, "The Problems of the Underdeveloped Countries," and Chapter 6, "Alternative Approaches—India and China."

HEILBRONER, ROBERT L., *The Making of Economic Society* (Englewood Cliffs, N.J., Prentice-Hall, 1962). A highly literate discussion of the history of economic development by the author of *The Worldly Philosophers*. Especially valuable for an understanding of the emergence of the market society.

HIGGINS, BENJAMIN, *Economic Development: Problems, Principles and Policies* (New York, Norton, 1959). A good introductory textbook on the problems of economic development. The author analyzes the general nature of the development problem and illustrates his findings by a number of case studies (Libya, India, Indonesia, Philippines, Mexico, and Italy). General theories of development are examined, including the classical theory of capitalist development, the Marxist model, Schumpeter's theory of trend, and the models of Harrod and Hansen. Historical theories of the rise of capitalism are reviewed and, in a final section, various policies of development are analyzed.

MILLIKAN, MAX F. and BLACKMER, DONALD L. M. (eds.), *The Emerging Nations: Their Growth and United States Policy* (Boston, Little, Brown, 1961). An instructive interdisciplinary study of the challenge presented to U.S. policy by the processes of development taking place in present-day world. The work examines the features of traditional societies, factors in social change and economic modernization, patterns and problems of political development, and the implications for policy.

NURKSE, RAGNAR, *Problems of Capital Formation in Underdeveloped Countries* (New York, Oxford University Press, 1961). An important work on the problems of saving and investment in the economically underdeveloped countries. The author examines the potential source of saving concealed in rural underemployment, the importance of agricultural productivity, and the obstacles to the saving process presented by the tide of rising expectations. Various courses of public action to combat underdevelopment are analyzed in the framework of economic theory.

ROSTOW, W. W., *The Stages of Economic Growth: A Non-Communist Manifesto* (Cambridge, Mass., Harvard University Press, 1960). An economic historian's generalization of modern history in a set of stages-of-growth. Five major stages are identified and illustrated from contemporary experience. Soviet and U.S. growth patterns over the last century are compared. The theory of stages is also applied to shed light on aggression and war.

WILCOX, CLAIR, WEATHERFORD, WILLIS, JR., AND HUNTER, HOLLAND, *Economies of the World Today: Their Organization, Development, and Performance* (New York, Harcourt, Brace & World, 1962). A simple, readable, informative account of current economic systems. Ideological issues are de-emphasized. The discussion centers on what is actually happening in present-day economies under the headings of organization (individualism, collectivism, market economies, command economies), stages of economic development, rates of growth, and quality of growth. The analysis of general principles is followed by an examination of the Soviet, Communist Chinese, Indian, and U.S. economies.

ZIMMERMAN, L. J., *Poor Lands, Rich Lands: The Widening Gap* (New York, Random House, 1965). An analysis of changes in the world distribution of income and of the economic structures of developed and underdeveloped countries. Using a wealth of statistical material, the author explains the differential rates of growth and the implications of the increasingly unequal distribution of world income.

ZIMMERMANN, ERICH W., *Erich W. Zimmermann's Introduction to World Resources,* HUNGER, HENRY L., editor (New York, Harper & Row, 1964). The book is an edited version of parts of E. Zimmermann's 1933 classic *World Resources and Industries.* The functional approach to resources is stressed throughout. There are excellent discussions of the relationship of resources to human wants, social objectives, well-being, and culture.

7

Democracy, Communism, and the Conflict of Method

IT WAS SUGGESTED IN CHAPTER 6 THAT names such as "capitalism," "socialism," "communism," and "fascism" applied to economic systems tend to be at best ambiguous, and at worst misleading. Capitalism, for example, means one thing to the rulers in the Kremlin and quite another to the owner of a department store in Toledo, Ohio; one thing in 1870, and another in 1970. The socialism of Stalin is not the same as the Soviet socialism of the late nineteen-fifties and early sixties. Both are fundamentally different from the socialism of Britain or Sweden. Communism as an ideal means one thing to the Soviets and another to the Chinese, and both these visions are a far cry from the communism of Plato or the communism of a monastery. The fascism of Adolf Hitler had many capitalist elements in it, and to make things just a little more tricky, the political movement which directed it described itself as "National Socialist." Present-day India calls itself a "Socialist Democracy" but in many respects it is more capitalist than the United States. There exist many varieties of "Marxism" and at least three operational interpretations of "Marxism-Leninism."

A somewhat similar problem arises when the attempt is made to tag specific names onto political constructs. The "People's Democracies" of Eastern Europe are certainly very different from the "Western Democracies." The word "liberal" means one thing in England and another in the United States, and the same holds true for the appellation "conservative." The British Labour Party and the Albanian Party of Labor are worlds apart. The list could be lengthened, but enough has been said to at least suggest that ours is the age of misnomers and semantic confusion. A not inconsiderable part of the world's chronic misunderstanding is, no doubt, traceable to the fact that the discussants mean different things by the same words.

The fundamental reason for this semantic chaos which has invaded the social sciences is that economic and political systems are not static dogmas that can be defined once and for all. They are in constant flux.

To recognize their essentially dynamic nature is the only meaningful way of looking at them. They are conceptual processes: evolution, transformation, mutation are of their very essence; immobility, rigidity, stagnation their greatest enemies. As man's intellectual creations, they can be modified or destroyed by man almost with the stroke of a pen. They reflect often conflicting conceptions of how men's affairs should be conducted in various countries and regions at various points in time. Static analysis of economic and political systems and of the underlying outlooks shows no more than does the flash picture of a man in motion. As yet we do not possess a scientific theory of social change that would not only explain the process but also indicate its direction. As we have seen in Chapter 6, the economic "theory" of convergence is really no more than a rather intriguing hypothesis.

These economic and political constructs are explicitly or implicitly recognized by the laws of the society to which they apply. Their existence and proper functioning are ensured by the concensus of society expressed in the body of laws and traditions. But these laws, too, are in constant flux. They are continually being tested, modified, adjusted, rejected, and others are being added, only to be tested, modified, adjusted, and possibly at some time rejected. Constant motion is the key to the understanding of modern societies. On the other hand, names applied to social constructs tend to acquire an immobility and emotionalism which only confuse the issue.

There are two main ways of dealing with the problem of semantic confusion. One is to carefully define each word in each and every phenomenon at every point of time and in each particular instance. This is the way of the encyclopedia-dictionary. It is long and tedious, and not especially fruitful. The one simple word "socialism" could take up volumes with the prospect of many more tomes to come. The conclusion which would, in all likelihood, emerge would be that there was no such thing as a socialism, but rather a mosaic of socialisms spread both geographically and over time. There might thus be $socialism_1$, and $socialism_2$, and $socialism_{1a}$, as well as $socialism_{1b}$. An endless task.

The other solution, the one used here, is to select a period of time (or several roughly comparable periods, the basis of the comparison being clearly spelled out) and a number of countries and to examine the ways in which a common set of problems was handled in this limited number of countries. Although far from perfect, this method has the merit of brevity and the advantage of pinpointing the problems involved. Above all, it is more meaningful. Essentially it is a "problems approach." Although terms such as "capitalism," "socialism," "communism," and "democracy," cannot be altogether avoided, they shall be used with discretion for reasons discussed at length in Chapter 6 and in this section.

THE BUILDING BLOCKS

The Importance of Economics

Even though the discussion will be general in scope, the main emphasis will be on economics. This is not to suggest that economic problems in some way determine the conduct of social life. It is perhaps just as well to make this clear from the very start: in the analysis which follows there is no suggestion of economic determinism.[1] The emphasis on economics is due to the fact, mentioned in Chapter 5, that over two-thirds of the world's people are vitally interested in problems of economic development, that competing solutions to this problem are being offered, that impressive economic growth had been achieved by Western societies in the last century and a half, as well as by the U.S.S.R. and Eastern Europe in more recent times, and that the problem of further growth is a major preoccupation of peoples in the developed countries. Moreover, much of the misunderstanding in the world today is traceable to differences in the developmental ages among nations. In the nuclear setting, the essence of the ideological conflict is in the comparative performance of the contending sociopolitical systems and in the effectiveness of the remedies which these systems offer for the nagging and explosive problem of poverty. Behind the clash of arms in Vietnam, the Congo, and the Caribbean there is the more intractable question of how to escape from the clutches of destitution, and which of the several possible solutions should be adopted. More than at any time in history, modern wars are the expression of deep-seated social and economic discontent and not just the symptom of territorial squabbles or of the pique of military men. Revolutionary ferment today carries with it the seeds of socioeconomic transformations in the very foundations of society, the adoption of radically different methods of economic development. Cuba had many revolutions before Castro, and China many peasant revolts before Mao. But the Castro and Mao revolutions were not mere palace affairs, not just a change in the occupants of the same socioeconomic structure. The old structures were torn down and new ones began to be built according to other designs and radically different specifications. To underestimate or ignore the economic ingredient of present-day world tensions is to misunderstand the problem. In the paragraphs which follow, the differences between democracy and communism and the competition between ideologies will be examined primarily in their economic content. That content, in turn, will focus on the urgent problem of competing solutions to the problem of development.

[1] See, Edwin R. A. Seligman, *The Economic Interpretation of History* (New York, Columbia University Press, 1961).

THE COUNTRIES

Three countries will occupy most of the space: the Soviet Union, Communist China, and India. Their experience will illustrate two basic approaches to the problem of development: the market approach (with some elements of command) and the command approach in two variants. Politically, the sample will reveal, in the one instance, efforts at government through consultation and discussion, and, in the other, government through *Diktat* from above in which consultation is reduced to a minimum. The discussion will also attempt to show the gradual changes that have been taking place in the market orientation and in command, as well as in the political equivalents of consultation and *Diktat*.

PERIODS

To be meaningful, comparisons of economic and political systems must cover roughly equivalent periods. It would serve little purpose, for example, to compare Communist China today with the United States of today. Such a comparison may, indeed, shed a good deal of light on the sources of conflict between the two countries, but it would do little to clarify the kind of economic and political processes taking place in each. Present-day Soviet Union and China will, in fact, be compared at one stage, but mainly in order to bring out some of the reasons for their noisy misunderstanding. The method adopted here is to compare the experiences of the three selected countries at roughly the same developmental age. This is far from easy and it must be admitted that the periods selected are, in many respects, rather arbitrary. In the case of India, the period chosen covers the years 1951–1966. For the Soviet Union, the comparable dates are 1929–1956, with additional remarks about developments since that time. China's experience is covered for the years 1949–1966, with special stress on the years 1958–1966. This is perhaps the best that can be done in what is generally a very imprecise situation. Quite clearly, the Soviet Union in 1929 was economically farther ahead than China in 1949 or even in 1958, and the same can be said of the U.S.S.R. and India. In the social sciences, however, the kind of exactitude displayed by the physical sciences is quite illusory and one must make do with uncomfortable, though illuminating, compromises. In defense of our classification it can be said that all three countries were faced, in the time periods covered here, with basically similar types of problems stemming from the retarded state of their economies. Their responses to the challenge in those years are, therefore, of inherent interest.

BASIC DIFFERENCES IN THE THREE APPROACHES

The difference between the Indian approach to the problem of poverty on the one hand, and the Soviet and Chinese approaches on the

EUROPE

S O V I E T   U N I O N
U. S. S. R.

TURKEY

LEBANON SYRIA
ISRAEL
JORDAN   IRAQ
KUWAIT

I R A N

SAUDI ARABIA

YEMEN
SOUTH ARABIA

MUSCAT
& OMAN

AFGHANISTAN

(WEST)
PAKISTAN

MONGOLIA

PEOPLE'S REPUBLIC OF CHINA

NORTH KOREA

SOUTH KOREA

JAPAN

JAMMU &
KASHMIR

NEPAL   SIKKIM
BHUTAN
(EAST)
PAKISTAN

I N D I A

TAIWAN

BURMA

NORTH
VIETNAM
LAOS

THAILAND

CAMBODIA   SOUTH
VIETNAM

PHILIPPINES

Independent in 1935

Independent since 1945

Not independent

ASIA

CEYLON

MALDIVE ISLANDS

M A L A Y S I A

SINGAPORE

I N D O N E S I A

TIMOR
(Port.)

other, in the periods under consideration, is the difference between gradualism and forced draft, voluntarism and compulsion, balanced and
unbalanced growth, *festina lente* and storming, or in the orthodox vocabulary, the difference between democracy and communism. Diffusion of
decision-making power in economics and politics characterizes the Indian
approach. Extreme concentration of that power typifies the Soviet and
Chinese ways. The differences in the degree of control over people's lives
in the two approaches are such as to constitute a difference in kind. The
Indian, Soviet, and Chinese manners of tackling the problem of widespread destitution and the political and social problems attendant upon
it thus constitute a microcosm of a pressing contemporary problem and
one, moreover, on which the world's major powers and philosophies
bitterly disagree.

This disagreement centers on the methods to be used and on the
institutional arrangements to be adopted in order to give effect to the
methods. In more familiar words, the difference between democracy and
communism, in both economic and political aspects, consists in divergent
strategies of economic growth and social development and in vastly different economic and political institutions employed to give effect to the
respective strategies.[2]

THE SOVIET WAY

It will be useful at this point to call to mind the three essential ingredients of economic development which were discussed at some length
in Chapter 6.

The first is capital accumulation, which implies second, the need to
drum up savings, and third, the need to direct those savings into growth-
yielding employments. It was suggested in Chapter 6 that these obstacles
can be negotiated in various ways and that the major difference between
those ways lies in the degree of compulsion. The important thing to bear
in mind, however, is that every underdeveloped country, whether it calls
itself Marxist or not, cannot escape the saving-investment process, the
need, that is, to accumulate capital both human and physical.

SOVIET STRATEGY

The Soviet strategy of economic development applied in the Soviet
Union from about 1929 to 1956 may be used as a good representative
sample of an operational "Marxist-Leninist-Stalinist" approach to economic and political realities. The reasons for this are:

(A) Economic development is pervasive. It involves more than just
strictly economic policy. Its ramifications extend to society's political

---

[2] See also above, Chapter 5, pp. 155–165, for a discussion of the ideological differences between the Soviet, Chinese, and Indian systems.

and constitutional framework, educational policy, and social philosophy. Legal constructs are involved as well as psychological attitudes and ideological preconceptions.

(B) The Soviet strategy of economic development of the years 1929–1956 was adopted by a number of countries in Eastern Europe during the first decade following World War II. The choice in this matter was not entirely free by reason of geographical location and the persuasive presence of Soviet troops. Whatever the circumstances, most Eastern European countries followed for a time the Soviet strategy to the letter and adopted Soviet-type social, legal, cultural, and political institutions. Officially, at least, Marxist ideology in its Soviet edition was proclaimed as the "correct" and only outlook. From 1953 to about 1958, Communist China, too, trod the Soviet path, as did North Korea and North Vietnam (after 1954). Yugoslavia broke away in 1948 but has not to this day rejected certain key features of the Soviet model.

(C) Most people when they think of communism still think mainly of this particular Soviet model. The trouble is, however, that the model seems to have outlived its usefulness in precisely those regions in which for decades it had been most steadfastly applied. It remains, nonetheless, the first example of operational Marxism, that is of Marxism applied in a particular way on a national, indeed, a continental, scale; and its relevance to the choice being made by underdeveloped countries at the present time remains undiminished.

The building blocks of the original Soviet (or, better, Soviet-Stalinist) strategy of economic growth are:

(1) Uprooting of existing social, economic, and political institutions and the reorientation of cultural values.

(2) Compulsion exercised by a highly centralized Party and State.

(3) Steep rates of forced saving, extracted from agriculture and the consumers.

(4) Steep rates of investment, including investment in human capital.

(5) A rigid system of investment priorities noted for its imbalance and "storming" of selected targets. In descending order these priorities comprise:

(i) First priority for the allocation of resources to industry (accelerated industrialization).

(ii) Within the industrial sector, emphasis on the rapid development of heavy industry, i.e., priority of investment goods over consumption goods.

(iii) High priority for the introduction of advanced technological processes in the investment goods industries and in a few other selected key sectors, or selected departments within the high priority sectors. This further emphasizes the imbalanced pattern of growth mentioned under (i) and (ii).

(iv) Relatively low investment priority for the development of consumer services, agriculture, residential housing, transport, and communications. In the case of agriculture, this low priority verges on neglect. Investment neglect in social overheads is compounded by intensive use of such overheads as are available.

(6) Relative neglect of foreign trade and comparatively small reliance on foreign economic assistance (elements of self-reliance or autarchy). Preference for exchanges with countries possessing similar socioeconomic and political structures. Bilateral agreements mainly on a cash or short-term credit basis. Until 1953, extraction of resources from dependencies in Eastern Europe. After 1953, a growing modest volume, but on a world scale, of assistance extended to allies and to selected underdeveloped countries outside the Soviet bloc.

These are the main elements of the Soviet-Stalinist strategy of economic development.[3] Since communism has so far been implanted in relatively underdeveloped countries (Russia, Rumania, Bulgaria, Poland, Hungary, the Baltic countries, China, North Korea, North Vietnam, Cuba), this method and its ramifications provide an excellent example of a certain type of "early" communism or Soviet-type Marxist socialism of the Stalinist *genre*. Czechoslovakia, even though more industrialized than its eastern and northern neighbors, was so only in its Czech part (Bohemia). Eastern Germany, while advanced industrially, was underdeveloped when compared to the rest of the country. Moreover, in 1945 it was in a state of physical destruction and its territory had been truncated.

Before examining in detail each of these major building blocks of the Soviet strategy of economic development and commenting on the relationship in which each stood to social and political structures, it may be useful to list the economic and political institutions which Soviet Stalinist Marxism-Leninism employed to give effect to this strategy.

Soviet Institutions for Development

Soviet economic and political institutions of the period 1929–1956 were essentially instruments of compulsion doctrinally rationalized as the "dictatorship of the proletariat," but in fact, the dictatorship of a few economic and political entrepreneurs over everyone else, including the proletariat. Socially, the compulsion aimed to transform the thinking and behavior of the citizens in a "correct," that is Party-defined, manner. The basic objective was to eradicate all vestiges of "bourgeois" individualism and to instill in one and all "proletarian" collectivism. Individual men

[3] Jan S. Prybyla, "Competitive Coexistence and Soviet Growth," in Harry G. Shaffer, ed., *The Soviet System in Theory and Practice* (New York, Appleton-Century-Crofts, 1965), pp. 200–207; "Soviet Economic Growth: Perspectives and Prospects," *The Quarterly Review of Economics and Business*, Vol. 4, No. 1, Spring, 1964, pp. 56–67; "The Economic Problems of Soviet Russia in Transition," *The Indian Journal of Economics*, Vol. XLV, No. 177, October, 1964, pp. 135–151.

were to love Men and work for Men in the upper case and in the plural. Even though material incentives to individuals could not be altogether abandoned, they were not to take the form of gratification through private ownership of the means of production. In the perspective of Soviet strategy men were first and foremost producers, or better still, individual human beings counted only in so far as they were the quotients of the collective factor labor—the State being the divisor. The producer mentality is mentality in the future tense. It is the distant, final product that matters, not immediate satisfaction of nagging wants. Postponement of present consumption is the key. Under Stalin, and immediately after the dictator's death, the Soviet Union was a land whose eyes were fixed on the future. Marxist dogma defined that future in vague, if attractive, terms. The "building of socialism," the doctrinal anteroom of full communism, came to be the recurrent theme of massive propaganda campaigns that pursued the citizen-producer into his very, and very cramped, home. Carefully organized spontaneous declarations of allegiance and manufactured pledges of redoubled effort were the constant attendants of every patriotic holiday. For those unable to mobilize the needed enthusiasm, there was the forced labor camp, the State prison, and the firing squad. There were men (their number has dwindled as far as Soviet history is concerned) in the relaxed and liberal West who dismissed all this as a pack of lies hatched up by the enemies of progress. Their simple faith suffered a grievous shock when Khrushchev himself in his famous anti-Stalin speech of February, 1956, supplied the proof in all its stark and terrible nakedness.[4]

Since Stalinist Marxism wanted to build anew, the uprooting of the old and the remolding of millions of men was part and parcel of what we have earlier described as the emergence of an outlook favorable to growth. The gruesome business was dispatched quickly, if not as thoroughly as had been supposed at the time. It was marked by impatience and excess. It cost the Soviet Union millions of people, including some of the more original thinkers, men of outstanding intellectual caliber, administrators, and the top military. The new mentality, which a Yugoslav observer labelled in 1964 as the mind of *Homo Sovieticus,* one which finds within itself the justification for the most heinous crimes in pursuit of an allegedly higher and nobler goal, was mass produced by terror.[5] Like the Teutonic knights of old, the Party cadres imposed their faith upon the nonbelievers and skeptics by sword, fear, and tedious repetition, in that order. It was inhumanity of man to man elevated to the rank of objective law and justified by dubious, allegedly all-powerful and irreversible Laws of History discovered by Marx. Throughout, the driving

---

[4] Harry G. Shaffer, ed., *supra,* Note 3, pp. 58–95.

[5] Mihajlo Mihajlov, "Moscow: Summer 1964," Part III, *The New Leader,* June 7, 1965, pp. 3–14. For Parts I and II see, *The New Leader,* Special Issue, March 29, 1965.

force was hate. The hate of class enemies which pervades Marxist theory became State policy under Stalin. Anyone who opposed or was suspected of opposing the will of the supreme authority became *ipso facto* an enemy of the people. As the Chinese were later to remind the Russians: "any obstacle on the people's road of advance must be removed." [6] Removed by physical liquidation, if need be. In not so many words, the innocent-looking prerequisite of industrialization, that outlook favorable to growth, was implanted in Soviet Russia by brute and merciless force.

Some of the institutions set up to attain this objective and to pursue the end of rapid saving and investment are, in the abstract, innocuous enough. The essence is public control through ownership of the means of production and distribution. Public ownership of the means of production and some control over the channels of distribution are not unknown in other parts of the world where they do not connote the sort of thing that they did, and to a lesser degree still do, in the Soviet Union. There are two important differences between public ownership in, let us say, India and the U.S.S.R. The first is the comprehensiveness of public ownership or, as has been pointed out in Chapter 6, the precise mix of the various agents of control over the allocation of scarce resources. The second is the extent to which the public authority is genuinely representative of the public or, to put the same thing the other way, it is the degree of effective control which the public through its elected representatives exercises over the public authority. This is the element of consultation mentioned in Chapter 6. In the Soviet case, public ownership is comprehensive and the element of consultation minimal. Since, by definition, individual preferences cannot be revealed, such agreement between the decision makers and the others as does exist must be attributed to the internalization by the people of what our Yugoslav author describes as the Soviet man's propensity to look to authority for major and even not so important decisions.

In summary, the institutions used by the Soviets to enforce the strategy of development outlined above, are:

(1) A totalitarian political system in which the Communist Party plays a decisive role. The word "party" is really a misnomer; by the Soviets' own admission it is a "party of a new type." This new type was given it by Lenin and was later fashioned and perfected by Stalin into a paramilitary affair of faithful and devoted, right-thinking and obedient, militant, and aggressive men and women whose primary task in Stalin's time was to see to it that the decisions arrived at on the summit of the pyramid were carried out. The basic principle of operation is known by another misnomer which happens also to be a contradiction in terms: "democratic centralism." The essence of democratic centralism, as it operates

---

[6] "Why Khrushchov Fell," by the Editorial Department of *Hongqi, Peking Review,* November 27, 1964, p. 6.

in practice rather than as it is defined in theory, is that authority flows from the top down but that responsibility is horizontal. Each individual on the ladder of authority accepts the decisions handed down from the rungs above him but is solely responsible for their execution. There can be horizontal discussion about how best to implement the orders, or better still, how to improve upon them. There can be no rejection or refusal to comply once the decision is reached ("unanimously") in the upper reaches. Decisions on methods of implementation are also supposed to be reached unanimously at each level after due discussion. In short, in the Soviet system as it operated in Stalin's time, and as it refuses to cease working today, criticism of a basic kind could flow downward in space and backward in time, but never up and forward.

The Party's role as the enforcer of central decisions did not, and does not, exclude its function as a transmission belt for information from the field, for carefully worded and ideologically safe suggestions, and for critiques of the mildest sort. But the flow of information and opinion was, and to the dismay of the present leaders, continues to be, essentially a fact-gathering exercise and the gymnastics of flattery. The facts themselves tend to be molded on their way up in a manner that appears to fit the leadership's preconceptions. Often the information fails to get through, in spite of crosschecks and counterchecks at each level. In the absence of a price mechanism which could transmit the relevant economic information, and without the ballot box (Soviet voting remains a farce) which would express broad political sentiments, in the primitive state and controlled nature of social public-opinion surveys, the leadership heard what it wanted to hear. Today when its mind has opened up a bit, it hears very little that is innovating and constructive. The habit of waiting for orders dies hard.

The apparatus of the State runs parallel to that of the Party and it gets about as much information for its pains. Interlocking Party-State directorships at all levels of the hierarchical pyramid are indispensable for the right hand to know what the left one is doing, but the price of this coordination is loss of touch with reality.

These are the negative features of the system. They make for a considerable amount of waste motion and produce unnecessary costs of all kinds. Yet the contemplation of the system's weaknesses should not blind one to the achievements, be they dearly bought. The Soviet Party and State, cumberous, bureaucratic, and obsequious though they are, have made a breakthrough from poverty in a relatively short space of time. As will be shown later, they are now trying to shed the rigidities of the take-off, a task no less complex than the earlier escape from destitution, but less painful to the mass of the people. It was mentioned in Chapter 6 that systems of constraint tend to be self-cancelling if the compulsion is used to promote economic growth. The Soviet Union and the countries of

Eastern Europe are excellent examples of the use of force for that purpose. In fact, Soviet-type Marxist-Leninist-Stalinist socialism consists in harnessing the power of a tightly organized totalitarian State and Party for the single-minded purpose of increasing the gross national product in the minimum of time. Soviet experience since 1956 suggests that once that product has expanded sufficiently to generate further self-sustained growth, the primitive method of brute force loses much of its economic rationale. In fact, it then becomes an obstacle to further progress.

(2) These reflections lead to the second major institution of the Soviet system. The allocation of resources is the prerogative of the central Party-State authority. This allocation reflects the central authority's scale of preferences which, in turn, mirrors the strategy of development outlined earlier. In the period 1929–1953, central planners' preferences meant, for all practical purposes, the preferences of Stalin and of his closest advisers.

Like the Party-State apparatus, centralization of decision making over the allocation of resources tended to produce rigidities and misallocations that were both costly and disruptive. Hence the unending Soviet pursuit of administrative reorganization that seems most of the time to lead nowhere. On the other side of the ledger, there is undoubted achievement. Provided the strategy of development is such as to result in large and rapidly rising increments of measurable growth, centralized resource allocation can be a powerful means of breaking out of the low level equilibrium trap. Soviet strategy has been just that. The allocation priorities current in the period 1929–1956 were partly a reflection of political desiderata and partly a rough calculation of incremental capital-output ratios. They resulted in lopsided growth, but in growth all the same.

(3) The nationalization of industry, domestic and foreign trade, financial institutions, and consumer services. In short comprehensive state ownership of the means of production and distribution. This important aspect of the Soviet system's institutional structure has been discussed earlier.

(4) The nationalization of land and the socialization of agriculture. Under Soviet-type socialism land is owned by the State and some of it is leased out to various cooperative bodies which, in turn, lease out small plots to the families of members of the collectives. The socialization of land is not an institution common to all countries that have adopted the Soviet model. Thus, for example, the greater part of the agricultural land in Poland and Yugoslavia is privately owned. In 1961, the nationalized sector represented only 10 percent of total agricultural land in Yugoslavia and 13.2 percent of that of Poland. In all the other countries of Eastern Europe, as well as in China, North Vietnam, and North Korea, socialization of agricultural land is practically complete.

In the Soviet command system the socialized sector of agriculture takes on two main organizational forms: the state farm and the collective farm. There are a good many distinctions between the two. About 70 percent of Soviet agricultural land is farmed by the collectives (or *kolkhozy*) and almost all of the remainder by state farms. At the present time there are over 50,000 collective farms in the Soviet Union, the average sown acreage being about 7,000 acres. The state farms are much larger (the average sown acreage is in excess of 20,000 acres) and are worked by about 1,000 laborers each. State farms tend to be highly specialized in the production of one or a small number of commodities, for the most part grains.

The most striking difference between state and collective farms, however, is not in their size, degree of mechanization, or commodity specialization. It is rather in the methods of payment for work done. The state farm is run very much like an industrial enterprise. It is owned and operated by the State and its employees are paid monthly wages based on a combination of piece and time rates. The collective farms are theoretically voluntary associations of producers who have transferred their land and implements as well as livestock to the collective and who work the jointly owned lands in common. In fact, theoretical voluntarism is a fiction and the collective farm democracy a myth. Collective farm managers are Party and State appointees whose appointment is confirmed by the general meeting of the collective farmers in one of those displays of unanimity we have met earlier. During the Stalinist period and until about 1958, the collective farmers were paid on a residual basis. The farm was given a production plan which, like all economic plans in the Soviet Union, had the force of law. A portion of the planned output had to be sold to the State at fixed (and usually very low) prices; another "above-quota" portion could be sold to the State at somewhat higher prices. Out of the remainder, if any, a part had to be set aside for future production, and another was used to pay the farm's income taxes and the services of special machine-tractor stations (MTS). Next, the wages of the manager, bookkeeper, controller, and other administrative officers were paid. If anything was left after all that, it was distributed among the collective farmers according to a rather complicated system of workdays (*trudodni*). The workday was a unit of account weighted to measure a farmer's contribution to the farm's production process: a day spent in one occupation could earn fewer or more workday units than a day spent in another. The farmer, in other words, got whatever was left over and could not be certain from year to year what amount a given input of workdays would fetch him. As a rule it fetched very little, and what little was coming took the form of payments in kind at harvest time. Cash payments were small and irregular.

In 1935, Stalin realized that the collective farmer could not live without an additional source of income. The farms were, therefore, authorized to lease to collective farm families small plots of land (about one acre per family). These the farmers were allowed to cultivate as they pleased, in their spare time. They were further allowed to dispose of the produce on the free (or collective farm) markets, at whatever price the produce would fetch. Incidentally, the collective farms were also permitted to sell any surplus produce on the free market. In time, the collective farmers' private plots became the major source of the farmers' cash income, while sales on the free market were also an important source of cash income for the *kolkhozy*. A significant part of the Soviet Union's supply of milk, butter, eggs, vegetables, fruit, and meat is today produced on the private plots of the collective (and state) farmers.[7]

The institution of the collective farm proved to be extremely inefficient and continues to be backward to this day. Although in the absence of regular and ascertainable payments to labor, cost accounting was practically nonexistent, unit costs were thought to have been high. Productivity per acre and per man was correspondingly low. The basic reason for this sorry state of affairs was, of course, the almost total lack of material incentives for collective farm work. To this day agriculture remains the Soviet Union's major economic problem.

But from another point of view, the institution of the collective farm was a success. In the setting of Stalin's industrialization drive, the institution's primary purpose and *raison d'être* was to extract as many resources as possible from the agricultural sector in exchange for next to nothing. The Soviet collective farms of Stalin's time were the Party-State's principal weapon of forced savings. The main preoccupation was to get the planned quantities of produce needed to feed the urban population and to supply industry with raw materials of agricultural origin. This produce was sold to the urban (and rural) consumers at prices which exceeded the cost to the State by a substantial margin. The margin (turnover tax) was then used for investment in industry, especially heavy industry. It is not an exaggeration to say that Soviet industrialization was made possible by the exploitation of the farmers or, alternatively, by forcing high savings rates out of the only sector potentially capable of some saving at the beginning of the industrialization drive. The collective farm, in other words, was the instrument of compulsion. The potential savers were placed in an institutional setting in which their marginal propensity to save and to consume was subject to effective control. The price of this vast forced saving was efficiency. Unlike the state farms, the collective farms were supposed to take care of themselves in regard to ploughbacks, social security for their members, and so on. As far as the State was concerned, they were of interest only as suppliers of savings.

A totalitarian Party and State structure, unquestioning obedience to

---

[7] Jan S. Prybyla, "Problems of Soviet Agriculture," *Journal of Farm Economics,* Vol. XLIV, No. 3, August, 1962, pp. 820–836; "Private Enterprise in the Soviet Union," *The South African Journal of Economics,* Vol. 29, No. 3, September, 1961, pp. 218–224.

orders from above, the nationalization of all sectors of the economy, and the collectivization of agriculture are the main institutions of a command economy of the Soviet Stalinist type. Between 1948 and 1956, these institutions were adopted by practically all communist countries, including China. They were the channels through which flowed the Soviet Stalinist strategy of economic development and social transformation. To this we must now return.

STRATEGY EXAMINED

Table 14 summarizes in a general way the Soviet breakthrough method. The data do not refer to any particular year. They are, however, fairly typical of what went on in the Soviet Union in the feverish period of early industrialization.

TABLE 14

Shares of Final Uses of Gross National Product in the Soviet Union and Patterns of Investment Typical of the Period 1929–1956

BASIS: CURRENT RUBLE FACTOR COST COMPUTATIONS	
I. *GNP Share Percent:*	
Gross Investment	27
Communal Services	11
Budgeted Defense Outlays	10
Government Administration, Including Secret Police	4
Household Consumption Outlays	48
II. *Pattern of Investment Percent:*	
Gross Investment	*100*
of which:	
Industry	55
Heavy Industry	45
Agriculture	13
Transport	17
Communications	1
Trade and Procurement	2
Other	12

The figures are cited merely as an expositional device. They are typical of the general approach to the breakthrough problem which the following comments will help clarify.

Except during World War II when defense outlays absorbed as much as one-third (and on occasion more) of GNP, gross investment in the

Soviet Union in the years 1929–1956 never descended below 23 percent of a rising gross national product. In nontechnical terms, the Soviets put aside year-in, year-out about one-quarter of current output for the explicit purpose of promoting growth. This fact alone goes a long way in explaining the prevalence of coercion during this time. The figure actually underestimates the investment rate because it fails to take into account the resources channelled into the formation of human capital. To arrive at a more precise idea of the magnitude of the investment effort, one should add to the gross investment figure a portion of the outlays on communal services. It was not until 1964, for instance, that enterprise expenditures on lecture halls and laboratories used by part-time and evening students were included in the enterprises' investment budget rather than counted as enterprise expenditures on communal services. Outlays on the secret police should also be viewed as an investment item. Many of the functions of the police were economic. Included among these were the detection and apprehension of economic saboteurs, that is, the eradication of all but the Party-State preference functions. A notable feature of the Soviet investment strategy during this time was the neglect of capital depreciation, a marked indifference to wear and tear and obsolescence. Men and machines were driven to the limit with little thought for replacement and repair. It was only after Stalin's death that the Soviets and the Eastern Europeans began seriously to take heed of the inhibiting effects on growth of their reckless depreciation policy.

Outlays on communal services are a reflection of, on the one hand, the Soviet stress on the formation of human capital and, on the other, of a particular consumption philosophy. Communal rather than individual consumption (trains, buses, taxis rather than private automobiles) is the goal which Soviet-type command systems hope to achieve one day. Communal consumption, in this view, contributes to the initiation of the people into communist principles of human relationships and fosters the "correct" attitude toward labor and public property.[8] All Soviet-type command systems have stressed this aspect of consumption and as a result have spared no efforts to develop a wide range and variety of social services and public facilities.[9] During the forced-draft industrialization drive, however, most of these services and facilities were not made available to the collective farm population.

Defense was and continues to be an important item. When the Soviet command system first took root in Russia, it considered itself surrounded by hostile powers whose one aim was to destroy the revolution. Rapid

[8] Jan S. Prybyla, "The Soviet Theory of Social Consumption Funds During the Transition from Socialism to Communism," *The Southwestern Social Science Quarterly,* Vol. 43, No. 1, June, 1962, pp. 47–56.

[9] Jan S. Prybyla, "The Soviet Consumer in Khrushchev's Russia," *The Russian Review,* Vol. 20, No. 3, July, 1961, pp. 194–205. Reprinted in Harry G. Shaffer, ed., *The Soviet Economy: A Collection of Western and Soviet Views* (New York, Appleton-Century-Crofts, 1963), pp. 252–260.

development of armament industries which later spilled over into space exploration became one of the top priorities in the strategy of development. Politically, the army was kept in line by its submission to the Party. Party political officers are present in every army unit, and political instruction ranks in importance next only to military drill.

Expenditures on government administration were not excessive considering the command character of the system.

Household consumption was kept at low levels throughout the period. This was achieved through a combination of rationing, high prices for consumer items, and relatively low money wages. Even so, suppressed inflation was characteristic of the whole industrialization drive. The policy of employing all available resources, especially labor, generated money income pressures on the limited supply of consumer goods which manifested themselves in long lines outside state and cooperative stores and other daily shopping frustrations. Occasionally, forced loans and currency reforms were used to wipe out surplus purchasing power.

The concentration of the bulk of investment on industry, especially heavy industry, and the relative neglect of investment in such sectors as residential and commercial construction is the most characteristic feature of the Soviet-type breakthrough strategy. It is the method of walking on one leg, as the Chinese would put it, or the theme of the leading sector. This theme was at one time summed up by Lenin in the slogan "Communism is Soviet political power plus electrification of the entire country." The industries emphasized were those which tended to yield much output for every unit of capital (i.e., industries the incremental capital-output ratio of which was low). They included such branches as metallurgy, machine-building, and power generation. In these priority sectors up-to-date technology was introduced in the key processes, while auxiliary processes (e.g., materials handling) were left to largely traditional, labor-intensive methods. Until Stalin's death, the industrialization drive favored the older industrial regions of European Russia rather than the newer Siberian areas. In short, growth was unbalanced as regards economic sectors, processes within the chosen sectors, and geographical location. Selected processes within a few chosen industries in a small number of areas were highly advanced, while the rest of the economy went its old Tsarist way. To this day, most communist countries present a striking contrast of the old and the new, of the latest techniques and outdated methods coexisting side by side. Added to this is the visible neglect of consumption and the vast, sprawling agricultural slum.

Soviet Growth Results

The object of all this was to be growth, and growth the Soviets did get. But the interesting thing is that the rates of growth in output were no more striking than those chalked up in a comparable period by systems using the market method. Even though the market-oriented systems did not shirk from using constraint, the degree of constraint was less than in the systems of command. In comparison with the Stalinist industrial revolution of the nineteen-thirties and forties, the British industrial revolution of the early nineteenth century and the American industrial upsurge of the late nineteenth and early twentieth centuries were child's play insofar as the thoroughness of constraint was concerned. Table 15 compares the average annual growth rates in output for the U.S.S.R. and the United States in roughly equivalent developmental periods. In looking at these figures one should remember that they say little about the sectoral balance in the economies listed. American growth was not only as fast as the Soviet, but it was better balanced. Even in moments of its most acute fever it did not exact from the individuals involved the price in personal freedom and dignity inherent in the Soviet method.

Several comments on Table 15 are pertinent.

(1) The growth rates refer to industrial output. In other words, they pertain to the favored Soviet sector.

(2) Growth rates in the last years of Tsarist rule were substantially lower than in the various periods of Soviet power. It should be remembered, however, that 1913–1915 were war years. In the period 1870 through 1913, the rate of Russian industrial growth was 5.3 percent.

(3) The Soviet and other command economies are not subject to business fluctuations of the kind that in the past have at frequent intervals plagued market-oriented economies. The growth in output (especially industrial output) has been, consequently, more even than that in market-oriented systems.[10] On the other hand, the concerted application of compulsion tends to produce a phenomenon which can best be described as "politically-induced economic cycles." Mass executions, purges, sustained terror against the citizens, and just plain exhaustion tend to affect output

10

Average Annual Growth Rates Percent

PERIOD 1870–1913	OUTPUT Russia or U.S.S.R.	OUTPUT PER HEAD OF POPULATION		
		U.S.A.	Russia or U.S.S.R.	U.S.A.
1870–1913	5.3	5.1	3.7	2.9
1913–55	3.9	3.7	3.3	2.4
1913–28	0.1	3.7	—0.5	2.3
1928–55	6.1	3.7	5.3	2.5
1928–40	7.4	1.8	5.9	1.0
1940–55	5.1	5.2	5.1	3.6
1928–37	10.9	1.3	9.9	0.5
1950–55	7.7	4.5	5.9	2.8

SOURCE: G. Warren Nutter, "The Structure and Growth of Soviet Industry: A Comparison with the United States," Joint Economic Committee, Congress of the United States, Part I, *Comparisons of the United States and Soviet Economies*, Washington, D.C., 1959, Table 3, p. 105. Soviet figures for 1913–55, 1928–55, and 1928–40 have been adjusted to exclude territorial gains.

TABLE 15

Growth Rates for Industry in Soviet Union and the United States. Output in Selected Comparable Periods

	AVERAGE ANNUAL GROWTH RATE		
Period for the U.S.S.R.	*Output Growth Rate*	*Period for the U.S.A.*	*Output Growth Rate*
1928–1955	6.1	1877–1904	5.6
1928–1940	7.4	1877–1889	7.0
1950–1955	7.7	1908–1913	8.0
1913–1915	3.9	1877–1919	5.0

SOURCE: G. Warren Nutter, "The Structure and Growth of Soviet Industry: A Comparison with the United States," Joint Economic Committee, Congress of the United States, Part I, *Comparisons of the United States and Soviet Economies*, Washington, D.C., 1959, p. 117, Table 6. On the basic problem of "what to compare," see, *ibid.*, pp. 103–104. *Cf.*, our discussion of "Periods" above.

rates in the short run, particularly the output rates of agriculture. The mass collectivization drive of the late twenties and early thirties was accompanied by fierce peasant resistance which included the burning of crops and the slaughter of animals. In fact, Soviet agriculture (especially animal husbandry) did not recover from that blow until well into the fifties. Moreover, the strategy of the breakthrough appears to lose its effectiveness as the economy expands. New breakthrough sectors have then to be created in rapid succession or, better still, simultaneously, a process which requires more refined instruments of measurement and incentive than brute force. The continued use of administrative constraint in a more complex system, in a system, that is, in which the range of choice is much wider and more varied, tends to exert a retarding effect on output, besides being prejudicial to the quality of output.[11]

THE SOVIET SYSTEM IN TRANSITION

There can be no doubt that Stalin's strategy of economic development and the political and social institutions which it employed have lifted Russia from underdevelopment and economic backwardness and brought it to within reach of the payoff stage. But to actually reach that stage, the system must be profoundly transformed. Today there is no need to squeeze resources out of the agricultural sector by force and by neglect of the farmers' wants. There seems to be a limit to the blood that

[11] Jan S. Prybyla, "The Quest for Economic Rationality in the Soviet Bloc," *Social Research*, Vol. 30, No. 3, Autumn, 1963, pp. 343–366; "The Economic Problems of Soviet Russia in Transition," *The Indian Journal of Economics*, Vol. XLV, No. 177, October, 1964, pp. 135–151; "The Soviet Economy: From Libermanism to Liberalism?" *Bulletin of the Institute for the Study of the U.S.S.R.*, July, 1966, pp. 19–27.

coercion can squeeze out of a stone, and that limit has, in fact, been reached. What Soviet agriculture lacks above all else is efficiency that cannot be made by threats and slogans. What the Soviet farmer needs today to lift his productivity and that of the collective land is not a whip, but a pension, not bombastic appeals to his collective conscience, but some tangible evidence that his work on the common lands is not a waste of time. The best tangible evidence, material incentive as the Russians put it, is higher and more regular income. To achieve this, agriculture can no longer be starved for lack of investment. For one, it must get more fertilizer and a more liberal allocation of building materials. This, in turn, means the development of chemical industries, but not to the exclusion of the building trades. An advanced country cannot go on forever hopping along on one economic leg. It must try and grow the other, or others; for an economy walks on a thousand legs, the movement of each being dependent on the health of all the others. In short, the Soviet economy (as the economies of other Soviet-type command countries which approach the payoff stage) has no choice but to move on a broad front, well beyond the few key industries which powered the takeoff from poverty. It needs not one, but many, leading sectors.

The allocation of resources in such a setting becomes a matter of close and careful calculation of the alternatives foregone (there now *are* such alternatives), a question of what Western economists refer to as "microeconomics." The system of administrative commands based on the whims of a dictator (even educated whims) has clearly outlived its usefulness. But careful calculation presupposes freedom to engage in such exercises. It means giving scope to economists and mathematicians, managers of enterprises, and collective farm chairmen. Yet scope, the free exercise of initiative and invention, is the very thing that Stalinism killed. Even today one can never be quite sure where the borderline between officially approved grassroots enterprise and illegitimate individual innovation lies. Moreover freedom is contagious: it cannot be limited to some leading sector and excluded from other spheres of activity. The mathematicians and the physicists need it in their work and so does the State— their respective needs meet. But the State thinks it needs those sycophants of atrophied socialist realism in art and literature, while writers and artists yearn for something else. The complex economy needs economists and economists need freedom to build a new theory of socialist microeconomics. The State needs the economists and the microeconomics but is hesitant about the freedom. There are many rigidities inherent in Stalinism, but none so severe and difficult to break as the totalitarian temper. Communal consumption is all very well provided it does not breed the habit of relying on the paternal State for every little thing. Investment in human capital is also an excellent idea, but the training of competent robots is not. In the long run it is better to have a thinking engineer than just an engineer. In the short run an engineer whose intellectual horizon is bounded by his profession and the Party's dogma is better than no engineer at all. In brief, freedom may come too early, but it can never come too late.

The Soviet leaders who followed Stalin seemed on the whole to have grasped the message, but the force of Stalinist habit had made them more timid than circumstances demanded. They moved boldly to end the second-class citizenship of the peasants, yet for a while (under Khrushchev) tried the old outplayed game of organizational reshuffle upon reshuffle. More recently, they announced a radical departure from the old faith in the beneficent effects of heavy industry, detailed central allocation of resources, and agricultural neglect.[12] The sudden turn was somewhat reminiscent of Khrushchev's storming of chemical heights and Stalin's attack on steel. What the post-Stalin leaders have not yet learned are the virtues of gradualism and the subtleties of carefully moving on all fronts at once. They keep on fuming against and storming now this, now that, special target. Their conception of strategy is still restricted by two, perhaps three, variables. Because Stalin killed economic science (and sociology, psychology, and political science, too), they are ignorant in the ways of general equilibrium. Yet, increasingly, their tenure of power comes to depend on their ability to run the economic system efficiently, on their success in providing the citizens not just with a pair of pants, but with one that fits, and perhaps an extra pair for the socialist bourgeois weekend. Collective farms, arbitrary Party rule, storming in politics and economics, less than full citizenship for nearly half the population, intellectual conformity at the lowest Party hack's common mental denominator, fairy tales about superiority where visibly there is none are no longer tools of growth, vehicles of the long march from poverty. They are now, and will increasingly become, the surest means of problem accumulation and an unequivocal invitation to stagnation. Having escaped from the low level equilibrium trap, the Soviets are now faced with the prospect of falling into the equally ensnaring trap of high level equilibrium. They are aware of the danger, but whether they can avoid it, only time will tell.

12 Since the removal of Khrushchev, compulsory farm deliveries of grain to the State procurement agencies have been reduced to 55.7 million metric tons (1964–1965), while the State requirements have been estimated at some 65 million tons. The 55.7 million tons represent from 35 to 40 percent of the total grain output. To get the remaining 9.3 million tons, the State has introduced a 50 percent bonus for wheat and rye supplied over and above the compulsory quota. This bonus comes on top of substantial increases in compulsory delivery prices. To reduce harvesting losses, tractor drivers and other machine operators are no longer to be paid on the basis of hours in the field or area harvested, but according to an incentive system. Under it the operators are paid in advance or are guaranteed a minimum wage for harvest work. Final adjustments, which include bonuses for reduction of harvest time and grain losses, are made after the harvest is in. See, Theodore Shabad, "Russians Hopeful on Grain Harvest," The New York Times, July 13, 1965, p. 4.

1962–1967: THE "LIBERMAN REFORMS"

On September 9, 1962, *Pravda,* the organ of the Communist Party of the Soviet Union, carried an article by a then little-known professor at the University of Kharkov, Y. Liberman, entitled "Plan, Profits, and Bonuses," in which the author advanced a series of proposals to reform the Soviet managerial incentives system. The article was followed by a second Liberman essay published in the economic periodical *Ekonom-icheskaya Gazeta* (November 10, 1962). Both articles gave rise to a lively discussion in the Party and government press during the next few years.

The interest of the Liberman proposals and of the ensuing discussion was that they were notably lacking in ideological dogmatism and that they addressed themselves pragmatically and realistically to the many ills which beset the Soviet economy. Perhaps the most curious sign of the times was that the Party and government allowed such proposals to be made in the columns of their monopolistic press and that the exchange of views on the suggestions was encouraged by the trustees of official truth. It was de-Stalinization come alive on a narrow front. Part of the explanation was in the fact that the Liberman proposals were well within the general bounds of orthodoxy. A further reason was that Stalin's administrative socialism had outlived its usefulness and that it was hampering the economy's striving for efficiency and quality of output as against the mere piling up of quantity. The time had come to translate Stalin's understanding of quantity into a more modern and wider grasp of quality. Growth at any cost had to yield place to careful calculations of the cost of growth.

The economy inherited from Stalin was indeed impressive in its quantitative performance, but there was much waste and inefficiency, and much too much useless motion. For example, in order to obtain its annual supply of ball bearings from the neighboring GPZ factory, the Moscow Likhachev Automobile Plant was at one time required to furnish 400 pounds of supporting documentation to fourteen planning agencies; after all the plans had been made, checked, and counterchecked, the Russian Republic Council of Ministers had to issue in 1958 over 100 statutory orders to secure additional supplies for Moscow City; the Novo-Krama-torsk Machine Factory counted 600 inspectors in a single year—and so on. With all that, a good portion of the output of Soviet farms and factories had to be regularly rejected as being below standard. Between 1955 and 1963 inventories of nonfood consumer goods in wholesale and retail trade had risen in monetary terms from 12,500 million rubles to 30,600 million rubles, much of the increase being accounted for by goods rejected by customers.

The conclusion reached by the post-Stalin leadership was that the Soviet economic problem consisted essentially of two basic ills: first, the central planning apparatus was too elaborate, too detailed, and too all-embracing. Second, at the firm level, managerial incentives were such as to distort managerial conduct.

The Soviet planning apparatus, it was found, had been using old-fashioned analytical tools to tackle a job of immense proportions. It attempted to control practically everything that went on in the economy, leaving little to the individual initiative of lower echelons and going about the task with almost prehistoric tools. Thus, the Russian Republic in 1966 counted over one million accountants fully engaged on adding and subtracting largely irrelevant information. A Soviet mathematical economist estimated in the early 1960's that unless something drastic were done about the way in which the economy was being run, by 1980 the whole adult population of the U.S.S.R. would have had to be employed in economic planning and administration. The introduction of better planning tools by itself was surely not enough. Economic planning means the flow of meaningful information, and the basic problem, therefore, was to make the information available to the planners better than heretofore and at the same time to see to it that this improved information was processed with better analytical tools. Since 1962 the Soviets have tackled both aspects of the planning problem. They have, on the one hand, tinkered with their unrealistic price structure, a structure inherited from the Stalin era of administrative socialism, and tried to make prices more representative of relative resource scarcities than they had been until then. On the other hand, they began experimenting with integrated computers, linear programming, and input-output procedures, and applying mathematical economics to some of the problems facing the planners. All this is highly nonideological business, only partly understood by professional Party committeemen. There is inevitably much divided opinion about it within the Party; some fear that decision-making power may be slipping through the Party's fingers. Yet the wastes of the present system are so obvious that, reluctant though some Party men may be about the reforms, there is a sort of historical necessity about doing away with an awkward and inefficient planning system.

As distinct from reform at the top of the economic pyramid, the Liberman proposals address themselves to reforming the bottom of the planning system. Liberman's argument is that the enterprise manager's behavior is distorted by the kind of "success indicators" imposed on the manager from above. The central planning agencies had been handing down to the manager a mass of targets which he was expected to fulfill or, better, overfulfill. These targets covered practically every aspect of the plant's operations but in the end boiled down to one overall success criterion: quantity of output. The net result was a general chase after quantity and an almost total disregard of quality. If a firm producing nails is given its target in terms of units, it will tend to produce very many very small nails; if the target is set in tons, it may theoretically produce one huge nail with beneficial effects on the manager's salary and workers' wages; if the target is expressed in rubles, an attempt may be made to use the most expensive materials available, and so on. The phenomenon is familiar to the Soviet economy and, of course, it is one which cannot be tolerated indefinitely. Administrative sanctions against wayward managers are not enough; in fact, they have been known to do more harm than good. Liberman's suggestion was to (a) reduce the number of production indices which the central planners hand down to the manager, and (b) to replace quantitative success indicators with a single indicator of success that would be more flexible and more comprehensive. Such an indicator, Liberman argued, was profit, or more exactly, the "profitability rate" calculated as a ratio of profits to the total capital of the enterprise. The main difficulty, however, is that the profitability rate criterion of success will tend to induce new distortions in managerial behavior, unless the price structure within which profits are calculated is thoroughly reformed. Managerial reform, in other words, cannot be divorced from price reform. In Stalin's time prices were set by the planners primarily with a view to serving as agents of accounting and control, not as allocating and signalling devices. Price reform, therefore, implies *ipso facto* some surrender of Party control over the economy in the interest of greater efficiency. That is a hard pill to swallow for many men brought up in the tradition of administrative socialism.

In a somewhat modified form, the Liberman suggestions were tried first in two plants producing consumer goods. In addition to the profitability criterion, an element of direct contracting between producers and retailers was introduced, and the plants' success was measured not only in terms of the profitability rate but also by output actually sold. In 1966, the experiment was extended to some branches of industry, and since 1967 to almost all industry. At the same time a thorough price reform has been initiated. The results of the experiment have apparently been favorable and it may be presumed that, short of a sudden change of heart, the Liberman reforms will be pursued in the years to come.

The Liberman-type experiments have often been misunderstood and misrepresented in the West as some sort of "return to capitalism." This is not so. Libermanism is merely an attempt to make Soviet-type socialism work more smoothly than hitherto. It introduces into what used to be very largely an administratively run economy, elements of economic calculation and a dose of cost-benefit rationality which it would be incorrect to saddle with any one label. Politically, it does tend in the direction of greater grassroots initiative, but still controlled grassroots initiative. It is a pragmatic response to the needs of a complex economic system, and not —as the Chinese are prone to say—an abandonment of the planning principle.

THE CHINESE WAY

In the midst of the Sino-Soviet dispute, in defending themselves against Chinese accusations of callousness, the Soviets remarked that they became "upset by a turn that had become apparent in the development of the Chinese national economy in 1958." This turn which upset the Russians so much was, in fact, the second Chinese Communist revolution, this one against Soviet influence. The revolution came to be known as the "Great Leap Forward," and though in many respects it was far from a howling success, it did give birth to a specifically Chinese method of economic development. This method is now being offered to whoever wants to try it in competition with both the Soviet and Western strategies. The Chinese method is a variant of the general command approach to economic development, but it contains many novel elements especially designed to fit the conditions of very backward, woefully poor, overpopulated Asian countries.

1949–1953: CONSOLIDATION OF POWER

From October, 1949, until the inauguration of the First Five-Year Plan in 1953, the Chinese followed the methods employed by the Soviets and the Eastern European communists just prior to the breakthrough industrialization drive. Naked force was used to radically transform the social relations in the countryside. Millions of landlords and so-called "rich peasants" were executed or deported to forced labor camps in Sinkiang and other outlying provinces. A temporary land reform was quickly pushed through giving the poor peasants and former agricultural laborers small, economically nonviable strips of land. The urban middle class was subjected to repeated campaigns of harassment and finally reduced to submission. Runaway inflation was brought under control by a series of monetary and fiscal reforms and the nationalization of banking. New roads, railroads, canals, and bridges were built, but most of the effort during this period was spent on repairing the devastation caused by years of foreign and civil war. The political administration of the country was reorganized along the Soviet pattern, the power of local feudal lords was effectively broken, control was extended over a number of disputed border areas (Sinkiang, Outer Mongolia), Tibet was incorporated as a province of China, and political opposition was silenced. In all these tasks frequent use was made of the army (the People's Liberation Army, or P.L.A.). As in other countries taken over by the communists, this was the period of economic reconstruction, seizure and consolidation of power, and the laying of foundations for a future system of command.

1953–1957: CHINESE STALINISM

From 1953 through 1957 (the period of the first Five-Year Plan), China followed the Stalinist method of economic breakthrough.

This is brought out by Table 16.

The resulting growth rates in China and the Soviet Union in these broadly comparable periods were fairly close. Officially, the Chinese claimed that in the period 1953–1957 the annual average rate of growth in the output of industry was 16.5 percent. The corresponding Soviet figure was 19.0 percent. There were, however, wide divergences in the growth performance of agriculture. The Soviet collectivization process was, as we have noted earlier, an extremely painful one. China's collectivization was carried out smoothly and without fuss, and the whole huge

TABLE 16

**Rates and Patterns of Investment in the Soviet Union
(1928–32) and in Mainland China (1953–57)**

	CHINA		SOVIET UNION	
	1953	*1957*	*1928*	*1937†*
Rate of Investment (per cent) *	16.0	20.0	21.0–23.0	19.0–23.0
Pattern of Investment (per cent)	Planned		Realized	
	China	Soviet Union	China	Soviet Union
Sector:				
Industry	61.8	40.7	56.0	49.0
Heavy Industry	. . . .	31.3	49.0	42.1
Agriculture	6.2	15.3	8.2	19.1
Transport	17.1	21.1	18.7	17.6
Communications	7.2	0.6	. . . .	1.1
Trade and Procurement	. . . .	. . . .	. . . .	1.8
Social-cultural Services and Administration	7.7	22.3	17.1	11.0

SOURCE: Alexander Eckstein, "The Strategy of Economic Development in Communist China," *American Economic Review*, Papers and Proceedings, Vol. LI, No. 2 (May, 1961), Table 1, p. 509.
* For China: gross investment as a ratio of gross national product. For the Soviet Union: the lower rates represent gross investment as a ratio of gross national product at established market prices, while the higher rates are in terms of adjusted factor costs.
† There are no reliable national income estimates for 1932; therefore 1937 as the end year of the second Soviet Five-Year Plan was taken as illustrative.

undertaking took less than a year (1956). These two very different collectivization experiences were reflected in the output rates: −4 percent for the U.S.S.R., and +4.5 percent for China. Such progress in agricultural production as the Chinese did make was offset to some extent by the rapid rate of population increase, which during this period was 2.2 percent (1.3 percent in the comparable Soviet period).

The institutions of constraint used in both countries were broadly similar—perhaps a little more thorough in China. The high rates of saving and investment were made possible by agricultural collectivization and the neglect of agriculture in the sense already discussed. The State planning and supervisory apparatus was modelled on that employed by Stalin and was, in fact, installed with the help of Soviet experts. Advanced technology was introduced only into a few selected sectors and into particular key processes within the chosen sectors. Consumption levels were kept low in much the same way as in the Soviet Union of the takeoff period. Intimidation of all suspected of opposing the system was much in evidence. Investment in social overhead was kept at an indispensable minimum. It was the Soviet strategy and the Soviet institutional structure all over again: a system of constraint from the center, the strategy of the leading sector, unbalanced growth, and all the rest.

Then in 1957 something happened to change all that. By 1958, the Chinese strategy of development and the tools used to put it into effect had significantly departed from the Soviet model. In addition, political and inter-Party relations between China and the Soviet Union deteriorated rapidly, and things have never been quite the same since. It is certainly not an exaggeration to say that the emergence of Communist China as a potentially important economic and political power and the dispute between China and the Soviet Union are two of the most interesting and significant events of contemporary history. In spite of much contradictory evidence furnished in anger by both sides to the monumental dispute, the exact reasons for the quarrel are still not crystal clear. As the mutual villification unfolded, new reasons and new irritants constantly appeared. There can be little doubt, however, that by 1957 the Chinese had come to the conclusion that the Soviet strategy and institutions of development were not suitable for China beyond the level of general principle and that the political price they were expected to pay for the privilege of applying the Soviet method was too high. Moreover, Stalin was gone and his successors began experimenting with forms of economic organization and political methods that seemed to the Chinese even less applicable to China than the original Stalinist model.

CAUSES OF SHIFT AWAY FROM STALINISM

The issues directly relevant to the sudden shift in Chinese strategy and tools of development may be summed up as follows:

(1) A country whose population increases at a rate of 2.2 percent per annum, whose agricultural land is limited, and whose agricultural output depends heavily on irrigation and flood control, cannot neglect agriculture for a couple of decades and get away with it unscathed.

(2) China's greatest potential asset and, at the same time, her greatest immediate burden is population. The first scientifically competent census in Chinese history carried out in 1953 showed a population in excess of 582 millions. About 80 percent were illiterate peasants who worked on the land only part of the year and whose productivity, when they did work, was very low. As an instrument for the mobilization of peasant masses, the collective farm system was only partly successful. Beyond supplying industry with resources at high cost, it contributed little to the industrialization process.

(3) The experience of the first five years had shown that farm production (in spite of inflated claims) barely kept up with the rate of population growth. Were this trend allowed to continue, it threatened to seriously impede the pace of industrial expansion.

(4) Soviet economic aid, all of it, had to be paid for by exports. This put an additional strain on agriculture and various consumer goods industries, the products of which were exported to the Soviet Union in payment for capital imports. Soviet aid, though not large by any count, was of great strategic importance to China. From 1950 through 1957, the value of Soviet exports to China was $4.9 billion. Commercial loans came to only $790 million and military assistance in the form of loans to just over $1 billion. In 1957, 50 percent of Soviet exports to China consisted of industrial machinery and equipment. Most of the remainder was made up of fuels, lubricants, metals, chemical fertilizers, and drugs. In that year, complete industrial installations represented 77 percent of the value of machinery and equipment imported by the Chinese from the Soviet Union. At the end of that year, Soviet-built enterprises accounted for 50 percent of China's coal output, 57 percent of steel production, and 100 percent of the output of synthetic rubber.[13]

When, after 1959, this source of capital imports was abruptly cut off, the Chinese were obliged to reorient their investment strategy to fit the new circumstances. Moreover, the sudden withdrawal of Soviet technical experts from China in mid-1960 was a serious blow to China's second Five-Year Plan, the original draft of which still copied the Stalinist method.

[13] Sidney Klein, "Recent Economic Experience in India and Communist China: Another Interpretation," *American Economic Review,* Papers and Proceedings, Vol. LV, No. 2, May, 1965, pp. 31–39; "On the Struggle of the CPSU for the Solidarity of the International Communist Movement," Report by Comrade M. A. Suslov on February 14, 1964 at a Plenary Session of the Central Committee of the C.P.S.U., *Pravda,* April 3, 1964, pp. 1–8.

1958–1960: THE GREAT LEAP FORWARD

The revolt against Soviet methods was violent in the extreme. In the first three years (1958–1960) all caution was thrown to the winds. During that time there was, strictly speaking, no well thought-out method, but merely political fever. The economy was run by administrative fiat and political absolutism. Even the pretence of economic planning could not be kept up for long.

The essence of the new approach to economic construction was total mobilization of rural labor. Every man, woman, and child in the countryside was put to work twelve hours a day, every day of the year. When farm work had been done, there were "subsidiary activities" like smelting iron in homemade backyard furnaces, repairing machinery and tractors, building dykes and reservoirs, roads, railroad lines, and bridges. It was a mobilization so total and so thorough as to constitute a phenomenon unprecedented in the history of mankind. For three years the countryside was in convulsions. Every day, in addition to regular farmwork organized on a military basis, 90 million peasants marched out into the fields to collect animal and human manure, another 90 million smelted iron in hundreds of thousands of improvised furnaces, 100 million tried their hand at deep ploughing, almost 80 million ran back and forth carting tons of earth to build irrigation ditches and dykes, and 60 million women tended to communal kitchens, sewing shops, nurseries, first-aid stations, and laundries. During leisure hours, prescribed by law to number eight per day, 500 million peasants engaged in organized activities which included military drill, calisthenics, reading and organized discussion of the works of Mao Tse-tung, and the singing of revolutionary songs.

The policy of the Great Leap was command pushed to its theoretical limit in a desperate attempt to cut the Gordian knot of poverty. Basically the policy drew inspiration from the old Soviet prescription of storming difficult problems, but it carried this assault well beyond what the Russians had ever thought possible, and it stormed many problems at the same time. It was movement along a broad front early in the process of economic development, using Stalinist methods sharpened and exaggerated a thousand times. In short, it was a combination of balanced growth and Stalinist storming without the benefit of economic calculation.

To make it possible, new tools were introduced. The first was permanent tension created by constant, sustained, repetitious, unending persuasion, a bloodless form of terror, an assault on the individual personality that went, and still goes, by the name of "socialist education." Dangers of foreign intervention were conjured up, visions of capitalist threats and revisionist subversion. The enemy was allegedly everywhere: in the person of the village laggard as well as in Moscow. The essence of Chinese socialist education was, and is, to keep everyone afraid all the time, afraid of something elusive and indefinable, yet real. On the positive side, socialist education means the harnessing of the people's pride in their country, of their desire to leave poverty and material degradation behind, the mobilization of nationalism and patriotism, and of resentment against past wrongs suffered at the hands of landlords, corrupt political bosses, and foreign powers. At the very time that the Chinese were raising permanent tension to the rank of a political and economic institution, the Soviets were hesitantly shedding the worst features of Stalin's reign of fear.

The second characteristic tool of the Great Leap was the People's Commune. This was a form of agricultural organization (eventually to be extended to urban industry) which the Chinese Communists regarded, and officially at least still view, as nearer the communist ideal than even the Soviet state farm and nationalized industrial enterprise. More immediately and practically, the People's Commune was a mobilizing and rationing device. Instead of some 750,000 scattered collective farms over which control was difficult (if much easier than over privately owned farms), some 27,000 large communes were set up in a matter of months. Whereas a collective farm in China comprised about 160 households, the number of households per commune averaged 5,000. It was hoped that this consolidation would achieve economies of scale of various kinds and make the task of mobilizing labor for specific agricultural and other tasks much easier than under the collective farm system.

The communes began to exercise many functions which had formerly been vested in local authorities: public health, education, commerce, public security, the management of local consumer and other light industries, the building of small and medium-sized reservoirs, and so on. Labor was organized in production brigades and smaller production teams. Work was assigned to these units by the commune's central leadership on the basis of instructions received from above. The discipline was modelled on the People's Liberation Army. In fact, many demobilized P.L.A. units were settled en masse in Sinkiang and Inner Mongolia in pioneer People's Communes. Half the income was distributed in the form of ration tickets redeemable in commune stores, communal dining halls, laundries, and tailoring establishments.

The commune experiment in its extreme form broke down in 1960. The tension was too great, the units too unwieldy, the fatigue too unbearable. Natural disasters made matters worse. Much of the steel output of the backyard furnaces was unusable and, more generally, the waste motion and resource strain were too costly even for a land in which labor was among the cheapest of commodities.

1961–1966: THE NEW ECONOMIC POLICY [14]

Three major events which occurred between 1958 and 1961 led to a rethinking of Communist China's approach to economic development. These were the economic disruption brought about by the ideologically determined policies of the Great Leap Forward (1958–1960), the natural calamities of the "three bad years" (1959–1961), and the abrupt withdrawal of Soviet experts (mid-1960).

The new policy, elaborated in the latter part of 1960 and applied from 1961 through 1966, has been characterized by gradualness, a modicum of intersectoral balance, an appreciation of the overwhelming rural realities of China's society, and a new understanding of quality as an important dimension of economic growth. However, the new policy of prudence, moderation, realism, and restraint has been accompanied by a renewed assault on the citizens' political consciousness. Launched earlier under the name of Socialist Education and culminating in 1966 in the so-called Great Proletarian Cultural Revolution, the campaign was aimed at preventing the essentially revisionist economic policies from seeping through into the realms of culture and politics and turning into the much-feared Soviet-type revisionism after the disappearance of the present generation of Chinese leaders. The campaign revealed the anxiety with which China's aging leaders viewed the possible future course of events in the country and the continued suspicion in which they held the rising generations of technocrats, engineers, and other experts. The campaign injected into the new economic course an element of tension and a suggestion of impermanence which may in the end threaten the real achievements made since the abandonment of the Great Leap.

The new economic policy is a reversal of both the policies current during China's first Five-Year Plan (1953–1957) and those applied in the course of the Great Leap Forward (1958–1960). Its major tenets may be summarized as follows:

I. Agriculture is the "foundation" of socialist construction.

II. Industry is the "leading factor" of this construction.

III. Scientific and technical education is an important element of economic development.

IV. Self-reliance is a basic virtue of socialist construction.

V. In matters of foreign trade, the rule is to "lean to all sides."

VI. In matters of population, restraint is the guiding principle.

Agriculture as the Foundation. In December, 1964, Chou En-lai summed up the new general approach to sectoral priorities in the following way: "The plan for national economic development should be arranged in

14 Jan S. Prybyla, "Communist China's Strategy of Economic Development 1961–1966," *Asian Survey,* October, 1966, pp. 589–603.

the order of priority of agriculture, light industry, and heavy industry. The scale of industrial development should correspond to the volume of marketable grain and the industrial raw materials made available by agriculture."

The tenet "agriculture as foundation" has been interpreted in six main ways:

(1) The *de facto* dissolution of the People's Commune as a production and accounting unit.

Although the ideological framework of the communes has been left in place and even though the commune still performs certain economic and administrative functions (e.g., local water and soil conservancy projects, running of repair shops, local government), since 1961 the basic agricultural production and income distribution unit has been the production team (20–30 households), a unit smaller than the classical production brigade or collective farm and bigger only than the individual household. Production team households were, until mid-1966, allowed to cultivate small garden plots (abolished during the Great Leap) and to sell the products of this sideline activity on the free market. The essence of the reform has been to stress feasibility, material incentives, and local conditions. This trend is now under attack.

(2) Emphasis on maximizing the area of high and stable yields in respect to staple crops.

The idea here is to concentrate on the development of existing high-yield farms rather than push ahead with ambitious land reclamation schemes at the present time. Consolidation implies four sets of priorities: food grains geared to the development of livestock (especially pigs), output of raw materials for industry (especially cotton), production of export crops (oil seeds, rice), and sideline production on household or team plots (mainly fruit, vegetables, oxen, poultry, and pigs).

(3) Mechanization and tool improvement.

This involves, on the one hand, the diversification of agricultural machinery (especially tractors), and on the other hand, the promotion of "semi-mechanization," that is, the introduction of small but important changes in production methods in the light of local means and conditions.

(4) Stress on the application of fertilizers, natural manure, pesticides, and insecticides.

Since 1961 the chemical industry has been among China's fastest growing industrial sectors. This is understandable: in 1962 Chinese agriculture used only 5 kilograms of fertilizer per hectare of cultivated land, as compared with 228 kilograms for Japan and 110 kilograms for Taiwan.

(5) Pushing ahead with water and soil conservancy on a local basis.

The aim is to minimize the effects of floods and drought which have plagued Chinese agriculture for centuries. The task devolves mainly on the communes and the stress is on (a) building small and medium-sized irrigation and flood control projects, and (b) putting the existing facilities into good repair and full use.

(6) Tightening-up of central control over the countryside.

By 1964 the central authorities got around to checking-up on the financial affairs and target reporting of the production teams, and the investigation apparently brought to light numerous irregularities in which the rural Party cadres were implicated. In short, the rural cadres sided with and abetted localism. A rural cadres rectification campaign was launched in September, 1964, as a by-product of the socialist education drive. It included central judicial investigations of alleged cadre corruption and involved the alliance of the central Party and government organs with the poorest sections of the peasantry against broad segments of the Party's rural administrative, technical, and supervisory elite. While it uncovered accounting and other malpractices here and there, the campaign also generated fear and distrust at the farm level, with adverse effects on production and productivity.

On the whole the results of the new course in agriculture have been satisfactory in the sense that by 1964 total grain output was back to the 1957 level, and the same was probably true of cotton, potatoes, and coarse grains. On a *per capita* basis, the picture was worse than in 1957, because population had in the meantime risen by about 100 million. Hence the need to import grain on a massive scale.

Industry as the Leading Factor. The slogan has been interpreted in four main ways:

(1) A moratorium on "the front of capital construction," especially in the manufacturing branches of heavy industry in 1961. The drop in the investment rate in 1960–1961 was estimated at 67 percent compared with the previous year. Steel appears to have been the sector most immediately affected. The investment cutback was paralleled by the closing down of many small and medium-sized plants hastily put up during the Great Leap. Beginning in 1962 investment in industry rose again, but until 1964 this rise appears to have benefited mainly the light industry which supplies the peasantry with consumer goods and producer goods for export. Investment rates in steel began to climb in 1963. By 1965 a gradual shift in investment from light to heavy industry could be detected, traceable in part to defense considerations. Stress has been put throughout on experimentation, diversification, and quality of output.

(2) Industrial construction must obey the so-called "Three Don'ts" and the "Four Musts."

The first instructs industry to conserve arable land and scarce peasant housing; the second requires of industrial planners to support such projects as increase the availability of water for agricultural use, extend agricultural electrification, and increase the supply of manure and pigwash.

(3) Educated youths should return to the countryside to spur agricultural production and productivity.

The great exodus from the land which characterized the 1953–1960 period is being reversed. Between 1961 and 1965 about 40 million young people were said to have returned to the countryside after gaining education in the cities. The movement has apparently caused some acute morale problems among the young whose urban ambitions and promising careers are being thwarted. The objective of the movement seems to be, in addition to its purely technical aspect, to prevent the reemergence of China's age-old problem of social alienation of the intellectuals from the laboring masses. It is part of the general movement of remolding through menial labor.

(4) In the absence of foreign scientific and technical assistance, industry must practice a vigorous "Combining of the Three."

The basic idea is to diffuse information and prevent the emergence of a meritocratic class structure. It means essentially the combining of the efforts of the political leadership, the workers, and the intellectuals in a great revolutionary fusion of muscle and intellect in conformity with Marxist-Leninist teaching about the integration of theory and practice. There are many variations on this theme (e.g., the combination of the work of intellectuals, soldiers, and workers or of workers, college teachers, and scientific and research personnel).

Scientific and Technical Education. One of the most salient characteristics of the new course has been the preoccupation with scientific and technical education, a matter rendered more urgent by the withdrawal of Soviet experts. The new drive has taken four main forms:

(1) The continued expansion of universities, colleges, technicums, and other institutes of higher learning, in the majority of which students receive instruction which prepares them to handle specific and relatively narrow technical or scientific tasks.

(2) The establishment of part-work, part-study schools all over the country in which academic courses are combined with work in the fields or the factory.

(3) The establishment of research and development departments in farms and industrial enterprises and of specialized research institutes under the Academy of Agricultural Sciences. Specialized research of this kind is supplemented by "mass research" and "spare-time research," both politically motivated but perhaps helpful in the setting of China's present conditions. The first is allegedly conducted by "the broad masses of peasants and workers" who are counted upon by the Party to keep a sharp lookout for any signs of wayward tendencies on the part of the specialists; the second is a commune and industrial enterprise responsibility and is apparently conducted by cadres, peasants, and workers in moments of

organized reflection in-between work at the lathe and in the field. As in other areas, the drive for economic rationality is here accompanied and, more often than not, hampered by the drive for cultural transformation of the Marxist-Maoist-Yenan type.

(4) To selectively learn from the foreigner is the duty of every revolutionary. Scientific and technical information must be imported from all sources while keeping an eye on the ideological content in which such information may be wrapped.

Self-Reliance. "We advocate regeneration through our own efforts," says Mao. "We hope there will be foreign aid, but we cannot count on it. We rely on our own efforts, on the creative power of the army and the people."

The doctrine of self-reliance, reiterated a hundred times since 1961, has been interpreted in two main ways:

(1) It means belt-tightening and asceticism in the early revolutionary tradition; capital formation from as yet meager resources, forced savings, and low consumption for many years to come. Industry and frugality are praised as "proletarian virtues" and their practice is said to represent the true "proletarian style."

(2) Self-reliance does not imply autarchy and fear of foreign economic contacts. On the contrary, as will be seen later, it fits in quite well with diversification of markets and sources of supply, and with selective aid to friendly or neutral countries.

Foreign Trade: Leaning to All Sides. The new course regards foreign trade as a component part of developmental policy. The common denominator is balanced diversity, which has three main implications:

(1) The termination of the 1949–1960 policy of "leaning to one side," i.e., toward the Soviet Union and other socialist countries. This has meant (a) the repayment of all commercial and other debts due to these countries by China, and (b) a reduction, both absolute and relative, of trade exchanges with the socialist world. In 1964 about 35 percent of China's trade was with communist countries and some 65 percent with non-communist countries, almost an exact reversal of the 1957 situation. The Chinese now lean to all sides, but on a strictly cash and barter basis.

(2) The pattern of exports and imports has been stabilized. Large-scale purchases of grain from abroad have become a familiar feature of the new course, amounting to about 5 million tons per year. An overall balance between exports and imports is being maintained, accounts are settled scrupulously, and any hard currency payments are made promptly out of earnings from Hong Kong, foreign exchange remittances by overseas Chinese, and occasional favorable balances in hard currency areas.

(3) Trade with and economic assistance to a number of economically underdeveloped countries of Asia and Africa is being promoted, in spite

of diplomatic reverses. Assistance is usually tied to the delivery of Chinese-made goods, long-term loans are for the most part interest-free, and aid projects are selected with a view to producing the maximum growth impact on the economy of the recipient country with the minimum of outlay. The recipients are carefully chosen, as is the political timing of the loan and grant offers.

Population Restraint. The new course approaches people as individuals in the matter of population policy and avoids the crudity and bluster of the 1956 birth control campaign. The elements of the new policy are advocacy of later marriages, the popularization of contraceptive methods, legalized, free abortion (if advised and permitted by a recognized physician), and sterilization. The emphasis is on marriage postponement, and the idea is to reduce the annual rate of natural increase from its present 2.5 percent or thereabouts.

Conclusions. On the whole, China's economic policies since the retreat from the Great Leap have been marked by prudence and restraint and have taken account of the underlying realities of the country's modest level of economic development. On the verbal front there was still much storming against internal and external foes, incipient traitors, revisionists, etc. So far the new course amounts to a rationalization of past errors, a vast rectification campaign which bears within itself no guarantee of permanence. It is quite possible that the Party has not yet made up its collective mind about the precise shape of future policies and that there is considerable debate and dispute on this subject in the innermost sanctum of the Party leadership. The present Five-Year Plan is certainly no long-term program in its present vague and undefined state. The unknown variables of both the domestic and international situations will certainly influence the shaping of future domestic policies. The Chinese have been quick to learn from their mistakes. Whether they will be in the years to come equally steadfast, yet flexible, in their solutions remains an open question.

CHINESE GROWTH RESULTS

The diffusion of statistical information that could be taken at face value is not one of the strong points of the Chinese Communists. As has been shown previously, during the first Five-Year Plan period the Chinese officially claimed an average annual increase in industrial output of 16.5 percent (and 15 percent in industry plus handicrafts) and 4.5 percent in the output of agriculture. The increase in the industrial value of product in 1958 (the first year of the Great Leap) was officially given as 66.3 percent. Western estimates for that year range from 19.6 to 30.3 percent. In 1959, the official increase was given as 39.2 percent (27 to 31.5 percent according to Western calculations). In 1960, the relevant official claim was 29 percent and the Western estimates pointed to about 16 percent.[15] According to Professor Wilfred Malenbaum,[16] China's GNP increased 86 percent from 1950 through 1957. From 1957 through 1959, the increase was said to have been 31 percent. These are, indeed, impressive results. So are the human costs.

THE INDIAN WAY

The solution to economic underdevelopment adopted by India from 1951 on differs radically from the methods employed by the Soviet Union and Communist China. The Indian way out of poverty combines the operation of markets with governmental planning and ownership and emphasizes political consultation between the decision makers and the rest of the community. The pace is more relaxed and the approach to growth more balanced than in the U.S.S.R. or even China after the Great Leap and until 1966. It is nothing short of the difference between communism and democracy.

In spite of appreciable government participation, the Indian model represents essentially a "mixed" system with considerable elements of the market. Private ownership of the means of production and distribution and private economic and political initiative are widespread, while constraint, though present, tends to be used as an inducement to individual efforts. Rather than uprooting the established political, social, and economic order, the Indians have tried, with varying success, to reform it, gradually to modernize the most obsolete institutions, and to build upon what was already there. In their efforts they have exercised a remarkable degree of restraint and respect for even the most "unprogressive" attitudes. Self-reliance in the Soviet and Chinese sense has tended, in the Indian setting, to give way to reliance on foreign economic assistance.

It should be repeated that in spite of India's stated intention gradually to expand the State sector to such industries as iron and steel, heavy electrical plant, coal, mineral oils, iron mining, air and rail transport, shipbuilding, public utilities, atomic energy, and munitions, and to compete with private enterprise in the production of machine tools, nonferrous metals, fertilizers, road and sea transport, and the mining of various minerals, India's economy at the present time is a mixture of market and indirect command, with the market (plus traditionalist) element

[15] Alexander Eckstein, "The Strategy of Economic Development in Communist China," *American Economic Review*, Papers and Proceedings, Vol. LI, No. 2, May, 1961, Table 2, p. 110; *cf.*, Nicolas Spulber, "Contrasting Economic Patterns: Chinese and Soviet Development Strategies," *Soviet Studies*, July, 1963, pp. 1–16.

[16] Wilfred Malenbaum, "India and China: Contrasts in Development," *American Economic Review*, Vol. XLIX, No. 3, June, 1959, pp. 284–309.

predominating. The ratio of government nondefense expenditures to total outlays is one of the lowest in the world (much lower, for example, than the United States). The country's 1956 Industrial Policy Resolution did not envisage the complete disappearance of the private sector even in the distant future.

INSTITUTIONS OF A MARKET ECONOMY [17]

What then are the tools used by the private sector of a mixed economy? What are their essential functions?

(1) Private Property

This means the individual (personal and corporate) ownership of the various means of production and distribution. Within certain broad limits defined by law, the institution of private property places the decision-making power over the allocation of resources in the hands of the many individual owners. The essential function of private property is to diffuse that power. Tendencies toward concentration are often combated by legislation of the antitrust type. The institution vests the saving and investment functions in private hands by guaranteeing the private saver and investor control over the proceeds of the saving and investment process. Private property is also supposed to take care of the conservation of wealth through private depreciation and maintenance policies.

(2) Inheritance

Inheritance means the right of the owner of wealth to designate the recipient at the owner's death and the right of the designated recipient to acquire that wealth. Inheritance is an indispensable corollary to the institution of private property. It perpetuates private property beyond the life span of the individual owner. As with private property, the institution of inheritance is subject to various social restrictions (e.g., inheritance taxes).

(3) Economic Rationality and the Profit Motive

Economic rationality means that the individuals who exercise decision-making power over resources through private property of the means of production and distribution act in a fundamentally similar and consistent way: they try to maximize their extra satisfactions and minimize their extra costs. In business decisions economic rationality takes on the pecuniary form of profit motive to action. The profit motive is quantified as the money difference between returns and expenditures. More strictly formulated (for purposes of economic theory), the assumption is that individual firms try to maximize their profits. In a market economy, the profit motive is *the* stimulus to action.

(4) Freedom of Individual Initiative

This institution vests in the individual the right to use his income as

[17] See William N. Loucks, *Comparative Economic Systems*, 5th ed. (New York, Harper & Row, 1957), Chap. 2.

he pleases, dispose of his labor and capital as he wishes, and act alone or in combination with others. Combined with the institutions of economic rationality, the profit motive, and private property, this institution is relied on in a market system to insure the most efficient possible allocation of all resources. As with other institutions of the market system, freedom of individual initiative is subject to social restrictions to the extent that individual preferences do not reflect many social preferences (e.g., factory legislation, provisions for social security, banking regulation, the control of public utilities, and so forth).

(5) Competition

This means the freedom for all buyers and sellers to enter or leave the market and to make such offers in the market as they consider consistent with their estimates of economic rationality and the profit motive. Competition is relied on to establish in the market a competitive price for every good and to assure productive efficiency by eliminating noncompetitive producers and noncompetitive buyers. In practice competition takes many forms (not always a price form) and is rarely pure.

(6) The Market

The market is merely any arrangement whereby buyers and sellers are kept in constant touch with one another. It is the "computer" which coordinates the various decisions taken by millions of individuals and expresses them in a mathematical equation system. The prices which emerge in the market are, on the one hand, the end-result of economically rational resource allocation decisions taken by the many buyers and sellers, and on the other, signaling devices on which buyers and sellers base their future actions.

THE INDIAN EXPERIMENT

Using a combined market and command economy, India's rate of gross investment (as a percentage of gross national product) rose from 9.3 percent in 1950 to about 13.6 percent in 1957. (The comparable figures for Communist China were 9.7 percent and 23.9 percent.) [18] The source of these investments has been predominantly private. However, the rate of domestic savings, both private and governmental, has risen only moderately. In fact, between 1956 and 1961 there was hardly any increase at all. In other words, the marginal propensity to invest has continued to be low, and the inducement to invest has failed to show any appreciable strengthening. Public revenues from taxation have increased slowly (7.5 percent of national income in 1956 to about 8.9 percent in 1961), and most of these were swallowed up by current State expenditures leaving little for State investment. According to the Government of India's 1961 publication *Third Five-Year Plan* (p. 59), public outlays in the three Five-Year Plans shaped up as follows (the figures for 1961–1966 are estimates):

18 Wilfred Malenbaum, *supra,* Note 16.

TABLE 17

Percentage Distribution of Plan Outlays in the
Public Sector

| | FIVE-YEAR PLANS | | |
| | I | II | III |
	1951–56	*1956–61*	*1961–66*
Agriculture and community development	15	11	14
Irrigation	16	9	9
Power	13	10	13
Village and small industries	2	4	4
Industry and minerals	4	20	20
Transport and communications	27	28	20
Social services and others	23	18	20
	100	100	100

Insofar as command is exercised in the Indian economy, it tends to spread itself much more thinly over the various sectors of the economy than in Soviet and Chinese type command systems. Although industry and transportation are emphasized, agriculture and village industries are not neglected to the extent that they are in the purer command models. In short, the philosophy of command in India is that of more balanced growth.

To finance its public sector investments, India has increasingly relied on foreign assistance. In the first Plan, foreign aid accounted for about 10 percent of public outlays; 24 percent in the second Plan, and 30 percent in the third.

As against China's full employment policy through force, India continues to suffer from serious rural unemployment and underemployment. In 1961, the combined unemployment and underemployment figure was in the region of 27 million out of a population of over 400 million. Hence the effort to stimulate handicrafts and village industries, a policy based on the creation of local opportunities rather than on the use of constraint. In this, the Indian planners have often had to overcome widespread passivity on the part of those for whose benefit the Plan had been elaborated. According to one study, fifteen years after the first Plan began, two-thirds of India's villagers did not even know that the country had five-year plans.[19] The study showed that "three-fourths of the people were

[19] The study was undertaken by the Agro-Economic Research Center of the University of Allahabad and published in December, 1966. See "Apathy Worries India's Planners," *The New York Times,* December 11, 1966, p. 9.

in a zone of complete indifference and did not care whether the plans failed or succeeded." Participation of the people in the execution of planned economic programs was said to have been "very nominal": most people favored working six days a week, six hours a day—a mere pittance in India's critical situation.

Indian Growth Results

As against China's and the "early" Soviet Union's single-minded drive for measurable growth, and good luck to welfare, the objectives of India's planners were, from the very beginning, more varied. Growth was certainly wanted and highly prized, but its significance was subordinated from the very start to social considerations of equity and to political motives that rejected the use of arbitrary force. The element of consultation was put high on the overall scale of priorities and existing sources of economic and political power, rather than being silenced, were given fairly free, if not unlimited, play. The net effect has been a rate of growth about 3.3 times lower than that of Communist China. India's GNP increased 26 percent from 1950 through 1957, that of China by 86 percent. From 1957 through 1959, the growth rates were 9 percent and 31 percent respectively. Even allowing for a considerable margin of exaggeration and pure bombast in the Chinese figures, the difference is striking. Equity and economic welfare cannot be measured with the same kind of precision. One very imperfect way of measuring them is the political ballot box, used in India but not in Communist China. In India it has so far registered the people's approval of the government's approach to the tough issue of poverty (insofar as they were aware of that approach) in spite of the relatively modest results in economically measurable terms. In China one can only guess, and the guess will depend upon one's particular political bias. However, the Indians themselves admit that "a great opportunity for kindling a mass upsurge" for national economic growth is being lost in a sea of popular indifference. A good part of China's totalitarian apparatus is geared full-time to precisely this task of "kindling a mass upsurge." The citizen of Communist China is not allowed for one moment to forget about the plan. The citizen of India is left alone, and more often than not, choses to think other than plan-construction thoughts. In spite of much progress in welfare economics, the individual's immediate and total well-being is not easily quantifiable. Habit and the present often militate against economic dynamics and the future. As has been pointed out earlier, things which are statistically measurable are not always the most important, though frequently very powerful in molding people's estimates of a regime. For those who believe that economic development can be achieved through a gradualistic combination of market and command, democracy and consulted constraint, the experience of India calls for close and sympathetic interest and support.

The three positions which follow illustrate the different approaches to economic development discussed in this chapter and evaluate the appeal of each of these approaches to the leaders of the developing countries.

POSITIONS

1. THE APPEAL AND DANGERS OF THE SOVIET MODEL

Alec Nove, a British economist and specialist in Soviet economic growth and development argues that in spite of its many shortcomings and dangers, the Soviet strategy of economic development does exert a strong appeal for countries seeking quick paths to development.[20]

A MODEL FOR UNDERDEVELOPED COUNTRIES?

One of the more important ways in which Soviet ideas exercise an influence on people in the uncommitted world is through the quite widespread belief that the USSR—and perhaps China also—demonstrates how it is possible rapidly to transform a peasant country into a great industrial power. In the earlier part of this chapter, we have seen that certain western economists who study problems of development outside the Soviet bloc recommend policies which are in some respects similar to those pursued in the USSR. It is also to some extent true that the obstacles which were so ruthlessly tackled under Stalin's rule exist in many underdeveloped countries. The Soviet Communist party smashed through the "interlocking vicious circles," to use Hirschmann's phrase again. They forced the peasants and other private interests to conform to the priorities and financial requirements of the plans for rapid industrialization. They imposed an industrializing ideology. Through a one-party state, through party organization, through the suppression of any persons or groups holding contrary opinions, they were able to mobilize the people to carry the process through despite heavy cost and much suffering. All this is another way of saying that the totalitarian aspects of Soviet rule, which we in the west find most distasteful, may actually be a source of attraction to some statesmen and intellectuals in underdeveloped countries, who find, for reasons analysed at some length elsewhere,* that they are unable to break out of the vicious circles, unable to mobilise their apathetic and sometimes obstructionist peasants, unable to overcome a variety of vested

20 *The Soviet Economy:* An Introduction by Alec Nove, New York, Frederick A. Praeger, Inc., Publishers, 1961, and London, George Allen & Unwin, Ltd., 1961. Reprinted by permission of the publishers, pp. 303–306.
* See Myrdal and Hirschmann, works cited. See also A. Nove, "The Soviet model and underdeveloped Countries," in *International Affairs,* January, 1961.

interests, unable to cope with the inflationary and balance-of-payments crisis which seems inevitably to accompany attempts at development. The practical consequences of the path advocated by Myrdal, Hirschmann and others of their way of thinking may, whether they wish it or not, lead far along the road of political despotism and ideological enthusiasm, because this path can be effectively followed only by a government which can take charge of much of the economy and pursues the aim of development with a fervour not usually associated with democracy or tolerance. It is interesting to note that Bauer, who opposes this whole approach, is aware of this and uses it as an argument against state-sponsored industrialization.*

Yet there are a number of features of the Soviet model which should serve as a warning rather than as an example. It must be recalled that, when the first five-year plan was launched in 1928, the Soviet Union already possessed some industry, considerable technical, scientific and statistical cadres, a fairly extensive railway system, and, perhaps most important, food surplus. This provided a basis and a margin which most overpopulated Asian countries do not possess. The disasters of compulsory collectivization led to a sharp drop in farm output in the USSR; there was in fact widespread famine in 1933. To follow the Soviet model of collectivization, to launch a struggle with the property-owning peasantry, might have fatal results in Asia, for people and regime alike. True, the Chinese experience seems to have been rather different, and it is also true that some government-induced change in archaic systems of farming may well be indispensable. But it is surely right to say that, while the peasant problem is indeed a major factor in the inter-locking vicious circles,† the Soviet way of solving it should not be a model for anyone. The Soviet-style industrializing ideology in fact tends to strengthen those elements which have contempt for peasants and are all too ready to neglect agriculture. Then the Soviet authorities largely destroyed handicrafts, the private small-workshop industry. This greatly contributed to the drastic fall in living standards in the first years of the thirties, and represents a loss in material and human terms which should surely be avoided. The same is true of the liquidation of the private trader, as part of the war on the "speculator," when the state was incapable (indeed is still in certain respects incapable in the USSR) of effectively replacing him. Last but not least, the too complete rejection of conventional economic rationality criteria, the reliance on the campaign approach, untrammelled by free expression of opinion by those adversely affected, led to waste on a scale which underdeveloped countries should surely do all in their power to avoid. Such slogans as "there is no fortress the Bolsheviks cannot take," and the many similar slogans directed in China against the so-called "rightists," open the door far too wide to policies which are irrational in terms of any criterion.

Part of the "magic" of the Soviet example also lies in the acceptance of official Soviet growth-rate statistics, which, were they really correct, would indeed be evidence of magic. It is the reluctance of western economists to believe that miracles happen in economics, even under a Stalin, which have led them

* See especially P. Bauer, *United States Aid and Indian Economic Development* (Washington, American Enterprise Association, 1959).

† On this whole question, see in particular A. Erlich, *op. cit.*

rightly to question these indices. Of course, rapid industrialization of the USSR is a fact. But, properly deflated, the figures compare reasonably with those of Japan, and remind us that there was also a Japanese road, neither western nor communist. But we cannot do more here than to mention it, in a book devoted to the Soviet Union.

Finally, it seems important to realise that, although the Soviet methods were crude and in important respects irrational, few will hearken to such warnings if those who utter them do not show awareness of the very serious problems which underdeveloped countries face on their road to modernization. The western path, a reliance on the free market, is often irrelevant, often leads nowhere. As one American economist put it, "laissez-faire will not do the job, and totalitarian physical planning is unlikely to do the job well." * Even if it were certain to do the job badly, men would still turn to it if other methods are ineffective. Hence the serious need for imaginative study both of problems of development in various countries and of the positive and negative features of the Soviet system at various stages of the industrializing process.

2. THE APPEAL OF THE CHINESE MODEL TO UNDERDEVELOPED COUNTRIES

During his visit to China in the midst of the Great Leap, Tibor Mende, professor of political science at the University of Paris, tried to gauge the appeal of the Chinese Communist method of economic development for visitors from the underdeveloped countries of Asia, Africa, and Latin America. In the paragraphs which follow, he presents his findings.[21]

A MODEL FOR HALF OF MANKIND?

While in *Peking Hotel,* I have tried hard to get into conversation with visitors from underdeveloped countries. I wanted to find out why they had come and what had impressed them most in what they had been shown. Some were critical. Some others considered themselves as mere tourists. Many more, however, were passionately interested in China's methods and results and did not hide their enthusiasm.

Their majority were earnest young men, idealists, and more or less influenced by their readings of Marxist literature. Nearly all were frustrated by their own experiences at home or because of the general performance of their countries. Whether they came from Latin America, Africa or from Asian countries, their stories were almost identical. There was unemployment while there was widespread and crying need. Both the ideal and the organization were lacking to exploit natural wealth. Tiny privileged classes were living in modern towns, attached to a way of living and thinking that completely cut them off from the misery and the stagnation of the rural areas where the majority lived. They all

* B. Higgins, *op. cit.,* p. 456.

[21] Reprinted by permission of Coward-McCann, Inc. from *China and Her Shadow* by Tibor Mende; © 1960 by Tibor Mende, pp. 271–275. Reprinted also by permission of Thames & Hudson, Ltd., London.

complained of corruption, of slow progress if any, or of complete dependence on foreign economic forces. In what they had been shown in China they professed to have found the answers to at least some of the problems of their countries. Whether it was a question of colour or of the brotherhood of still visible backwardness, most of them appeared to be more spontaneously attracted to China's rather than to the Soviet Union's example. And one could almost see them returning to their countries as carriers of arguments and of convictions which, in the long run, were bound to exert considerable influence.

A young Brazilian teacher shared with me his enthusiastic discovery that his country's problems were comparable to those of China. With similar methods, he thought, Brazil too could become a great power within a generation. A negro trade-unionist from Guinea seemed to be particularly impressed by China's ability to train technicians fast and on a large scale, and with persistency he explored how the Chinese students' time was divided between school and workshop. An Indian economist, a young man from the South, was overwhelmed by China's mobilization of her labour. "Imagine, no unemployment in China," he repeated. "If all the idle hands could be put to work in our country . . . ." When I objected that climate, if nothing else, made Indians perhaps less capable of the sustained physical effort the Chinese were putting up with, he bitterly swept aside my objection: "That may be so. But if the Chinese could advance from ten to thirty, with similar methods we might have gone from ten to twenty. Yet we haven't advanced beyond fifteen . . . !"

All these, of course, were generalizations. Also, most of the residents of *Peking Hotel* were selected on the basis of their receptivity. Yet all the enthusiasm was symptomatic. It only helped to confirm my conviction that by now, the Chinese experiment must be regarded as far more revolutionary in its scope, and far more interesting for the future of the world's poor areas, than the Soviet Union's experience. And at least three main reasons seem to justify that impression.

Unlike the Soviet revolution, China's has a peasant base and the overwhelming majority in all underdeveloped countries is made up of cultivators. The change in leadership and in social organization in China did not come from a shift of power within the urban, commercial minority, but from its transfer from those tiny privileged groups to the peasant majority who, for the first time, were organized and educated for that purpose.

In the second place, no government in any of the underdeveloped countries, democratic or totalitarian, has as yet found a method to turn to constructive use the energies wasted through large-scale unemployment or under-employment in the countryside. With the organizational innovation of the Communes, not only has unemployment disappeared but under-employment too has been transformed into productive effort. The Commune system, even if a few more years will be needed to assess its balance-sheet, appears workable in China. Adapted to local conditions, its variants may serve the same purposes in other overpopulated, predominantly agrarian countries.

Finally, and as a result of the previous two innovations, China's experiment is revolutionary also in its emphasis on the simultaneous development of modern and small-scale, decentralized industry. In most underdeveloped coun-

tries either there is a one-sided and sentimental emphasis on large-scale industries—which may provide symbolic satisfaction but few openings for employment
—or on archaic cottage-industries, as in India, which are wasteful, uncompetitive,
and fail to prepare the rural masses for modern industrial pursuits. China's
experience permits the introduction of relatively modern manufacturing processes into rural surroundings without prohibitive investments. It encourages the
utilization of local raw materials. Moreover, it exerts all the sociological influence desirable to prepare the skills and the way of thinking of the peasants for
times when large-scale industry reaches their region. This same experiment permitted in China a vast increase in the supply of tools and of simple equipment
which, in other underdeveloped countries, are expected from urban industries
only. And while small-scale but modern rural industries already contribute to
overall industrial progress, they also help to transform the attitudes of a peasantry which have been immobile and imprisoned in traditions for centuries.

Social transformation with the peasant majority as its armed vanguard;
rural industries as agents of the mental and material modernization of the
countryside; and the massive investment of idle labour as a means to accumulate
capital for development—these are, simplified to the extreme, the three major
characteristics of the Chinese model.

They are primarily economic in character. Though Communist organization
and indoctrination may have been decisive in their realization, they were secondary in importance behind the imperatives which have dictated the main lines
of the solutions to given problems.

Yet besides these principal characteristics of the Chinese model, distinguishing it from that of the U.S.S.R., observers from underdeveloped countries may
find a number of supplementary features likely to claim their attention.

While in Russia the Communist Revolution established itself through continued mass arrests and executions aimed at the elimination of the condemned
upper and middle classes, China has been making great efforts, and with some
success, to win them over to collaboration with the new régime. There had been
mass executions of landlords and there have been waves of terror. But their aim
and duration was limited. At the same time everything was done to facilitate the
integration of those capable to comply. Quite often former industrialists and
merchants now are directing State-enterprises or occupy other important posts.
Though they may be closely supervised by a less qualified but politically more
reliable cadre, their lot is still enviable compared with that of their Russian
counterparts in their mass-graves. As late as 1956 there were claimed to be 65
people in China with an annual income of over U.S. $400,000, capitalists who
had the wisdom to go into partnership with the State in good time. Then, one
may come across processions of "reformed exploiters," demonstrating with flags
and banners their change of heart. "They were unfortunate to be born capitalists," a Chinese was reported to have remarked on their passage. All these, of
course, may be no more than exotic exceptions. Yet their existence is symbolic of
an attitude, one that basically differs from the absolute solutions employed in
the Soviet Union.

Of course China's present rulers can be extremely cruel when they have no
alternative. But, as a rule, they prefer to convince or to shame before they

employ force. And this addiction to persuasion may not be lost upon observers from underdeveloped countries especially when they compare Soviet and Chinese experience.

Should one add to all this China's success in avoiding the excessive urbanization which characterized Soviet development; the steady encouragement of peasant initiative and inventiveness; the State's continued ability to command the selfless devotion of large masses; or that unprecedented venality has been replaced by almost puritanic honesty, permitting the world's lowest insurance rates, then, it may be admitted that, in the eyes of a visitor from an underdeveloped country the result is infinitely more subtle than Slavic Communism. For the same reason the Chinese model may seem tempting to many who are dismayed by the inability of their countries to overcome their backwardness, or even to those who are already disillusioned by the Soviet Union.

China is the second backward, agrarian country being transformed by Communism into a great power and within one generation. For the time being no underdeveloped country has found a satisfactory answer to this challenge. Whatever the merits of alternative methods may be, hitherto their results have not been comparable either in quantity or in speed. So long as the answer to that challenge will be lacking, China's example will continue to help to expand her influence in the world. And the impact of that formidable weapon, the power of her example, will only be enhanced by the lever provided by China's growing economic weight.

3. INDIA AND CHINA: DIFFERENT MODELS OF DEVELOPMENT

The authors of the selection quoted below examine the role of ideology in economic progress and compare the economic achievements of the two countries since 1950.[22]

Since the aspirations of the people in the poor countries as well as the urgings of popular leaders require that these nations pay heed to whatever methods and procedures promise to increase their rate of economic advance, the present competition between democratic and Communist models has inevitably given economic programs for accelerating a nation's growth a significant political dimension. Ideological alternatives are thrust upon the less-developed nations. Even where the ways of totalitarianism are repugnant to leaders and to traditions —as is certainly true in many such lands—domestic political pressures demand an open mind, perhaps an open door.

Leaders in the new and underdeveloped countries are bound to ask: Are totalitarian regimes more adept at initiating a process of continuous economic growth than democratic governments? If the methods of communism do in fact promise a surer or less expensive route to economic well-being, some of these nations, deeply committed as they are to a free society, may also ask: How much

22 Wilfred Malenbaum and Wolfgang Stolper, "Political Ideology and Economic Progress: The Basic Question," *World Politics*, April, 1960, Vol. XII, No. 3, pp. 413–420. Reprinted by permission of the publisher.

more economic progress in five or ten years, say, for how much less freedom? The relevance of these questions is clear. These nations need material progress; they are confronted with alternative roads differentiated on ideological grounds.

*   *   *

COMPARATIVE PERFORMANCE

History now provides the material for some judgment on the role of ideology in economic progress under today's conditions. In each of two pairs of compara-ble lands—India and China, West Germany and East Germany—there is available reasonably documented experience of some ten years of effort to achieve more rapid rates of economic growth from essentially the same starting points. India and West Germany chose paths under democracy; in both lands, government places a high premium upon private property and individual privilege. In East Germany and in China, on the other hand, the methods used can be traced directly to the totalitarian experience of the Soviet Union; in the development effort, as in other aspects of the social order, individual rights are completely subordinated to those of the state.

In 1950 both India and China had per capita incomes of about $50—lower than in any other large nation. The two countries initiated their development operations at about the same time and from the same type of economic structure. In both, at least 80 percent of the working force was in agriculture and small-scale enterprise. If anything, India gave promise of greater progress in view of its advantages in basic resources per man, in transport facilities and modern indus-try, and in training and leadership attributes. Thus, India apparently had greater scope for using its surface water potential and for exploiting the inten-sive margins of agricultural cultivation. With the same relative efforts, therefore, larger returns could be anticipated in India than in China. So, at any rate, did it seem in the pre-Plan period.*

Yet by 1959 per capita gross national product in India was only some 12–15 percent above its 1950 level, while in China it had expanded to about double the earlier figure. Almost half (45 percent) of this difference in performance can be associated with the proportionately greater investment made in China; the remaining difference measures the extent to which each additional unit of capital in China was associated with larger flows of current income.

With an initial gross investment ratio just below 10 percent, absolute real investment in China had increased by 1958 to five times the 1950 level; in India it about doubled. Foreign aid did not explain this difference: indeed, China's investment was more nearly financed from its current output than was India's. Communist methods made possible a relatively large (40 percent) feedback of new output into China's domestic investment. But India's voluntary performance in this respect was impressive also. During favorable harvest years, marginal sav-ings rates in India may well have exceeded those in China.

* For an analysis of the comparative pre-Plan status and subsequent performance of the two countries, see Wilfred Malenbaum, "India and China: Development Con-trasts," *Journal of Political Economy*, LXIV, No. 1 (February, 1956), pp. 1–24; and *idem*, "India and China: Contrasts in Development Performance," *American Economic Review*, XLIX, No. 3 (June, 1959), pp. 284–309.

The Chinese put more effort into expanding physical output as against services; a larger proportion of new capital was allocated to agriculture and small industry; the degree of utilization of resources, and especially of labor, was increased significantly. Over the whole period, government played a much larger role in economic life in China than in India. And of course, compared with India's, China's producers and consumers had limited freedom of choice—in techniques of production, in final goods for consumption. Greater regimentation in China was accompanied by considerable flexibility on the part of government. In response to actual developments in the economy, relative emphasis was shifted away from the initial concentration on heavy industry, for example. By and large, China's economic progress has been steady. In India, government adheres to models of growth which are permissive; comparatively few restraints are imposed on individuals whose usual ways of life did not in the past generate economic expansion. There have been impressive spurts of industrial output in India's essentially private modern industry sector, as well as some record crops in years with favorable monsoons. The total performance has been less even; the degree of plan fulfillment has not increased steadily, for example.

* * *

Underlying Factors

China's ties to a Russian model of rapid, large-scale industrialization did not impede early recognition of the emptiness of industrialization without agricultural advancement in a nation where most people will long remain rural; of the complementarities rather than the competitiveness, of large industry and many types of small enterprises suitable to a heavy endowment of labor. Important deviations from Communist economic lore were soon made in the allocation of large percentages of investment resources to agriculture and the small-scale sector. A form of communal organization was created with continuous and strong guidance and controls to assure the change that the economy on its own could not generate.

The government of India's models of growth are largely derived from the patterns and relationships found in Western capitalist societies; neither the concepts, nor the values, of the multipliers relevant to a market-conscious economy in the throes of expansion are directly applicable in an institutionalized and static society. The major task of rural improvement and growth was placed upon a national community development and extension scheme. While this action recognized the need, especially in the initial years, of injecting into rural India a new force for change, government did not provide the programs with sustained, strong leadership. In modern industry, where the parallels between Western nations and India were greatest, borrowed doctrine was often in conflict with India's own formulation of the needs of a socialist state. India tries to allocate 50–60 percent of all investment to the government sector while expecting the private sector to produce more than 90 percent of total product. These contrasting ratios are not necessarily in conflict; but they do demand close scrutiny of day-to-day investment and production developments to assure that the drive to high levels of investment in the public sector does not impede continued performance and expansion in the private sector.

This examination of underlying factors permits an interesting conclusion. The two more successful nations—Communist China and democratic West Germany—operated on the same sets of technical determinants of growth as did India and East Germany. Their relative success was due to the degree to which they geared their development programs to the existing structure of their economies. Cold and objective appraisals were made of the stages necessary to achieve a state of continuing progress from inadequate starting points. Throughout, they demonstrated flexibility in selecting courses of action. Only those were finally adopted in which practice gave promise of the changes needed in savings rates and in technical input-output coefficients. In democratic India and Communist East Germany, on the other hand, governmental operations on these basic parameters have manifested much less objectivity and flexibility. Indeed, India, where growth under democracy demands a greater interplay of new and old relationships in the society, evidenced less of an experimental and flexible approach to its problem of expansion than did China.

SELECT BIBLIOGRAPHY

BERLE, A. A., JR., *The 20th Century Capitalist Revolution* (New York, Harcourt, Brace & World, 1954). An examination of the impact of the modern corporation on the structure of capitalism. The author advances the interesting hypothesis that the modern corporation has developed a social conscience and has increasingly tended to assume the role of a political institution.

CHU-YUAN, CHENG, *Communist China's Economy, 1949–1962* (South Orange, N.J.: Seton Hall University Press, 1963). An authoritative analysis of China's economic construction since 1949. Note especially the chapters dealing with the collectivization and communization of agriculture. A good source of statistical information on the performance of the Chinese economy.

COMMITTEE FOR ECONOMIC DEVELOPMENT, *How Low Income Countries Can Advance Their Own Growth* (New York, C.E.D., September, 1966). An excellent statement on the internal aspects of economic development which addresses itself to the question of what low income countries can do through self-help measures to achieve sustained high rates of growth in per capita income. A good "Western" view of the "self-reliance" thesis, which the Communists usually claim as their own special invention.

GALBRAITH, JOHN KENNETH., *American Capitalism: The Concept of Countervailing Powers* (Boston, Houghton Mifflin, 1956). A novel approach to the study of the nature and mechanics of American capitalism. The theory of countervailing power developed by the author argues that private economic power under American-type capitalism is held in check by the countervailing power of those who are subject to it: the power of strong sellers is checked by the power of strong buyers.

HIRSCHMAN, ALBERT O., *The Strategy of Economic Development* (New Haven, Yale University Press, 1958). The author presents the case for unbalanced growth and other interesting views on the economic processes of underdeveloped countries.

LAIRD, ROY D. and CROWLEY, EDWARD L. (eds.), *Soviet Agriculture: The Permanent Crisis* (New York, Praeger, 1965). A first-rate collection of essays on the problems of Soviet agriculture. The topics covered include: administration and the peasant, regional peculiarities, economic advances (note especially the essay on peasant incomes), and the politics of Soviet agriculture.

MENDE, TIBOR, *China and Her Shadow* (New York, Coward-McCann, 1962). An excellent eyewitness account of China's frantic economic construction. The study gives instructive insights into such problems as the total mobilization of China's peasantry, the devious course of population policy, massive social engineering, foreign policy, and China's ambition to serve as a model for half of mankind. Tibor Mende, a well-known political commentator, is Professor of Political Science at the University of Paris and author of many authoritative studies on Asian affairs.

MENDEL, ARTHUR P. (ed.), *Essential Works of Marxism* (New York, Bantam, 1965). A useful reprint of the classics of Marxism in its various forms and at different points in time. The compendium, introduced by a perceptive essay on the formation and appeal of "scientific socialism," includes selections from the writings of Marx, Engels, Lenin, Stalin, Djilas, Kolakowski, the New Program of the Communist Party of the Soviet Union, and Mao Tse-tung. Useful for the understanding of the development and variety of communist theory.

MONSEN, JOSEPH R., JR., *Modern American Capitalism: Ideologies and Issues* (Boston, Houghton Mifflin, 1963). The author examines the major group ideologies used at the present time to explain and defend American capitalism. These include the classical capitalist ideology, the managerial ideology, that of countervailing power, people's capitalism, and enterprise democracy. Great emphasis is put on the analysis of the basic ideological issues of modern American capitalism such as the allocation of resources and consumer sovereignty, the government and consumer sovereignty, efficiency, the problem of bigness, and stability.

SCHUMPETER, JOSEPH A., *The Theory of Economic Development* (New York, Oxford University Press, Galaxy Book, 1961). A penetrating treatment, that has become a classic of economic theory, of the process of economic development.

SHAFFER, HARRY G., editor. *The Soviet System in Theory and Practice* (New York, Appleton-Century-Crofts, 1965). A representative and judicious selection of Western, Western Marxist, and Soviet views on various aspects of the Soviet system. The areas covered include Communist ideology and morality, the reign of Stalin and views on Stalin's performance both during and after his life, Soviet life today, economic planning, peaceful coexistence, and the economic challenge, living standards, education, freedom and democracy in the U.S.S.R., the position of the creative artist in Soviet society, Soviet law, and Soviet aid to the underdeveloped countries.

WELLISZ, STANISLAW, *The Economies of the Soviet Bloc* (New York, McGraw-Hill, 1964). An explanation of how resources are allocated in Soviet bloc economies. Stress is on broad issues, achievements, and difficulties. Frequent comparisons are made with market economies. The book is particularly useful for the study of the Polish economy from which most examples used in the work are drawn.

WINT, GUY, *Communist China's Crusade: Mao's Road to Power and the New Campaign for World Revolution* (New York, Praeger, 1965). An absorbing account of Communist China's emergence as a world power and of the Sino-Soviet dispute. The author, member of St. Anthony's College, Oxford, and known writer on Asian affairs, stresses Peking's two major tenets: national expansion and the seizure of the revolutionary initiative in the underdeveloped countries.

ZEBOT, CYRIL A., *The Economics of Competitive Coexistence: Convergence Through Growth* (New York, Praeger, 1964). A comparative, interesting study of economic growth in the newly developing countries, the Soviet orbit, and the West. Professor Zebot argues that the major economies of the world are becoming increasingly similar. This trend toward convergence in economics has its counterpart in the capitulation of the extremist ideologies of individualism and collectivism. The emerging economic convergence is seen as having far-reaching implications for the future peace of the world. A thought-provoking statement of the convergence hypothesis.

8

Coexistence, Security, and the Organization of Peace

THE COMPETITION BETWEEN DIFFER-
ent political and economic systems is one of the most challenging phenomena of our times, involving the destinies of all of us. In the preceding
chapters, the main emphasis has been on economic institutions and on the
assets and liabilities of different patterns of economic development. But
the competition has particular significance for the field of international
politics inasmuch as the major world powers see in it opportunities to increase their influence and followings among the developing countries, and
particularly among the over sixty new states which have achieved independence since World War II.

One of the most baffling questions associated with the competition
between different political and economic systems relates to the possibility
of peaceful coexistence between these systems. With communist leaders
preaching the inevitability of the collapse of capitalism, with Western
leaders confident of the universal appeal of democracy, and with both
sides seemingly convinced that their long-range security requires the
world-wide acceptance of their respective ideologies, peaceful coexistence
seems like a contradiction of terms. "Competitive coexistence" may be a
more realistic term, but this likewise raises many questions.

To Westerners, coexistence suggests a peaceful "live-and-let-live"
relationship in which countries with different political and economic
systems do not attempt to interfere in one another's affairs and can settle their differences through normal channels of discussion and negotiation. It would presumably do away with expansion at the expense of
independent peoples as well as with efforts to subvert or infiltrate governments in other countries. Since it envisages a "live-and-let-live" relationship of mutual toleration, it would not assume (although it might
conceivably hope) that any one system would inevitably triumph over
all others.

Some of the ideas expressed by communist leaders also seem to imply
that they envisage peaceful coexistence as a condition of peaceful rela-

tions between states with different political and economic systems. By emphasizing principles of mutual respect, nonaggression, and noninterference in the internal affairs of other states, they seem to be agreeing with the "live-and-let-live" concept of peaceful coexistence. Thus the program of the Communist Party of the Soviet Union, adopted in October, 1961, declares:

Peaceful coexistence implies renunciation of war as a means of settling international disputes, and their solution by negotiation; equality, mutual understanding and trust between countries; consideration for each other's interests; noninterference in internal affairs; recognition of the right of every people to solve all the problems of their country by themselves; strict respect for the sovereignty and territorial integrity of all countries; promotion of economic and cultural co-operation on the basis of complete equality and mutual benefit.[1]

Many people in the noncommunist world would welcome evidence that the communists are prepared to accept a "live-and-let-live" relationship with other countries. Yet, since communism frequently portrays itself as a world revolutionary movement which will inevitably replace capitalism and Western democracy, it is exceedingly difficult to conclude that communist leaders regard peaceful coexistence as anything more than a temporary stratagem during the period prior to the anticipated triumph of communism. How long this temporary period might last is not clear although on a few occasions Soviet leaders have given the impression that it might extend until approximately the end of the twentieth century. Khrushchev, for example, in a television interview with three American news correspondents in Moscow in 1957 declared:

And I can prophesy that your grandchildren in America will live under socialism. And please do not be afraid of that. Your grandchildren . . . will not understand how their grandparents did not understand the progressive nature of a socialist society.[2]

He went on to explain the kind of peaceful competition he envisaged between capitalism and socialism:

Now, as far as competition between capitalist and socialist ideologies is concerned, we have never made a secret of the fact that there will be an ideological struggle going on between these two ideologies, but we never believe that that is the same thing as a war, because this would be an ideological struggle in which the system which will have the support of the people . . . will come out on top.

At the present time your American people do not support the Marxist-Leninist theories. They are following the bourgeois political leaders, but is that a reason for war? Is that a reason for any enmity between us and the United

[1] *Programme of the Communist Party of the Soviet Union* (Moscow, Foreign Languages Publishing House, 1961), p. 56.
[2] *The New York Times*, June 3, 1957, p. 6.

States? No. Let us live in peace. Let us develop our economy. Let us compete. Let us trade with each other. Let us exchange experience in agriculture, in industry, in the field of culture, and as far as the question of which system will come out on top, let history, let our peoples decide that. I think this is a good way.

We believe that our socialist system will be victorious, but that does not mean under any conditions that we want to impose that system on anyone. We simply believe that the people of each country themselves will come to realize that that system is best for them. That is up to the people concerned to decide. We have no intention of imposing our ideas on anybody.

In recent years, Soviet leaders have frequently reiterated their position that peaceful coexistence applies only to the interstate relations between socialist and nonsocialist countries, and that it does not apply to matters of ideological conflict and does not mean any renunciation of either the class struggle or the need for revolution. Furthermore, it does not involve any reconciliation with "imperialism" or any slackening in support for wars of national liberation against colonialism in all its forms. Soviet leaders have apparently felt obliged to say this strongly and repeatedly in order to counter the sharp criticism from the Chinese Communists of the whole theory of peaceful coexistence.[3] In its long letter of July 14, 1963, replying to the Chinese challenge, the Central Committee of the Soviet Communist Party declared:

Everyone in any of our political discussion circles knows perfectly well that when we speak of peaceful coexistence, we mean by this the state relations of the socialist countries with the countries of capitalism. The principle of peaceful coexistence, naturally, cannot in the slightest degree extend to relations between antagonistic classes within the capitalist states; it is impermissible to extend it to the struggle of the working class against the bourgeoisie for its class interests, to the struggle of oppressed peoples against the colonialists. The Communist Party of the Soviet Union resolutely opposes peaceful coexistence in the province of ideology. These are elementary truths, and it is time for everyone who considers himself a Marxist-Leninist to master them.[4]

This does not sound like a "live-and-let-live" relationship, but more like a kind of armed truce between the various antagonistic systems. Major thermonuclear war is to be avoided in the interest of mutual survival (see Chap. 1), but the ideological and economic struggle goes on as the different systems attempt to demonstrate their avowed superiority both at home and abroad. The struggle takes such forms as propaganda, psychological warfare, political influence through foreign economic aid, infiltration, subversion, and the encouragement of "liberation" movements among the peoples of the rival regimes.

[3] The Chinese criticism is summarized on pages 161–163 above. A detailed statement of the Chinese views on coexistence is presented in Position 2 at the close of this chapter. The Soviet answer to the Chinese criticism is given in Position 3.

[4] Translation from the *Current Digest of the Soviet Press*, August 7, 1963, pp. 22–23.

Insofar as coexistence is viewed as applying to relations between states, its meaning will be determined by the national security requirements of the states concerned more than by the principles of ideology. The leaders of the communist and Western democratic governments alike are custodians of their respective states as well as the protagonists of certain ideologies. While attempting repeatedly to demonstrate the ideological appeal of democracy or communism, they usually do not push these principles to the point where they jeopardize the safety of their states. National security, in practice, takes precedence over ideological principles, and the possibilities of accommodation and adjustment between conflicting national interests enter the picture.

Ideological systems, like religious principles, tend to become dogmatic and uncompromising, and their most ardent supporters usually see problems in terms of "black" and "white" or "right" and "wrong." This is the characteristic view of international affairs from the vantage point of ideological principles. Yet it is not the approach which the head of a government or a foreign minister can usually take when he feels primarily responsible for the immediate security and welfare of his state. He may acknowledge the theoretical validity of ideological principles, but if their application at a particular time would expose his state to danger or to a possible reduction in its power or influence, he will probably decide not to apply those principles at that time.

These points can be seen operating in the Chinese-Soviet dispute, one of the main factors of which seems to be their different assessments of the dangers and likelihood of thermonuclear war. Neither side seems likely to press its ideological principles to the point of consciously precipitating a thermonuclear war and thereby jeopardizing its future security. But the Soviet leaders seem more disposed to acknowledge the possibilities of such a war, and hence to be more concerned with avoiding it. The Chinese, on the other hand, seem more confident that there will be no nuclear war, feeling that the combined strength of the socialist-communist states will deter it. They therefore feel, more than do the Russians, that communism can be advanced through greater use of local wars and wars of national liberation without the dangers of a world war. This is why they seem more militant in the prosecution of their ideology and why they accuse the Soviet Union of watering down the program of revolution by their preoccupation with peaceful coexistence.[5]

[5] Soviet leaders have accused the Chinese Communists of ignoring the disastrous consequences of a thermonuclear war and of believing that a greater civilization could be built on the corpses and ruins of such a war. (See Position 2 at the close of this chapter.) The Chinese have described such charges as "slanderous" and denied that they wanted a thermonuclear war. They cite a statement by Mao Tse-tung in November, 1957, to the effect that the international situation has now reached a new turning point and that the forces of socialism are now "overwhelmingly superior to the forces of imperialism." Because of this, Mao Tse-tung expressed the view that a major war would not break out, and he chided those who feared such a war. If, however, his pre-

SECURITY AND THE ORGANIZATION OF PEACE

The problem of security, then, is essentially the problem of accommodation and adjustment between sovereign nation states. This may involve the discovery of common interests and consensus—as illustrated by the nearly universal approval of the limited nuclear test ban treaty of August, 1963, or the agreement in December, 1964, to establish permanent United Nations machinery to deal with the problems of international trade and development.[6] Or, in case deep differences between the contending states prevent agreement on the principal issues and produce a stalemate, security and the avoidance of war may depend on the precarious balance of power between the rival states or possibly on the presence of some United Nations peacekeeping mission which has interposed itself between the contending parties to prevent fighting and maintain some kind of truce while efforts are made at negotiation and peaceful settlement.

Germany and Korea are examples of stalemates in which the avoidance of war hinges largely on the balance of power between the contending states. Germany remains divided today because the Soviet Union and the Western powers have not been able to agree on terms of unification and are unwilling to see the country united in any way which might orient Germany politically towards either the East or the West. Korea, likewise, has been politically divided since World War II, although mili-

---

diction proved incorrect, and the imperialist powers should insist on fighting a major war, the whole imperialist system would be razed to the ground. Although as many as half the world's population might be killed in a nuclear war, in Mao Tse-tung's estimate, the survivors would become "socialist" and would "create on the ruins of imperialism a civilization thousands of times higher than the capitalist system and a truly beautiful future for themselves." (See the Chinese Government statement of September 1, 1963, in the *Peking Review*, September 6, 1963, pp. 7–16, at pp. 9–10.) The Chinese Communist Party Central Committee, in its famous letter of June 14, 1963, to the Soviet Party Central Committee, distinguished between world wars and wars of national liberation or civil wars in these words:

"Certain persons say that revolutions are entirely possible without war. Now which type of war are they referring to—is it a war of national liberation or a revolutionary civil war, or is it a world war?

"If they are referring to a war of national liberation or a revolutionary civil war, then this formulation is, in effect, opposed to revolutionary wars and to revolution.

"If they are referring to a world war, then they are shooting at a nonexistent target. Although Marxist-Leninists have pointed out, on the basis of the history of the two world wars, that world wars inevitably lead to revolution, no Marxist-Leninist has held or ever will hold that revolution must be made through world war." (*Peking Review*, June 21, 1963, pp. 13–14.)

6 Following the meeting of the United Nations Conference on Trade and Development during the summer of 1964, the General Assembly, on December 30, 1964, decided unanimously to establish the Conference as an organ of the General Assembly. A fifty-five member Trade and Development Board was also created as a permanent organ of the Conference, and a permanent, full-time Secretariat was authorized. See General Assembly Resolution 1995 (XIX), *U.N. Monthly Chronicle*, January, 1965, pp. 33–34.

tary efforts were made unsuccessfully by both sides during the Korean War of 1950–1953 to achieve their respective concepts of unification. The consequences of this have been a military stalemate with two governments still in control of the northern and southern sections of the country, and with peace dependent upon the balance of power between United States and Communist Chinese forces in that region.

In the case of the continuing dispute over Palestine between Israel and her Arab neighbors, the dangers of war have been substantially lessened by the presence since 1956 of a United Nations peacekeeping force of approximately 5,000 men along the frontiers of Israel and the United Arab Republic (Egypt). Originally despatched to bring about and supervise the cessation of hostilities in Egypt, resulting from the Anglo-French-Israeli invasion of Egypt, the UN Force has remained to patrol the frontiers between Israel and Egypt, prevent border incidents, and discourage any attempt by either side to invade the territory of the other. The almost complete absence of border incidents along the lines patrolled by the UN Force, coupled with the periodic occurrence of incidents along Israeli frontiers with Syria and Jordan where no UN Force is present, testifies to the usefulness of such a force in reducing the dangers of conflict. The basic causes of Arab-Israeli hostility have not yet been removed, but the dangers of war have been lessened by the presence of the UN Force.

Likewise in Cyprus, the civil strife which broke out in December, 1963, between Greek and Turkish Cypriots threatened to involve both Greece and Turkey and possibly other states in a serious international war. Great Britain, with the consent of Cyprus, quickly interposed some of its troops between the Greek and Turkish Cypriot communities, but this had only limited success in stopping the fighting, and it soon became evident that a larger international force, either supplied by several NATO members or set up by the United Nations, would be needed. Because of Cypriot unwillingness to accept a force composed mainly of NATO members, it was finally decided to create a UN Force under the Security Council. On March 4, 1964, the Council authorized such a force to be sent to Cyprus to interpose itself between the Greek and Turkish Cypriot forces, prevent a recurrence of fighting, and contribute to the maintenance and restoration of law and order. The force succeeded in maintaining an uneasy truce, although the basic issues in the civil strife remained unsolved.

While the presence of UN forces in a few cases such as the Israeli-Egyptian frontiers, Cyprus, and the Congo has served to keep conflicts localized and to lessen the danger of war, it is the balance of power between the major contending states of the world which in practice has been relied on principally to maintain the peace. This is seen in the balance between the NATO alliance system and the Soviet alliance system in Europe and to a lesser extent in other regions of the world. It is also seen in the Far East in the developing balance between Communist China and the United States.

The balance of power system is as old as the system of sovereign states itself, evidences of it being seen in the city-state systems of ancient Greece as well as in the nation-state systems of modern times. While it has in practice been reasonably effective under favorable circumstances [7] for considerable periods of time, it also breeds intense competition, generates rival alliance systems, and in the long run may culminate in war itself. World Wars I and II are regarded by many observers as the results of the struggle for power and the systems of rival alliances generated by the balance of power system.[8]

The belief that the traditional pattern of balance of power finally culminated in two world wars led many statesmen to support the organization of a different system for the regulation of power among states, namely, the system of collective security, embodied after World War I in the League of Nations and after World War II in the United Nations.

COLLECTIVE SECURITY

The essence of collective security is the familiar principle, "All for one and one for all." Drawing on the lessons of the history of the balance of power, the founders of the League and the United Nations attempted to provide for an overwhelming array of collective power always to be available to maintain the peace. If a member state were the victim of aggression, all other members would come to its aid. The preponderance of force thus mobilized would theoretically be so great that no state, however powerful, could undertake aggression with impunity.

The League and the United Nations, particularly the latter, were intended to be much more than just organs of collective security, although the latter function was probably viewed at the outset as the most important responsibility of the two organizations. Other major responsibilities of the United Nations include:

(1) The promotion of peaceful settlement of disputes through negotiation, mediation, conciliation, and arbitration, as well as through the

[7] These would include such conditions as: (1) the existence of several major states and the diffusion of power among them; (2) the possibility of making foreign policy decisions on the basis of power calculations alone, without any inhibitions from public opinion or ideological principles in accepting necessary compromises or compensations; (3) the existence of a broad consensus among the various states that the existing political order should be preserved, that the objectives of war be limited and not envisage the total destruction of one's enemies; and finally, (4) the presence of some major power which can play the role of holder of the balance (such as Great Britain has traditionally done), intervening as need be to check the potential domination by any one power or group of powers. For further discussion, see Inis L. Claude, Jr., *Power and International Relations* (New York: Random House, 1962), pp. 90–91.

[8] *Ibid.*, p. 66 ff. See also pp. 54–55 in Chapter 2, above.

supervision and observation of areas of tension and conflict. (See Articles 2, 10, 11, 14, 33–38 of the UN Charter.)

(2) The organization of economic, social and cultural cooperation, including the promotion of universal respect for human rights and fundamental freedoms. (See Articles 55, 56, 61, 62 of the Charter.)

(3) The exercise of trusteeship and other supervisory functions regarding certain non-self-governing territories and the promotion of conditions which would facilitate the progressive development of free political institutions and self-government in all dependent territories. (See Articles 73, 75–77, 85–88 of the Charter.)

As matters have developed in practice, collective security in the sense of coercive action by the United Nations against an aggressor has proved to be one of the least employed functions of the organization. It has been used only once, in the Korean War, and even here its application was facilitated by the temporary absence of the Soviet Union from the Security Council which enabled the Council to act quickly without any delays due to a Soviet veto.[9]

The explanation of this nonuse of collective security lies in (1) the disintegration of the Big Three unity which had existed in 1945 when the United Nations was formally established; (2) the Charter provisions (notably the veto powers in the Security Council) which made it inevitable that the Security Council would never be able to apply coercive measures or collective action against one of the five permanent members of the Council; and (3) the extreme unlikelihood that the basic assumptions of a collective security system could be realized in practice.

There are three assumptions underlying the effective operation of a collective security system:

(1) The collective security organization must be able to mobilize such overwhelming strength that an aggressor or group of aggressors would be deterred from challenging the organization or attacking one of its members.

(2) To be able to mobilize such overwhelming strength, the member states, in sufficient numbers, must recognize an equal interest in the maintenance of peace and the prevention of aggression whenever and wherever necessary. They must also feel an equal interest in maintaining the security of each individual member of the organization.

(3) All member states must be willing, if necessary, to subordinate their respective national interests to the common interest implied in the collective defense of any of their number who is the victim of aggression.[10]

---

[9] The Soviet Union at this time (June–July, 1950) was not attending meetings of the Security Council and other UN organs in protest against the fact that Communist China had not been seated in the UN.

[10] For a more detailed discussion of the problems involved in applying the principles of collective security, see Hans J. Morgenthau, *Politics Among Nations*, 4th edition (New York, Knopf, 1967), Chap. 24, and Inis L. Claude, Jr., *Power and International Relations* (New York, Random House, 1962), Chaps. 4 and 5.

If these assumptions can be met, collective security can function effectively. The chances, however, of getting a large enough number of states to join in collective military action seem rather small, given the usual reluctance of sovereign states to become involved in situations where their immediate security interests may not be directly at stake. In the one case to date of United Nations collective security action, the Korean War, only 17 out of the 60 members sent military forces in response to the Security Council's request for assistance. Of these, the United States and the Republic of Korea furnished over 90 percent of all the military forces and supplies, while the other 15 supplied much more limited amounts of military assistance. Twenty-three additional states supplied economic, medical, or other forms of aid, making a total of some 40 states which assisted in one way or another. Another 10 states offered various forms of material or financial aid, but for one reason or another it was not accepted or was never actually sent. Finally 10 states (the 5 communist bloc states and 5 others) gave the United Nations no help at all; and of these, the 5 communist states actually opposed the United Nations and supported North Korea.[11]

There have been three broad patterns of reaction to this demise of the system of collective security: (1) the development of regional systems of security such as NATO; (2) the increased use of the General Assembly and the establishment of peacekeeping machinery; and (3) the attempt to develop supranational institutions, either along the lines of world government or regional economic and political communities such as the European Economic Community.

REGIONAL ALLIANCES

Following the realization in the late 1940's that Big Three unity had disappeared and been replaced by the cold war, the United States and its Western allies developed regional systems of security such as the North Atlantic Treaty Organization (NATO) and the Southeast Asia Treaty Organization (SEATO) to bear the main burden of defense against the Soviet Union, Communist China, and other communist states.

NATO came into being in April, 1949, in the wake of the Truman Doctrine (American aid to Greece and Turkey), the Marshall Plan, the German peace treaty stalemate, and the Berlin Blockade. In the United Nations Security Council, 30 Soviet vetoes had been cast up to January, 1949, including 6 on various resolutions designed to stop Yugoslavia, Albania, and Bulgaria from aiding the communist guerrilla forces in the Greek civil war.[12] It seemed obvious that any future efforts by the Security

11 *Yearbook of the United Nations,* 1952, pp. 214 ff.
12 U.S. Congress, Senate, Subcommittee on the United Nations Charter, *Review of the United Nations Charter,* Senate Doc. No. 87, 83rd Congress, 2nd session, pp. 577–579.

Council to deal with what the West regarded as Soviet threats to security would be blocked by Soviet vetoes.

Faced with this situation, the United States, Canada, and 10 Western European countries joined together in what became one of the strongest and most integrated military alliances in history. For the United States, this was its first military alliance in 150 years, the last having been the Franco-American Alliance of 1778 concluded during the American Revolution and abrogated by the United States in 1798. In contrast to the more general and uncertain clauses of the UN Charter providing for action only after appropriate decisions by the Security Council or the General Assembly, Article 5 of the North Atlantic Treaty declared:

> The Parties agree that an armed attack against one or more of them in Europe or North America shall be considered an attack against them all; and consequently they agree that, if such an armed attack occurs, each of them, in exercise of the right of individual or collective self-defense recognized by Article 51 of the Charter of the United Nations, will assist the Party or Parties so attacked by taking forthwith, individually and in concert with the other Parties, such action as it deems necessary, including the use of armed force, to restore and maintain the security of the North Atlantic area.[13]

Action under this was to be reported to the Security Council and terminated if the Security Council took the necessary measures to restore international peace. But NATO action was not dependent on Security Council authorization, and, since NATO consisted of a limited group of states with strong common interests in collective defense against any potential Soviet expansion, it was presumed that the alliance would be able to operate quickly and effectively in case any signatory were attacked.

NATO members held that the alliance was compatible with the United Nations Charter since Article 51 of the charter recognized "the inherent right of individual or collective self-defense" if an armed attack occurred against a member of the United Nations, until the Security Council had taken the necessary steps to maintain peace and security. The Soviet Union, on the other hand, claimed that the North Atlantic Treaty violated the Charter since Article 51 recognized the right of collective self-defense only *after, not before,* an armed attack had occurred. The Soviet Union also pointed to Article 53 of the Charter which provided that no enforcement action should be taken by regional organizations without authorization by the Security Council. Since NATO action was not to be dependent on Security Council authorization, the Soviet Union held that this was a second reason why the North Atlantic Treaty violated the United Nations Charter.

Despite the Soviet-Western controversy over its legality, NATO dur-

[13] Text in U.S. Department of State, *NATO: Its Development and Significance,* Department of State Publication 6467 (Washington, Government Printing Office, 1957), pp. 58–61.

ing the 1950's developed a high degree of intergovernmental cooperation in joint defense planning and the establishment of joint defense forces. Although NATO was not a "supergovernment," but only an alliance between sovereign independent states, elaborate organizational machinery was established to facilitate the consultations needed to implement the treaty. Among its major organs were the North Atlantic Council, the top policy-making body, comprising high-level diplomatic representatives from each member state; the International Staff or Secretariat headed by the Secretary-General; and the three Supreme Allied Commands for Europe, the Atlantic Ocean, and the English Channel areas. Greece and Turkey joined NATO in 1952, and in 1955 special arrangements were concluded whereby West Germany also became a member.

Maintaining a reasonable degree of unity among fifteen states on military and political cooperation has not been easy or at times entirely successful—despite the common security interests which have bound them together since 1949. One of the principal controversies has centered on the issue of giving the European members of NATO a greater share in the decisions regarding the use of nuclear weapons by NATO. Thus far, the United States has retained control over all nuclear warheads stationed overseas, and the warheads can be fired only by agreement of both the United States and the host country. Yet some of the European NATO members have questioned whether the United States could be relied upon to use these nuclear weapons to defend some remote European frontier since it would at once expose the United States itself to the dangers of Soviet nuclear retaliation. Would the United States, for example, risk a Soviet attack on New York or Washington by using nuclear weapons to defend Berlin or Paris? The multilateral character of the alliance is in practice not very real, it has been argued, so long as the United States insists upon exerting 100 percent control over all nuclear operations and thus subordinates the defense of Europe to the criteria of United States national interests.[14]

To meet these objections, the United States offered various proposals for a multilateral nuclear force under NATO in which European manpower and resources could play a greater part within the alliance. Yet this encountered very strong opposition from President de Gaulle of France who was most reluctant to subordinate French forces to NATO authority and who preferred instead to develop an independent nuclear force for France which he felt would be more reliable than the guarantees of the United States.

In the spring of 1966, President de Gaulle further widened the

[14] For a fuller discussion of NATO and these problems, see Robert E. Osgood, *NATO, The Entangling Alliance* (Chicago, The University of Chicago Press, 1962); Alastair Buchan, *NATO in the 1960's* (New York, Praeger, 1963); and Robert Kleiman, *Atlantic Crisis* (New York, Norton, 1964).

breach between himself and the other NATO allies by announcing that France intended to cease placing its forces at the disposal of NATO and participating in the integrated commands of NATO. He also insisted that in the future all forces and bases on French soil must come under French rather than NATO command. He did add, however, that, subject to the above conditions, France still desired to remain a party to the North Atlantic Treaty.[15] Behind this statement of policy seemed to lie the belief that the European situation was much more stable and secure in 1966 than it had been in 1949, that some kind of accommodation with the Soviet Union was possible in view of the Soviet-Chinese split, and that therefore NATO was in need of appropriate modifications.

Despite the painful difficulties of maintaining unity among its members, NATO has perhaps been the most potentially effective regional alliance created to supplement the collective security provisions of the UN Charter. While it has never been formally invoked, the alliance has probably been an important factor in stabilizing the political and military situation in Europe, providing a counterforce to Soviet military power in that area, and assuring a reasonably cohesive group of states to negotiate with the communist bloc, either directly or in the United Nations and other international bodies.

On the other hand, it may also have had the negative effect of freezing the East-West division and making it more difficult to develop flexible alternatives for bridging the East-West gap and facilitating greater all-European unity. In 1955, the Soviet Union and its Eastern European allies formed a similar mutual security system, the Warsaw Pact, the provisions of which duplicated the wording of the North Atlantic Treaty at many points.[16] The confrontation of these two military systems, each attempting to offset the other, illustrates the extent to which European security has rested more on the traditional pattern of balance-of-power principles than on the newer principles of universal collective security envisaged by the United Nations.

In September, 1954, the United States, the United Kingdom, and France, along with Australia, New Zealand, the Philippines, Thailand, and Pakistan established the Southeast Asia Treaty Organization. This followed the termination of the French war in Indochina and the establishment of the independent states of Laos and Cambodia and the partition of Vietnam. Modeled loosely after NATO and designed to check potential expansionism of Communist China, SEATO recognized that armed aggression in Southeast Asia against any one of its members would endanger the peace and safety of the other members, who in turn agreed

[15] *The New York Times,* February 22, 1966, pp. 1 and 6. By 1967, NATO headquarters had moved from France to Belgium.

[16] Text of the Warsaw Pact of May 14, 1955, may be found in Royal Institute of International Affairs, *Documents on International Affairs,* 1955 (London, Oxford University Press, 1958), pp. 193–197.

to act to meet the common danger. The signatories also agreed to extend the same guarantees to Laos, Cambodia, and Vietnam, although these countries were barred by the 1954 Geneva Accords on Indochina from joining any military alliances.

SEATO has been plagued from the beginning with even greater disunity than NATO, and this has kept it from becoming an effective regional system of security. In the case of the Vietnam war in the 1960's, its members were so divided over how best to deal with the situation that no agreement could be reached on any common SEATO program of military assistance to South Vietnam. As of mid-1967, for example, only 4 of the 8 SEATO members besides the United States (Australia, New Zealand, the Philippines, and Thailand) had given combat assistance to South Vietnam. France was so opposed to United States policies in Vietnam that its representative took no formal part in the 11th annual meeting of the SEATO Council of Ministers in June, 1966, and disassociated himself from the final communique. Pakistan was reported to have pressed for peace at almost any price in Vietnam, while the British Labour Prime Minister, Harold Wilson, although approving American objectives in Vietnam, had disassociated his government from the American bombing of North Vietnamese oil depots in the areas of Hanoi and Haiphong.[17]

Furthermore, SEATO's stature as an Asian regional security system has been lessened by the fact that only three Asian states—the Philippines, Thailand, and Pakistan—belong to it. Most other Asian states look upon SEATO as a Western-oriented alliance like NATO and have felt that their own security would be more effectively promoted by nonalignment with either of the two rival military systems. Even Cambodia and Laos have repudiated the protection pledged them by the SEATO members in 1954. While SEATO has thus not become an improvement over the uncertainties of United Nations collective security action, some observers feel, nevertheless, that the SEATO machinery has had some advantages in (1) the preparation of its members for joint action against future aggression in Asia, and (2) the economic and cultural aid programs which it has promoted among its members.[18]

INCREASED USE OF THE UN GENERAL ASSEMBLY AND THE ESTABLISHMENT OF PEACEKEEPING MACHINERY

As a second method of getting around the difficulties in obtaining Security Council action in some collective security situations, steps were taken to make greater use of the General Assembly. As early as 1947, when

[17] Robert S. Elegant, "SEATO Talks End with Wider Split on Policies in Asia," *The Philadelphia Inquirer,* June 30, 1966, p. 1.
[18] Tillman Durdin, "SEATO Has Its Points," *The New York Times,* July 3, 1966, Sec. 4, p. 3.

Soviet vetoes prevented the Security Council from adopting resolutions to check outside aid to the communist guerrilla forces in the Greek civil war, the question was transferred to the General Assembly, which was able, under its two-thirds majority voting procedure, to recommend actions which had been vetoed in the Security Council.[19]

Again during the Korean War, similar procedures were followed.[20] This time, the Security Council, owing to a strange combination of circumstances, was not paralyzed by the veto in setting its machinery for collective security into motion. The Soviet Union was not attending sessions of the Security Council or other United Nations organs at this time, in protest against the refusal of these organs to accept the Communist Chinese as the legal representatives of China. Hence, when the Korean War started in June, 1950, and the Security Council was summoned into immediate emergency session, it was able within a few hours to adopt a resolution calling for a cease-fire. North Korea ignored the resolution, and the Council two days later adopted a second, calling on all United Nations members to help repel the armed attack. Even before this had been adopted, the United States government had announced that it was furnishing air and naval forces to support the South Koreans.

In July, 1950, the Security Council established a Unified Command for all forces placed at the disposal of the United Nations, and shortly thereafter General Douglas MacArthur was designated commander of these forces. The Soviet Union, perhaps surprised at the vigorous response of the United Nations, returned to the Security Council in August, 1950, but by that time all the necessary machinery of collective security had been set up. However, from then on, the Soviet Union was in a position to block any Security Council decisions of which it did not approve. In September, 1950, it vetoed a resolution calling on all countries to refrain from assisting the North Koreans. In November, 1950, after Communist China had entered the war, the Soviet Union vetoed another resolution calling for the withdrawal of Chinese forces from Korea. It also vetoed two other resolutions, calling for impartial investigation of communist charges that United Nations forces were waging bacteriological warfare in Korea.

Confronted with these vetoes, the other members of the United Nations turned to the General Assembly. In October, 1950, it was the General Assembly which approved the extension of military action in Korea north of the 38th parallel, in order to achieve a united democratic country. Again in February, 1951, it was the Assembly which, after unsuccess-

[19] For a summary of United Nations action in this case, see United Nations, *Everyman's United Nations*, 7th ed. (New York, United Nations, 1964), pp. 157–159.

[20] A summary of U.N. action on the Korean question appears in *Ibid.*, pp. 99 ff. The Uniting for Peace Resolution, adopted by the General Assembly, November 3, 1950, is discussed in *Ibid.*, pp. 64–65.

ful efforts to obtain a cease-fire from the Chinese Communists, declared Communist China guilty of aggression in Korea. In May, 1951, the Assembly went further and called on all United Nations members to embargo the shipment of a list of strategic war materials to that country. By June 30, 1951, 30 member states and 3 nonmember states reported that they had complied with the request.

In this way, the General Assembly took over certain of the enforcement functions that the Security Council was unable to perform because of the veto. Perhaps the most significant action of the Assembly (from the long-run standpoint), in interpreting its jurisdiction broadly, came in November, 1950, when it adopted the "Uniting for Peace" Resolution. Under this resolution, the General Assembly modified its rules of procedure to permit its being called into emergency session on 24-hour notice in the event that the Security Council was unable to discharge its responsibilities for the maintenance of peace. The Assembly, under such circumstances, might recommend whatever action was necessary to deal with a case of aggression. A Peace Observation Commission was appointed under the Assembly to observe and report on any situation where there might be a threat to the peace. The resolution also called upon United Nations members to maintain certain units of their armed forces for prompt availability as United Nations units if need arose.

Through the Uniting for Peace Resolution, the United Nations was attempting to make certain that, in the event of future aggression, the General Assembly would be able to speak for the organization, even if the Security Council could not. The Assembly could, of course, do no more than make recommendations, but it at least would provide a channel through which the majority of its members could act if they so desired. The Soviet Union has contended that this is a violation of the Charter, since it permits the General Assembly to usurp the functions of the Security Council.

The supporters of the Uniting for Peace Resolution acknowledge that the procedure was not contemplated at the time the Charter was drafted in 1945, but they argue that it is not out of line with a broad interpretation of the Charter and its purposes. In defense of their position, they point specifically to Article 11 of the Charter, which authorizes the General Assembly to discuss any question regarding the maintenance of peace and to make recommendations on the subject provided that it is not at the moment on the agenda of the Security Council. Advocates contend that a broad construction of the meaning of the Charter is necessary to enable the United Nations to meet changed circumstances in world affairs not anticipated in 1945. So far as this broad interpretation is accepted by a two-thirds majority of the General Assembly, and to the extent that the procedures of the Uniting for Peace Resolution are followed, it would seem that the United Nations has found a practical method either for promoting the peaceful settlement of disputes or for organizing a system of collective security without being obstructed by the veto power of one country.

Since 1950, the General Assembly has been used on several occasions to recommend action for the restoration or maintenance of peace when the Security Council could not reach the necessary agreement.

The Suez Crisis. Following the British-French-Israeli invasion of Egypt in 1956 in the wake of the crisis occasioned by the Egyptian nationalization of the Suez Canal, the General Assembly took up the question under the Uniting for Peace Resolution procedures, following British and French vetoes of action by the Security Council. The Assembly urged an immediate cease-fire, called upon the British, French, and Israeli forces to withdraw their forces from Egypt, and established a United Nations Emergency Force to be stationed along the Israeli-Egyptian borders to replace the British, French, and Israeli forces and assure general compliance with the United Nations resolutions. The British, French, and Israeli governments all complied eventually with these resolutions.[21]

The Hungarian Crisis. Simultaneously with the Suez crisis, the General Assembly was called upon to deal with the equally serious crisis resulting from the Soviet intervention in Hungary in October, 1956. Starting early in November, 1956, after the Soviet Union had vetoed a Security Council measure calling for the end of Soviet military action in Hungary, the General Assembly passed some thirteen resolutions on the Hungarian question. They called on the Russians to stop their armed attack, withdraw their troops, end the deportation of Hungarians, permit the holding of free elections under United Nations auspices, and permit the admission of United Nations observers to Hungary. Other resolutions authorized an emergency relief program for Hungarian refugees and urged all members to provide medicines and other supplies. On December 12, 1956, after the Soviet government had declined to heed any of these resolutions, the General Assembly, by a vote of 56 to 8 (the Soviet bloc), with 13 abstentions, condemned the Soviet Union for violating the United Nations Charter "in depriving Hungary of its liberty and independence and the Hungarian people of . . . their fundamental right." Throughout the debate, the Soviet Union argued that the Hungarian problem was essentially a question within the domestic jurisdiction of Hungary itself and that the United Nations had no right to interfere in such matters. Inasmuch as none of the other United Nations members was prepared to apply further measures of coercion against the Soviet Union to force her out of Hungary, the United Nations action amounted only to a moral protest. The Soviet action, however, did lead some Asian powers to speak more critically of the Soviet Union than they had ever done previously. In this way,

[21] United Nations, *Everyman's United Nations,* 7th ed., pp. 80–83.

the Soviet reputation throughout the world may have been damaged by the intervention in Hungary, even though the Soviet Union was not actually forced to withdraw from the country. The publication in the summer of 1957 of a United Nations committee report, based on the testimony of Hungarian refugees, provided a detailed, documentary foundation for further condemnation of the Soviet intervention in Hungary by many governments.[22]

A special session of the General Assembly met in September, 1957, and adopted a resolution endorsing the report, condemning the Soviet action in Hungary, and appointing a special United Nations Representative to do what he could to secure compliance with the various United Nations resolutions on the Hungarian question. The United Nations Special Representative was never successful in achieving these objectives, but the Assembly continued for the next five years to adopt resolutions annually deploring the continued disregard by the Soviet Union and Hungary of the Assembly's recommendations.[23]

The Lebanese Crisis. In August, 1958, the General Assembly again met in emergency session following the inability of the Security Council, due to a Soviet veto, to act on the Lebanese crisis. In May, 1958, Lebanon had complained to the Security Council that personnel and military supplies from the United Arab Republic were being infiltrated into Lebanon to aid groups which were trying to overthrow the Lebanese government.[24]

The Security Council despatched a UN Observation Group to Lebanon in June, 1958, to ensure that no infiltration took place, but while it was there an anti-Western *coup d'état* occurred in neighboring Iraq which so alarmed the Lebanese government that it requested the United States to send troops to Lebanon to help forestall a possible similar *coup* against the Lebanese government. The United States immediately despatched forces to Lebanon, and, a few days later, the British landed troops in Jordan following a request for aid from that government.

The Soviet Union now called upon the Security Council to condemn the American and British armed intervention in Lebanon and Jordan and to demand that their troops be withdrawn at once. Most of the Security Council members did not support this Soviet proposal, but preferred instead to send the Secretary General to the Middle East to try to resolve the difficulties. A resolution to this effect, however, was vetoed by the Soviet Union because it did not contain a clause condemning the American and British "aggression."

[22] *Report of the Special Committee on the Problem of Hungary,* United Nations, General Assembly Official Records, Eleventh Session, Supplement No. 18 (A/3592).

[23] UN action on the Hungarian question is summarized in United Nations, *Everyman's United Nations,* 7th ed., pp. 165–170.

[24] Internal difficulties had arisen in Lebanon because its pro-Western President Chamoun wanted to amend the constitution to permit himself to be re-elected for a second term.

The case was thereupon transferred to the General Assembly. During the eight days of its deliberations, moderate forces were brought to play which enabled the Assembly to work out a resolution which satisfied all parties concerned, including the Soviet Union, and was therefore approved unanimously, August 21, 1958. Included in its various provisions were: (1) assurances by the Arab states not to attempt to change one another's systems of government, (2) an appeal to all UN members to respect one another's territorial integrity and sovereignty in accordance with the UN Charter, and (3) an authorization to the Secretary General to make practical arrangements which would uphold the Charter principles in Lebanon and Jordan and thereby facilitate the withdrawal of foreign troops from the two countries.[25]

This resolution is one of the best examples of how—under auspicious circumstances—the General Assembly may be able to reach a consensus and resolve a stalemate which has previously halted Security Council action. The resolution was subsequently implemented, and by November, 1958, American and British troops had been withdrawn from Lebanon and Jordan.[26]

The Congo Crisis. Most of the United Nations action in this case, including the establishment of the UN Force in the Congo, was initially authorized by the Security Council. But in September, 1960, a constitutional crisis developed in the Congolese government after the Congolese President had dismissed Premier Lumumba and full power was assumed by Colonel Joseph Mobutu, who proceeded to terminate various policies of Lumumba which were regarded as pro-Soviet. Lumumba had also differed sharply with Secretary General Hammarskjöld because the latter had refused to allow the UN Force to assist Lumumba in putting down the secession of Katanga Province headed by Moise Tshombe. Because Secretary General Hammarskjöld accepted the dismissal of Lumumba as being within the constitutional prerogatives of the Congolese President, and because he thereafter continued to consult with the President regarding the operation of the UN Force in the Congo, the Soviet Union strongly criticized Hammarskjöld's action as improper and illegal. It subsequently demanded his resignation and refused to contribute further to the costs of the UN Force in the Congo.

This was the background against which the Soviet Union vetoed a Security Council Resolution in September, 1960, which would have (1) urged the Secretary General vigorously to implement previous Council resolutions regarding the Congo; (2) called upon all Congolese to seek a speedy and peaceful solution to their internal differences; and (3) requested all states to refrain from any action which might impede the restoration of law and order or undermine the territorial integrity or in-

[25] UN action on the Lebanese case is discussed in United Nations, *Everyman's United Nations*, 7th ed., pp. 89–91.

[26] The election of a compromise presidential candidate in Lebanon in the fall of 1958, in place of Chamoun, contributed greatly to a relaxation of tension in the region.

dependence of the Congo. The resolution also called upon all states not to give military assistance to the Congo except through the United Nations.

In view of the inability of the Security Council to take action, an emergency session of the General Assembly was at once convened to take up the question. Three days later, in the early hours of September 20, 1960, the Assembly unanimously approved a resolution virtually identical to the one which had been vetoed previously in the Security Council. The Soviet Union, apparently because it realized it could not prevent the adoption of the resolution, abstained, as did the other communist bloc states, France, and South Africa. Once again, the Assembly succeeded in producing a consensus following a stalemate in the Security Council.[27]

During the regular 1960 Assembly Session, which followed immediately after the close of the emergency session, Soviet Premier Khrushchev demanded the resignation of Secretary General Hammarskjöld and his replacement by a three-man body (the so-called "troika plan") representing each of the three main groups in the Assembly. However, the General Assembly members, aside from the Soviet bloc, stood strongly behind the Secretary General and refused to be moved by Khrushchev's hysterical table-pounding tactics. It was a good example of how the Assembly could make its influence felt, this time in behalf of the independence and integrity of the Secretary General against the pressure of a big power.[28]

United Nations Peacekeeping Operations. While only one instance of collective security enforcement action by the United Nations has thus far occurred—the Korean case, a number of peacekeeping operations have been undertaken in which UN forces have performed a kind of "policeman" role to hold local conflicts in check and prevent their expanding into wider wars. The principal examples of this have been (1) the United Nations Emergency Force in the Middle East which since 1956 has been interposed between Israel and the United Arab Republic and has effectively prevented border disturbances between the two countries; (2) the United Nations Force in the Congo which, between 1960 and 1964, helped maintain stability and order within the Congo and, in all probability, prevented the internal strife in that country from escalating into a Korean-type, cold war conflict; and (3) the United Nations Force in Cyprus which since 1964 has maintained an uneasy truce in the civil strife on that island and prevented a serious military clash between Greece and Turkey.[29]

[27] UN action in the Congo is summarized in United Nations, *Everyman's United Nations,* 7th ed., pp. 143–151. A more complete account of the Assembly action is given in the *United Nations Review,* December, 1960, pp. 40–42. In April, 1961, the Assembly adopted three further resolutions on the Congo question. See *United Nations Review,* May, 1961, pp. 5–6.

[28] Khrushchev's statement and Hammarskjöld's reply are given in *United Nations Review,* November, 1960, pp. 37–40.

[29] See above, p. 290.

These peacekeeping operations differ from collective security action in that they do not involve the UN forces in fighting or enforcement operations against a recognized aggressor. Instead, the UN forces are sent at the request of the host government to assist in "policing" the disturbed areas and preventing the eruption of further hostilities. They are authorized to resort to arms only in self-defense if attacked. Thus the UN Force in the Middle East was stationed there with the consent of Egypt, Great Britain, and France, and without objection from Israel. The UN Force in the Congo was despatched at the request of the Congolese government, and the UN Force in Cyprus was sent with the approval of the governments of Cyprus, Greece, and Turkey.[30]

In view of the difficulty of getting sufficient consensus among a large number of United Nations members to undertake major enforcement operations, it may be that the "policeman-type" peacekeeping operations are the most politically feasible steps the United Nations can undertake as alternatives to collective security. Insofar as they can keep local conflicts from becoming major ones and provide time for the slow processes of conciliation and accommodation to lessen the underlying causes of tension, they represent a significant contribution by the United Nations to the prevention of another major war.

The United Nations has, however, encountered a major constitutional problem in attempting to establish peacekeeping operations. This centers on the question as to whether the General Assembly as well as the Security Council may legally establish such operations and levy assessments to finance the costs. The key article of the Charter on this is Article 24, which confers on the Security Council "primary responsibility for the maintenance of international peace and security." The Soviet Union and France hold that the words, "primary responsibility," mean "exclusive responsibility," and that therefore only the Security Council, where each of them as permanent members has a veto, may lawfully authorize such operations.

The United States, the United Kingdom, and many other United Nations members contend, however, that primary responsibility is not exclusive responsibility, and that therefore the Assembly may legitimately recommend peacekeeping operations if the Security Council is unable to discharge its responsibilities.[31]

This controversy lay behind the refusal of the Soviet Union and its communist allies to pay the assessments levied by the Assembly for the costs of the UN forces in the Middle East and the Congo. France has re-

[30] For a fuller discussion of UN Peacekeeping Operations, see Burns, A. L. and Heathcote, N., *Peacekeeping by U.N. Forces from Suez to the Congo* (New York, Praeger, 1962).

[31] For a fuller discussion, see John G. Stoessinger and Associates, *Financing the United Nations System* (Washington, The Brookings Institution, 1964), Chaps. 5 and 6; and the *UN Monthly Chronicle*, October, 1964, pp. 47–50.

fused to pay its assessments for the Congo operation, although it has made its payments for the Middle East Force. The Arab states have not paid their assessments, for the most part, contending that the burden of payment for peacekeeping operations should fall on the states whose "aggression" or other action necessitated the establishment of the peacekeeping forces in the first place. None of these constitutional or legal objections have complicated the financing of the UN Force in Cyprus inasmuch as this operation was to be paid for with voluntary contributions. Nor have these objections affected the payment by states of their main assessments for the regular budget of the United Nations except in the case of a few small items. Here, the Soviet Union and its communist allies, along with France, have for the past few years deducted a few small amounts from their main budget assessments, representing those items relating to peacekeeping operations which they consider illegal. But apart from this, they have paid all of their assessments for the regular budget on time.

The financial and constitutional crisis reached unprecedented heights in 1964 when the unpaid Soviet assessments for peacekeeping operations reached a level (some $54,700,000)[32] which exceeded the total of all assessments levied by the Assembly on the Soviet Union for all UN activities for the preceding two years (1962 and 1963). This created a situation in which certain penalties prescribed by Article 19 of the Charter for nonpayment of assessments seemed applicable. Article 19 specifies that a state which is in arrears to an extent equalling or exceeding the amount of contributions due from it for the preceding two full years shall lose its vote in the General Assembly for such time as it continues this much in arrears. As the time for the General Assembly approached in the fall of 1964, the United States took the position that unless the Soviet Union paid its overdue assessments it should be deprived of its vote in the General Assembly under Article 19.

The Soviet Union argued that it was not in arrears inasmuch as the special assessments for peacekeeping operations were, in its view, unconstitutional. A complete stalemate resulted over this issue, and, rather than have a showdown at that time, the General Assembly agreed not to take any action during the 19th session (1964–1965) except that which could be done by unanimous consent.[33] The General Assembly which since 1950 had been playing an ever-increasing role in United Nations activities now became virtually paralyzed as neither the Soviet Union nor the United States showed any signs of compromise.

Eventually, in August, 1965, the United States, in response to the feeling of an overwhelming majority of United Nations members that the

[32] UN Document, ST/ADM/SER. B/189, 15 July 1964. Table II. Several other states also had reached the point in 1964 where their accumulated unpaid assessments for peacekeeping operations exceeded the total assessments due from them for the preceding two years.

[33] UN Monthly Chronicle, November, 1964, p. 88, and January, 1965, p. 3.

General Assembly should not be paralyzed for a second year, announced that it would no longer object to the resumption of normal voting procedures during the forthcoming 20th session of the Assembly. The United States emphasized at the same time that it was not abandoning its position that nonpayment of assessments should mean the loss of voting rights in the Assembly.[34] This concession by the United States permitted the Assembly to conduct a regular and reasonably normal session from September to December, 1965.

A special committee of the Assembly has been at work since early 1965 trying to resolve the controversy, but as yet no solution has been found. If any compromise is reached, it is likely to involve recognition of the principle that any future peacekeeping operations established by the General Assembly will have to depend on voluntary contributions rather than on compulsory assessments. Only if the Security Council has approved the operations is it likely to be feasible to have the Assembly levy binding assessments.

Thus a limit seems to have been reached on the extent to which the General Assembly may act in the area of peace and security. If a two-thirds majority wishes to act, it must at the same time be able to raise the necessary funds through some formula of voluntary contributions, without trying to compel payments from states which have opposed such Assembly action.

THE DEVELOPMENT OF SUPRANATIONAL INSTITUTIONS

The limitations on the potential powers or influence of the United Nations as an organ for the maintenance of peace have prompted some observers of international affairs to propose a much more radical alternative to collective security, namely, the establishment of some form of supranational institutions either on a world-wide basis or on a more limited regional basis. This view is based on the belief that no dependable system of international cooperation for the maintenance of peace can be built on the foundations of the sovereign nation-state—that the principles of unlimited national sovereignty are incompatible with any comprehensive system of international law enforcement because each of the world's 120 sovereign states insists on having the final word on all matters which it regards as vital. Each also is in most cases unwilling to be bound against its will by the decisions of any international organization or arbitral body. This insistence by each state on virtually unlimited freedom of action, it is argued, makes treaties and agreements both unreliable and unpredictable since states are unlikely to carry out any undertakings

---

[34] *The New York Times*, August 17, 1965, pp. 1, 6. *UN Monthly Chronicle*, August–September, 1965, p. 17 ff. summarizes the discussions.

which may subsequently conflict with their interests. It may undermine the dependability of mutual assistance pacts such as NATO and SEATO if the various members have divergent ideas on how the pact is to be applied or not applied. This is clearly seen in the current attitude of France towards NATO and SEATO which in turn reflects French doubts concerning the reliability of the American commitment to defend Europe. It is also illustrated by the unwillingness of the Soviet Union and France to pay UN assessments for peacekeeping operations to which they are opposed. And, as a result of the Soviet and French attitudes on UN financing, even the United States has since August, 1965, indicated that it might, under some future circumstances, wish to reserve the same right to withhold payments for peacekeeping operations to which it might object.[35]

The creation of a world government with effective power to prevent nation-states from resorting to war, it is argued, is the only way to overcome the weakness of the United Nations and the undependability of alliances or balance of power systems. The establishment of the United States federal government in 1789 is sometimes cited as an example of how a loose confederation of sovereign states (under the Articles of Confederation, 1781–1789) might form "a more perfect union" with a central government of limited but effective powers over matters of concern to the entire nation. Likewise, the relations of the thirteen American states with one another under the Articles of Confederation are sometimes compared with the relations between nation-states today.

Under the Articles, for example, each state had explicitly retained its sovereignty, freedom, and independence (Article II). The thirteen states had banded together to form a "firm league of friendship" for their common defense, the security of their liberties, and their mutual welfare (Article III). The principal organ of the central government was a one-house Congress in which each state had one vote (comparable to the United Nations General Assembly), and a majority of nine votes was required for action on major questions. The Congress, however, had only limited and incomplete power. It lacked authority to collect taxes directly from the citizens and had to rely instead on assessments and requests for funds from the various state governments, which often failed to make their payments (a relatively worse financial dilemma than even that of the United Nations). Congress also lacked power to regulate interstate commerce, and consequently the states adopted many trade barriers and obstacles to the free flow of commerce. Congress was empowered (Article IX) to act in some areas of national concern such as declaring war, concluding peace, conducting foreign relations, making treaties, requesting men and money from the states, borrowing and coining money, fixing the size of the army and navy, and conducting a postal system. But, generally speaking, it was

[35] *Ibid.*

a weak form of government, and the principal sources of authority still rested with the thirteen states. It was, of course, considerably more of a government than the United Nations, and there was a much broader degree of consensus among the thirteen states, due to their common language, historical background, and culture, than exists among the nations of the world today. Even so, many of the fundamental weaknesses of the United Nations were also evident in the government of the Articles of Confederation. Since the United States Constitution of 1789, with its division of powers between the national and state governments, corrected many of the weaknesses of the Articles, it is argued that the same remedy is needed today on a world basis to correct the weaknesses of the United Nations and regional defense systems such as NATO.

Some very specific plans for establishing a federal form of government on either a world-wide or regional basis have been made. One of these would transform the present North Atlantic Treaty Organization into an Atlantic Federal Union.[36] It is suggested that an Atlantic constitutional convention be assembled, patterned after the United States Constitutional Convention of 1787, with delegates from the several states in the North Atlantic Treaty Organization. Such a convention would draft a constitution establishing a defense, political, and economic union among the members. This would include a bill of rights guaranteeing the citizens of the union all the fundamental freedoms they now enjoy in their respective countries. It would confer upon the union government certain delegated responsibilities including the establishment of a union defense force, a union free market, a union currency, a union postal system, a union citizenship (in addition to national citizenship), and a system of union taxation on its citizens to raise the funds to carry out the preceding powers. As under the United States Constitution, those powers in the realm of purely domestic jurisdiction of the several national states such as education, social services, internal economic matters, and police would be reserved to the states belonging to the Atlantic Union.

The Atlantic Union would not replace the United Nations or any other existing international institutions aside from NATO, but would provide a means whereby those members within the United Nations which so desired could form a stronger political, economic, and defense union among themselves. The union as a whole would become a member of the United Nations, and efforts would be made to have it retain the voting power now held in the United Nations by the NATO powers joining the union.

36 These ideas have been set forth in Clarence Streit, *Freedom's Frontier; Atlantic Union Now* (New York, Harper & Row, 1961), and have been actively espoused by an organization, Federal Union, Inc., in Washington, D.C. The latter publishes a monthly periodical, *Freedom and Union*. Streit's basic principles had been previously outlined in *Union Now* (New York, Harper & Row, 1939), which called for a federal union of the Western democracies and most British Commonwealth members.

Because the powers of this proposed Atlantic Union are extensive, its supporters recognize that its membership would need to be limited for the time being to those states which already have a high degree of common interests and consensus—*i.e.,* the states of the North Atlantic and West European region with a strong tradition of Western democratic institutions.

A second comprehensive plan for an international government has been suggested by an organization known as the United World Federalists (UWF).[37] Unlike the proposal for an Atlantic Federal Union, the UWF plan would attempt to attract a much wider membership from all parts of the world, including the communist and nonaligned nations, but would limit the powers of the world federal government to the enforcement of comprehensive disarmament and the prevention of international violence. By leaving all powers over trade, currency, postal matters, immigration, and citizenship in the hands of national governments as at present and restricting the powers of the new world federation to the development and enforcement of a world law forbidding international violence, it is hoped to attract a nearly universal membership of states which, despite their wide differences in political and economic institutions, have a strong common interest in preventing the holocaust of nuclear war.

The new system would be brought into being by revising the United Nations Charter so as to abolish national military forces (aside from purely domestic police establishments) and create in their place a United Nations Military Force strong enough to maintain peace and security for all. The General Assembly would be reorganized as a kind of international parliament with representation based on such factors as population and economic strength rather than on the principle of "one state, one vote." It would have powers by majority vote to enact binding legislation in the matters of enforcing disarmament and maintaining peace, including the power to apply penalties against individuals as well as governments failing to comply with its laws. The Assembly would also be authorized to raise, through collaborative arrangements with the member states, sufficient and reliable revenues to finance these activities. The United Nations Security Council would be reconstituted as an Executive Council, chosen by and responsible to the Assembly, to act as the executive arm of the Assembly in respect to the maintenance of international peace. The veto power of the present Security Council would be dropped.

There are many further provisions in this plan for a world federal government, but enough has been said to give a general idea of its character. Although both this plan and the plan for Atlantic Union have at-

[37] The details of this proposal have been developed in Grenville Clark and Louis B. Sohn, *World Peace through World Law,* 2nd ed. rev. (Cambridge, Mass., Harvard University Press, 1962).

tracted some support from various intellectuals, professional and business groups, and some legislators, neither has yet gained significant political support from governments. On the other hand, the principles of international government have, in a number of significant cases, been accepted and applied at the regional level, especially in the fields of economics and trade. These efforts at regional integration are a subject in themselves, and will be explored more fully in the following chapter.

The concluding section of this chapter will present several positions on the question of peaceful coexistence, including the Soviet and Chinese views, as well as the more detached observations of the distinguished British historian Arnold J. Toynbee. Two further positions will deal with the effectiveness of the United Nations in preserving international peace and security.

POSITIONS

1. THE SOVIET CONCEPTS OF PEACEFUL COEXISTENCE

The following are excerpts from Nikita S. Khrushchev's opening speech to the 20th Congress of the Communist Party of the Soviet Union in February, 1956. In his speech, Khrushchev introduced two significant modifications in Marxist-Leninist theory as it had been interpreted by Soviet leaders previously: (a) that wars were not necessarily inevitable while capitalism still existed; (b) that the proletariat under certain circumstances might achieve political power by peaceful, parliamentary means, rather than by violent revolution. It seems highly probable that these views of Khrushchev reflected his increasing awareness of the implications of major nuclear warfare.[38]

THE WORLD-WIDE EMERGENCE OF COMMUNISM
AND THE FIGHT FOR PEACE

The principal feature of our epoch is the emergence of socialism from the confines of one country and its transformation into a world system. Capitalism has proved impotent to hinder this world-historical process.

The simultaneous existence of two opposed and world economic system[s] . . . capitalism and socialism, developing according to different laws in the opposite direction, has become an irrefutable fact. . . .

The forces of peace have grown considerably with the appearance in the world arena of the group of peace-loving states in Europe and Asia, which have proclaimed non-participation in blocs to be the principle of their foreign policy.

As a result, an extensive "zone of peace," including both Socialist and non-Socialist peace-loving states of Europe and Asia, has appeared on the world arena.

[38] *New York Times*, February 15, 1956, p. 10. ©, 1956, by the New York Times Company. Reprinted by permission.

This zone extends over a vast area of the globe, inhabited by nearly 1,500,000,000 people, or the majority of the population of our planet. . . .

Today many Social Democrats are for an active struggle against the war danger and militarism, for closer relations with Socialist countries, and for unity of the labor movement. We sincerely welcome the Social Democrats, and are ready to do everything possible to unite our efforts in a fight for the noble cause of the defense of peace and the interests of the working people. . . .

We believe that if the famous five principles of peaceful coexistence were made the basis of relations between the U.S.S.R. and the United States, this would be of truly outstanding significance for all mankind and would, of course, be no less beneficial to the people of the United States than to the peoples of the U.S.S.R. and all other nations. . . .[39]

We want to be friends and to cooperate with the United States in the effort for peace and security of . . . [all] peoples. . . .

If good relations are not established between the Soviet Union and the United States, and mutual distrust exists, this will lead to an arms race on a still greater scale and to a still more dangerous growth of the forces on both sides.

We intend to continue to work for the further improvement of our relations with Great Britain and France.

We welcome the desire of the people of the Arab countries to uphold their national independence. . . .

Counterposing the slogan of the North Atlantic pact: "Let us arm," we advise the slogan: "Let us trade."

The Leninist principle of peaceful coexistence of states with differing social systems was, and remains, the general line of our country's foreign policy. . . .

THE MEANING OF THE WORLD-WIDE TRIUMPH OF COMMUNISM

When we say that in the competition between the two systems of capitalism and socialism, socialism will triumph, this by no means implies that the victory will be reached by armed intervention on the part of the Socialist countries in the internal affairs of the capitalist countries.

We believe that after seeing for themselves the advantages that communism holds out, all working men and women on earth will sooner or later take to the road of the struggle to build a socialist society.

We have always asserted and continue to assert that the establishment of a new social order in any country is the internal affair of its people.

Such are our positions, based on the great teachings of Marxism-Leninism. . . .

As will be recalled, there is a Marxist-Leninist premise which says that while imperialism exists wars are inevitable.

While capitalism remains on earth the reactionary forces representing the

[39] "These principles [the "famous five principles of peaceful coexistence"] proclaim that countries different from one another politically, socially, and economically can and must cooperate on the basis of mutual respect, and non-interference in each other's home affairs, and must abide by the policy of active and peaceful coexistence in the common desire to attain the ideals of peace and the improvement of man's living conditions." From the Joint Statement of N. A. Bulganin, N. S. Khrushchev, and Jawaharlal Nehru, December 13, 1955, in *Report to the Supreme Soviet on the Visit to India, Burma, and Afghanistan* (New York, New Century Publishers, 1956), p. 32.

interests of the capitalist monopolies will continue to strive for war gambles and aggression, and may try to let loose war.

There is [however] no fatal inevitability of war.

Now there are powerful social and political forces, commanding serious means capable of preventing the unleashing of war by the imperialists, and—should they try to start it—of delivering a smashing rebuff to the aggressors and thwarting their adventuristic plans. . . .

The enemies are fond of depicting us, Leninists, as supporters of violence always and in all circumstances. It is true that we recognize the necessity for the revolutionary transformation of capitalist society into Socialist society.

This is what distinguishes revolutionary Marxists from reformists and opportunists. There is not a shadow of doubt that for a number of capitalist countries the overthrow of the bourgeois dictatorship by force and the connected sharp aggravation of the class struggle is inevitable.

But there are different forms of social revolution and the allegation that we recognize force and civil war as the only way of transforming society does not correspond to reality.

Leninism teaches us that the ruling classes will not relinquish power of their own free will.

However, the greater or lesser degree of acuteness in the struggle, the use or not of force in the transition to socialism, depend not so much on the proletariat as on the extent of the resistance put up by the exploiters, and on the employment of violence by the exploiting class itself.

In this connection the question arises of the possibility of employing the parliamentary form for the transition to socialism. For the Russian Bolsheviks, who were the first to accomplish the transition to socialism, this way was excluded.

However, since then radical changes have taken place in the historical situation that allow an approach to this question from another angle.

Socialism has become a great magnetizing force for the workers, peasants and intelligentsia in all lands. The ideas of socialism are really conquering the minds of all toiling mankind.

At the same time, in a number of capitalist countries, the working class possesses in the present situation realistic opportunities of welding under its leadership the overwhelming majority of the people and of insuring . . . [the] transition of the principal means of production into the hands of the people.

The right-wing bourgeois parties and the Governments they form are becoming bankrupt more and more often.

In these conditions, by rallying around itself a toiling peasantry, the intelligentsia and all the patriotic forces, and by meting out a determined rebuff to opportunistic elements incapable of abandoning a policy of conciliation with the capitalists and landlords, the working class has the possibility of inflicting a defeat on the reactionary anti-popular forces and of gaining a firm majority in parliament, and converting it from an organ of bourgeois democracy into an instrument of genuinely popular will.

In such an event, this institution, traditional for many highly developed capitalist countries, may become an organ of genuine democracy, of democracy for the working people.

The winning of a stable parliamentary majority, based on the mass revolutionary movement of the proletariat and the working people, would bring about for the working class of a number of capitalist and former colonial countries, conditions insuring the implementation of fundamental social transformations.

Of course in countries where capitalism is still strong and where it controls an enormous military and police machine, the serious resistance of the reactionary forces is inevitable.

There the transition to socialism will proceed amid conditions of an acute class revolutionary struggle. . . .

2. COMMUNIST CHINESE CONCEPTS OF PEACEFUL COEXISTENCE

The Communist Chinese challenge to Soviet views on communist theory and practice has been set forth in many places. One of the strongest and most comprehensive statements of the Chinese position was the letter of June 14, 1963, from the Central Committee of the Communist Party of China to the Central Committee of the Communist Party of the Soviet Union. Portions of this dealing particularly with the Chinese attitudes towards peaceful coexistence and the possibilities of peaceful transition to socialism are given below.[40]

(1) The general line of the international communist movement must take as its guiding principle the Marxist-Leninist revolutionary theory concerning the historical mission of the proletariat and must not depart from it.

The Moscow Meetings of 1957 and 1960 adopted the Declaration and the Statement respectively after a full exchange of views and in accordance with the principle of reaching unanimity through consultation. The two documents point out the characteristics of our epoch and the common laws of socialist revolution and socialist construction, and lay down the common line of all the Communist and Workers' Parties. They are the common programme of the international communist movement.[41]

It is true that for several years there have been differences within the international communist movement in the understanding of, and the attitude towards, the Declaration of 1957 and the Statement of 1960. The central issue here is whether or not to accept the revolutionary principles of the Declaration and the Statement. In the last analysis, it is a question of whether or not to accept the universal truth of Marxism-Leninism, whether or not to recognize the universal significance of the road of the October Revolution, whether or not to accept the fact that the people still living under the imperialist and capitalist system, who

[40] *Peking Review,* June 21, 1963, pp. 6–22. Full text also in *The New York Times,* July 5, 1963, pp. 6–9.

[41] The Moscow Declaration of November, 1957, was a statement by the twelve communist parties in power in their respective countries. It was a compromise statement designed to restore unity among the various communist parties following the Hungarian and Polish uprisings against Soviet domination of their regimes in late 1956. The Moscow statement of December, 1960, was another broad compromise statement of principles agreed to by eighty-one communist parties from all over the world.

comprise two-thirds of the world's population, need to make revolution, and whether or not to accept the fact that the people already on the socialist road, who comprise one-third of the world's population, need to carry their revolution forward to the end.

It has become an urgent and vital task of the international communist movement resolutely to defend the revolutionary principles of the 1957 Declaration and the 1960 Statement.

Only by strictly following the revolutionary teachings of Marxism-Leninism and the general road of the October Revolution is it possible to have a correct understanding of the revolutionary principles of the Declaration and the Statement and a correct attitude towards them.

(2) What are the revolutionary principles of the Declaration and the Statement? They may be summarized as follows:

Workers of all countries, unite; workers of the world, unite with the oppressed peoples and oppressed nations; oppose imperialism and reaction in all countries; strive for world peace, national liberation, people's democracy and socialism; consolidate and expand the socialist camp; bring the proletarian world revolution step by step to complete victory; and establish a new world without imperialism, without capitalism and without the exploitation of man by man.

This, in our view, is the general line of the international communist movement at the present stage.

(3)

* * *

This general line is one of resolute revolutionary struggle by the people of all countries and of carrying the proletarian world revolution forward to the end; it is the line that most effectively combats imperialism and defends world peace.

If the general line of the international communist movement is one-sidedly reduced to "peaceful coexistence," "peaceful competition" and "peaceful transition," this is to violate the revolutionary principles of the 1957 Declaration and the 1960 Statement, to discard the historical mission of proletarian world revolution, and to depart from the revolutionary teachings of Marxism-Leninism.

* * *

(10) In the imperialist and the capitalist countries, the proletarian revolution and the dictatorship of the proletariat are essential for the thorough resolution of the contradictions of capitalist society.

* * *

Social democracy is a bourgeois ideological trend. Lenin pointed out long ago that the social democratic parties are political detachments of the bourgeoisie, its agents in the working-class movement and its principal social prop. Communists must at all times draw a clear line of demarcation between themselves and social democratic parties on the basic question of the proletarian revolution and the dictatorship of the proletariat and liquidate the ideological influence of social democracy in the international working-class movement and among the working people. Beyond any shadow of doubt, Communists must win over the masses under the influence of the social democratic parties and must win over those Left and middle elements in the social democratic parties who are willing to oppose domestic monopoly capital and domination by foreign imperialism, and must unite with them in extensive joint action in the day-to-day struggle of the working-class movement and in the struggle to defend world peace.

In order to lead the proletariat and working people in revolution, Marxist-Leninist parties must master all forms of struggle and be able to substitute one form for another quickly as the conditions of struggle change. The vanguard of the proletariat will remain unconquerable in all circumstances only if it masters all forms of struggle—peaceful and armed, open and secret, legal and illegal, parliamentary struggle and mass struggle, etc. It is wrong to refuse to use parliamentary and other legal forms of struggle when they can and should be used. However, if a Marxist-Leninist party falls into legalism or parliamentary cretinism, confining the struggle within the limits permitted by the bourgeoisie, this will inevitably lead to renouncing the proletarian revolution and the dictatorship of the proletariat.

(11) On the question of transition from capitalism to socialism, the proletarian party must proceed from the stand of class struggle and revolution and base itself on the Marxist-Leninist teachings concerning the proletarian revolution and the dictatorship of the proletariat.

Communists would always prefer to bring about the transition to socialism by peaceful means. But can peaceful transition be made into a new worldwide strategic principle for the international communist movement? Absolutely not.

Marxism-Leninism consistently holds that the fundamental question in all revolutions is that of state power. The 1957 Declaration and the 1960 Statement both clearly point out, "Leninism teaches, and experience confirms, that the ruling classes never relinquish power voluntarily." The old government never topples even in a period of crisis, unless it is pushed. This is a universal law of class struggle.

In specific historical conditions, Marx and Lenin did raise the possibility that revolution may develop peacefully. But, as Lenin pointed out, the peaceful development of revolution is an opportunity "very seldom to be met with in the history of revolution."

As a matter of fact, there is no historical precedent for peaceful transition from capitalism to socialism.

Certain persons say there was no precedent when Marx foretold that socialism would inevitably replace capitalism. Then why can we not predict a peaceful transition from capitalism to socialism despite the absence of a precedent?

This parallel is absurd. Employing dialectical and historical materialism, Marx analysed the contradictions of capitalism, discovered the objective laws of development of human society and arrived at a scientific conclusion, whereas the prophets who pin all their hopes on "peaceful transition" proceed from historical idealism, ignore the most fundamental contradictions of capitalism, repudiate the Marxist-Leninist teachings on class struggle, and arrive at a subjective and groundless conclusion. How can people who repudiate Marxism get any help from Marx?

It is plain to everyone that the capitalist countries are strengthening their state machinery—and especially their military apparatus—the primary purpose of which is to suppress the people in their own countries.

The proletarian party must never base its thinking, its policies for revolution and its entire work on the assumption that the imperialists and reactionaries will accept peaceful transformation.

The proletarian party must prepare itself for two eventualities—while preparing for a peaceful development of the revolution, it must also fully prepare for a non-peaceful development. It should concentrate on the painstaking work of accumulating revolutionary strength, so that it will be ready to seize victory when the conditions for revolution are ripe or to strike powerful blows at the imperialists and the reactionaries when they launch surprise attacks and armed assaults.

If it fails to make such preparations, the proletarian party will paralyse the revolutionary will of the proletariat, disarm itself ideologically and sink into a totally passive state of unpreparedness both politically and organizationally, and the result will be to bury the proletarian revolutionary cause.

(15)

* * *

The emergence of nuclear weapons can neither arrest the progress of human history nor save the imperialist system from its doom, any more than the emergence of new techniques could save the old systems from their doom in the past.

The emergence of nuclear weapons does not and cannot resolve the fundamental contradictions in the contemporary world, does not and cannot alter the law of class struggle, and does not and cannot change the nature of imperialism and reaction.

It cannot, therefore, be said that with the emergence of nuclear weapons the possibility and the necessity of social and national revolutions have disappeared, or the basic principles of Marxism-Leninism, and especially the theories of proletarian revolution and the dictatorship of the proletariat and of war and peace, have become outmoded and changed into stale "dogmas."

(16) It was Lenin who advanced the thesis that it is possible for the socialist countries to practise peaceful coexistence with the capitalist countries. It is well known that after the great Soviet people had repulsed foreign armed intervention the Communist Party of the Soviet Union and the Soviet Government, led first by Lenin and then by Stalin, consistently pursued the policy of peaceful coexistence and that they were forced to wage a war of self-defence only when attacked by the German imperialists.

Since its founding, the People's Republic of China too has consistently pursued the policy of peaceful coexistence with countries having different social systems, and it is China which initiated the Five Principles of Peaceful Coexistence.

However, a few years ago certain persons suddenly claimed Lenin's policy of peaceful coexistence as their own "great discovery." They maintain that they have a monopoly on the interpretation of this policy. They treat "peaceful coexistence" as if it were an all-inclusive, mystical book from heaven and attribute to it every success the people of the world achieve by struggle. What is more, they label all who disagree with their distortions of Lenin's views as opponents of peaceful coexistence, as people completely ignorant of Lenin and Leninism, and as heretics deserving to be burnt at the stake.

How can the Chinese Communists agree with this view and practice? They cannot, it is impossible.

Lenin's principle of peaceful coexistence is very clear and readily comprehensible by ordinary people. Peaceful coexistence designates a relationship between countries with different social systems, and must not be interpreted as one pleases. It should never be extended to apply to the relations between oppressed and oppressor nations, between oppressed and oppressor countries or between oppressed and oppressor classes, and never be described as the main content of the transition from capitalism to socialism, still less should it be asserted that peaceful coexistence is mankind's road to socialism. The reason is that it is one thing to practise peaceful coexistence between countries with different social systems. It is absolutely impermissible and impossible for countries practising peaceful coexistence to touch even a hair of each other's social system. The class struggle, the struggle for national liberation and the transition from capitalism to socialism in various countries are quite another thing. They are all bitter, life-and-death revolutionary struggles which aim at changing the social system. Peaceful coexistence cannot replace the revolutionary struggles of the people. The transition from capitalism to socialism in any country can only be brought about through the proletarian revolution and the dictatorship of the proletariat in that country.

In the application of the policy of peaceful coexistence, struggles between the socialist and imperialist countries are unavoidable in the political, economic and ideological spheres, and it is absolutely impossible to have "all-round co-operation."

It is necessary for the socialist countries to engage in negotiations of one kind or another with the imperialist countries. It is possible to reach certain agreements through negotiation by relying on the correct policies of the socialist countries and on the pressure of the people of all countries. But necessary compromises between the socialist countries and the imperialist countries do not require the oppressed peoples and nations to follow suit and compromise with imperialism and its lackeys. No one should ever demand in the name of peaceful coexistence that the oppressed peoples and nations should give up their revolutionary struggles.

The application of the policy of peaceful coexistence by the socialist countries is advantageous for achieving a peaceful international environment for socialist construction, for exposing the imperialist policies of aggression and war and for isolating the imperialist forces of aggression and war. But if the general line of the foreign policy of the socialist countries is confined to peaceful coexistence, then it is impossible to handle correctly either the relations between socialist countries or those between the socialist countries and the oppressed peoples and nations. Therefore it is wrong to make peaceful coexistence the general line of the foreign policy of the socialist countries.

3. SOVIET REPLY TO THE CHINESE CRITICISM

In a lengthy letter of July 14, 1963,[42] the Central Committee of the Communist Party of the Soviet Union replied to the Chinese criticisms set

---

[42] Original in *Pravda*, July 14, 1963, pp. 1–4. Translation from the *Current Digest of the Soviet Press*, published weekly at Columbia University by the Joint Committee on Slavic Studies, appointed by the American Council of Learned Societies and the Social Science Research Council. Copyright 1963, Vol. XV, No. 28, by the Joint Committee on Slavic Studies. Reprinted by permission, pp. 16–25.

forth in the Chinese letter of June 14, 1963, portions of which were presented in the preceding position.

. . . The letter of the C.P.C. Central Committee contains baseless, slanderous attacks on our party, on other Communist Parties, on the decisions of the 20th, 21st and 22nd Congresses and on the C.P.S.U. Program. . . .

In April, 1960, the Chinese comrades openly revealed their differences with the world Communist movement by publishing a collection of articles under the title "Long Live Leninism!" This collection, the basis of which consisted of misrepresentations and truncated and incorrectly interpreted postulates from well-known works by Lenin, contained postulates directed in essence against the principles of the Declaration of the 1957 Moscow conference, which had been signed by Comrade Mao Tse-tung on behalf of the C.P.C.; against the Leninist policy of peaceful coexistence between states with different social systems; against the possibility of averting a world war in the contemporary epoch; and against the use of both peaceful and nonpeaceful ways of developing socialist revolutions. The C.P.C. leaders began forcing their views on all the fraternal parties. . . .

What is the essence of the differences between the C.P.C. on the one hand, and the international Communist movement on the other? . . .

In fact, at the center of the dispute are questions that involve the vital interests of the peoples.

They are questions of war and peace, the question of the role and development of the world socialist system; they are questions of the struggle against the ideology and practice of the "cult of the individual"; they are questions of the strategy and tactics of the world workers' movement and the national liberation struggle. . . .

The C.P.S.U. Central Committee considers it its duty to tell the Party and the people with all frankness that in questions of war and peace, fundamental differences of principle with us and with the world Communist movement have arisen in the C.P.C. leadership. The essence of these differences lies in the opposing approach to such important problems as the possibility of averting a world thermonuclear war, the peaceful coexistence of states with different social systems, and the relationship between the struggle for peace and the development of the world revolutionary movement.

Our party, in the decisions of the 20th and 22nd Congress, and the world Communist movement, in the Declaration and the Statement, placed before Communists as a first-priority task the struggle for peace, the averting of a world thermonuclear catastrophe. We appraise the balance of forces in the world realistically, and we have drawn from it the conclusion that, although the nature of imperialism has not changed and the danger of the outbreak of war has not been eliminated, in modern conditions the forces of peace, the chief bulwark of which is the mighty commonwealth of socialist states, can through united efforts avert a new world war.

We also appraise soberly the radical qualitative change in the means of waging war, and consequently its possible consequences. The missiles and nuclear weapons created in the middle of our century have changed the former ideas about war. These weapons possess unprecedented destructive force. Suffice it to say that the detonation of only one powerful thermonuclear bomb exceeds the explosive force of all the munitions used in all preceding wars, including World Wars I and II. And there are many thousands of such bombs in the stockpiles!

Do Communists have the right to ignore this danger? Must we tell the people the whole truth about the consequences of thermonuclear war? We think that we certainly must. This cannot have a "paralyzing" effect on the masses, as the Chinese comrades assert. On the contrary, the truth about modern war mobilizes the will and energy of the masses in the struggle for peace and against imperialism, the source of the war danger.

The historic task of the Communists is to organize and lead the struggle of the peoples to avert world thermonuclear war.

The averting of a new world war is a fully realistic and feasible task. The 20th Congress of our party came to the extremely important conclusion that in our time war between states is not fatally inevitable. This conclusion was not the fruit of good intentions but the result of a realistic, strictly scientific analysis of the relations of class forces in the world arena; it is based on the gigantic might of world socialism. Our views on this question are shared by the entire world Communist movement. "World war can be prevented"; "The real possibility of excluding world war from the life of society will arise even before the complete victory of socialism on earth, with capitalism still existing in part of the world," the Statement emphasizes.

This Statement bears the signatures of the Chinese comrades, too.

But what is the position of the C.P.C. leadership? What can the theses it is propagandizing mean: War cannot be eliminated while imperialism still exists; peaceful coexistence is an illusion, it cannot be the general principle of the foreign policies of the socialist countries; the struggle for peace impedes the revolutionary struggle?

These theses mean that the Chinese comrades are moving counter to the general course of the world Communist movement on questions of war and peace. They do not believe in the possibility of averting a new world war; they underestimate the forces of peace and socialism and overestimate the forces of imperialism; in essence, they ignore the mobilization of the popular masses in the struggle against the danger of war.

It emerges that the Chinese comrades do not believe in the capability of the peoples of the socialist countries, the international working class and all democratic and peace-loving forces to frustrate the plans of the instigators of war and to achieve peace for our generation and future generations. What lies behind the ringing revolutionary phrases of the Chinese comrades? Lack of faith in the forces of the working class, in its revolutionary capabilities, lack of faith both in the possibility of peaceful coexistence and in the victory of the proletariat in the class struggle. All peace-loving forces are united in the struggle to avert war. They differ in their class composition and in their class interests. But they can be united in the struggle for peace, for averting war, because the atomic bomb does not observe the class principle—it destroys everyone who comes within range of its destructive action.

To enter upon the path proposed by the Chinese comrades means to alienate the popular masses from the Communist Parties, which have won the sympathies of the peoples through their persistent and courageous struggle for peace.

In the consciousness of the broad masses, peace and socialism are now inseparable!

The Chinese comrades clearly underestimate the full danger of thermonuclear war. "The atomic bomb is a paper tiger," it is "by no means terrible," they assert. The chief thing, they say, is to do away with imperialism as rapidly as possible, but how this is to be done and the losses involved are, it would seem, questions of secondary importance. For whom, may we ask, are they of secondary importance? For the hundreds of millions of people who would be doomed to die if a thermonuclear war broke out? For the states that would be wiped from the face of the earth in the first hours of such a war?

No one, including the big states, has the right to play with the fates of millions of people. Those who do not wish to exert their efforts to exclude world war from the life of the peoples, to avert the mass annihilation of people and the destruction of the values of human civilization, merit condemnation.

The C.P.C. Central Committee's letter of June 14 has much to say about "inevitable sacrifices" allegedly in the name of revolution. Some responsible Chinese leaders have also mentioned the possibility of sacrificing hundreds of millions of people in war. In the anthology "Long Live Leninism!" that was approved by the C.P.C. Central Committee, it is asserted that "The victorious peoples will create rapidly on the ruins of dead imperialism a civilization a thousand times higher than that under the capitalist system, will build their own truly beautiful future."

One might ask the Chinese comrades if they are aware of what sort of ruins would be left behind by a nuclear-missile war?

The C.P.S.U. Central Committee—and we are convinced that our whole party and all the Soviet people support us in this—cannot share the views of the Chinese leadership about the creation of "a civilization a thousand times higher" on the corpses of hundreds of millions of people. These views are in fundamental contradiction to the ideas of Marxism-Leninism.

One might ask the Chinese comrades: What methods do they propose for the destruction of imperialism?

We fully support the destruction of imperialism and capitalism. We not only believe in the inevitable death of capitalism but are doing everything possible for it to be accomplished through class struggle and as quickly as possible. Who should decide this historic question? First of all, the working class, headed by its vanguard—the Marxist-Leninist party, the working people of each country.

The Chinese comrades propose something else. They say outright: "On the ruins of dead imperialism"—in other words, as the result of the outbreak of war—"a beautiful future will be built." If we accept this, then indeed the principle of peaceful coexistence and the struggle to strengthen peace will have no pertinence. We cannot enter upon such an adventurist path; it contradicts the essence of Marxism-Leninism.

Everyone knows that in modern conditions a world war will be a thermonuclear war. The imperialists will never agree to leave the stage voluntarily, to climb voluntarily into the grave without resorting to the use of the most extreme means they have at their disposal.

Clearly, those people who call thermonuclear weapons a "paper tiger" are not fully aware of the destructive force of these weapons.

We take this soberly into account. We ourselves make thermonuclear weapons and have manufactured a sufficient quantity of them. We are well aware of their destructive force. And if imperialism unleashes a war against us, we will not stay our hands from using these terrible weapons against the aggressor. But if we are not attacked, we will not be the first to use these weapons.

Marxist-Leninists are striving to achieve peace not by begging for it from the imperialists but by rallying the revolutionary Marxist-Leninist parties, rallying the working class of all countries, rallying the peoples who are struggling for their freedom and national independence, by relying upon the economic and defense might of the socialist states.

We would like to ask the Chinese comrades, who propose building a beautiful future on the ruins of the old world destroyed in a thermonuclear war: Have they consulted on this question with the working class in those countries where imperialism reigns? The working class in the capitalist countries would certainly answer them: Are we asking you to unleash a war and, in eliminating imperialism, to destroy our countries also? After all, the monopolists, the imperialists are a small handful, while the major part of the population of the capitalist countries consists of the working class, the toiling peasantry, the working intelligentsia. The atomic bomb makes no distinction between where the imperialists are and where the working people are—it strikes whole areas, and therefore millions of workers would be killed for each imperialist. The working class, the working people ask such "revolutionaries": What right have you to solve for us the questions of our existence and our class struggle? We, too, are for socialism, but we wish to win it through the class struggle and not by unleashing world thermonuclear war.

* * *

The next major question standing at the center of the differences is the question of the ways and methods of the revolutionary struggle of the working class in the countries of capitalism and of the national-liberation struggle, the question of the ways of the transition of all mankind to socialism.

As the Chinese comrades represent the differences on this question, they appear thus: One side—that is, they themselves—stands for a world revolution, while the other side—the C.P.S.U., the Marxist-Leninist parties—has forgotten the revolution, even "fears" it, and instead of revolutionary struggle is concerned about such things, "unworthy" of a true revolutionary, as peace, the economic development of the socialist countries and improving the living standards of their peoples, such things as the struggle for the democratic rights and vital interests of the working people of the capitalist countries.

In fact, however, the divide between the views of the C.P.C. and the views of the international Communist movement lies on a completely different plane: Some—that is, the leaders of the C.P.C.—argue about the world revolution in and out of place, parade the "revolutionary" phrase on every occasion and often without occasion, while others—in fact those whom the Chinese comrades are criticizing—approach the question of revolution with all seriousness and instead of pronouncing ringing phrases labor persistently in an endeavor to find the methods for the victory of socialism that are most right and most in accord with the conditions of the era, wage a persistent struggle for national independence, democracy and socialism.

Let us examine the basic views of the Chinese comrades on the questions of the contemporary revolutionary movement.

Is the transition of countries and peoples to socialism helped by the aim of ending the fight for peace in the name of the "world revolution," of renouncing the policy of peaceful coexistence and peaceful economic competition, renouncing the struggle for the vital interests of the working people and democratic reforms in the countries of capitalism? Is it true that the Communists of the countries of socialism, in coming out for peace and pursuing a policy of peaceful coexistence, are thinking only of themselves and have forgotten their class brothers in the countries of capital?

Everyone who ponders the meaning of the present struggle for peace and against thermonuclear war understands that the Soviet Communists and the fraternal parties of the other socialist countries are by their policy of peace rendering invaluable aid to the working class, the working people of the capitalist countries. And this is not a matter solely of averting a nuclear war—that is, of saving from destruction the working class, the peoples of entire countries and even continents—although this in itself is enough to justify our whole policy.

Beyond that, such a policy is the best means of helping the international revolutionary workers' movement in achieving its basic class goals. And indeed, is it not an enormous contribution to the working-class struggle when the countries of socialism, in the conditions of peace they themselves have won, are achieving remarkable successes in the development of the economy, are achieving newer and newer victories in science and technology, are constantly improving the living and working conditions of the people and are developing and perfecting socialist democracy?

Looking at these successes and victories, each worker in a capitalist country will say: "Socialism is proving by deeds that it is better than capitalism. This is a system worth fighting for." In present conditions, socialism is conquering the hearts and minds of people not just through books but primarily by its deeds, by its living example.

The 1960 Statement sees the chief distinguishing feature of our time to be that the world socialist system is becoming the decisive factor in the development of human society. All the Communist Parties participating in the conference arrived at the common conclusion that at the center of the modern era stand the international working class and its offspring, the world system of socialism.

The solution of all the other tasks of the revolutionary movement depends in enormous measure on the consolidation of the world system of socialism. Therefore the Communist and Workers' Parties have pledged themselves *"to strengthen tirelessly the great socialist commonwealth of peoples whose international role and influence on the course of world events grow every year."* Our party sees in the fulfillment of this most important task its supreme internationalist duty.

V. I. Lenin taught that ". . . *we exert our chief influence on international revolution through our economic policy. . . . In this area the struggle is transferred to a worldwide scale. Once we accomplish this task we shall win on an international scale once and for all"* ("Works" [in Russian], Vol. XXII, p. 413).

This behest of the great Lenin has been firmly assimilated by Soviet Communists and is being followed by the Communists of the other countries of socialism. But now it turns out that there are comrades who have decided that V. I. Lenin was wrong.

What is this—a lack of faith in the ability of the countries of socialism to defeat capitalism in economic competition? Or is this the position of people who, having encountered difficulties in building socialism, have become disenchanted, do not see the possibility of exerting the chief influence on the international revolutionary movement through their economic successes, through the example of the successful construction of socialism in their own countries? They want to reach the revolution sooner, by other, what seem to them shorter, routes. But a victorious revolution can consolidate and develop its successes, can prove the superiority of socialism over capitalism, by the labor and only by the labor of the people. True, this is not easy, especially if the revolutions are accomplished in countries that have inherited an underdeveloped economy. But the example of the Soviet Union and many other socialist countries convincingly demonstrates that even under these conditions, if there is correct leadership, it is possible to achieve great successes and show the entire world the superiority of socialism over capitalism.

Further, which conditions are more advantageous for the revolutionary struggle of the working class of the capitalist countries—conditions of peace and peaceful coexistence, or conditions of constant international tension and "cold war?"

There can be no doubt as to the answer to this question. Who does not know that the ruling circles of the imperialist states are utilizing the "cold war" setting to inflame chauvinism, war hysteria and shameless anticommunism, to place in power the most rabid reactionaries and profascists, to abolish democracy, to do away with political parties, trade unions and other mass organizations of the working class?

The Communists' struggle for peace vastly strengthens their ties with the masses, their authority and influence, and thereby helps to create what is called the political army of the revolution.

The struggle for peace and the peaceful coexistence of states with different social systems does not in the least delay, does not postpone, but on the contrary provides the opportunity for developing in full measure the struggle for the achievement of the ultimate goals of the international working class.

4. TOYNBEE'S VIEW OF THE POSSIBILITIES OF PEACEFUL COEXISTENCE

The following position is taken from an article written by the well-known British historian, Arnold J. Toynbee [43] in *The New York Times Magazine,* July 24, 1955, entitled "The Question: Can Russia Really Change?"

. . . Can the present indications of a change on the Russian side signify something more than a mere political maneuver? Is it reasonable to hope that, this time, a more sincere and more durable change may be on the way? Can the Soviet Government make a genuine change in its policy without repudiating

43 © 1955 by The New York Times Company. Reprinted by permission of the publisher and author.

some of the fundamental tenets of Marxism? These are some of the questions that we have to ask ourselves. I will give the gist of my own answer at once, before explaining how I arrive at it.

It seems to me unlikely that any of the fundamental tenets of Marxism will be, or could be, repudiated in a country in which this ideology has been the officially established faith now for nearly forty years. At the same time, it seems to me possible that a sincere and durable change in Russian policy may be on the way. This seems possible because there have been cases in the past in which hallowed tenets have unavowedly been put into cold storage.

Let me illustrate what I mean by taking two familiar examples.

One of the tenets of Islam is that the Islamic world is in a permanent state of war with the non-Islamic world, and that this war is a holy war because the conquest of hitherto non-Moslem countries is the Moslems' religious duty. One of the tenets of the Roman Catholic Church is that, in carrying out its mission to bring all mankind into its fold, it ought to call in the aid of the secular arm, when the secular arm is willing to put its force at the church's purpose. Today, both these tenets are, in practice, "dead letters." We no longer worry about them, as we are worrying now about the tenets of Marxism.

But, in the days before Marx was born, the waging of the Holy War and the invocation of the secular arm were as great a menace to "unbelievers" as the Marxian world revolution has been to "capitalists" in our time.

Vienna was besieged by the Turks no longer ago than 1683. The Edict of Nantes was revoked by Louis XIV no longer ago than 1685. What has happened since the Sixteen Eighties to two tenets that, as recently as the seventeenth century, were still capable of setting the world in a blaze?

So far as I know, neither tenet has ever been repudiated by the official custodians of the faith. If, in 1955, one were to ask a doctor of the Islamic law whether the jihad [Holy War] was still incumbent on Moslems, I believe he would be bound to reply that it was. If one were to ask a Roman Catholic theologian whether it was still the church's duty to invoke the secular arm, I suspect that it might be difficult for him to reply that it was not.

There have, in fact, quite recently been sporadic examples of the persecution of Protestants being supported, or at any rate being countenanced, by the Government of a Catholic country, and of the jihad being waged by a Moslem people. It was waged, for example, by the Sudanese from 1882 to 1898.

These local outbreaks show that there are still people who believe in trying to propagate a religion by force. They believe in this with sufficient conviction to act on it.

All the same, these latterday outbreaks of Christian and Moslem fanaticism do not keep us awake at night. We take them calmly, because we feel sure that, in our time, the great majority of Moslems and Christians are not going to take up arms in the cause of religion, as they have done so often in the past. . . .

So we feel ourselves safe from a peril that haunted our seventeenth-century ancestors. Our confidence is founded on guesswork. It might be difficult for us to prove that we had appreciated the position correctly. Yet our common sense would reject the suggestion that the Islamic Holy War is one of the major perils of the twentieth century. . . .

Is it not conceivable that the Marxian doctrine of the World Revolution may go the same way as the Islamic doctrine of the Holy War? It may never be repudiated. It may still be cherished by some fanatics. But it may become a "dead letter," all the same. The power and the will to apply it on the grand scale may vanish, "softly and silently," like Lewis Carroll's snark.

Let us try to assess the forces in the Soviet Union that are working for and against a genuine change in Soviet policy.

The greatest force working for a change is surely the Soviet Union's need to give first place to its own vital interests. Ever since the Bolsheviks seized power in 1917, there has been a tension in the Soviet Union between Russia's interests and communism's. Is Russia to be communism's tool, or communism to be Russia's? This was the issue between Trotsky and Stalin, and, in that round, Russia's interests won.

It is one of the ironies of the situation that the issue becomes acute when another great country, besides Russia, is converted to communism by Russian efforts.

This problem would have confronted the Kremlin in 1923 if Germany had gone Communist in that year, and it confronts the Kremlin now, since China did go Communist after 1945. What does it profit Russia to spend her resources on building up the strength of another great Communist country that might repay Russia, one day, by snatching from her the leadership of the Communist world?

Perhaps this risk might be worth running for the sake of acquiring a first-class ally. But what profit is there in an alliance if it is going to lead to an atomic war in which everybody is going to be wiped out? The Soviet Union needs all its resources for its own development. Like the United States in the nineteenth century, the Soviet Union has a subcontinent to open up.

But, unlike nineteenth-century America, twentieth-century Russia cannot borrow resources from abroad. Her fidelity to Marxism has ruled out that. The Soviet Union has to depend on herself; and this makes it all the more irksome for her to lend Russian resources for developing other underdeveloped Communist countries.

The Soviet Union's forced march to catch up with the West in technology and industrialization is arduous enough in itself. The whole enterprise is a tour de force. If important parts of it have miscarried, that would not be surprising or discreditable. But it would mean that Russia now had two urgent needs.

One of her needs would be to husband her resources for her own development. Another of her needs would be peace, to give her a chance of repairing the miscarriages and carrying the enterprise through to completion. This looks like a powerful force in favor of a genuine change in foreign policy.

There is an allied force working in the same direction. Industrialization is the Soviet Government's aim. You cannot industrialize a primitive peasant country without calling a new class of workers into existence. You must have plenty of managers, designers and engineers, and you must have trained foremen and skilled technicians in vast numbers.

You must not only have them; you must have them doing their work effectively; and you cannot get this kind of work out of human beings by the brutal methods that are effective (more or less) for making a galley slave row or a plantation slave hoe. Skilled work cannot be exacted by force; it has to be coaxed out of people by inducements.

So the Soviet Government has a choice. It can cling to the Russian governmental tradition of coercion at the cost of falling behind in the technological race; or it can go ahead with technology at the cost of giving its technicians the modicum of freedom without which they will not do what is wanted of them. This looks like a powerful force in favor of a genuine change in domestic policy. But domestic policy and foreign policy cannot be kept in separate water-tight compartments nowadays.

Of course, there are also forces working the other way. Doctrinaire Marxism is, no doubt, still a living force in the Kremlin. But in a seat of government an ideology must surely be a wasting asset. Academic doctrine is a diet for political exiles. They have to live on it as a medieval chameleon lived on air. But as soon as the Bolsheviks were translated from the British Museum Reading Room to the Kremlin, they found other fare to live on and other things to think about.

The first concern of every Government in power is to keep itself going. If ideology gets in the way of *raison d'état,* so much the worse for ideology. If this diagnosis is correct, we may expect to see doctrinaire Marxism fight a stubborn rearguard action in Russia but fail, in Russia, to hold its own.

An ideology's everlasting mansions are not to be found in a converted country. . . . Doctrinaire Marxism is likely to survive in Bloomsbury and Greenwich Village longer than in Moscow or Peiping.

Another force in Russia that might work against a change of policy is the traditional Muscovite appetite for the acquisition of more territory. This is a force with a formidable momentum, for it has been at work since the fourteenth century.

For six hundred years the Muscovite grain of mustard seed has been steadily growing into the tree that now overshadows the earth. The Muscovite empire has spread from the suburbs of Moscow to the Bering Straits and the Pamirs and the Oder-Neisse Line. Can the men of the Kremlin break this inveterate habit of adding field to field?

Undoubtedly this might have been difficult if Russia had remained the peasant country that she used to be. But a government that already possesses a great estate and that has decided to go in for industrialization is perhaps likely to give priority to the development of its existing assets. Twentieth-century Russia, like nineteenth-century America, may be inclined to turn her attention inward to the exploitation of her own subcontinent.

These are, perhaps, some of the more obvious pros and cons. An analysis of them will not give us any conclusive answer to our question. We shall still be left guessing; and, in dealing with the Russians in this critical year, we shall therefore be feeling our way in the twilight, as human beings have to do in so many episodes of practical life, public and private.

At any rate, the situation today is not analogous to the situation in the Nineteen Thirties. Unlike Nazi Germany, the Soviet Union does not need *Lebensraum.* It is not faced with a choice between war and downfall. And, in the atomic age, war could no longer bring victory either to the Soviet Union or to any other belligerent. It could bring nothing but annihilation for us all.

In these circumstances, it is evidently possible that Russian policy may have changed bona fide. The West's decision to explore this possibility must surely be right.

5. THE UNITED NATIONS PROGRAM OF COLLECTIVE SECURITY IS IMPRACTICAL AND IS BASED UPON UNSOUND ASSUMPTIONS

The following position is that of Hans J. Morgenthau. Professor Morgenthau does not question the theory of collective security, but he strongly criticizes its basic assumptions.[44]

In a working system of collective security the problem of security is no longer the concern of the individual nation, to be taken care of by armaments and other elements of national power. Security becomes the concern of all nations, which will take care collectively of the security of each of them as though their own security were threatened. . . . One for all and all for one is the watchword of collective security.

We have already pointed out that the logic of collective security is flawless, provided it can be made to work under the conditions prevailing on the international scene. For collective security to operate as a device for the prevention of war, three assumptions must be fulfilled: (1) the collective system must be able to muster at all times such overwhelming strength against any potential aggressor or coalition of aggressors that the latter would never dare to challenge the order defended by the collective system; (2) at least those nations whose combined strength would meet the requirement under (1) must have the same conception of security which they are supposed to defend; (3) those nations must be willing to subordinate whatever conflicting political interests may still separate them to the common good defined in terms of the collective defense of all member states.

It is conceivable that all these assumptions may be realized in a particular situation. The odds, however, are strongly against such a possibility. There is nothing in past experience and in the general nature of international politics to suggest that such a situation is likely to occur. It is indeed true that, under present conditions of warfare no less than under those of the past, no single country is strong enough to defy a combination of all the other nations with any chance for success. Yet it is extremely unlikely that in an actual situation only one single country would be found in the position of the aggressor. Generally, more than one country will actively oppose the order collective security tries to defend, and other countries will be in sympathy with that opposition.

The reason for this situation lies in the character of the order defended by collective security. That order is of necessity the status quo as it exists at a particular moment. Thus the collective security of the League of Nations aimed necessarily at the preservation of the territorial status quo as it existed when the League of Nations was established in 1919. But in 1919 there were already a number of nations strongly opposed to that territorial status quo—the nations defeated in the First World War, as well as Italy, which felt itself despoiled of some of the promised fruits of victory. Other nations, such as the United States

[44] From *Politics Among Nations*, second edition, by Hans J. Morgenthau, pp. 388–393. Copyright, 1948, 1954, by Alfred A. Knopf, Inc. Reprinted by permission. Professor Morgenthau's position remained unchanged in the 4th (1967) edition of *Politics Among Nations*, pp. 397–402.

and the Soviet Union, were at best indifferent toward the status quo. For France and its allies, who were the main beneficiaries of the status quo of 1919 and most anxious to defend it by means of collective security, security meant the defense of the frontiers as they had been established by the peace treaties of 1919, and the perpetuation of their predominance on the continent of Europe. Security for the dissatisfied nations meant the exact opposite: the rectification of those frontiers and a general increase in their power relative to France and its allies.

This grouping of nations into those in favor of the status quo and those opposed to it is not at all peculiar to the period after the First World War. It is, as we know, the elemental pattern of international politics. As such it recurs in all periods of history. Through the antagonism between status quo and imperialistic nations it provides the dynamics of the historic process. This antagonism is resolved either in compromise or in war. Only under the assumption that the struggle for power as the moving force of international politics might subside or be superseded by a higher principle can collective security have a chance for success. Since, however, nothing in the reality of international affairs corresponds to that assumption, the attempt to freeze the particular status quo by means of collective security is in the long run doomed to failure. In the short run collective security may succeed in safeguarding a particular status quo because of the temporary weakness of the opponents. Its failure to succeed in the long run is due to the absence of the third assumption upon which we have predicated the success of collective security.

In the light of historic experience and the actual nature of international politics, we must assume that conflicts of interest will continue on the international scene. No nation or combination of nations, however strong and devoted to international law, can afford to oppose by means of collective security all aggression at all times, regardless of by whom and against whom it may be committed. The United States and the United Nations came to the aid of South Korea when it was attacked in 1950 because they had the strength and interest to do so. Would they make themselves again the champions of collective security if tomorrow Indonesia should be the victim of aggression, or Chile, or Egypt? What would the United States and the United Nations do if two different aggressors should start marching at the same time? Would they oppose these two aggressors indiscriminately, without regard for the interests involved and the power available, and would they refuse to violate the principles of collective security and refrain from taking on only the one who was either more dangerous or easier to handle? And if tomorrow South Korea should turn the tables and commit an act of aggression against North Korea or Communist China, would the United States and the United Nations then turn around and fight South Korea?

The answer is bound to be either "No," as in the last-mentioned hypothetical case, or a question mark. Yet according to the principles of collective security, the answer ought to be unqualified "Yes." These principles require collective measures against all aggression, regardless of circumstances of power and interest. The principles of foreign policy require discrimination among different kinds of aggressions and aggressors, according to the circumstances of power and interest. Collective security as an ideal is directed against all aggression in the abstract; foreign policy can only operate against a particular concrete aggressor. The only question collective security is allowed to ask is "Who has committed aggression?" Foreign policy cannot help asking: "What interest do I have in opposing this particular aggressor, and what power do I have with which to oppose him?"

. . . In other words, what collective security demands of the individual nations is to forsake national egotisms and the national policies serving them. Collective security expects the policies of the individual nations to be inspired by the ideal of mutual assistance and a spirit of self-sacrifice which will not shrink even from the supreme sacrifice of war should it be required by that ideal.

This third assumption is really tantamount to the assumption of a moral revolution infinitely more fundamental than any moral change that has occurred in the history of Western civilization. . . .

Men generally do not feel and act, whether as individuals among themselves or as members of their nations with regard to other nations, as they ought to feel and act if collective security is to succeed. And there is, as we have tried to show, less chance today than there has been at any time in modern history that they would act in conformity with moral precepts of a supranational character if such action might be detrimental to the interests of their respective countries. . . .

In the light of this discussion, we must conclude that collective security cannot be made to work in the contemporary world as it must work according to its ideal assumptions. Yet it is the supreme paradox of collective security that any attempt to make it work with less than ideal perfection will have the opposite effect from what it is supposed to achieve. It is the purpose of collective security to make war impossible by marshaling in defense of the status quo such overwhelming strength that no nation will dare to resort to force in order to change the status quo. But the less ideal are the conditions for making collective security work, the less formidable will be the combined strength of the nations willing to defend the status quo. If an appreciable number of nations are opposed to the status quo and if they are unwilling to give the common good, as defined in terms of collective security, precedence over their opposition, the distribution of power between the status quo and anti-status quo nations will no longer be overwhelmingly in favor of the former. Rather the distribution of power will take on the aspects of a balance of power which may still favor the status quo nations, but no longer to such an extent as to operate as an absolute deterrent upon those opposed to the status quo.

The attempt to put collective security into effect under such conditions—which are, as we know, the only conditions under which it can be put into effect—will not preserve peace, but will make war inevitable. And not only will it make war inevitable, it will also make localized wars impossible and thus make war universal. . . .

By the very logic of its assumptions, the diplomacy of collective security must aim at transforming all local conflicts into world conflicts. If this cannot be one world of peace, it cannot help being one world of war. Since peace is supposed to be indivisible, it follows that war is indivisible, too. Under the assumptions of collective security, any war anywhere in the world, then, is potentially a world war. Thus a device intent upon making war impossible ends by making war universal. Instead of preserving peace between two nations, collective security, as it must actually operate in the contemporary world, is bound to destroy peace among all nations.

6. THE UNITED NATIONS HAS BEEN THE DECISIVE FACTOR FOR PEACE SINCE WORLD WAR II

The following position is taken from the book, *UN: The First Twenty Years,* by Clark M. Eichelberger. The author is Executive Director of the United Nations Association of the United States of America. The book was written on the occasion of the twentieth anniversary of the founding of the United Nations and represents an appraisal of the world organization's work up to that time.[45]

The last twenty years have been years of unparalleled change, danger, defeat, and bold adventure. Scientific horizons have been penetrated. A great part of the world has won its political independence. An effort is being made to provide a society of abundance for all mankind.

At the same time, many efforts at improvement were chilled by the paralyzing effect of Communism, which, at least for the first ten years after the war, continues to expand. The problem was made even more difficult by the fact that the Soviet Union made the first foray into outer space.

What has kept the peace in these fantastic years? The Marshall Plan? It saved the West from bankruptcy. NATO? It may well have saved Western Europe from invasion. The Organization of American States? Certainly it continued to keep the protective mantle of the Monroe Doctrine around the nations of the southern part of the Western Hemisphere. The Baghdad Pact and the Eisenhower Doctrine? Their beneficial effects are questionable. The nuclear stalemate? Here is the peace of fear, for each side in the bipolarized world knows that an initiative on its part would be met by instant retaliation and the destruction of all.

However, the decisive factor for world peace has been the United Nations. It has made the difference between the uneasy peace in which the world has lived and a third world war. Every day since the Second World War ended there has been spasmodic fighting somewhere on earth, but these conflicts have not resulted in a third world war. The United Nations has made the difference. It is hard to define the many specific and subtle influences of the United Nations on the side of peace. One phrase, however, may best describe it—"moral unity."

Suppose the nations had entered the atomic age in a world of anarchy. The author knows from interviews with the late President Franklin D. Roosevelt that he feared a repetition of the reaction of 1920 that kept the United States out of the League of Nations. He was determined that at least a provisional United Nations be created before the fighting ended.

What if the United Nations' allies had not carried out President Roosevelt's intention? What if the nations had not formally adopted principles of good conduct with laws against war? Suppose they had not created a common meeting place, with machinery for the peaceful settlement of disputes? Suppose they had not provided a forum in which the peoples dominated by colonialism could petition peacefully for their freedom? Suppose the newly created United Nations and Specialized Agencies had not set in motion a process for the relief of economic and social misery? If these things had not been done, it is doubtful that the world would have survived this long. The changes in the postwar period were so great and so terrible in their potential for destruction that without the unifying force of the United Nations the world might well have destroyed itself.

So far the United Nations has survived one defiance after another, one neglect after another, and has seemingly emerged stronger than ever. Nations may ignore it for a moment, but usually return to it as the only means to meet world problems.

As the third decade of the United Nations opens, one hundred fourteen nations [46] are bound by the obligations of the Charter. More will be so bound in the next few years. The peace of the world is dependent upon their becoming increasingly integrated into an international society by the many bonds that the United Nations provides. It is essential that the moral unity be strengthened every day by devotion and common usage.

The ever-present danger is that the member nations may fragmentize their concerns by alliances and bilateral action, that they may lose the vision of world society. It was so in 1955, in 1960, and it is true in 1965. The United Nations has passed through repeated crises, some of them so serious that commentators predicted the death of the organization. The fourteenth year of the United Nations (1959) closed with the Secretary-General reporting to the Fourteenth General Assembly: "The past year has been characterized by intense diplomatic activities mainly outside the United Nations although in some cases within its precincts or in informal contact with the Organization." The Security Council had had only five meetings in that entire year. There were no emergency meetings of the General Assembly.

The tragic collapse of the Summit Conference between President Eisenhower and Chairman Khrushchev in May, 1960, ended these particular bilateral negotiations outside of the United Nations. The problems of the Congo brought the major attention of the world back to the Security Council.

The United Nations begins its twentieth year with problems equally serious or even more so than those of the previous years. The refusal of some nations to pay their special assessments for United Nations peacekeeping forces threatens the organization with bankruptcy. The African states are in danger of permitting racial hatred to blind them to obligations that they assume as members of the organization. War is raging in the Indochinese peninsula without having been brought to the attention of the United Nations as the Charter obligates. The NATO powers seemingly see no inconsistency in discussing a multilateral nuclear force while the General Assembly and the Geneva Disarmament Conference discuss ways to stop the proliferation of nuclear weapons.

The world will have peace if the sense of moral unity imposed on the

[46] AUTHORS' NOTE: As of early 1967, U.N. membership was 122 nations.

nations by the Charter and the habits of cooperation developed in nineteen years are strong enough to prevail against the forces of fragmentation. The history of the last nineteen years would justify one in believing that the present crisis, too, will pass and the United Nations will emerge with greater physical and moral strength.

SELECT BIBLIOGRAPHY

ASPATURIAN, VERNON V., *The Soviet Union in the World Communist System* (Stanford, Stanford University, 1966). A provocative analysis of the role of the Soviet Union in the world communist system and its failure to evolve successfully as the nucleus for a world communist state. The assertion of Great Russian hegemony within the facade of Soviet federalism and the efforts of Soviet leaders to dominate other Communist Party states have diminished the attractiveness of the Soviet model for a world communist union.

BAILEY, SYDNEY D., *The United Nations* (New York, Praeger, 1963). An excellent introductory analysis of the United Nations, its organization and operation, its major programs and problems, by a British scholar who has had extensive first-hand experience at the United Nations.

CLAUDE, INIS L., JR., *Power and International Relations* (New York, Random House, 1962). An extremely lucid and thought-provoking analysis of the problem of managing power in international relations. The systems of balance of power, collective security, and world government are carefully examined and appraised.

CORDIER, ANDREW W. and FOOTE, WILDER (eds.), *The Quest for Peace* (New York, Columbia University Press, 1965). A series of lectures concerning the United Nations and world problems delivered in various centers of learning around the world as a memorial to the late Secretary General of the United Nations, Dag Hammarskjöld. Many of the eminent contributors worked closely with Mr. Hammarskjöld during his service at the United Nations.

GARDNER, RICHARD N., *In Pursuit of World Order* (New York, Praeger, 1964). A well-written discussion of the work of the United Nations in the various phases of international peace, security, economic and social welfare. Special emphasis is placed on the role of the United States in the United Nations. The author, a Professor of Law at Columbia University, had, at the time of writing this book, been serving for three years as Deputy Assistant Secretary of State for International Organization Affairs.

GROSS, ERNEST A., *The United Nations: Structure for Peace* (New York, Harper, 1962). An excellent interpretation of the role of the United Nations in the maintenance of international peace. The author, who served for several years prior to 1953 as Deputy United States Representative to the United Nations, gives a realistic insight into the workings of the United Nations.

JACOB, PHILIP E., and ATHERTON, ALEXINE L., *The Dynamics of International Organization* (Homewood, Illinois, Dorsey Press, 1965). A comprehensive, problem-oriented text dealing with international organization and world order. It treats both the international institutions and activities to maintain peace and security as well as those concerned with the promotion of economic development and social welfare.

JACOBS, DAN W. (ed.), *The New Communist Manifesto and Related Documents*, 2nd edition (New York, Harper & Row, 1962). A useful collection of documents relating to international communism, including the Communist Manifesto of 1848, Khrushchev's "secret" speech of February, 1956, Mao Tsetung's "Hundred Flowers" speech of 1957, the 1960 Statement of 81 Communist Parties, and the latest (1961) Program of the Soviet Communist Party.

KENNAN, GEORGE, *On Dealing with the Communist World* (New York, Harper & Row, 1964). A readable, stimulating discussion of the feasibility of coexistence with the communist world as compared with the implications of policies designed to destroy that world. The author is a leading American scholar in Soviet studies, and a former United States Ambassador to the Soviet Union and to Yugoslavia.

KHRUSHCHEV, NIKITA S., *For Victory in Peaceful Competition with Capitalism* (New York, Dutton, 1960). A collection of speeches and statements by the former Soviet Premier on international affairs and peaceful coexistence. Useful for providing a better understanding of the Soviet outlook on world affairs.

KISSINGER, HENRY, *The Troubled Partnership* (New York, McGraw-Hill, 1965). A reappraisal of the Atlantic alliance system prepared for the Council on Foreign Relations by a distinguished professor of government at Harvard. The current causes of disunity among NATO members are analyzed, together with the changed nature of the Atlantic system resulting from the decline of American preeminence and the emergence of a stronger, more self-confident Europe. The author feels that the principal danger to the Atlantic alliance lies in the tendency to persist in patterns of action which were appropriate for the period of American preeminence but are unsuited for the new conditions today.

MILLIS, WALTER, and REAL, JAMES, *The Abolition of War* (New York, Macmillan, 1963). A stimulating examination of the factors in international society which make it probable, in the eyes of the authors, that war will be laid aside as a major instrument in world politics. Suggests that the potentially destructive character of nuclear war makes a demilitarized world both necessary and practicable. The task is to make men realize this.

9

Regional International Organization

MOTIVATION

Since the end of World War II, regional international organizations have multiplied rapidly and have attained a cohesion unprecedented in modern history. The two most striking examples are the European Economic Community (EEC) comprising six Western European countries and the Council of Mutual Economic Assistance (COMECON, CMEA), embracing a number of countries of Eastern Europe. At first glance Europe seems to be a rather infertile and hostile ground for experiments in anything more than national organization. For centuries the European continent had been torn by national rivalries that created deep wounds and almost insuperable obstacles to cooperation. The cultural and linguistic differences between nations have had ample time to become accentuated through wars, foreign domination, and mutual persecution to the point where the word "European" meant little beyond a geographical reference. Antagonisms ran deep. Vast income inequalities and the Great Depression made matters worse. To top it all, the savage nationalism of Hitler's Germany unleashed its destructive forces over the length and breadth of the torn continent leaving behind it a legacy of hate and a thirst for revenge.

But there was also weariness and a deeply-felt need to stop the recurring carnage once and for all. What had been done could not be undone, but perhaps steps could be taken to avoid similar mistakes in the future. The weariness and the need were not new—they had been experienced and voiced in the past, apparently without avail. In part the reasons for this failure to do what so clearly needed to be done were due to the inadequacy of the institutions which had been used in the past to bring about international understanding and cooperation. The age-old machinery of diplomacy, the occasional meetings of heads of state, pious treaties of friendship and nonaggression had broken down in the face of ardent, militant, unyielding nationalism and the expansionist urges of unscrupulous demagogues. Europe, which possessed a twentieth-century capacity for self-destruction, conducted its social and political affairs with the tools of the sixteenth. The institutions of international law and order were no more than deliberative and advisory bodies. They set down rules of international conduct, but had not the power to enforce them. And even these rules were often just polite compromises, watered-down versions of meaningful original drafts, diluted to cater to the objections of this or that sovereign member. Europe before 1939 was like a great city without municipal government. The individual homes were highly organized (often on the basis of uncompromising paternalism), but confusion and terror reigned in the streets.

Hitlerism embodied in the power of an advanced industrial state was merely the extreme manifestation of that disorder. It brought untold suffering to millions of innocent men, women, and children. It killed six million Jews, four million Poles, and close to twenty million Russians. It divided the human species into the human and the subhuman on the basis of hair texture, facial features, and national origin. The subhumans were marked for destruction in a speedy, clean, and scientific way; no mess, no fuss, and no disruption of orderly process. It bullied and threatened, despised, tortured, and hated. It imposed on masses of faithful followers caught in the euphoria of power and success a willful ignorance, a surrender of self and self-respect that were not matched even by the *Homo Sovieticus* of Stalin's bloody reign. It showed how thin was the veneer of culture, how skin deep the thousand-year civilization. It stamped men with fear and distrust and suspicion. It was the dregs of society's gutter come to the top, raised to the rank of national principle and tasted with delight by many till the very moment of truth. Its most concentrated cruelty was reserved for Eastern Europe, where it ravaged and pillaged and wallowed in a blood bath that will not be forgotten for many generations. To ignore the legacy of Hitlerism is to misunderstand just about 90 percent of contemporary political history of Eastern Europe and to endow Soviet Russia and her brand of communism with a power and cunning they do not possess. The fear of Germany is a fact of Eastern European life besides which the excesses of local communist leaders fade into insignificance.

It is against this background that, when peace came, a few men of vision tried to build anew, on foundations more solid and more stable than those that had collapsed under the oppressive weight of the immediate past. It was a Herculean task, and the end is not in sight. The first motivation for this work of reconstruction and reorganization of international relations in Europe's own backyard was, therefore, to prevent the future from repeating the horrors of the past. The second and third were common defense and joint economic construction. Before saying more under those headings a few marginal remarks on the nature of cooperation are in order.

COOPERATION AND INTEGRATION

COOPERATION

In the present state of international relations the way out of disunion and the wayward wanderings of exclusive, hermetically closed national units can take two main forms: that of cooperation between sovereign national entities and that of fusion or integration. The former is the time-sanctioned manner of tackling the problem. It has shown itself to be not overly effective in preventing repeated outbursts of collective anger and hysteria. International cooperation, as the name implies, is the building of a few bridges between national units. The existence of ravines of disagreement is explicitly recognized—hence the bridges. The persistence of forms of national organization is equally admitted. In fact, the nation-state is taken as the starting point, the basic assumption. It is because the interests and objectives of nation-states tend on occasion to clash that the bridges are needed. These bridges, institutionalized in periodic meetings of heads of state, joint consultative assemblies, diplomatic get-togethers and the like, are really arrangements whereby conflicting points of view get a chance of being discussed across the conference table rather than over the cadavers of former combatants. It is a nice, civilized way of settling disputes on a distinguished-person-to-distinguished-person basis, and it may even lead to lasting personal friendships between those who have savored the joys and the sorrows of the round table. It has its merits. It recognizes the existence of real disagreements and acknowledges the validity of the sources of tension. Since in the present constellation of world forces these disagreements tend to have a national origin, its appeal is precisely in that it refuses to blind itself to the fact that in the course of centuries, political, social, and economic contacts between men had evolved from the intimate stage of person to individual person, to state and state, and that the state is not just an aberration but a valid and often useful cultural, ethnic, linguistic, and temperamental association of people. Some states are, of course, less closely knit than others, but not, for all that, less chauvinistic. In fact, their chauvinism, their need for self-identification and self-assertion, tends to be in inverse ratio to their national age and in direct ratio to past nationalist frustrations.

As a matter of historical record, the states of Eastern Europe have been in times past switched and shunted like boxcars. Nationalist feelings, repressed and denied for generations, run deep. Under the stress of events, cooperation at the state level had in recent years proceeded slowly, often painfully, always against a background of distrust and fearful hesitation. Since "liberation," the peoples and leaders of the Eastern European countries have been told repeatedly, and told by Moscow, that they are now the citizens of one big ideological fraternity, Marxist-Leninists one and all, the East Germans and the Poles, the Czechs and the

Slovaks, the Magyars and the Rumanians. They had, they were further told, one common foe: bourgeois imperialism, the rapacious capitalists— German, French, American, no matter. But if Budapest, Warsaw, and East Berlin are any indication, they continued to think that the Russians in Soviet dressing were still national poison, just like the Russians of the Tsars. And while about it, they had built over the years little iron curtains along their national frontiers. In Stalin's time and long after his death, it was as difficult for a Czech to cross the political-ideological border to West Germany as it was for him to get to fraternal Poland. East German troops are still not welcome on Polish territory in spite of ritualistic public political embracings and leadership kisses on both cheeks. Flowers in the Soviet manner do not yet friendships make. But the flowers and the handshakes and the comings and goings of Party and State officials, the endless conferences and committees, the congresses, treaties, and agreements, the ayes and noes with the leaders, the orchestrated applause, the joint statements and pledges, and the fraternal greetings are symptoms of cooperation, attempts to build bridges over gulfs of incomprehension and distrust. And yet, if questioned in the relative privacy of their cramped homes, the citizens of Eastern Europe's nation-states still think of all this feverish activity as something rather distant and unreal. If "they" want to do it, let them—that is what "they" are for. As for real issues, there are plenty close at hand: a bigger apartment, with running water if possible, and fresh vegetables in winter.

The trouble with old-fashioned cooperation is that it always seems so distant, that it never somehow filters down to the level of individual daily life. It is something in the papers or on the radio or in the movies on a Saturday night just before the real program begins. In the absence of bridges, life does indeed get disrupted. But when you pass over them every day, you do not stop to weave elaborate theories about them.

INTEGRATION

Integration is something else again. It implies the pooling of sovereignties, the surrender of strategic political and economic decision-making powers to a supranational body. It means the gradual transformation of individual nation-states into a larger political and economic organization and the vesting in it of the prerogatives formerly exercised at the state level.

Where the integration of previously separate states or peoples has taken place on the basis of consent, it has usually been based on the principles of federalism, drawing its inspiration from the American or Swiss model. Federalism involves the establishment of centralized institutions which take over various key powers in areas of concern to the state as a whole, such as defense or foreign commerce. In the long run, federalism assumes the yielding of unlimited sovereignty by nation-states, the acceptance of a kind of intermediate-level sovereignty over purely national and local matters, and the emergence of some form of superstate of world-wide or continental proportions with supreme authority to prevent violent conflicts between its constituent units.

Integration is not historically new, although it has in past centuries more often been based on conquest rather than consent and has taken the form of empires rather than federations. Because the experience of empires has not always been a happy one, the legacy of imperialism weighs heavily on modern attempts at integration, even when done on a voluntary basis. There is the ever-present anxiety about who will eventually dominate the federated authority. Even though all the integrated members are theoretically equal, history shows that for various reasons some tend to be more equal than others. Much steam was taken out of the Western European drive toward integration by the suspicion prevalent among some participants that an integrated Europe would tend to be dominated by Western Germany, a possibility not especially appealing to those who had had the mischance of living through two world wars. Some more zip was taken out of the integration movement by the thinly disguised attempt of France to do that very thing, a maneuver which, if successful, would be a source of serious worry to those who harbor misgivings about France's inherent capacity for political stability and the will behind her military deterrent. In Eastern Europe, shared ideology notwithstanding, efforts at integration have been time and again blocked by the timid but obstinate reservations of local national communists about the ultimate locus of leadership. The economically poorer potential members of the socialist commonwealth have argued that hasty integration would subject them to the command of the economically more advanced. Since Eastern Germany and the Soviet Union are among the latter, there is much understandable dragging of feet. Yugoslavia was the first to voice these premonitions at a time when Soviet thinking ran more along autarchic and imperial lines. After 1956, stepped-up attempts at integration based on the principle of equality met with redoubled hesitations. In the Albanian *cahier de doléances* (list of complaints) there are long passages about alleged Soviet "new colonialism"; and the Rumanians, even though in the Soviet camp, give all indications that they think the Albanians have a point.[1]

REGIONALISM

Where cooperation has moved beyond bridge building, it has done so on a regional level. There are indeed those whose federalist philosophy embraces the whole world (United World Federalists), but it must be

[1] Jan S. Prybyla, "The Economic Causes of the Soviet-Albanian Quarrel," *Bulletin of the Institute for the Study of the U.S.S.R.*, March, 1963, pp. 11–19.

said in all fairness that even the most ardent among them have few illusions about the feasibility of their project in anything but a dim future. The practical obstacles in the way of world political and economic integration are real and formidable. They are not just blindness and ill will, but are rooted in the belief that there does not yet exist a sufficient level of consensus among the nation-states of the world to accept any comprehensive system of world law or government in place of the existing national systems of defense and security. The best that can be hoped for is some kind of agreement on traffic rules to minimize collisions and keep the more reckless drivers off the world's political highways. But on a more modest scale, the dream of venturing beyond cooperation into the unexplored regions of integration is not as wild as some would have it. In fact, it verges on the feasible. It is not easy, but it can be done. It is not political mythology but politics—the art of the possible.

The regions are usually defined by political and economic considerations rather than pure geography. Europe, for instance, stretches geographically from the Atlantic to the Ural Mountains, yet for all practical purposes there are at present two very distinct and very different Europes. Western Europe includes geographically eastern Greece and non-European Turkey. Eastern Europe has in it such very Western cities as Prague, Budapest, and Warsaw. The concept is quite obviously political and in cold war language is often referred to as the "free" and the "communist" or, when originating on the other side, as "capitalist" and "democratic." Economically, Western Europe has its inner six and outer seven, besides those who are neither of the sixes nor the sevens. Geographically, the Soviet Union is mostly an Asian land, yet the Chinese, for reasons of their own, choose to see it as a distinctly European, white power.

The present regional organization of Europe dates back to the immediate post-World War II years, and more will be said about that later. The point being made here is simply that regional organization is feasible precisely because it corresponds to certain commonly felt political needs and economic demands. These needs and demands, of course, change over time, and by this very fact make the course of regional organization uncertain. One more point should be made at this stage. Recent history seems to show that there is nothing like an acutely felt common threat to make countries crowd together. But, at the same time, common threats are not enough. There is also the need for a friendly prod from a richer and more powerful ally. It is no exaggeration to say that the idea of Western European unification is as much the brainchild of the Europeans as of the Americans. Were it not for gentle but firm American prodding in the years following World War II, Europe would very probably have gone its merry nation-state way for decades to come. The prod was economic and political: a promise of material aid and of defense on the clear condition that the Europeans get together, stop squabbling, and start building jointly. As Europe's war-caused poverty declined and her military capability increased, American influence waned. The initial impetus was, however, sufficient to keep the unification idea alive.

For a time it was vigorous and promising, but from overindulgence in the material comforts of life and overconfidence, it grew sluggish and its health suffered. Today it is in a state of crisis, torn between the temptation to return to the old, tried, if not always promising ways, and the desire to move ahead into new, largely unexplored, and uncertain fields. The provincialism which for centuries marked the nation-state mentality has imperceptibly crept into the philosophy of federalism. The inner six are jealous of the outer seven, and all thirteen grow touchy at the mention of links across the Atlantic. Organizationally, Europe has always tended to turn inward, and now the habit has been multiplied by thirteen. For those who think regional integration represents a progressive political and economic idea, all hope is not lost. It was said earlier that economic forces, though by no means the most important in shaping men's lives, are without a doubt the most powerful. Although there may be no such thing as a scientifically ascertainable law of the dynamics of history, there is the very real and measurable principle of economies of scale. As early as 1776, Adam Smith formulated it in his "division of labor is limited by the extent of the market." Like it or not, the state of modern technology and the direction in which that technology is moving require large economic units. Now, rising expectations are not restricted to the citizens of the developing countries. Because they appear more attainable and because many of the benefits of modern economic systems have, in fact, been tasted by the peoples of Western Europe (and increasingly by those of Eastern Europe, too), there is a growing impatience with those ideas which, when translated into policy, retard the process of mass and high consumption. Among such ideas is narrow economic nationalism. The facts of the matter are that many of the material things that the peoples of Europe want are attainable only through an enlargement of the market, the pooling of resources, and bold social experimentation. Philosophers may disagree on the moral and ethical validity of such expectations, but the great mass of those who hurry and scurry through life in pursuit of less lofty ideals does not exhibit such qualms.

Such regional organization as the Eastern Europeans have so far developed is also largely due to pressures from outside. Considerations of common defense came first, the demands of economic rationality a little later. Behind both was the Soviet Union.

ECONOMIC PRESSURE

Between the two world wars, especially in the thirties, Europe, with an exception or two, was a patchwork of trade restrictions, economic retaliations, tariffs, quotas, and payments regulations. Economic and political boundaries coincided, and self-sufficiency was the rule. The only serious attempts to stop the process of economic disintegration were the Belgium-Luxembourg Economic Union of 1922 and the 1933 London World Economic and Financial Conference held in the deepening shadow of the Great Depression. The Conference ended in total failure.

After the war, and until 1947, little progress was made to end the prewar atomization of Europe's economic life. In fact, by 1947, a new factor—the growing hostility between the West and the U.S.S.R.—threatened to bring about new divisions, as it in fact did. From 1945 to 1947, reconstruction in both East and West proceeded on a national level and made relatively little headway. The old tools of reparations payments began to be used all over again, bringing into play ancient hostilities and promising acute problems for future years. The Soviet Union, for one, pursued a frankly colonialist policy toward its beaten opponents in Eastern Europe: it extracted heavy reparations payments from East Germany, Bulgaria, Rumania, and Hungary, incorporated into its territory vast stretches of Poland and Rumania (something that the Rumanians are now discreetly protesting), swallowed up the Baltic countries once again, and carried away from friends and former foes alike what its soldiers and railroads could carry. Joint stock companies were formed in East Germany, Rumania, Hungary, Bulgaria, China, Albania, and Czechoslovakia in which the Soviets had a controlling interest, to which they contributed little beyond the "enemy capital" already there, and which exercised effective control over the key sectors of the economies in almost all Eastern European countries. Moreover, beginning in 1948, the Soviet Stalinist model of economic development and the Soviet Stalinist forms of economic organization were adopted by every Eastern European country except Yugoslavia. Even in Yugoslavia, however, the political organization of Party and State followed the Soviet example. On the face of it, by 1948 Eastern Europe had a number of common features which might have seemed capable of promoting economic cooperation of more than a purely formal, state-based kind. The opposite was nearer the mark. Economic integration is not advanced merely because everyone is pumped by the same fraternal power. Moreover, as we have seen in Chapter 7, the Stalinist Soviet economic model was essentially one of autarchic growth. What did, in fact, happen was that from 1948 on, the countries of Eastern Europe began to build, each behind closed doors, many little replicas of the closed Soviet model. Instead of eight jealous little countries, there came into being eight jealous little Soviet Unions, each with its own heavy industry and its own problem-ridden agriculture. Contacts between them were ideological (at the leadership level). Economically, the channels of communication were bilateral and took the form of strictly balanced commodity exchanges. Multilateralism was regarded as a bourgeois prejudice incompatible with Stalin's interpretation of proletarian internationalism.

The steadily mounting disagreement between the West and the Soviet Union finally came into the open in 1947–1948. From then on all hope of creating a comprehensive European union became pious yearning in the future conditional. The nations of Western Europe and those of the European East henceforth turned their attention to the possibility of establishing some sort of closer economic cooperation, perhaps even integration, within the boundaries delimited by political and ideological conflict.

THE MARSHALL PLAN, OEEC, OECD, ECA, NATO, WEU

The iron curtain which descended on Europe after 1948 made economic reconstruction the more urgent. From the Soviet standpoint the curtain was necessary to isolate from "capitalist" influences the countries of what began to be called the "socialist camp." Within that camp the Stalinist strategy of economic development and Soviet-type social and political institutions could henceforth be installed without fear of international embarrassment or interference. The era of forced growth began. There can be little doubt that from the very beginning the Soviets had no intention of letting their plans for the socialist transformation of their newly acquired sphere of influence be diluted by participation in non-socialist economic organizations that went beyond the old type cooperation (or what we have earlier called bridge-building). As soon as economic integration schemes began to take hold in the West, the Russians literally ordered the Eastern Europeans to cease and desist. The Stalinist method, it must be remembered, was socialism in one country. After 1945, the doctrine simply became socialism in one country multiplied by as many countries as there happened to be in the Soviet sphere of political influence.

That the idea of economic integration did take hold in the West by 1947 is clear from the Western European response to Secretary George Marshall's June 5, 1947, Harvard speech in which he urged all European countries to draft a plan for joint economic action to speed up economic recovery. True, the Secretary's invitation might well have fallen on deaf ears had it not been for one very practical fact. The United States, Mr. Marshall assured the Europeans, would underwrite such joint efforts in a convincingly tangible manner. If the Europeans could only forget their differences, cast aside their age-old propensity to nationally turn inward in times of peril, and get together for a heart-to-heart economic talk, the vast resources of the United States would be tapped, and tapped generously, in support of joint European recovery. Specifically each European country was asked to draw up a plan for economic reconstruction, estimate the resources needed for the task, and coordinate its figures with those of each and every other country. This last step was as novel as it was important. To put it bluntly, it was the *sine qua non* of American aid. By pooling together, the Europeans were likely to lessen duplication and reduce their resource deficit. The difference between what the joint European effort could provide and what was needed for reconstruction would be supplied, the Secretary promised, by the United States. It was an act unprecedented in the annals of world history: far-sighted and generous, humane and couched in terms least likely to offend the sensibilities of old relations fallen on hard times. It was an initiative of the government of the United States, later confirmed by the people through Congress, addressed to the governments (many of them socialist) of wartorn Europe. It met with favorable response from the vast majority of the governments and peoples of Western Europe, and if the facts were known, from that of the peoples of Eastern Europe as well. The communist parties the world over raised hue and cry about American imperialism, the devious schemes hatched up in Washington, the evil power of Wall Street, and the rest. They were not listened to except in regions occupied by Soviet troops and ruled by native political leaders most of whom had been trained in Moscow.

There is no doubt that the Marshall Plan, as it came to be known, was in the American interest. But to see clearly takes a good deal of courage and keen vision. Of course, the United States government is not empowered by the American people to act against the interest of the United States. Yet, the true greatness of the Plan was that it saw through the haze and confusion of the moment, that it had the sheer guts to discount present costs against future benefits, and that in the setting of a society enamored of private enterprise and individual initiative, it did not shirk from using the agency of the State to do what was urgently needed. But to grant the element of American interest in the economic health of Europe is not to belittle the underlying generosity of the act, the willingness to extend a helping hand in moments of need. Few nations can honestly say that in their long history they had been capable of something even vaguely similar. Whatever the future course of events, the impetus to European unification came from across the Atlantic much more than from the Europeans themselves.

The fact that the Western Europeans responded should not be underrated. They had more trouble in jointly accepting than the Americans in singly giving. The Eastern Europeans, as we have seen, largely against their will, were spared this not too onerous embarrassment by Soviet veto. The Marshall invitation was addressed to all nations of Europe. A conference held in Paris in July, 1947, and attended by sixteen European nations, none of them communist, set up an intergovernmental coordinating and clearing body, the Organization for European Economic Cooperation (OEEC), which by September submitted to Washington a preliminary balance sheet of reconstruction needs and resources. Czechoslovakia was tempted to come to Paris; it vacillated, wavered, and finally decided against it. The Poles accepted readily, and then on second Russian-sponsored thoughts, withdrew. The ideological and political division of Europe was translated into the realities of economics.

In April, 1948, President Truman signed into law the Foreign Assistance Act, the purpose of which was to extend during the first fiscal year $5 billion in aid to the members of OEEC. The agency through which this and future aid was to flow was set up at that time under the name of the Economic Cooperation Administration (ECA). The Marshall Plan, or the European Recovery Program (ERP), as it came more formally to be known, lasted in its original form from 1948 through June, 1951. During that time the United States furnished the countries of Western Europe, members of the OEEC, $11.7 billion (out of a total allotment of $12.5 billion) for economic reconstruction in Europe's first joint venture. About 76 percent of this aid was given as outright grants, 15 percent in conditional aid, and 9 percent in long-term loans. Results exceeded expectations. The industrial production index of OEEC countries (1950 = 100) rose from 80 in 1948 to 127 in 1954, while the volume of intra-European trade increased from 48 in 1947 to 135 in 1954.

The OEEC was not a supranational economic planning body. It was essentially an intergovernmental agency, a permanent conference of governmental representatives of independent nation-states charged with coordinating European reconstruction and allocating American financial aid. Its decisions taken under the rules of unanimity were implemented by the individual governments. In arriving at decisions, each government had one vote and the power of the veto. The exercise of the veto power by any member did not in all circumstances prevent the other member governments from implementing the decision in their own countries.[2] In 1961, the OEEC was replaced by the Organization for Economic Cooperation and Development (OECD). Like its predecessors, the OECD is an intergovernmental agency the primary task of which is to encourage economic growth in member countries, coordinate economic policies, and work toward the progressive elimination of trade barriers. In addition, the OECD emphasizes aid to underdeveloped countries and collects, analyzes, and diffuses statistical information concerning trends in the member countries.[3] The membership of OECD is broader than was that of OEEC. All Western European countries except Spain and Finland participated in the work of the OEEC and benefited from U.S. aid. Membership in the OECD comprises, in addition to all Western European countries (Finland excepted), the United States and Canada. Japan,

[2] Seymour E. Harris, *Convention for European Economic Cooperation* (Paris, 1948).

[3] *Convention on the Organisation for Economic Cooperation and Development,* Paris, 1960; *Annual Reports of OEEC/OECD,* 1949 ff.; *OEEC/OECD Economic Surveys of Member Countries,* 1945 ff.

EUROPE

● Reykjavik
ICELAND

N O R W A Y
S W E D E N
F I N L A N D

Oslo ●
Stockholm ●
Helsinki ●   ○ Leningrad
○ Tallinn
ESTONIAN REP.

LATVIAN
REP. ○ Riga
● Moscow

○ Glasgow
Belfast
IRELAND   ○
Dublin ●
○ Manchester
DENMARK
Copenhagen ●

LITHUANIAN REP.
○ Vilnius
○ Minsk

WHITE RUSSIAN
REP.

GREAT BRITAIN

Amsterdam ○
London ●   The Hague ●   ● Hamburg
HOLLAND
Berlin ●
Warsaw ●
P O L A N D
○ Kiev   ○ Kharkov

Brussels ●
BELGIUM   ● Bonn
LUXEMBURG
EAST
GERMANY
Paris ●
WEST
GERMANY
○ Prague
C Z E C H O S L O V A K I A
○ Lvov
UKRAINIAN REPUBLIC

Munich ○
Vienna ●
Berne ●
○ Bordeaux   Lyons ○
SWITZERLAND
AUSTRIA
● Budapest
HUNGARY
RUMANIA

○ Milan
Y U G O S L A V I A
Belgrade ●
Bucharest ●

PORTUGAL
Marseille ○
I T A L Y

● Lisbon   ● Madrid   Barcelona ○
S P A I N
○ Seville

Rome ●
Sofia ●
BULGARIA

○ Naples
Tirane ●
ALBANIA
Ankara ●

T U R K E Y

G R E E C E
● Athens

● Nicosia
CYPRUS

MALTA

Common Market Countries

345

Yugoslavia, and Finland take part in OECD's work on an associate member basis. On the American side, the ECA was the agency set up under the Foreign Assistance Act of 1948 to administer the aid funds allocated by Congress for purposes of European recovery.

Shortly after the formation of the OEEC and ECA (1949), the Western nations, again on American initiative, set up the joint defense organization known as NATO, discussed in Chapter 8.[4] Out of this, among other things, was to come an abortive attempt to create an integrated European army among the West European powers. The United States, fearful that another Korea-type war might be launched by the Communist powers in Europe, sought in the early 1950's to strengthen the European defense system by including West Germany and forming twelve German divisions to help breach the gap in European defenses created by the withdrawal of several American divisions for service in the Korean theater of operations.

The French objected to this since they were apprehensive about any steps which might lead to the revival of an independent German army and military establishment. In 1952, however, they proposed an alternative plan for the establishment of a European army under a central command in which German soldiers might participate without setting up an independent national German military staff, to which the French were opposed. The integrated European army was to comprise elements of the armed forces of every member nation, including a West German force. In May, 1953, a treaty establishing the European Defense Community (EDC) was signed by the foreign ministers of France, Belgium, Italy, Luxembourg, and West Germany. Concurrently, plans were set on foot for the creation of an integrated European political authority. The proposed European Political Community (EPC) was to have been, for all practical purposes, a supranational government based on a popularly elected European parliament. It was the federal principle pushed to its theoretical limit. In August, 1954, the French National Assembly refused to ratify the EDC treaty and, by the same token, put an end to hopes for the formation at that time of a federated European political union. The failure of the federalist idea in 1954 was due in no small measure to the fact that it came too early. Also, political and military integration has an immediate and direct impact on nation-state sovereignty that is readily understood by everyone and which, therefore, tends to provoke violent and emotionally charged responses. The defeat of the proposed EDC and EPC stimulated a search for other, perhaps less obvious, more complex, but not less real, methods of integration. Attention, not unnaturally,

---

[4] The NATO Handbook (Paris, 1962); NATO Facts (Paris, 1962); P. H. Spaak, Why NATO? (London, Harmondsworth, 1959); M. Margaret Ball, NATO and the European Union Movement (London, Stevens, 1959).

turned to economics. As will be seen later, economic integration proceeded with relative ease until it reached the political stage, as sooner or later it had too.

In 1955, West Germany was admitted to NATO through a back and somewhat neglected door, the Brussels Treaty of 1948. The treaty signed by Britain, France, the Netherlands, Belgium, and Luxembourg in March, 1948, was a fifty-year alliance for "collaboration in economic, social, and cultural matters, and for collective self-defense." At the end of 1954, following the demise of EDC, the Brussels Treaty powers and the U.S.A. decided to invite Germany and Italy to join the treaty, henceforth to be known as the Western European Union (WEU, formally inaugurated in May, 1955), to end the occupation of Germany, to allow that country limited rearmament, to establish an agency to control the rearmament efforts of the WEU countries, and to admit West Germany to NATO.[5] It should be added that already in 1950, the Brussels Treaty defense organization had been merged with NATO.

It was the Consultative Council of the Brussels Treaty Organization which in January, 1949, decided to create a Council of Europe consisting of a Committee of Ministers and a Consultative Assembly, both of which came into being in May, 1949.[6] The aim of the Council of Europe is "to achieve a greater unity between its members for the purpose of safeguarding and realizing the ideals and principles which are their common heritage and facilitating their economic and social progress." This aim is pursued, innocuously enough, "by discussion of questions of common concern and by agreements and common action in economic, social, cultural, scientific, legal, and administrative matters and in the maintenance and further realization of human rights and fundamental freedoms." Matters pertaining to national defense do not fall within the purview of this body. Today the Council counts among its members all Western European countries including Greece, Turkey, and Cyprus. The Council of Europe Assembly is, as its name implies, a consultative body consisting of representatives of each member country elected by its parliament or appointed in such manner as that parliament may decide. The Council's Committee of Ministers consists of the foreign ministers of member countries. The Council of Ministers considers recommendations submitted to it by the Consultative Assembly but may also take action on its own initiative. All important decisions require the unanimous vote of the foreign ministers. The Council of Europe represents an early attempt to

5 *Documents Agreed on by the Conference of Ministers held in Paris 20–23 October, 1954* (London, H. M. Stationery Office, 1954), Cmd. 9304.

6 K. Lindsay, *Towards a European Parliament* (Strasbourg, Council of Europe, 1958); A. H. Robertson, *The Council of Europe*, 2nd ed. (London, Stevens, 1961); K. Lindsay, *European Assemblies* (London, Stevens, 1960); Council of Europe, *Ten Years of the Council of Europe* (Strasbourg, 1960).

combine the federalist and functional approaches to European unification. The Consultative Assembly of members of national parliaments has, occasionally, displayed a boldness and a European-mindedness unusual even for post-World War II Europe. However, this courage must not be exaggerated. It is due in part to the fact that members of the Assembly know that their recommendations have to be filtered through the essentially nation-state oriented Council of Ministers and that consequently there is little chance of conflict between European courage and national loyalty, between ideal and reality. As for Assembly resolutions, they seem to hurt nobody. They are, in fact, merely public expressions of sentiment, important enough to be sure, but largely inoperative. In the world as it is presently constituted, moral force is all very well, but more often than not, it is a far cry from policy. The Council of Europe does, however, have some concrete achievements to its credit. In 1953, a Declaration on Human Rights went into effect. Not only is this declaration bolder and more comprehensive than that of the United Nations, but provisions have actually been made to implement it. A Council of Europe Commission on Human Rights (elected by the Committee of Ministers, but not in any sense "representing" the contracting parties) was established. Its stated function is to receive and consider applications by individuals who believe their rights to have been infringed by their governments. A European Court of Human Rights was set up in 1959.

The Council of Europe in its years of operation thus far has a number of solid accomplishments to its credit. In all, about thirty European conventions have been concluded through its agency. These conventions cover such matters as patents, extradition, compulsory insurance against civil liability in respect to motor vehicles, social security, equivalence of diplomas for admission to universities, the academic recognition of university qualifications, and so on.

Essentially, the OEEC, OECD, NATO, the Brussels Treaty, WEU, and the Council of Europe are examples of the functional approach to unity. It is cooperation pushed to a fairly advanced stage, but it is in no sense integration. The only attempts at integration among the efforts just described were the EDC and EPC, and both, as we have seen, did not even reach the organizational stage. There are, however, in most of these post-World War II cooperation attempts some elements of integration (e.g., the Supreme Allied Command within NATO, the Consultative Assembly of the Council of Europe). None of these elements are allowed to shape supranational policy. From the standpoint of the movement toward integration, the organizations reviewed do represent a distinct advance over the prewar period, if only because of their relative permanence. The fact remains that the decision-making mix remains biased in favor of the traditional nation-state.

COMECON (1949)

Soviet reaction to the developments in the West was not long in coming. The response was economic and political. In 1949, the Soviet Union took the initiative in establishing a rather loose and ill-defined agency for Eastern European economic cooperation known as the Council for Mutual Economic Assistance (COMECON or CMEA).[7] At the time, the step was intended to act as counterpoise to the OEEC. Until the mid-1950's COMECON was not much to speak of. Fundamentally, the idea of economic integration conflicted with the Stalinist theory and practice of autarchic socialism and with the Stalinist predilection for unity through direct rule. As has been mentioned earlier, until Stalin's death in 1953, and in spite of the COMECON, the Soviet conception of unity was direct intervention which took the form of war reparations, joint companies, and the stationing of Soviet advisers in almost every Eastern European country. Politically, integration to the Soviets meant strict copying in every dependency of the Soviet social and political model and the imposition on all countries of governments led by men faithful to and trained in Moscow. It was integration of a crude and primitive kind, a hardly disguised variety of colonialism. It has been estimated that between 1946 and 1953 the Soviet Union, besides imposing on every Eastern European country the Soviet-Stalinist socioeconomic model, extracted from its former wartime allies and enemies, goods and services equivalent to $21 billion (in current U.S. prices). This figure probably represented no more than half the real but unreported total.[8] The countries covered by this estimate include East Germany, Hungary, Rumania, Poland, Finland, Italy, and Manchuria. This sum of $21 billion compares with the $12 billion given by the United States to Western Europe under the Marshall Plan in the period 1948–1951. It is an interesting comment on the later course of Sino-Soviet relations, that the pillaging of Manchuria by Soviet troops and "experts" (in the guise of "war reparations" from Japan) was never quite forgotten by the Chinese Communists. Nor, of course, was it forgotten by the Poles, the Hungarians, the Rumanians, and others within the Soviet camp.

Until Stalin's death, COMECON's functions were limited to lending a semblance of international respectability to bilateral trade agreements

[7] Nicolas Spulber, "The Soviet Bloc Foreign Trade System, *Law and Contemporary Problems,* Summer, 1959, pp. 429–432. F. L. Pryor, "Forms of Economic Cooperation in the European Communist Bloc," *Soviet Studies,* October, 1959, pp. 173–185; Alfred Zauberman, "Economic Integration: Problems and Prospects," *Problems of Communism,* July–August, 1959, pp. 23–29; "The CMEA: A Progress Report," *ibid.,* July–August, 1960, pp. 57–58.

[8] G. Warren Nutter, *The Growth of Industrial Production in the Soviet Union* (Princeton, N.J., Princeton University Press, 1962), pp. 214–216, 351–354.

concluded between its members. In the setting of centrally planned, command economies integration through trade was just about the most ineffective way of going about the business. Economic integration in such economies means, if it means anything, the integration of investment plans and not the sponsorship of essentially autarchic bilateral trade exchanges. But then, until 1953, COMECON was no more than a propaganda reply to the OEEC. Real integration was a one-way affair based on the philosophy of pumping the weak.

In one sense, the Soviet economic response to the OEEC was a Stalinist rendering of the cooperation principle. Such integrations as there were took the old-fashioned form of imperialism. To put the same thing in different words, imperialism of a rather crude kind was practiced in the name of ideologically fraternal economic cooperation. After Stalin's death, three factors converged to radically alter this approach. In the first place, the Soviet Union had grown prosperous enough to afford a measure of economic goodwill toward its ideological neighbors. For example, it had found large deposits of oil within its own territory which made it possible to relax pressure on Rumania and noncommunist Iran. Second, the pace of forced savings and the accompanying bureaucratic control of every aspect of Eastern European life had, by 1955, given rise to widespread discontent in Poland, Hungary, and East Germany. The disappearance of Stalin and the squabbles among his successors in the Kremlin seemed to supply an opportune moment for the expression of that discontent. Already in 1953 trouble had erupted in East Berlin. Immediately it took on an anti-Soviet, indeed, anti-Russian, coloring. In the fall of 1956, a revolution in Poland was averted only by the restoration to Communist Party leadership of the "national communists" headed by W. Gomulka. The Hungarian revolution which erupted in November, was crushed by Soviet tanks. It became obvious to the Soviets that the old method of economic unification through equal exploitation had become unworkable. If communist rule in Eastern Europe was not to fall apart, the countries of that region had to be helped rather than drained. Moreover, the Stalinist autarchic model was clearly unsuited to each and every country in which it had been applied. Not only were the Russians beginning to realize that the usefulness of the model was progressively diminishing for the Soviet Union but they also became convinced that in other countries where it had been tried, its meaningfulness was even less. The doctrine of "different roads to socialism" was invented to rationalize the situation, and the Soviet economic grip on the Eastern European countries began gradually to relax. The third factor which contributed to the change in Soviet policy toward the countries of Eastern Europe was the success of Western European economic reconstruction and the visible progress that was being made there toward economic integration. From the mid-1950's on, this changed Soviet approach to socialist camp economics was reflected in the transformations that were operated in the Council for Mutual Economic Assistance. We shall later return to this subject.

THE WARSAW TREATY

The Soviet response to NATO, especially to the admission of West Germany to that organization, was the signing in May, 1955, of a twenty-year treaty of friendship and collaboration between the U.S.S.R., Albania, Bulgaria, Czechoslovakia, East Germany (German Democratic Republic, as it came to be officially known), Hungary, Poland, and Rumania. A few days before the conclusion of the Warsaw Treaty, the Soviet Union had annulled its twenty-year treaties of alliance with Britain (concluded in 1942) and France (signed in 1944). The Warsaw Treaty powers agreed to set up a joint command of such armed forces as were placed at the disposal of this command by agreement between the powers, and used on the basis of jointly established principles. The headquarters of the Warsaw Treaty forces is located in Moscow. Without being formally expelled, Albania was no longer invited to Warsaw Pact meetings after 1962. At the present time about 25 Soviet divisions are stationed in East Germany, two or three divisions in Poland, and four in Hungary (including two air divisions). Rumania has become increasingly restless about the arrangement and in 1966 reportedly made veiled threats about leaving the alliance if it continued to be obliged to share in the financing of Soviet troops stationed in Eastern Europe without any say in their command.

WESTERN ECONOMIC INTEGRATION SCHEMES

In spite of occasional setbacks the movement for European economic integration gained momentum after the mid-fifties. This development was as true of Western as it was of Eastern Europe. Regional economic integration may take four main forms, the degree of integration rising as one proceeds from the first to the fourth.

(1) Free Trade Area

The free trade area represents the lowest form of economic integration on a regional level. Within the area the movement of goods between countries is free. Each country removes tariff and quota barriers which separate it from its trading partners within the free trade area but retains those that regulate its trade with countries outside the area.

There are, at the present time, two examples of this type of economic integration: the European Free Trade Association (EFTA) and the Latin American Free Trade Association (LAFTA).[9]

---

[9] A. Lamfalussy, *The United Kingdom and the Six* (Homewood, Ill., Irwin, 1963); F. V. Meyer, *The Seven: A Provisional Appraisal of the European Free Trade As-*

EFTA came into being in 1960, following the breakdown of attempts to establish a European Free Trade Area which would have linked the European Economic Community (see below) with Britain and the other members of OEEC. The EFTA Stockholm Convention (ratified by Austria, Denmark, Norway, Portugal, Sweden, Switzerland, and Britain—the "outer seven"—on May 3, 1960, and to which Finland subscribed on an associate basis in March 1961), makes provision for the progressive elimination of customs duties, tariffs, and quotas on industrial goods traded among its signatories. The Convention does not cover agricultural goods. However, it does make it possible for member countries to conclude bilateral agreements aimed at freeing trade in agricultural products. A bilateral agreement of this type has in fact been signed between Britain and Denmark. A first tariff reduction on industrial goods of 20 percent was made in July, 1960, and other reductions followed. EFTA is managed by a Council with the cooperation of a small Secretariat. It was hoped at the outset that EFTA would one day merge with the more integrated European Economic Community. In 1961, Britain began negotiations with the Community with a view to membership, but in 1962, France vetoed Britain's entry into the Community. EFTA is a regional organization formed for a specific purpose; it makes no provision for any effective supranational authority.

The Latin American Free Trade Association (LAFTA) was set up in Montevideo in 1961 by Argentina, Brazil, Chile, Mexico, Paraguay, Peru, and Uruguay. Colombia and Ecuador joined later in the year. The formation of LAFTA was facilitated by the United Nations Economic Commission for Latin America. Because of continuing political instability and nagging economic problems in the member countries, LAFTA's aim to reduce and eventually eliminate tariffs and other obstacles to trade has not to date progressed very far.

(2) Customs Union

This represents a somewhat higher degree of economic integration on a regional level. A customs union abolishes all tariffs and other trade barriers between the members of the union and imposes a common tariff on imports from nonmember countries.

An example of a customs union is the Belgium-Netherlands-Luxembourg Economic Union, or BENELUX.[10] The history of this union goes back to the formation in 1922 of the Belgium-Luxembourg Economic Union. The union was made at the insistence of Luxembourg, which

---

sociation (London, Barrie & Rockcliff, 1960); Emile Benoit, *Europe at Sixes and Sevens* (New York, Columbia University Press, 1961).

[10] J. Viner, *The Customs Union Issue* (London, Stevens, 1950). James E. Meade, *Negotiating for Benelux: An Annotated Chronicle 1943–56* (Princeton, Princeton University Press, 1956); W. Robertson, "Benelux and Problems of Economic Integration," *Oxford Economic Papers*, February 8, 1956, pp. 45–50; A. C. L. Day, "The European Free Trade Association," *Times Review of Industry*, London, December, 1959.

found itself economically nonviable following its severance from the German Zollverein (customs union) after World War I. In 1944, in London, preparations were made for a more comprehensive union, to include the Netherlands, which it was hoped would materialize after the end of World War II. In 1948, the BENELUX customs union was, in fact, put into effect. In quick succession customs duties and quota restrictions on the exchange of industrial goods among the three countries were abolished and a common external tariff was set up. In 1949, progress was made toward reducing the restrictions on trade in agricultural commodities. A year later, consumption taxes in the three countries were harmonized and conventions were signed for the purpose of harmonizing social security legislation and facilitating a freer movement of labor. Close cooperation was also achieved in the use of port facilities, joint action was taken on freight costs, and progress was made in standardization of statistical procedures. Between 1948 and 1957, intra-BENELUX trade tripled in value terms. In 1958, a Treaty of Economic Union was signed and went into effect in 1960. The treaty brought together the various *ad hoc* unification measures taken in the intervening years and formalized the aim of an eventual full economic union.

Even though different in name and less comprehensive, the Central American Common Market (CACM) represents another instance of the customs union approach to economic integration. CACM was brought into being by the Managua Treaty (December 13, 1960), concluded between El Salvador, Guatemala, Honduras, and Nicaragua. It provides for the equalization of import duties and other charges on trade between its members and for the establishment of a Central American Bank for Economic Integration.

(3) Common Market

The characteristics of a common market are (a) elimination of all trade barriers within the market area, (b) the imposition of a common external tariff, (c) free movement of labor and capital within the market area.

This is an advanced form of regional economic integration, just short of total union. Because (a), (b), and (c) are closely bound up with national political decisions, the common market will usually contain considerable elements of supranational authority which enable it to initiate, coordinate, and harmonize policies affecting the whole region.

The principal examples of the common market stage of economic integration are the three Western European Communities, i.e., The European Coal and Steel Community (ECSC), the European Atomic Energy Community (EURATOM), and the European Economic Community (EEC). The last of these is designed to pave the way to the highest stage of integration, that of economic union. More will be said later about each of the three main European communities.

(4) Economic Union

An economic union is economics turned political economy. It has all the characteristics of a common market plus the following: (a) common monetary, fiscal, and countercyclical policies, (b) a supranational authority empowered to take decisions on economic policy for the union as a whole, (c) integration of political and social policy, i.e., the establishment of a supranational government and parliament. In effect, an economic union means the creation of a single economic and political unit out of a number of formerly separate economies and politically independent countries.

The European Coal and Steel Community [11]

The ECSC represents a sectoral approach to European economic integration. On May 9, 1950, French Foreign Minister Robert Schuman presented a plan which proposed that France and Germany pool their steel and coal production and subject it to a common supranational authority. At the same time the plan suggested that membership in the community be left open to any country that wished to join and was ready to subscribe to the terms of the community's charter. A treaty was worked out in due course and took effect in August, 1952, following ratification by the parliaments of France, West Germany, Italy, Belgium, Luxembourg, and the Netherlands.

The main initial task of the community was to establish a common market for coal, iron ore, scrap steel, and special steels. A free trade zone for coal, steel iron ore, and scrap was, in fact, put into effect in 1953. At the same time a number of currency restrictions between the member countries was abolished. The following year the free trade zone was extended to special steels.

The ECSC has three major institutions. The most important of these is the High Authority, made up of 9 members. Eight of these are elected for six-year terms by the 6 member nations, and one by the elected members. The functions of the High Authority are to direct the coal and steel industries of the member nations. The decisions of the Authority are not subject to veto by national governments. The Authority has its own source of finance in the form of a levy on coal and steel producers. In short, the High Authority of the ECSC is Europe's first truly supranational executive. The second institution of the community is the Consultative Committee, composed of 51 representatives of coal and steel producers, labor unionists, merchants, and consumers. The third institution is the Council of Ministers, whose functions are (1) to approve certain basic decisions of the High Authority by majority vote, (2) to give opin-

11 W. Diebold, Jr., *The Shuman Plan: A Study in Economic Cooperation 1950–59* (New York, Praeger, 1959); Louis Lister, *Europe's Coal and Steel Community: An Experiment in Economic Union* (New York, Twentieth Century Fund, 1960); A. H. Robertson, *European Institutions* (London, Stevens, 1959).

ions on every other decision of the Authority, and (3) to determine the salaries of all members of the High Authority. In short, the Council of Ministers (6 foreign ministers, one from each member country) tries to harmonize supranational with national policy but does not exert on supranational policy the kind of brake that the Council of Ministers of the Council of Europe in fact does. Its powers, while important, are considerably reduced compared with those exercised by the nation-states within other international bodies. The fourth institution of the ECSC was the Common Assembly, a parliamentary body made up of 78 members elected by the six national legislatures. The European Assembly of the EEC has, since 1958, served both the ECSC and the EEC. The Assembly is composed of 142 members distributed as follows: 36 each from France, West Germany, and Italy, 14 each from Belgium and the Netherlands, and 6 from Luxembourg. The Council of Ministers of the ECSC is obliged to consult the Assembly before making final decisions on certain basic Authority proposals. Like its predecessor, the smaller ESCS Common Assembly, the European Assembly, has quickly developed a European as distinct from a national perspective, with representatives tending to group themselves according to party affiliation (Socialist, Christian Democrat, Liberal) rather than national origin. The Assembly meets each month for a period of about four days. The fifth institution of the ECSC (shared since 1958 with EEC and EURATOM) is the Court of Justice, composed of 7 judges and 2 advocates general. The judges are chosen on the basis of their competence, stature, and independence. The principal functions of the Court are (1) to insure the supremacy of law in the interpretation and implementation of the ECSC treaty, (2) to consider, on application, approve, or nullify any decisions or acts of the High Authority, the Council of Ministers, or the Assembly.

The ECSC is the first example of meaningful integration. Its success over the years has not been seriously questioned. Steel production has risen very substantially, and a coal crisis which developed in 1959 was handled on a truly regional basis. In time, however, its supranational prerogatives, as also those of the EEC, have come up against growing national opposition, mainly from the French quarter.

EUROPEAN ECONOMIC COMMUNITY (EEC) [12]

The EEC came into being on January 1, 1958, after the ratification by the parliaments of France, West Germany, Italy, Belgium, Netherlands, and Luxembourg (the original "six" of the Coal and Steel Com-

---

[12] *General Report on the Activities of the Community* (Brussels, Annual from 1958); *Bulletin of the EEC* (bi-monthly); Isaiah Franx, *The European Common Market* (New York, Praeger, 1961); Paul Minet, *Full Text of the Rome Treaty and an ABC of the Common Market* (London, Christopher Johnson, 1962); Finn B. Jensen and Ingo Walter, *The Common Market: Economic Integration in Europe* (Philadelphia, Lippincott, 1965); European Communities, Information Service, *The European Community—Coal, Steel, Common Market, Euratom: The Facts* (Brussels, EEC, 1959).

munity) of a treaty signed in Rome on March 25, 1957. Essentially, at the present stage, the EEC is a common market for a large and, until 1965, growing number of commodities and services. Its major aim, however, is to work toward an economic union, a task which the Treaty of Rome envisaged as employing the better part of twelve years. In 1960, the pace of integration was stepped up; measures were agreed on tending to free the movement of labor within the Community, consultative agreements were reached on such matters as commercial policy and transport, and anti-trust measures were adopted. In 1962, deep differences over agricultural policy were resolved by the Community's Council of Ministers, and the way seemed clear toward the next stage, that of political unification. At this point, however, the Community idea ran into serious trouble. From the point of view of the proponents of a European union, the culprit, once more, was France, the France of de Gaulle. In 1965, disagreement over common agricultural policy was used as a pretext for the French government to put the brakes on the Community's drive toward a decisive surrender of national sovereignty. But the troubles of the EEC are not all of French Gaullist making. Germany, too, has been noticeably less enthusiastic about a United Europe since the retirement from active politics of Chancellor Adenauer. German industrialists, elated by years of prosperity, began to find in trade with Eastern Europe a potentially attractive source of income and growth and chafed at what they thought might be the restrictions on such trade resulting from full membership in a Western European economic union. The Dutch, for their part, had watched the French attempts to dominate the common market with rising apprehension, and their enthusiasm for the whole project waned in direct ratio to France's growing national self-reassertion.

The basic objective of the EEC is to serve as a stepping stone to economic and political union. To reach this objective, the Treaty of Rome envisaged the following major steps: (1) elimination of all trade restrictions within the market area and the establishment of a uniform external tariff between the EEC and the rest of the world; (2) coordination of transportation systems of the member countries, especially as regards freight rates and other transport costs; (3) coordination of monetary and fiscal policies with the aim of promoting high employment levels, relative price stability, and equilibrium in the balance of external payments; (4) coordination of laws governing competition among enterprises so as to prevent the emergence of monopolistic combinations other than those regarded as contributing to the economic welfare of the community; (5) the establishment of free movement of labor and capital within the community; (6) increase in agricultural productivity through technical progress and the rational utilization of resources; (7) assurance to the farm population of a fair standard of living; (8) stabilization of agricultural markets; (9) assurance of regular and sufficient supplies of farm produce; (10) reasonable prices of agricultural products for consumers. These 10 tasks were to be accomplished in three main stages of four years each, with 1972 being fixed as the latest date for the achievement of full economic union, and 1969 as the proximate date.

In addition to the European Parliamentary Assembly and the European Court of Justice which the EEC shares with the ECSC and EURATOM, the Community has a political executive (Council of Ministers—one member from each national government), an administrative executive (the Commission—9 members appointed by national governments), a series of consultative committees (e.g., a 101-member Economic and Social Committee shared with EURATOM, and committees on economic policy, monetary affairs, and transportation), several administrative departments (external relations, economic and financial affairs, internal market, competition, social affairs, agriculture, transport, overseas countries and territories, and administration), and three special agencies (the European Investment Bank, the European Social Fund, and the European Development Fund). The EEC Commission is the Community's equivalent of the ECSC High Authority. It makes recommendations to the Council of Ministers and is responsible to the Assembly for its decisions reached by simple majority vote. The initiative rests with the Commission, not with the Council. The Council must either approve or reject the Commission's recommendations in the original form. If it wishes to amend a recommendation, it can do so only by unanimous vote. On one occasion, at least, the Council did, in fact, reverse a Commission decision—the case was the famous "chicken war" with the United States. The Commission had proposed a reduction of EEC tariffs on imports of poultry from the United States, but the Council voted unanimously to increase these duties. Nominally, the Commission is independent of national pressures, but in fact it often tempers its supranational *élan* in response to national sentiments.

The French intransigence during 1965, which threatened to slow down the pace of unification and turn the EEC into a free-trade area instead of an economic union, was due less to the ostensible disagreement over agricultural policy than to the fact that as of December 31, 1965, the voting on important matters concerning transportation, commerce, and agriculture within the Council of Ministers was to change from unanimity to qualified majority. A qualified majority would have meant the abandonment of national veto powers and would have represented an important step toward the internationalization of the Council. Within the Council, France would have had four votes (the same number as Germany and Italy), Belgium and Holland two votes each, and Luxembourg one. A qualified majority is defined as twelve out of the possible seventeen votes. Although in 1965, the French did not withdraw from EEC, they abstained from participating in the work of a number of EEC committees, thus grinding the movement toward greater integration to a virtual halt. In fact, de Gaulle's conception of European unification seems to have moved close to the original British functional position. The trouble is, that in the meantime, British thinking had evolved in a federalist sense.

The farm controversy is nevertheless real. The disagreements are due in part to the significance of agriculture in the economic life of the member nations and to the very different policies which each country had for years pursued toward its agricultural sector. Thus, except for tropical and subtropical products, France is almost self-sufficient in agricultural produce and exports grain on a large and rising scale. French agricultural prices have been kept above world prices through subsidies to producers and exports have often been subsidized. Italy needs grain imports and wishes to export freely its fruit and vegetables. Italian grain producers are protected, and France's (as well as Netherland's) desire to free trade in grain places the Italian government in a delicate position vis-à-vis its grain farmers who would very likely be hurt by such liberalization. The Germans have a complicated system of farm production and are not anxious to open the floodgates of free trade in grain which would have serious short-run repercussions on the welfare of the country's important farm bloc. Much the same is true of Belgium. The Netherlands, on the other hand, is anxious to export its fruit, vegetables, and dairy products with the least hindrance from foreign tariffs and other restrictions. In short, any EEC decisions on agricultural integration tend to have important political repercussions at the national level. Hence the hesitations and conflicts that have on occasion threatened the very existence of the Community. Eventually these thorny problems have to be resolved by political integration, which at present appears a very distant proposition indeed.

The Atomic Energy Community (EURATOM) [13]

EURATOM was formed on January 1, 1958, by the Rome Treaty signed the previous year. The objective of the Community is to promote common efforts among its six members in the development of nuclear energy for peaceful purposes. The executive organ of EURATOM is a 5-member independent Commission, advised by a Scientific and Technical Committee composed of 20 members and an Economic and Social Committee shared with EEC. Important decisions rest in the hands of the Council of Ministers (one member from each country). In 1959, EURATOM introduced a common market for nuclear products. The Community has its own research centers in Ispra (Italy), Mol (Belgium),

[13] Louis Armand, et al., A Target for Euratom (Brussels, Euratom, 1957); EURATOM Bulletin, Brussels (quarterly from January, 1962); General Report on the Activities of the Community (Brussels, annual from 1958).

Petten (Netherlands), and Karlsruhe (Germany). EURATOM has concluded a number of agreements with other countries (e.g., U.S.A., Canada, Britain, Brazil) covering joint power and research projects, work on natural uranium, heavy water moderated reactors, and general cooperation.

NEW LIFE FOR COMECON

It became apparent to the Soviet Union that the progress toward economic integration in Western Europe after the mid-1950's threatened to leave the U.S.S.R. and its Eastern European allies out in the cold so far as international competition and economic rationality were concerned. Moreover, after the death of Stalin, the whole Stalinist strategy and tactics of economic development, with their insistence on a strict copying of the Soviet autarchic model of the thirties, came up for serious reappraisal. The costs inherent in the atomization of the communist bloc became a source of acute dissatisfaction to the new leaders of the Soviet Union bent as they were on "catching up and surpassing" the most advanced capitalist powers and, incidentally, raising the standard of living of their own people. This desire for new ways of running the economy and new methods of intrabloc economic and political cooperation, coincided with the emergence in the Eastern European countries of national-communist leaders and the resurgence of nationalism stifled during years of Stalinist rule. Soviet professions of honorable economic intentions had to overcome deep suspicions bred of years of Stalinist exploitation and the unwelcome presence of Soviet troops. In the new slogan of "united but equal" the Soviets stressed the "united" and most of the Eastern Europeans the "equal." Albania was first to go overboard. Its quarrel with the Soviet Union was to a considerable extent political and ideological in nature, but a strong economic element was also present. The Albanians were extremely sensitive about the Soviet sponsorship, under the auspices of the CMEA, of a socialist division of labor under which they saw themselves producing raw materials and agricultural products for the rest of the budding communist commonwealth. The Rumanians, too, responded unfavorably to COMECON attempts to impose on them what they considered to be a rather narrow industrial specialization (especially in petroleum products and refinery equipment) at the expense of their well-advanced plans for the establishment of heavy industry and the progressive industrialization of the country. Against this trend of resurgent nationalism, the powers of COMECON were generally strengthened to include first attempts at coordination of national long-range investment plans. A Bank for Multilateral Payments and Investment was set up and a number of joint projects was completed within a few years. The projects included an international oil pipeline stretching from Kuybyshev in the U.S.S.R., to Poland, East Germany, Czechoslovakia, and Hungary, the construction of a number of natural gas feeders between Hungary and Rumania, and the installation of an electric power grid between a number of COMECON countries. Thus, a greater measure of national and ideological independence went hand in hand with efforts at supranational economic planning, even though conflicts and recurrent setbacks were as common here as they were in Western Europe.[14]

OTHER REGIONAL ORGANIZATIONS

There are a number of other regional international organizations, most of them created for the purpose of common defense, economic development, and political understanding. All of them are instruments of cooperation rather than agents of integration.

THE COLOMBO PLAN [15]

The Colombo Plan for Cooperative Economic Development in South and Southeast Asia came into being in 1951. As originally formulated the Plan was to provide a framework for the development programs of Asian member countries and was to end in 1957. Successive extensions have moved the date of termination to 1966. The Plan has a Consultative Committee composed of Australia, Canada, Ceylon, India, Malaysia, New Zealand, Pakistan, Britain, South Vietnam, Cambodia, Laos, Burma, Nepal, Indonesia, Japan, the Philippines, and Thailand. The United States attends the meetings of the Committee as a full member. The principal aim of the Plan is to pool the resources of its members for purposes of economic development, to review national economic development programs, and to foster technical cooperation. Since its inception, the Plan has received substantial financial assistance from the United States (*ca.* $1.5 billion) and the UN International Bank for Reconstruction and Development (*ca.* $1.5 billion). Plan members (especially Britain, Australia, Canada, and New Zealand) provide technical training facilities for citizens of member countries and send experts in various fields for service in the Plan area.

SOUTHEAST ASIA COLLECTIVE DEFENSE TREATY (SEATO)

As discussed in Chapter 8, this treaty was concluded between Australia, France, New Zealand, Pakistan, the Philippines, Thailand, Britain, and the United States in 1954, with the aim of establishing a collective defense system in Southeast Asia. In 1965, largely due to differences over

[14] Jan S. Prybyla, "Eastern Europe and Soviet Oil," *The Journal of Industrial Economics,* March, 1965, pp. 154–167; Ghita Ionescu, *The Break-up of the Soviet Empire in Eastern Europe* (London, Penguin Books, 1965).
[15] *The Colombo Plan* (London, H.M.S.O., 1950, 1952), Cmd. 8080; *Change in Asia: The Colombo Plan* (Colombo, Colombo Plan Bureau, 1959).

policies regarding Vietnam and Communist China, France ceased to co-operate in the work of this organization, even while retaining membership.

Central Treaty Organization (CENTO)

CENTO is a pact for mutual defense concluded in Baghdad in 1955 between Turkey and Iraq. The organization was later joined by Britain and Iran. The United States became a member of the economic, counter-subversion and military committees in 1956 and 1957. Iraq left the organization in 1959. In addition to its military role, CENTO has an economic development program which covers road construction, port development, railway building, and disease prevention and cure. In addition, the CENTO countries have established joint programs of technical cooperation.

The Arab League

The League, a loose organization of Arab states, came into being in 1945. Its main purpose is to mediate disputes between member countries and take joint military action in face of external threat.

French Community (Communauté Française)

The concept of the "French Community" is embodied in the 1958 Constitution of the Fifth French Republic. The Community, headquartered in Paris, is essentially an alliance of France with her former African colonies on matters of defense, economic and financial policy, and foreign affairs. Implicitly, the Community acknowledges the benefits for all concerned deriving from a common cultural heritage and the continuation of close cultural contacts between France and French-speaking Africa. In some respects the Community concept is modeled on the British Commonwealth of Nations.

Afro-Malagasy Union for Economic Cooperation (UAMCE)

UAMCE is an organization of some French-speaking African states (Cameroun, Dahomey, Gabon, Malagasy Republic, Mauritania, Rwanda, Senegal, and Togo) formed in April, 1964, for the purpose of promoting the economic integration of French-speaking Africa. UAMCE had repeatedly charged Ghana (at the time of Mr. Nkrumah's presidency of that country) with sheltering, arming, and training subversive elements from the member countries who had taken refuge in Ghana. The post-March, 1966 Ghanaian government confirmed that these allegations had, in fact, been true. Seven members of UAMCE boycotted the summit meeting of the Organization of African Unity held in Accra (Ghana) in October, 1965.

ORGANIZATION OF AFRICAN UNITY (OAU)

On May 25, 1963, the representatives of 32 African governments meeting in Addis Ababa (Ethiopia) decided to set up an organization to promote the political unity and economic development of Africa, defend the sovereignty of member nations, and eliminate the remnants of colonial rule from the continent. By 1965, the membership had grown to 36. One of the leading members of the organization was Nkrumah's Ghana. In 1965, OAU went through a severe crisis amounting to a split and traceable to civil strife in the Congo, the attitude to be adopted on the Sino-Soviet dispute, and allegations of subversion levelled against Ghana by the Afro-Malagasy Union. The Organization has a number of committees (e.g., the Economic and Social Committee, the Scientific, Technical and Research Committee), and a Council of Ministers which meet periodically to discuss items of common interest and make recommendations affecting all members. Meetings of heads of state ("summit meetings") are scheduled from time to time. The October 21–27, 1965, OAU summit meeting in Accra (Ghana) was attended by only 18 of the 36 member states. The Organization has called for a trade boycott of Rhodesia, South Africa, and the Portuguese territories in Africa and has protested to Communist China against that country's continued trade with South Africa.

ECONOMIC COMMUNITY OF EASTERN AFRICA (ECA) [16]

The terms of association of the Economic Community of Eastern Africa were signed in Addis Ababa (Ethiopia) on May 4, 1966, by ministers and ambassadors from Burundi, Ethiopia, Kenya, Malawi, Mauritius, Somalia, Tanzania, and Zambia. The signing ceremony brought into being an Interim Council of Ministers and gave assent to a set of principles which was to govern cooperation among the member states until such time as the treaty establishing the Community has been negotiated. The aims of the Community are to promote coordinated economic development of the member states, especially in industry, agriculture, transport, communications, trade, manpower, and natural resources. The Community will also aim at progressive reduction of customs and other barriers to trade between the members and will act to obtain more favorable terms of trade for the products of its members in world markets.

ALLIANCE FOR PROGRESS

The Alliance for Progress (*Alianza para Progresso*) was proposed by President John F. Kennedy on March 13, 1961, in Washington, D.C., and founded on August 17, 1961, at Punta del Este, Uruguay, by representa-

---

[16] "The Economic Community of Eastern Africa," *East Africa Journal*, June, 1966, pp. 28–30.

tives of all the Latin American countries with the exception of Cuba. To some extent the Alliance idea owes a debt to the success of the Marshall Plan under which American assistance made a crucial contribution to the rehabilitation and reconstruction of Western Europe following World War II. It is, however, an incontestable fact that the problems and issues involved in Latin America of the 1960's and 1970's are different and more intractable than those facing Western Europe in the late forties and early fifties. The problem is not to rebuild, but to build, not on a tradition of democratic institutions that had been temporarily overthrown (as in Western Europe), but against a background of age-long instability and right-wing rule. The principal aim of the Alliance is to promote the economic development of Latin America and solve its most urgent social problems within the framework of Western democratic institutions which, in many instances, have to be built up from scratch. The program, involving some $20 billion in U.S. assistance, is optimistically envisaged to take ten years, for a start. Up to 1967 the United States had spent some $5 billion for the Alliance and cautious optimism was being aired in both Washington and in the capitals of the recipient countries. The Inter-American Economic and Social Council (IAECOSOC) reported in 1963 that 10 out of the 19 Latin American countries participating in the Alliance had met or surpassed their goals of 2.5 percent per capita growth rates. On a per capita basis, U.S. aid to Latin America is second only to that rendered to South Vietnam. By June 30, 1964, U.S. assistance through the Alliance had helped build 222,600 homes, 23,400 classrooms, 1,056 water systems and wells, and 2,900 miles of roads. It also helped to produce 6,810,000 schoolbooks, build 554 health centers, hospitals, and mobile health units, train 47,930 teachers and 5,660 public administrators, make 207,000 agricultural credit loans, and establish or develop the resources of 16 development banks or funds, 910 credit unions, and 74 savings and loan associations. Progress was made in improving tax systems, with eight countries passing major tax reform legislation. Governmental expenditures on education have been increasing at an annual rate of about 10 percent.

CONCLUSIONS

In order to reduce political tension, promote economic growth, and assure common defense, a number of regional international organizations have come into being since the end of World War II. Some of these have inevitably come in conflict with other organizations of a similar type. All represent a trend away from narrow economic and political nationalism, but their history reveals the strength and durability of the nation-state concept. The greatest advance toward integration, as distinct from cooperation in the sense discussed earlier in this chapter, has undoubtedly been made in Western Europe. Substantial progress has also been registered by the countries of Eastern Europe. Elsewhere, international regional organization still follows the simple cooperation principle, and the aim of integration remains distant and uncertain.

POSITIONS

1. TREATY ESTABLISHING THE EUROPEAN ECONOMIC COMMUNITY

The Treaty of Rome establishing the European Economic Community, or "Common Market," was signed on March 24, 1957 by representatives of France, Belgium, the Netherlands, Luxembourg, Italy, and the Federal Republic of Germany, and was ratified by all the signatory countries within a few months. The EEC thus came into being on January 1, 1958. Although primarily an economic document, the Treaty clearly addresses itself to increasing political, social, and military convergence of the member countries. This implication of the Treaty was put in question by France eight years later.[17]

ARTICLE 1

By the present Treaty, the HIGH CONTRACTING PARTIES establish among themselves a EUROPEAN ECONOMIC COMMUNITY.

ARTICLE 2

It shall be the aim of the Community, by establishing a Common Market and progressively approximating the economic policies of Member States, to promote throughout the Community a harmonious development of economic activities, a continuous and balanced expansion, an increased stability, an accelerated raising of the standard of living and closer relations between its Member States.

ARTICLE 3

For the purposes set out in the preceding Article, the activities of the Community shall include, under the conditions and with the timing provided for in this Treaty:

(a) the elimination, as between Member States, of customs duties and of quantitative restrictions in regard to the importation and exportation of goods, as well as of all other measures with equivalent effect;

17 Intergovernmental Conference on the Common Market and Euratom, *Treaty Establishing the European Economic Community and Connected Documents* (Brussels, Secretariat of the Interim Committee for the Common Market and Euratom, 1957).

(*b*) the establishment of a common customs tariff and a common commercial policy towards third countries;

(*c*) the abolition, as between Member States, of the obstacles to the free movement of persons, services and capital;

(*d*) the inauguration of a common agricultural policy;

(*e*) the inauguration of a common transport policy;

(*f*) the establishment of a system ensuring that competition shall not be distorted in the Common Market;

(*g*) the application of procedures which shall make it possible to co-ordinate the economic policies of Member States and to remedy disequilibria in their balances of payments;

(*h*) the approximation of their respective municipal law to the extent necessary for the functioning of the Common Market;

(*i*) the creation of a European Social Fund in order to improve the possibilities of employment for workers and to contribute to the raising of their standard of living;

(*j*) the establishment of a European Investment Bank intended to facilitate the economic expansion of the Community through the creation of new resources; and

(*k*) the association of overseas countries and territories with the Community with a view to increasing trade and to pursuing jointly their effort towards economic and social development.

ARTICLE 4

1. The achievement of the tasks entrusted to the Community shall be ensured by:

     —an ASSEMBLY,
     —a COUNCIL,
     —a COMMISSION,
     —a COURT OF JUSTICE.

Each of these institutions shall act within the limits of the powers conferred upon it by this Treaty.

2. The Council and the Commission shall be assisted by an Economic and Social Committee acting in a consultative capacity.

ARTICLE 5

Member States shall take all general or particular measures which are appropriate for ensuring the carrying out of the obligations arising out of this Treaty or resulting from the acts of the institutions of the Community. They shall facilitate the achievement of the Community's aims.

They shall abstain from any measures likely to jeopardise the attainment of the objectives of this Treaty.

ARTICLE 6

1. Member States, acting in close collaboration with the institutions of the Community, shall co-ordinate their respective economic policies to the extent that it is necessary to attain the objectives of this Treaty.

2.   The institutions of the Community shall take care not to prejudice the internal and external financial stability of Member States.

Article 7

Within the field of application of this Treaty and without prejudice to the special provisions mentioned therein, any discrimination on the grounds of nationality shall hereby be prohibited.

The Council may, acting by means of a qualified majority vote on a proposal of the Commission and after the Assembly has been consulted, lay down rules in regard to the prohibition of any such discrimination.

Article 8

1.   The Common Market shall be progressively established in the course of a transitional period of twelve years.

The transitional period shall be divided into three stages of four years each; the length of each stage may be modified in accordance with the provisions set out below.

2.   To each stage there shall be allotted a group of actions which shall be undertaken and pursued concurrently.

3.   Transition from the first to the second stage shall be conditional upon a confirmatory statement to the effect that the essence of the objectives specifically laid down in this Treaty for the first stage has been in fact achieved and that, subject to the exceptions and procedures provided for in this Treaty, the obligations have been observed.

This statement shall be made at the end of the fourth year by the Council acting by means of a unanimous vote on a report of the Commission. The invocation by a Member State of the non-fulfilment of its own obligations shall not, however, be an obstacle to a unanimous vote. Failing a unanimous vote, the first stage shall automatically be extended for a period of one year.

At the end of the fifth year, the Council shall make such confirmatory statement under the same conditions. Failing a unanimous vote, the first stage shall automatically be extended for a further period of one year.

At the end of the sixth year, the Council shall make such a statement acting by means of a qualified majority vote on a report of the Commission.

4.   Within a period of one month as from 'the date of this last vote, each Member State voting in a minority or, if the required majority vote has not been obtained, any Member State, shall be entitled to require the Council to appoint an Arbitration Board whose decision shall bind all Member States and the institutions of the Community. The Arbitration Board shall be composed of three members appointed by the Council acting by means of a unanimous vote on a proposal of the Commission.

If the Council has not within a period of one month from the date of such requirement, appointed the members of the Arbitration Board, they shall be appointed by the Court of Justice within a further period of one month.

The Arbitration Board shall appoint its Chairman.

The Board shall give its award within a period of six months from the date of the vote by the Council referred to in paragraph 3, last sub-paragraph.

5. The second and third stages may not be extended or curtailed except pursuant to a decision of the Council acting by means of a unanimous vote on a proposal of the Commission.

6. The provisions of the preceding paragraphs shall not have the effect of extending the transitional period beyond a total duration of fifteen years after the date of the entry into force of this Treaty.

7. Subject to the exceptions or deviations provided for in this Treaty, the expiry of the transitional period shall constitute the final date for the entry into force of all the rules laid down and for the completion of all the measures required for the establishment of the Common Market.

2. EEC: A BRITISH VIEW

President de Gaulle's refusal to go along with the supranational implications of the European Economic Community is analyzed critically by *The Economist,* a leading British periodical. *The Economist* sees in de Gaulle's insistence on national sovereignty and bilateral cooperation arrangements a danger to the future peace of Europe and, as emphasized here, for one of the most constructive international ideas to emerge from postwar Europe.[18]

THE WAR FOR EUROPE

No one can yet say for sure whether the European community is going to emerge alive from what is now its open war with General de Gaulle, or what shape it will be in if it does. But it is easier to see it disintegrating under his bludgeon blows in the coming months than surviving as a major force in the western world. As after the veto on the British attempt to enter the common market in 1963, the watchword in Brussels is Business as Usual. But the watchword comes eerily, as from men whistling in the dark. In 1963 there was a widespread hope that, though General de Gaulle might do his worst, generals come and go but institutions live on forever. Today there is a sadder and wiser disposition to recognize that institutions can be assassinated after all.

And everything at present points to the general's will to assassinate them. The ruthless way in which the French dropped the guillotine on June 30th, the immediate freezing of the common market by withdrawing French representatives from its meetings, the tendentious way in which the French farmer is being told that the foreigner is refusing to pay him his due—all denote a carefully prepared campaign. General de Gaulle's design is clear: to remove the only effective restraint on his nationalism. This is the European community and the widespread commitment of Europeans, including many Frenchmen, to its integrationist ideals.

His tactics, too, foreshadow further diplomatic violence. A frozen common market is a contradiction in terms and cannot last. By the time, probably this autumn, when the freeze sets in and cools the present ardour of indignation,

[18] Reprinted from *The Economist* (London) of July 10, 1965, pp. 109–111. By permission.

shivering businessmen, farmers and politicians will all be saying they want to live with a better prospect than that. One of two pressures will then be felt by the Five and the European Commission. Either they will say, as they have done hitherto, "We must save the common market at all costs." General de Gaulle can then impose his terms. Or they will say, "We must fight"; and then the general can present himself to the French electorate as a Roland standing at the pass for the integrity of France.

The odds are against their caving in. Not that they will fail to seek a compromise. But the process set in train is against one being achieved. The right card for the Five and the European Commission to play now is undoubtedly to offer to finish the talks cut off in their prime on June 30th. A compromise on the basis of the negotiations as they stood at that moment would be the best possible outcome. It would be exactly what they have said is possible all along. But, after all the rancour that has been generated, they can hardly settle for less. And why, after all the drama, could General de Gaulle not ask for more? He is far more likely to raise the stakes than call quits. He could well insist that the full French demand—an agreement now on farm financing—be accepted without anything being said about community budgets or the powers of the European Parliament. The Five might be able to justify this further retreat on the ground that it is better to live and fight another time. But more likely their humiliation and alarm would make them think the game is not worth the candle. Already this year General de Gaulle has shown the Germans he might sacrifice their interests to his desire for an agreement with Russia: he has also offended the Italians. Both are angry.

He might even add insult to injury and suggest turning the common market into a customs union without political aspirations. In this way, the old dream of a European-wide free trade area could rear its unexpected head in the most unlikely capitals. For some time, there has been talk in Paris that the French, including even industrialists, are less opposed to a free trade arrangement than they were. General de Gaulle must also calculate that, if the other five countries lose hope of a deal, they will tend to look politically to Britain and economically to their own trading interests. Thus, whether the French or others lead the way, a free trade area proposal from within the frontiers of the Six seems the most plausible outcome of the present crisis: the end of integration for Efta and anon.

Lest some in Britain should be moved to raise a cheer, it is worth remembering that the last of General de Gaulle's victories of disintegration was the rejection of a European army in 1954. This was followed soon afterwards by German national rearmament, theoretically controlled by a loose Western European Union which in fact has never begun to come to life. If a free trade area were created, it might function better than that, because individuals, not governments, carry on trade. But for a long time to come, the essential achievement of General de Gaulle would be the political vandalism of breaking up the world's one successful postwar attempt to organize international negotiation on a fairly civilized basis. This is what the European ideal has been about. In the present mood of the nations, there is precious little hope that, once killed, it would easily be revived after General de Gaulle had gone.

The general sees things otherwise. He probably feels that in clamping down on the common market he is freeing himself, the only independent European, from the embrace of America and its knock-kneed satellites, and thereby ending the cold-war division of Europe into two hostile blocks. Once the Germans have got over the initial shock, he reckons, they will sadly but inevitably abandon their American connection. But once they do that, Paris will always be better in with Moscow than Bonn can possibly be. The East will be France's ally against Germany, and so perhaps will Britain. Germany will be powerless to disturb the concert of powers revived in the heartland of world civilization. Not least, the hero of the operation will be General de Gaulle.

The trouble with this characteristically grand but contemptuous design is that it creates chaos now, and you cannot build on chaos. By bringing to a halt the development of the European community, General de Gaulle would shatter many people's hopes. Most of all, he would throw a cracking blow at Germany's psychological stability. The idea of belonging to a unified west Europe has played a central part in Germany's political and moral recovery from the nadir of Hitler's *Götterdämmerung*. It has offered the Germans moral dignity in building up a community with other Europeans, and security for the future. By taking the place of the old purgatory of 1945, it has acquired some of the moral imperatives of paradise. To destroy these for narrowly French reasons not only removes the restraints on a possible resurgence of German nationalism; it even gives it bitter justification. After all, Germany is more powerful than France and has the only real grievance of any country in Europe.

Moreover, free trade or no free trade, a break-up of the common market would restore instability over a far wider area than Germany alone. General de Gaulle has opened up a Pandora's box of horrid questions. Is the next step for Britain and France to line up on one side, America and Germany on the other? Will three of them team up in a developing Atlantic alliance and isolate France? Will America deal directly with Russia? Or Russia with France or Germany? A great deal of the unusual calm in Europe for the last decade has been due to the stability created by the common market and the hopes of broader unity to come. With attitudes to Russia changing throughout the West, this unity did not exclude better relations with the East. If anything, it created a firmer base for them. At a time when nationalism is raising its head all over the continent, the loss of these restraints would enormously increase everybody's uncertainty and mistrust.

Even the immediate consequences of a break-up of the common market, if it comes to that, seem an odd consummation for a man as devoted to Europe as General de Gaulle is. They would be to reinforce the tendency of European states to seek special bilateral relationships with the United States. But, plainly, an organized Europe would make a better and more influential partner for the United States than a balkanized Europe teeming with competing states. It is all very well to revive the concert of powers. But where's the power? From this viewpoint, the general's hubris invites the classical Greek nemesis of disunity all over again. Does General de Gaulle really want to go down in history as the perpetuator of European weakness?

There is too much at stake here for the other Europeans to let General de Gaulle succeed in doing what he is willing to do. And among these other Europeans the British have a particular duty. For the moment, the best British policy is to shut up and do nothing. But, some time, a rescue operation in which there would be a part for Britain to play may be unavoidable, and Mr. Wilson should be ready for it. He should resist the temptation to think solely in terms of reviving a European-wide free trade area; this is certainly one way of picking up the pieces, but it is not the best one, and circumstances may allow other approaches. The best way would be to stand ready to offer Britain as a member of a recognized European community which, shorn of France, could have an agricultural policy less alarming to the British consumer and the Treasury and to farmers in New Zealand and Australia. The biggest valid British objection to the common market would then disappear. Nobody really wants France to be isolated, and General de Gaulle will manoeuvre to prevent it. But people may yet get fed up with placating the implacable. Britain could then have a second chance to play a constructive part in the building of Europe.

3. UNIFICATION VERSUS SOVEREIGNTY IN EASTERN EUROPE

Stalin's empire in Eastern Europe is crumbling under the onslaught of nationalism. But fear of Germany still exerts a strong unifying pressure. The author of the paragraphs cited below was a high government official in pre-1946 Rumania. Presently he is a Nuffield Fellow in Eastern European Politics at the London School of Economics and Political Science.[19]

In the introduction we justified the expression "Soviet Empire." Now that the history of this empire has been retraced it only remains to see how far it is fair to speak of a "break-up." Does what has happened to the zone of Soviet military, economic and ideological domination in Eastern Europe amount to a "disintegration, decay, collapse, dispersal"? *

From an ideological point of view, the most recent events, as described and interpreted by the communist media themselves, provide the most conclusive proof. The "disintegration" or "dispersal" of the CPSU's authority as set up by Lenin and consolidated by Stalin over the entire communist movement, including the Soviet bloc in Eastern Europe, is now a fact. The communiqué issued at the end of the abortive conference of the nineteen communist parties on 1–5 March, 1965 was a most humiliating occasion for the Soviet Union and a veritable funeral oration for communist authority.

*   *   *

As far as regional discipline under the aegis of the CPSU is concerned, it has become more and more evident that COMECON will remain a dead duck. Moves were made, especially on Polish and Hungarian initiative, to continue further integration of the economies, without—or even perhaps to spite—the Rumanian Workers' Party. (For instance the creation of INTERMETAL, an organization linking the steel industries of Poland, Hungary and East Germany.) But the tendency among members of COMECON to increase their trade with

[19] Ghita Ionescu, *The Break-up of the Soviet Empire in Eastern Europe* (Harmondsworth, Middlesex, Penguin Books, 1965), pp. 150, 153–157. Reprinted by permission.
    * *Oxford English Dictionary.*

the non-communist markets is constantly growing. The most amazing instance of this remains the promise of future collaboration between Gomulka's Poland and the big West German concern, Krupp, of Essen. This entails the setting up by Krupp on Polish territory of industrial plants and factories in which imported raw materials will be manufactured by Polish workers and the goods re-exported to West Germany and to other non-communist markets. In any circumstances the formation by communist states and capitalist firms of such mixed companies would seem odd. (It was known that during the economic negotiations between communist Rumania and the United States in 1964, the Rumanian delegation had offered to set up with American firms such mixed companies.) Even more surprising is that this time the capitalist concern involved is Krupp, a name which in the world at large and in Eastern Europe in particular still bears the fearful reputation of having been the main armament factory for the Kaiser's and Hitler's wars of aggression. The fact that the communist country which is now prepared to consider such a collaboration is Poland, which suffered most from German aggression, and where communist propaganda's most effective weapon is still fear of Germany, makes the proposed deal even more significant.

It vividly demonstrates two things. On the one hand it shows how nonconformist and pragmatic the Soviet bloc countries can now be in the field of foreign trade. On the other it shows how acutely they must need to tap the financial and industrial resources of the West, whence alone they can hope to acquire what is unavailable in the pool of COMECON but is needed to develop the overall economic resources of the bloc as a whole. While criticizing the Rumanian Party and Government for the unorthodox trade policies they have adopted since 1960, the Poles, Czechoslovaks, Hungarians and indeed the East Germans have tried hard in the last five years to emulate and, if possible, to outdo them in their successful overtures to the West. In the economic sector, too, centrifugalism has come to stay.

There remains the military sphere. Here collaboration between the Peoples' Democracies and Soviet Russia is more stable (though other spheres are bound to influence trends to some extent) for two reasons. First, the communist parties in power in all these countries are anxious to preserve the myth that the entire region is united under the friendly wing of the first communist state in world history—Soviet Russia. It is clear that all the adaptations, reforms and national variations introduced by the communist governments of Eastern Europe have been in response to popular pressure; and the greater a government's sensitivity to this native pressure, the prompter its effort to find some compromise between the Russian Leninist-Stalinist models and the national reality. Sooner or later, though, all the communist parties of Eastern Europe had buttressed popular support for themselves by stressing their particular value as intermediants between Russia and their own peoples. Yet the governments remain aware that Russia's influence over the whole region is indispensable for them if they are to maintain power; and therefore they believe that while they should acquire for themselves as much freedom as possible in order to make their administrations smoother, more efficient and more palatable, they are nevertheless ultimately linked with the Soviet Union, her fate and her evolution by a basic common problem.

This problem is the "fundamental dilemma" * of any communist state: how to enable the people to participate in the decision-making process in the life of

* The expression used by Professor Mihal Markovic of Belgrade University.

the state, without once more being drawn irresistibly into the obvious institutions of free elections and multi-party systems which could lead to the loss of power of the "monolithic" party. In developed industrial or semi-industrial societies, the multiple influences of the component groups in society are bound to conflict with the monolithic party and its rule. The problem of representation and of participation in the debate on the nation's economic life without a corresponding participation in the debate on political life creates the "dilemma" common to all these states. From the Soviet Union as the conservative archetype to Yugoslavia as the most advanced and boldest innovator in various experiments and compromises, the communist governments in Europe must all walk the same tightrope. This is perhaps what unites the communist governments most closely with that of the Soviet Union. Each of them is trying separately and will continue to try to work out some device by which the dictatorship of the monolithic party can "wither away" and transmute itself into "the state of the whole people," which has already been proclaimed to be in existence since the 22nd Congress and yet is still indistinguishable from the mixture as before.

The second reason for the stability of the military collaboration between the eastern European countries and the Soviet Union is that the Soviet Union still carefully maintains the overall military control of the area which it established by the Warsaw Treaty. As has been shown earlier, at the height of the trend to de-Stalinize and bring new flexibility into the relations between the U.S.S.R. and the former Stalinist satellites, the leaders of the U.S.S.R. always clung to the Warsaw Treaty Organization as the main instrument of their political, diplomatic and strategic influence in Europe. To the U.S.S.R. the issue is a simple and strategic one. It has to maintain its communications with its military base in Europe, East Germany, as free and elastic as possible. The *de facto* military control of the area by the Soviet Union and her firmness in maintaining it have ensured a stable situation hitherto, regardless of East European views. On the other hand, the natural instinct of the East European nations is to try to attain a status of neutrality comparable in some respects to that of Austria or Finland, or to Yugoslavia's neutralism. (A distinction must however be drawn here. Though it may be true to say that all the peoples of Eastern Europe regard the possibility of achieving neutral status as one of their principal political aspirations, the same is not true of all the communist governments.)

The past history of their relations with Germany enables the Polish and Czech governments to keep alive in their peoples an awareness that the alliance with the Soviet Union and the other countries of the Soviet bloc is a welcome safeguard against the dangers of their vicinity with *any* kind of Germany. But the Hungarian or Bulgarian or even Rumanian communist governments have less reason to "fear" the West. Recent developments have shown Kadar conjuring up the possibility under some conditions of the withdrawal of Soviet troops from Hungary. And Rumania, on her own, has taken the unprecedented step of reducing the duration of military service, which in all the Warsaw treaty countries lasts for two years, to sixteen months. By this solitary move the Rumanian communist government has shown that fear of military aggression from the West will not inspire it to increase its military expenditure and deprive its industrial development of the massive contingents of manpower kept in the forces. It is here, in the obscure realm of their relations with the Warsaw treaty organization, that the next round between the more centrifugal communist governments and the Soviet government will be played out. It is here that the new definitions of "national sovereignty" and of "the communist commonwealth" will probably be tested.

The Warsaw treaty organization is the last survivor of Stalin's attempt to build up a Soviet Empire in Eastern Europe. The communist governments, in their quest for fuller sovereignty, realize that this is now the main obstacle in their path, for the issue of war and peace is not under their ultimate control, and the representative of the Soviet Union is the ultimate commander of their military forces. It is also here that the Soviet Union shows the greatest obduracy; and the fact that Imre Nagy fell between the clamour of the people for neutrality and the adamant refusal of the Soviet Union to consider allowing Hungary to leave the Warsaw treaty organization provides a measure of the extent of the conflict.

Can the Soviet Union accept that it is possible for a communist commonwealth to survive in Europe, without its members being subordinate, even in military matters, to the dominating power? And will other members of the commonwealth join Yugoslavia, non-aligned between the military blocs of the world, even if this further undermines the U.S.S.R.'s old Stalinist precepts: Soviet military security based on the creation of this pivotal buffer zone and jumping-off board? Finally, bearing in mind that except in East Germany—the last, and perhaps by now crumbling, bastion of Stalin's empire—all the other zones of Russian influence have undergone profound changes, can we now say that Stalin's empire has indeed broken up?

The answers must be yes. Indeed, it is inconceivable that, in any circumstances, Soviet Russia could have built a lasting empire in a part of Europe which by its very nature is a cradle of nationalism and a permanent cause of conflict of interests between the powers of the world. The years of Stalin's truly imperial rule over these peoples were short, violent, and precarious; the failure was implicit in the attempt.

SELECT BIBLIOGRAPHY

DALLIN, ALEXANDER, *Diversity in International Communism: A Documentary Record, 1961–63* (New York, Columbia University Press, 1963). A thorough and instructive collection of documents emanating in communist sources, showing the increasing diversity of communist systems. Professor Dallin is a recognized authority on communism as a theory and a movement.

FISCHER, GALATI, S. *Eastern Europe in the Sixties* (New York, Praeger, 1963). A historical account of the polycentrist and a-centrist forces at work in Eastern Europe in the last decade. The author analyzes the motive forces behind the growing diversity of communist systems and estimates their potential impact on future developments in the area and on the international communist movement.

IONESCU, GHITA. *The Break-up of the Soviet Empire in Eastern Europe* (London and Baltimore, Penguin Books, 1965). The author traces Stalin's construction of an empire in Eastern Europe, the rise of revisionism in post-Stalin Russia, Poland, and Hungary, the dogmatic counteroffensive (China, Albania), the position of Cuba, and the development of European "communist neutralism" (e.g., Rumania). Chapter 4 contains an interesting account of Rumania's attitude toward the COMECON.

JENSEN, FINN B., WALTER, INGO. *The Common Market: Economic Integration in Europe* (Philadelphia, Lippincott, 1965). A good summary of the history, institutional framework, trade, monetary, agricultural, and regional problems and policies of the European Economic Community. Note particularly the discussion of "The EEC and the Less Developed Countries" (Chapter 7), "The Common Market and the United States" (Chapter 12), and "Some Aspects of European Political Integration" (Chapter 13).

LINDBERG, LEON N. *The Political Dynamics of European Economic Integration* (Stanford, Calif., Stanford University Press, 1963). An examination of the relationship of politics to Western European economic integration and the problems which this relationship poses.

URI, PIERRE. *Partnership for Progress* (New York, Harper & Row, 1961). An account of Western European integration efforts and their relevance for the trans-Atlantic alliance.

10

Conclusion —The Race Against Time

THE STUDY OF WORLD AFFAIRS IS NOT an elementary exercise learned in six easy lessons. Not only are there divergent views on international problems—recall the variety of judgments revealed in the "Positions" at the end of each chapter—but there is the further complexity of the interdisciplinary approach. Even the most modestly sophisticated insight now requires familiarity with the contributions of the historian, economist, political scientist, anthropologist, sociologist, psychologist, and social psychologist. To this list probably should be added the philosopher and the student of religion. Yet despite this imposing challenge, some comprehension of the facts of international life is within the grasp of the student and citizen willing to devote some effort to it. This volume has endeavored to set forth a framework of thinking which enables one to look at contemporary world tensions with some understanding, some sense of the basic forces at work, and some realization that simple solutions will not be forthcoming.

A second major emphasis in this study has been the rapidly changing character of the international environment in which foreign policy must be conducted. Not only has the dawn of the nuclear era rendered war a much more destructive and deplorable means of resolving intergroup conflict, but it has made the price for the survival of civilized man intolerably high. There are those who argue that nuclear bombs will not be used because the potential users are well aware that they cannot escape frightfully destructive retaliation. The fact that for almost twenty years two atomically armed powers with divergent goals and policies have avoided atomic war is no guarantee that in some new "Berlin" or "Cuba" crisis zealous, optimistic, distracted, or frightened officials will not press the button igniting the holocaust. The world has been the happy beneficiary of cautious leadership in Washington and Moscow and of not a little good luck during the last two decades. Moreover, the world is now entering an age of nuclear proliferation in which a growing number of independent, sovereign governments will possess this weapon as their

375

last resort of policy in a lawless community of nations. And if faced with destruction, governments historically have demonstrated neither squeamishness about the use of what they deem survival weapons nor concern for the general and ultimate effect of their policies upon mankind. Thus the problem of war looms as the most formidable and lethal issue of our time—even more than that of unchecked population growth. We do in fact live with the sword of Damocles suspended above our heads—whether the heads be those of residents of Canton, Ohio, or of Canton, China.

Yet the technological revolution, even if the single most powerful agent of change, is not the whole story. It must be noted that at the very time when questions are being raised about the effectiveness of the nation-state as a viable political unit, the number of nation-states is rapidly multiplying. Since World War II, over sixty new sovereign governments have emerged, almost all on the wreckage of the Western colonial empires in Asia and Africa. These newcomers have outlooks and problems of their own quite apart from those which engage the older states and are bound to occupy an increasingly important, but unpredictable, part of the world stage. Furthermore, as has been emphasized especially in Chapters 5–7, this new array of developing countries is the major field in which competing economic and political systems are presently vying for support.

Finally and ironically, despite the intolerable price of nuclear conflict, there seems at present to be no politically acceptable formula or plan which might completely and permanently solve the problem of war. A system of world federation would obviously go a long way towards ending the condition of anarchy in international relations which presently leaves each sovereign community free to resort to war to protect or advance what it believes to be its interests. But world federation, or even regional political integration, involves restrictions on a state's freedom of action which few statesmen or citizens appear willing to accept even when staring at the hydrogen bomb. We seem destined, therefore, to live for a long time under conditions of intense international tension and rivalry with no assurance that this competition will be confined to peaceful forms or that nuclear war will be avoided.

From time to time, this international situation may be mitigated by international agreements on current problems such as Vietnam, Korea, and Germany, a more effective approach to economic development, the prohibition of nuclear tests, the nonproliferation of nuclear weapons, and the peaceful uses of outer space. But agreements which "solve" these problems will probably be long in coming, and then will have only limited effects on the overall world crisis.

We therefore face the frustrating prospect of living with uneasy stalemates and many unsolved problems, each of which is potentially explosive. Under these circumstances, the question of peace in the foreseeable future depends on strengthening every conceivable institution and imaginatively utilizing every channel of diplomatic negotiation which may prevent such stalemates and disputes from precipitating war or from expanding local conflicts into major ones. In this way, sufficient time may be gained to permit the divergent interests of the various antagonists to give way ultimately to some form of mutually tolerated compromise. The disputes and conflicts over Germany, Vietnam, Korea, Cyprus, and Palestine, although seemingly insoluble on a mutually acceptable basis today, may be easier to resolve ten, twenty, or thirty years from now, provided we are granted the necessary interval of time. In cases like Germany and Korea, the cautious application of the balance-of-power system, supplemented by perceptive diplomacy, although admittedly risky and dangerous, may be the best hope for those situations. In Cyprus and the Arab-Israeli dispute the presence of United Nations peacekeeping forces interposed between the contending parties has been an effective restraint. The possibility of using such international peacekeeping and observation forces in other trouble spots to deter violence and create conditions in which moderating influences are strengthened by the presence of representatives of the international community should be seriously considered.

In these ways increased opportunities will materialize for the gradual evolution of that consensus among nations which may provide the basis for progressively effective institutions of international law, order, and government. Thus the race for time may ultimately be won.

APPENDIX

PREPARATION OF A "POSITION PAPER" ON SOME CURRENT PROBLEM OF AMERICAN FOREIGN POLICY

NATURE AND PURPOSE OF THIS PROJECT

One of the best ways of integrating one's knowledge of world affairs is to prepare an analysis of some international problem, together with a recommended line of policy for the solution of it. Putting oneself in the position of a government official in the Department of State, for example, who has to formulate American foreign policy, is an extremely realistic way of studying and understanding that policy.

As the concluding exercise in this study of world affairs, therefore, it is suggested that a policy paper be prepared, comparable in substance and method to the policy papers which might be prepared within the Department of State. It should deal with some current problem of American foreign policy and should cover (a) a definition of the problem; (b) an analysis of the background of the problem; (c) a discussion of alternative policies which the United States might adopt in dealing with the problem; and (d) a recommendation of the specific policy that seems best designed to cope with the problem.

Within the Department of State, a policy paper—or position paper, as it is sometimes called—is usually drafted first by a committee of officials in the lower or middle echelons of the Department who have the most direct interest in the problem under consideration. When the paper has been approved by this committee, it is referred to the top officials in the Department of State and to the Secretary of State for a decision.[1] The purpose of the paper is to provide the Secretary of State and his top associates with the necessary information and background on all possible policy alternatives, in order to help them make the wisest foreign policy decision for the United States.

In preparing such a paper, the reader should therefore try to put himself as completely as possible in the position of a Department of State committee which has been asked to prepare a policy recommendation for the Secretary of State or the President. Considering all relevant aspects of the problem—historical, political, economic, psychological, technological, military—he will quickly

---

[1] Final decisions on major foreign policy problems are not usually made by the Secretary of State alone but by the President of the United States. Before making such decisions, the President obtains the advice of other key executive departments and agencies involved in foreign affairs, such as the National Security Council, Central Intelligence Agency, United States Information Agency, Department of Defense, Treasury Department, Department of Commerce, Atomic Energy Commission, and the Export-Import Bank.

find that he is applying the interdisciplinary approach to which frequent reference has been made in this book. Although he will not, of course, have access to the type of classified or confidential information available to government officials, his study will not be unduly restricted, nor will the value of his experience be reduced in preparing a policy recommendation. A very high proportion of government intelligence, perhaps 90 percent or more, consists of research and analysis based on nonconfidential materials available in any good library. The important function is the careful study of this information and the intelligent use of it in examining all implications of the various policy alternatives under consideration.

SUGGESTED OUTLINE

In order to assure some consistency and uniformity of organization, it is suggested that the paper be organized in the following manner:

Title

State the title in question form.

Example: What Should United States Policy Be
Regarding the Unification of Germany?

A. Statement of the Problem

This should be a concise statement of the foreign policy problem under consideration. Usually three or four sentences will suffice.

Example. If German unification is the topic, the problem might be stated as follows:

Since the end of World War II, the Soviet Union and the Western powers have been unable to agree on the terms for the reunification of Germany, thereby leaving unresolved what is perhaps the most critical current problem of Europe. Whether German unification can be accomplished without a heightened danger of communist infiltration or whether any Western concessions on such points as neutralizing Germany or restricting German rearmament should be made in an effort to reach a compromise agreement are some major unresolved aspects of the problem. The United States is interested in any possibility of breaking the stalemate on German unification, and the problem now is to determine whether progress in this direction is more likely to result from maintaining the present American policy or from making certain modifications in it.

B. Background of the Problem

This should be a reasonably detailed account of how the problem originated and developed. It should indicate the main factors contributing to the issue and list the principal events or actions that have taken place. If major proposals have been previously discussed for dealing with the problem, appropriate reference should be made to them. The viewpoints of the major governments interested in the problem might also be relevant. The purpose of this background statement is to provide the necessary information on which an intelligent discussion of policy alternatives can be based. It should be approximately five or six pages in length. It should include footnotes to indicate sources of the main points of information.

Example. With the problem of German unification again as an illustration, the background statement might appropriately cover such points as (1) the basic postwar agreements on the division of Germany; (2) an explanation of Germany's political, economic, and potential military significance in Europe, together with the reasons why both the Soviet Union and the Western powers have felt that Germany could not be allowed to come under the domination of the other side; (3) a summary of the major proposals regarding German unification that both sides have advanced since 1946; (4) the reactions or replies of the various governments to these proposals; (5) an explanation of German official and public opinion views on unification; (6) an analysis of the current positions of the different governments and the chief points of disagreement at present.

C. Alternative Policies

At least three alternative policies should be presented for dealing with the problem under consideration. These should be proposals the United States might be reasonably expected to adopt, that is, they should be proposals that a United States official might reasonably defend as being in the best interest of United States security and welfare. The arguments pro and con regarding each alternative should be indicated. Footnotes should be used to indicate sources of main ideas or arguments. This section will normally be five to six pages in length.

Example. In the case of German unification, such alternative policies as the following might be suggested, with a pro and con analysis for each alternative:

1. The United States should continue its present policy of insisting on free, impartially supervised elections throughout Germany, with the right of any freely elected German government to decide its own future policies on such questions as NATO membership, rearmament, or neutralization.

2. In an effort to secure Soviet acceptance of the principle of free elections throughout Germany, the United States should agree to support the neutralization of Germany and/or abandon any plans for the sharing of nuclear weapons with the Federal Republic of Germany.

3. In an effort to secure Soviet acceptance of the principle of free elections throughout Germany, the United States should agree to merge the NATO alliance with the East European security system (Warsaw Pact) and form a regional all-European security pact under Article 51 of the United Nations Charter. A united Germany would be a member of this all-European security system.

D. Recommended Policy

This concluding section should indicate the policy it is recommended that the United States adopt. The reasons for making the recommendation should be given, together with the reasons why various alternative policies do not seem desirable. This final policy recommendation may be one of the alternative policies discussed in Section C, or it may be a combination and synthesis of two or more alternatives. If it is one of the alternatives already presented, it is not necessary to repeat in full the arguments in favor of the policy. A brief summary will suffice.

FOOTNOTES

Notes should be numbered consecutively and may be placed either at the bottom of each page or on a separate page at the end of the paper. They should generally conform to the following style:

Books

Fred Warner Neal, *War and Peace and Germany* (New York, 1962), p. 89.

If the following footnote also refers to the same book, it is not necessary to repeat the author and title, but simply to write *Ibid.,* p. 102. If, after a different reference has been listed in a subsequent footnote, the Neal book were again to be cited, the reference could be as follows: Neal, *op. cit.,* p. 106.

Periodicals

Tang Tsou and Morton H. Halperin, "Mao Tse-tung's Revolutionary Strategy and Peking's International Behavior," *The American Political Science Review,* March, 1965, p. 80.

Newspapers

The New York Times, June 15, 1966, p. 3.

Documents

U.S. Congress, Senate, Committee on Foreign Relations, *Background Information Relating to Southeast Asia and Vietnam,* Committee Print, 89th Congress, 1st Session, January 14, 1965, p. 28.

GENERAL REFERENCES

The following list of references may be helpful in gathering information on the general background of various foreign policy problems:

Public Affairs Information Service. An index to books, pamphlets, articles, and government documents on various topics in public affairs. Very useful guide, especially for finding references to documents and similar studies.

Department of State Bulletin. Weekly publication of the United States Department of State including major statements, speeches, and articles on U.S. Foreign Relations by U.S. officials, as well as selected correspondence with other governments and texts of important agreements.

Readers' Guide to Periodical Literature. An index to periodical articles.

International Index to Periodicals. Similar to the *Readers' Guide* but includes references to some foreign periodicals and to some of the scholarly journals. In April, 1965, the title of this index was changed to *Social Sciences & Humanities Index.*

New York Times Index. An index to all articles in *The New York Times.* Very useful sometimes in checking details or locating public speeches and documents.

Facts on File. An excellent index and summary of all main current events, year by year.

Council on Foreign Relations, *The United States in World Affairs.* Annual surveys of major developments in U.S. foreign policy.

Council on Foreign Relations, *Documents on American Foreign Relations.* Annual series of documents on events of the year. Prior to 1952, the volumes were published by the World Peace Foundation.

Royal Institute of International Affairs, *Survey of International Affairs*. Annual survey of all major international problems.

Royal Institute of International Affairs, *Documents on International Affairs*. Annual series.

United Nations Yearbook. Annual report on all UN activities. Excellent, comprehensive accounts of all issues that have come before the UN.

United Nations Review. Monthly periodical on current UN activities.

U.N. Monthly Chronicle, successor to the *United Nations Review* since May, 1964.

Foreign Policy Association, *Headline Series*. A series of booklets on a wide range of international problems. Objective and popular in style. Approximately six are published each year.

INDEX